ULTRA

ULTRA

THE UNDERWORLD OF ITALIAN FOOTBALL

TOBIAS JONES

HEAD
of ZEUS

This is an Apollo book, first published in the UK in 2019 by Head of Zeus Ltd
This paperback edition first published in 2020 by Head of Zeus Ltd

IMAGE CREDITS:
Image 5 via Facebook, Image 6 via *Il Romanista*, Image 7 ANSA,
Image 11 ANSA, Image 12 Getty / Matthew Ashton, Image 13 via Twitter
Other images are courtesy of Tobias Jones
Every effort has been made to credit the copyright owner of the images

Map © Jeff Edwards

Epigraph: *Psalms* 88:4

9 7 5 3 1 2 4 6 8

A catalogue record for this book is available from
the British Library.

ISBN (PB): 9781786697370
ISBN (E): 9781786697356

Typeset by Adrian McLaughlin

Printed and bound in Great Britain by
CPI Group (UK) Ltd, Croydon CR0 4YY

Head of Zeus Ltd
First Floor East
5–8 Hardwick Street
London EC1R 4RG

WWW.HEADOFZEUS.COM

Contents

PART TWO

The idea for this book was gifted to me by the great Jon Riley. I dedicate it to him, and to my sport-loving brother, Paul, and his family – Marija, Theodore and Kristian – with gratitude and admiration.

'... ormai sono annoverato fra quelli che
scendono nella fossa...'

Author's Note

Although I love football – playing it, watching it, talking about it – I've always thought the fans were more intriguing than the players. Maybe it's an ideological inclination towards the masses rather than the elite; or else a belief that the meaning of sport resides not in the champions but in those who are being championed.

In many ways this isn't a book about football at all, but a portrait of an enduring Italian subculture inspired by it. For over fifty years now, the ultras have turned the *curve* (the 'curved' ends behind the goal) into fairground mirrors of Italian society, offering both a reflection and a distortion of the country. The ultras are a fascinating way to understand not football as such, but why it means so much to people and why a mere rectangle of grass can inspire religious fundamentalism. They are often compared to punks, Hells Angels, hooligans or the South American *Barras Bravas*, and there are elements of all those groups within the evolving movement. But in truth, it's a thoroughly Italian phenomenon drawing on much deeper influences within Italian history.

It is, though, the antithesis of a national movement. The foundation stone of every ultra group is topophilia (love of place) or *campanilismo* (the attachment to one's local bell-tower). An ultra is a patriot of his or her patch, of a specific town, city or suburb. It's about rootedness and belonging: the sort of pride that persuades people to boast that their forgotten nowhere is actually *caput mundi*, the 'capital of the world'. Being an ultra is not simply about love for your own town or city, but hatred of the others, especially those close by or even in the same city.

That necessarily creates a problem for a writer attempting to trace the characteristics of a country-wide phenomenon: the ultra world is strangely incomprehensible if you look at it as a national movement, skating across the surface of hundreds of different groups. To do so has the same effect as to study colours (a key ultra concept) by mixing them all together and ending up with none. That's why I decided to go deep into one particular setting. Whilst always keeping an eye on the national picture, I've concentrated on a small, ignored city in the deep South, trusting that the provincial can often be universal.

The choice of Cosenza requires a brief justification. Writers are, understandably, drawn to newsworthy events, and the ultras have always made the news. For decades they have been connected to murders, missing persons, bank jobs and drug-dealing, quite apart from the almost routine punch-ups and petty thefts that happen on match days. Yet those *cronache nere* – 'black chronicles' – are only partially representative of the ultra world. I actively sought out a *curva*, or terrace, which might balance the scales, which might even offer some 'white chronicles' as well. Cosenza, I had heard, was a place where the ultras squatted buildings confiscated from the Mafia, giving beds to hundreds of immigrants and destitute Italians. The Cosenza ultras had opened a foodbank for the poor and created Italy's first play park for disabled children. One of the most influential fans in the *curva* was a Franciscan friar. In an era when so many terraces find inspiration in fascism, Cosenza remains devoutly anti-fascist. If anyone was looking for a place to find a counterbalance to the ultra stereotype, Cosenza was clearly it.

The more I went back, the more I felt that the city was an expression of the idealistic origins of the movement back in the late 1960s and early 1970s. It was playful, charitable, chaotic and spectacular. I often met Donata Bergamini, the sister of a Cosenza midfielder murdered in 1989, on the terraces. Thirty years after his death, she would be there in the rain with the ultras, supporting a team a thousand kilometres from her home near Ferrara. 'I truly feel bad,' she told me, 'when I'm far from the city and its red-blue colours.'

And because Cosenza is a team that has never enjoyed much footballing or financial glory (it has bounced between the lower divisions of Serie D, C and B, going bust now and again), it doesn't draw fans from across the country, let alone the globe. There's no money to be made. Cosenza's fans are decidedly local and, therefore, offer a far better insight into the rootedness, even poverty, of the ultras than do fans of more decorated teams. Ultras are implacably opposed to the robed dignitaries of modern football, and there was nowhere, I felt, more gloriously ragged than Cosenza.

I've concentrated on other teams and cities for reasons that will, hopefully, become obvious. One draw has, strangely, been grief. Passion is an integral part of fandom but much more so in its original sense of suffering. When human tragedies far surpass, whilst still reflecting, sporting ones, the ultras' role becomes sacred, tending the memory of lives lost and mourned. Another reason I've been drawn to certain places was a hypothesis, possibly absurd, that ultra groups reflect their topography, so the more beguiling a city (like Genova or Catania) the more curious I was about their crews. I've been drawn to cities like Rome where there are local rivalries on the asphalt as much as there are on the grass. But I'm aware that many other famous groups (from Fiorentina, Napoli, Atalanta and elsewhere) are under-represented and I wouldn't pretend that these pages are anything like exhaustive. Research has been skewed by my personal interests. Clubs with English and Welsh links, a *capo-ultra* with distant Hollywood connections, places with the best songs, supporters with the most unlikely yarns – on the long journey south to Cosenza I've often been led astray.

But I realize that I have also been drawn to ultra groups that help explain one of the most urgent topics of the early twenty-first century: the resurgence of far-right extremism. The ultras offer a unique vantage point to understand how and why fascism has re-emerged into the mainstream. As you go back through the years, it becomes obvious how hard certain ultras were rubbing the lamp before the genie reappeared. In many ways, the ultras of certain clubs anticipated, by decades, the rhetoric, methods and ideologies that are now dominating political discourse in Italy and elsewhere. If, occasionally, I seem to go off topic it's because fascist revivalism is a constant subplot informing and polluting the ultra world.

There has also been a problem of veracity during research. Oral stories contain both richness and unreliability. I've often worried that the first evaporated in translation, then fretted that the second threatened truthfulness. The ultras have certain dates etched in their memory: Canaletta ('Drainpipe') has '338' tattooed on his forearm (the number of away games he's been to) along with '28/8/2016' (the date of the match when Cosenza beat their local rivals, Catanzaro, 0–3). Many ultras are prouder of their recall than a preacher quoting the Good Book. But just as often they've forgotten when certain things happened, or confuse what they heard about with what they saw with their own eyes. They are incessant raconteurs, relishing and embellishing. For many of them, the last fifty years are a bit of a haze. If you ask them for a year, let alone a precise date, they often roll their eyes. I've been told a lot of stories that are hard to verify, and I've sadly had to edit out plenty of fine ones because of lack of proof or probability. But I've also chosen to repeat some stories that, just by their very existence, underline the legends that they live by. That's not swapping accuracy for story telling, I hope, but offering glimpses of the stories the ultras tell themselves and joining dots where the only sources are ageing humans who have lived very hard.

I've also frequently quoted from ultra banners, the so-called *striscioni*. These curt couplets are how sometimes secretive groups present themselves – their cause, their stories and their controversies – to the world. That's why they've been compared to Chinese *dazibao*, the posters used for quick communication. These blunt, invariably rhyming slogans appear at every game and are the distillation of hours of heated meetings. Although they are often superficial or extremist, they can also be witty, profound and thought-provoking. I wanted them to punctuate the text in the same way as they do the terraces.

Ultras reputedly abhor *protagonismi* (individual grandstanding) and many have legal travails and relational problems within their own terraces. Many only agreed to talk on condition of anonymity. I've duly left many unnamed, or else have rendered them unrecognizable by changing their names or nicknames. Others insisted I kept their true identity, so in the end there's a mixture of real and invented appellations.

———

There's inconsistency in Italian, let alone in English, about the spelling of 'ultra'. In Italian, the word used to be accented: *ultrà*. Accented word endings are never normally pluralized in Italian ('many cities', for example, is *molte città*) and the word *ultrà* originally stood for both singular and plural. But because of their admiring nod to British fans and hooligans, *ultrà* groups have always loved anglicizations, and *ultrà* has often been pluralized to *ultras*. In academic discourse, some sociologists have used that pluralization (written '*UltraS*', their upper case), to distinguish a new phalanx of extreme right-wing gangs that they consider separate to the traditionally apolitical groupings of *ultrà*. Often the singular is now used in Italian without an accent. How to render such variations in English is an unsettled question, so I've decided to keep it very simple: 'ultra' singular, 'ultras' plural, and no accent unless I'm using the word in Italian (as in 'Casa degli Ultrà'). I've kept the names of football teams exactly as they appear in Italian even though that raises an inconsistency: because some teams were founded by the English and have English names (*Genoa* and *Milan*), I've left the name of those cities (*Genova* and *Milano*) in Italian in order to distinguish one from the other. I've remained loyal to team spellings elsewhere (*Roma* and *Torino*), so that their cities, for clarity, are actually anglicised (*Rome* and *Turin*). As is standard practice, I refer to Internazionale, the other team from Milano, as Inter, and Torino, sometimes, as Toro.

Glossary

CasaPound: a neo-fascist movement, named after Ezra Pound, founded in 2003.

Celtic cross: an encircled plus-sign, frequently used by the far right.

Curva: the (usually curved) terraces behind the goal that are the spiritual home of (almost all) ultras. Plural *curve*. Often distinguished by adding the points of the compass: Curva Nord (the north terrace), Curva Est (east), Curva Sud (south), and Curva Ovest (west). The word has taken on mythological depth: its rotundity leads people to give it a sense of pagan fertility (it's a breast or womb), and its horse shoe shape suggests at an inclusivity towards the entire political spectrum.

Daspo: a stadium ban (from '*Divieto di Accedere alle manifestazioni SPOrtive*'), a measure introduced into law in December 1989. Bans can last up to eight years. The acronym often becomes a verb, **daspare** ('to ban'), and an adjective, **daspato** ('banned').

Derby: a game between two teams within the same city, or else between two teams based in close proximity (Cosenza against Catanzaro, for example).

Diffidato: literally someone who has received an official warning. For simplicity I have translated it as 'mistrusted'. It implies someone banned from stadiums.

Duce / Dux: a cognate of 'duke' and 'doge', it means 'leader', 'warlord' or 'guide'. An appellation orginally used to compliment Giuseppe Garibaldi and Gabriele D'Annunzio, it is now associated solely with Benito Mussolini.

Fascism: notoriously hard to define, it was the name given to the totalitarian movement founded by Benito Mussolini. The 'fascia' was the binding of an axe within rods, the original symbol of the lictors, the officers of ancient Rome. It implied strength in unity, and the protruding blade implied the power of life or death over subjects. Michael Mann defined fascism as 'the pursuit of a transcendent and cleansing nation-statism through paramilitarism'. Robert Paxton called it: '... a form of political behaviour marked by obsessive preoccupation with community decline, humiliation, or victimhood and by compensatory cults of unity, energy, and purity, in which a mass-based party of committed nationalist militants, working in uneasy but effective collaboration with traditional elites, abandons democratic liberties and pursues, with redemptive violence and without ethical or legal restraints, goals of internal cleansing and external expansion'.

FIGC: the 'Federazione italiana giuoco calcio'. The Italian Football Association.

Forza Nuova: A neo-fascist party founded in 1997 by Roberto Fiore and Massimo Morsello.

Fossa: the 'pit' or 'ditch', but also implying the trenches, the grave and hell. A common name for ultra groups in the early days.

Goliardia: high spirits, transgression, satire or fun-and-games. A word invariably used by ultras to describe their excesses.

Gradinata: literally a 'flight of steps' or a 'staircase'. Sometimes used to describe the terraces. Genoa's Gradinata Nord is the most famous.

Lupi: Wolves (used to describe the players, or fans, of Roma and Cosenza, amongst others)

Maglia: the shirt. An object of mystical reverence.

Mentalità: the 'mentality'. Frequently invoked to suggest that there is a unique mindset to being an ultra.

Movimento Sociale Italiano-Destra Nazionale: the Italian Social Movement-National Right, usually known as the MSI. Founded in 1946 and dissolved in 1995, it was Italy's post-war fascist party.

Nuclei Armati Rivoluzionari: known as NAR, the 'nuclei of armed revolutionaries'. A fascist terrorist group, operative from 1977 to 1981.

Nostalgico: a 'nostalgic', someone yearning for the return of Mussolini's regime.

Predappio: the birthplace of Benito Mussolini in Romagna. Now a place of pilgrimage for those who want to visit his family home, school and tomb.

Questura: the central police station.

RSI: the 'Repubblica Sociale Italiana', also known as the 'Repubblica di Salò'. It was the puppet government, set up by Nazi Germany and headed by Benito Mussolini, between September 1943 and April 1945. The centre of the flag had an eagle's claws holding a lictor's bundle.

Runes: letters of the runic alphabet, a pre-Latin alphabet of the Germanic languages which are now routinely used by far-right groups as symbols and codes.

Scontri: fights, punch-ups, brawls, rucks etc.

Scudetto: the Serie A title (literally the 'little shield' worn on the shirts of the championship-winning team).

Serie A: the top division of Italian football.

Serie B: the second division of Italian football.

Serie C: the third division of Italian football, also known as the 'Lega Italiana Calcio Professionistico', or just Lega Pro. It is subdivided into three leagues according to geography: north, centre and south.

Sfottò: an insult or banter.

Squadre d'Azione: 'action squads' composed, mainly, of World War I veterans. They were later absorbed into Mussolini's fascist movement. Their violence – often allegedly in defence of property and law and order in the face of a Bolshevik insurgency – was particularly acute in 1919-20 and gave rise to the word '***squadrismo***'.

Striscione: a banner, usually containing slogans, jokes and insults (plural ***striscioni***). It can also refer to the 'herald' which announces the name of an ultra group. The desire to capture or defend these heralds is at the root of many fights.

Tessera del Tifoso: the hated 'loyalty card' introduced to prevent troublemakers from going to games.

Tifo: the support: '***il tifo era piatto***' – 'the support was flat'.

Tifoseria: the fans in general.

Tifoso: a fan (plural: ***tifosi***). A ***tifoso*** of Milan is called a ***Milanista***; of Inter an ***Interista*** etc.

Tribuna: the main stand of the stadium (the long side of the rectangle, or of the oval) where the tickets are more expensive and the fans more genteel. A few ultra groups now sit in the ***tribuna***, but almost all are behind the goals.

Ventennio: the (roughly) twenty years in which Benito Mussolini was in power (1922–43, then 1943–5 in Nazi-controlled northern Italy).

Some cities and football teams referred to in the text

Preface

Boxing Day, 2018

Dede was in the usual pub, Cartoons, on Via Emanuele Filiberto in Milan. Cartoons was an English-style boozer, with dark, shiny wood and framed cartoons on the walls. The place was packed now with Inter ultras. It was only a couple of hours until the match kicked off against Napoli.

Dede wasn't an Inter ultra. He was a thirty-nine-year-old tiler from Varese, 60 kilometres northwest of Milan. He had a wife and two kids and worked out in a martial arts club where he had won a few tournaments in 'short-knife fencing' using daggers. He had ten years of stadium bans behind him. Dede had got a bit tubby recently but he could still hold his own in a fight. He was there with other ultras from Varese, part of a group called Blood&Honour that was twinned with Inter ultras.

They weren't the only outsiders that the various Inter ultras – the Boys SAN, the Irriducibili and the Vikings – had invited for the fight. Nice's Ultras Populaire Sud were in the pub too, since they had a beef with the Neapolitans from a fight a few years before.

Blood&Honour is also a neo-Nazi organization. It was founded in England in 1987 by Ian Stuart Donaldson, the lead singer of the white-power rock band, Skrewdriver. The name came from the motto of the Hitler youth, *Blut und Ehre*. After Donaldson's death in a car crash in 1993, Blood&Honour became an international movement with chapters throughout Europe and America. In 1998 a new ultra group in Varese had decided to use the Blood&-Honour name, in English, and employ the same Oþalan rune as their logo, a symbol that had been used by both the Waffen-SS and by a banned Italian fascist organization, Avanguardia Nazionale.

There was a ruthlessness to the Blood&Honour group that had rarely been seen even on the Italian terraces. Hammers, axes, baseball bats and knives had all been used in fights before, but now they were being backed up by a Nazi ideology in which force was the only language. Within three years, the men from Blood&Honour had defeated Varese's traditional ultra groups and become the bosses of the terrace, hanging their banner – black with white lettering – more centrally than all the others.

But it was a gang beset by legal problems. Many members were arrested for drugs and arms offences, for bank jobs and beatings. Although one of their leaders survived a shooting, others were less fortunate: a man called Claudino was stabbed to death outside the bar where he worked, and Saverio – on the run in Spain – was stabbed in Torremolinos. One member of the gang now lived between Morocco and Spain and was involved with the 'Ndrangheta, the Calabrian Mafia, importing tonnes of hashish through the port of Genova.

The Blood&Honour gang, though, had a political affinity with the Inter ultras. The 'SAN' of Inter's Boys SAN – one of Italy's oldest ultra groups – stands for *squadre di azione nero-azzurro*, an echo of Mussolini's *squadre d'azione*. The leader of Boys SAN was called 'Il Rosso' ('Red') and, with other ultra leaders, he had planned this attack on the Neapolitan ultras with precision. For weeks some of his crew had infiltrated the Neapolitan's social media accounts. Look-outs on mopeds waited to catch sight of the Neapolitans' convoy as they came off the ring road. Other Inter ultras sat in another pub, the Baretto, to distract the under-cover cops.

When the call came through – 'They're turning into Via Novara now' – about a hundred men in twenty cars raced to Via Fratelli Zoia, a road that runs perpendicular to Via Novara. It was the ideal place for the ambush because it was near the stadium and a couple of large, dark parks were good for getting lost in or for dumping weapons. None of the ultras were packing anything: all the weapons – billhooks, lump hammers, crowbars – were being stored at the site of the ambush.

The Neapolitan ultras were travelling in three nine-seater minibuses and two cars. The attack started with a homemade hand grenade – what Italians call a 'paper bomb' – chucked in front of the first car. About a hundred Inter ultras now ran onto the road. Red flares were thrown onto the dual carriageway. Both lanes were lit up by the hissing sticks. Against that glare, silhouetted men – holding bars, bats and with faces covered by hoods, scarves and balaclavas – raced towards the vehicles.

'Come on, come on,' many were shouting, their arms raised. The noise sounded like a war cry, an ululation of playful disdain. More paper bombs were thrown. Car alarms were now going off, giving a rhythm to the chaos. Dogs were barking.

The Neapolitans piled out of their vehicles and it kicked off. Hooded silhouettes raced towards each other, punching, jab-bing, kicking, jeering. Metal bars were thrown, rattling as they cartwheeled across the asphalt.

It was hard to see anything now. The firecrackers and flares created a dense fog. One of the Neapolitans' vehicles pulled into the other lane and hit something. It felt as if the van was driving over a couple of spongy speedbumps. People were shouting, smashing their palms on the side of the van.

'He's yours, he's yours,' the Neapolitans screamed to the Inter ultras.

'Truce, truce,' others shouted.

And there it came to a standstill. They stopped fighting as if it had all been just a game. The Neapolitans stepped back and let some Interisti through to retrieve the body. Dede's legs seemed twisted unnaturally and his ribcage looked wrong. Three men picked him up but it was like lifting a soggy cardboard box. What should have been rigid was too soft to carry properly.

When Dede died that night in Milan's San Carlo hospital, it was yet another death to lay at the door of the ultras. The story had everything necessary to depict them as the embodiment of evil. Here were drug-dealing neo-Nazis who had planned an almost military ambush. The fact that the Neapolitan defender, Kalidou Koulibaly, was racially abused throughout the subsequent match only seemed to confirm the impression that the ultras were scum.

But behind the headlines, the story was far more subtle. When police looked at footage of the fight, filmed from balconies and captured by security cameras, it became obvious that there was actually minimal contact between the groups. They mostly stood apart, insulting each other and throwing metal bars. Considering that there were about a hundred Interisti armed with sharp and heavy tools used for forestry and building, the list of injuries was exceptionally short. The one fatality was accidental, not intentional. Many eye-witnesses even said that the Inter ultras applauded the Neapolitans for handing over the dying man, as if the whole aggression was contained within a ritualistic, role-playing framework that could be paused when real life, and death, intervened.

It suited everyone to exaggerate the violence. It was a great story for journalists. It suited the police narrative that the ultras were part of a menacing mob. Even the ultras themselves tried to depict the encounter, with embellishment and bravado, as an epic confrontation in which, as one said, 'we showed ourselves worthy of honour'. In speaking about 'slicing up the faces of the enemy', they made themselves feared. The ultras are actually, often, happy to be blamed for what they don't do because it adds to their reputation amongst the only people whose judgement they care about – other ultras.

The more you investigate, though, the more you see a conspiracy of disinformation on all sides. Nothing is quite as it seems. The story told by the police is invariably the complete opposite to the story told by the ultras. And because it's far easier, and safer, for journalists to talk to the police, it's usually only the official narrative that is heard. The ultras become scapegoats and they, in turn, scapegoat the police and journalists. But for all their devil-may-care attitude, the ultras are weary of being misunderstood. Unlike Sonny Barger, the Hells Angel leader who once told Hunter S. Thompson 'nobody never wrote nothin' good about us, but then we ain't never done nothin' good to write about', the ultras – whilst never denying the violence and mayhem they create – believe they have done a lot of good. But to see this, you have to be with them, to live alongside them. 'You'll never understand us,' they always say, 'unless you're with us.'

PART ONE

Present Day, Pescara: Siena v. Cosenza in the Lega-Pro (Serie C) Final

Ciccio Conforti is overlooking a horseshoe of 12,000 Cosenza fans from high up in the *curva*. He's in his mid-fifties now, with curly grey hair and aviator shades. His pregnant partner is by his side. Back in the glory days of the 1980s he was one of the brains behind the Cosenza ultras. In any other city he would have been called a *capo* but Cosenza is too anarchic and egalitarian for bosses. He's just known as Zu Ciccio ('Uncle Ciccio').

Almost all his old gang are here for this massive game. It's the grand final to reach the promised land of Serie B, Italy's second division. It's been decades since Cosenza was last promoted to this division. It's a hot evening in June and there's a sense that this year, at last, luck is on the side of the small Calabrian city. There are ultras from Genoa and Ancona here too, to support the Cosenza groups with whom they're twinned. The only ones missing are the *diffidati*, the 'mistrusted' who are excluded from the stadiums for years at a time.

Diffidati sempre presenti! Goes up the chant, repeated throughout the game with a hand-clap echo of the syllables: 'The mistrusted are always present!'

Ciccio's group was called *Nuclei Sconvolti* (the 'Deranged Nuclei'). It sounded deliberately like a sleeper cell of stoners. Their symbol was that spikey green leaf so well known to tokers. But beyond all the provocation, they felt that there was something profound to what they were doing.

'For me "ultra" was a sacred word,' Ciccio says wistfully. 'I would have done everything and more for that world. I was an ultra long before I was a fan.'

The word 'ultra' meant, originally, 'other' or 'beyond', like the Italian *altro* and *oltre*. To be an ultra implies that you're an insurgent, a revolutionary, a brigand, a partisan, a bandit, a radical and a rascal. To the bourgeois, an ultra is way beyond the pale, the wrong side of the tracks and then some.

Marco Zanoni (one of the leading figures in Verona's Yellow-Blue Brigade) once said: 'I think that someone who frequents the *curva* is an idealist. At the end of the day, he goes to support the team of his city and we know that an idealist can, in certain circumstances, become a tough, even an extremist.' That's the other meaning of ultra: 'extreme', like the English 'ultra-hardline'. The ultras are the extremists, the guerrillas, of Italian football.

Of the 12,000 in the *curva* this evening, probably only a few hundred are ultras (official estimates suggest there are about 40,000 ultras in the whole country, although ultras themselves say the figure is far higher). They're the ones at the centre of the *curva*, singing incessantly to dissipate the tension: *oh, la vinciamo noi*, they sing repeatedly ('we're going to win').

The game kicks off. Immediately, Siena are putting Cosenza, playing in white with a red-and-blue trim, under pressure. Siena's midfielders are running beyond their bearded striker, pulling the Cosenza defence this way and that.

'*Sono puliti, cazzo*,' says Ciccio. 'Fuck, they're neat.'

If you look at the clothing, it's obvious who is an ultra. 'You'll never have us as you want us' say their T-shirts. The ultras say they're fighting brutal state repression, and that their insurgency is a quasi-sacred act: *la fede non si diffida* say many of the other T-shirts, meaning 'you can't mistrust the faith'. Most of their headline concepts sound strangely spiritual: 'congregation', 'sacrifice', 'presence'.

Weirdly, one of the ways to spot the ultras is that many aren't paying attention to the game. The skinny man leading the singing with a megaphone is called Lastica (Elastic) and he has his back to the game, as do almost all his lieutenants. They are watching the troops. The more long-in-the-tooth ultras work the *curva* like hosts at a party. They chat and argue on the walkways, often only looking over each others' shoulders at the pitch every now and again to see what all the noise is about. Being an ultra isn't about watching the football, but watching each other: admiring the carnival on the *curva*, not the game on the grass.

The contrast between their self-perception and what the *bienpensant* say about them could hardly be more marked. The vast majority of Italians consider the ultras degenerate fuck-ups who have nothing decent to contribute to society. They are often described as sub-humans ('animals' is a common insult, as is *pezzi di merda*, 'pieces of shit'). The President of Genoa, Enrico Preziosi, in one prolonged rant, once said that 'certain ultras should be wiped from the face of the earth'. 'In Italian football,' the football manager Fabio Capello once complained, 'the ultras are in control.' Throughout their fifty-year history, the ultras have been, critics say, masked and violent criminals, sacking cities at every away game. They embody suspect or dangerous traits: blind loyalty, tribal affiliation, *omertà* towards the police, caveman masculinity and brute muscle. At worst they have become the willing foot soldiers of both organized crime and of Italy's fascist revival.

The ultra world is so contradictory that there's truth in both portraits. Those contradictions are constantly in evidence. They are football fans who don't much care about football. They're adamant that politics should be kept out of the terraces, and yet many terraces are profoundly politicized. It's a druggy world which has, however, often helped people stay clean. The ultra milieu overlaps with the Mafia, but the ultra world has, far more often, been a sanctuary from it. The ultras are intolerant but can also be incredibly inclusive. Violence is integral to them but so is altruism. They are responsible for acts of great charity at times when the Italian state has been, as it often is, absent. The ultras embody many of the themes that intrigue us as humans: they're obsessed by loyalty and affiliation and belonging; they reflect solidarity and cohesion as well as crime, violence and greed. They constantly seem to be asking the question of what it is to be a man in a world in which muscle and manliness are, for understandable reasons, considered suspect.

Suddenly, a goal. The stadium is going berserk. There's a forward surge, and people fall forwards, catching each other and hugging all at once. The goal was at the far end, a simple cut-back from Tutino (on loan from Napoli) and Bruccini stuck it away. People are bouncing now, jumping up and down, rewinding the songbook.

'*Che bello è, quando esco di casa,*' we sing ('How beautiful it is, when I get out of the house...'), '*per andare allo stadio, a tifare Cosenza...*' ('to go to the stadium to support Cosenza...'). The simple, stirring music was taken from the chorus of a drab pop song by the Italian singer, Noemi.

There are dozens of ultra groups in Cosenza but they come together in two different umbrella groupings: the Curva Sud 1978 and the Anni Ottanta (a tribute to the glory years of the 1980s). They have been feuding and fighting all season. Claudio, one of the wise heads of the city with friends in both camps, says that 'ultra' means *superunismo* ('superunity'). But despite that, almost all stadiums are divided into different sectors for warring ultras who support the same team. The splits occur for all sorts of reasons. The main factor is simply the defining stance of the ultra: it's all about being intransigent, uncompromising and unflinching. You never step backwards. *Mai in ginocchio*, is another slogan ('never on your knees'). And so, just like Italian politics, groups splinter and fight each other. Today, though, there's a peace agreement. In this show-piece game for the big prize, there's an armed truce between the rival groups.

Something astonishing happens after half-time. The action is at the far end where Siena have a free kick. It comes to nothing and suddenly Tutino, way inside his own half, has brought the ball down with the outside of his left foot and is sprinting towards us. No one's near him. Two, three touches, lunging forwards. Still no one near him. A couple more nudges, he's outside the area but, fuck it, he smacks it so hard with the outside of his left boot that it bananas away from the Siena keeper and into the very top corner of the goal. The score is 2–0.

The rush of adrenalin and love and ecstasy is intense. Chill is shaking his fist at me, as if berating me for not believing. Everyone is hugging, singing, reaching for their phones to call friends and send videos, trying to capture this once-in-a-generation moment when fate is smiling on the absolute underdogs.

The ecstasy doesn't last long. Siena are awarded a penalty and it's 2–1 before you've even caught your breath. This whore of a team, the man behind us is saying, has betrayed us so many times, we know the way it's going to go. The black shirts of Siena keep pounding away at that goal, so far away from this end that you can barely see what's happening.

It's suddenly tense but not as tense as it should be. The ultras are singing and singing. I can see Left-Behind there, screaming like it's his last night on earth. That's their way of dissipating the dread that the dream is over. They really thought it was their year. And now it's slipping away and all they can do is bear witness to their presence by being as loud as possible.

This new song is an old favourite, apparently started (although the provenance and dates of all ultra inventions are hotly debated) by Torino ultras. To the tune of the Beach Boys' 'Sloop John B', we're singing what has been an anthem all year: 'It seems impossible, that I'm still here with you, this is an illness that never leaves. I want to go away, away from here, but I can't survive far from you.' It's a song that seems to encapsulate much of what this ultra life is like: it's an addiction or illness, something you can't do without. The 'here' is less about the team than the terraces.

Everyone says that being an ultra is a way of life. But it's a way of life that has evolved, mutated, regenerated and reinvented itself. And it's the evolution of the ultra world that makes Ciccio so melancholic.

'It truly, truly hurts me to see what happens on the terraces now,' he says, ignoring the game. 'It makes me suffer greatly. Because I know we're responsible. It was us who created this world. But the thing has got out of hand. There's been an escalation, and we've gone from fist-fights to knives, from knives to flares, from flares to ambushes, to Molotov cocktails, to bombs and to pistols. It keeps getting worse.'

———

Ten months earlier, Cosenza
(Casa degli Ultrà)

It's the Tuesday night before the first game of the season. Everyone is gathering in the squatted building for the Curva Sud's weekly meeting. The air is dense with smoke from cigarettes and spliffs. There are about twenty to thirty people. A few come late and a few storm off, so it's hard to be precise. There are half a dozen women: Susi Sete ('Boozy Suzy'), MonSicca ('SkinnyMon') plus a few others. But the atmosphere is highly testosteronic.

The Curva Sud broke into this abandoned building last winter. Squatting is usually done by far-leftists for the creation of 'social centres' and, more recently, by far-right extra-parliamentarians like CasaPound. But it's unusual for an ultra group to take possession of an empty building. The group quickly rechristened the place 'The House of the Ultras'. They painted all the radiators and steps red and blue. They cleared out spillikin needles left by heroin-users and stripped out what was left of the bathrooms. They issued a press release and dealt with a flutter of interest from the Calabrian papers.

Their slogan was '*fuori le curve dagli stadi*' ('get the terraces out of the stadiums'). It is the sort of rallying cry that can cut in all sorts of different ways, according to what is meant by 'the terraces'. The Curva Sud group says the slogan means taking the ethics of the *curva* into the streets: a party atmosphere to battle repression, exclusion and intolerance.

The building was in the shadow of the old centre of Cosenza, the hill the other side of the Busento river. The ultras' new 'house' was central and anyone could reach it on foot. But there was plenty of parking around about for the days when hundreds met there and piled into minibuses for away matches.

Inside, it's identical to most ultra dens: a computer with the group's Facebook page open, paper and biros used to add up how many are going to the game, who has paid up, who is owing. There are beer bottles and ashtrays everywhere, as well as sofas and speakers wired up to cracked phones.

Súrici ('Mouse') must be in his early twenties. He's walking in the middle of the circle, swinging a metal baseball bat. He's doing it playfully but there's an edge about it too. Sometimes he puts the bat down and picks up the industrial stapler, pretending to staple someone's neck. 'Bam,' he shouts, and everyone laughs.

U Lisciu ('Chill'), a fifty-something man with pen and paper behind the bar, calls everyone to order. He explains the cost of the minibuses going to Monopoli on Saturday. Everyone loves Chill. He used to come to games, for years, with one small banner: 'Fantastic World'. Then Mouse gives a little speech. He wants to get things clear from the start. He's short and paunchy, with close eyes and an exuberant energy that slips from good humour to fury in an instant.

'None of you has to come with us,' says Mouse. 'I'll never force you to fucking come with us. You go wherever the fuck you want…' He pauses, rotating the bat slowly above his head like a scarf. 'But if you come with us, we're a group. United. Together. Compact. Shoulder to shoulder. This season we're going to serious piazzas. We're going up against the Catanesi, against the Reggini…'

'The Leccesi,' someone chucks in.

'The Leccesi.' Mouse smiles at the thought. 'We're up against the Catanzaresi.'

'Mouse,' says Lastica ('Elastic'), '*aspè*' ('wait up').

Pent-up anger explodes. Now everyone is shouting who they think should speak. 'Let Mouse finish' or 'Go on, Elastic.' In the end, it's Elastic who is left standing after the verbal brawl. He is tense with a taut face. He probably got his nickname because he's rubbery and can hurt you with a flick of his fist.

'Why are we going in a minibus', Elastic asks, 'if we said ten days ago we were going to take the train?'

'Who the fuck said we were taking the train?' Mouse whispers the question, stretching his neck and scowling. 'Did I say that?' The place is very silent now.

Elastic is knocked back. He had made an assumption without running it by Mouse.

'Was it decided in *sede*?' Mouse is still whispering. The *sede* (like the 'seat' of a government) is the grandiose name for this squat.

Elastic feels insulted. He's steaming now, as he is during the games when the team – the *lupi* or 'wolves', after their team logo – are playing like shit. 'It was on the chat,' he says limply.

'Fuck the chat,' Mouse explodes, smashing the baseball bat onto the tiles. 'Fucking chat chat chat chat chat. We decide everything here, together.'

'Sounds to me it was all decided before we came in,' Elastic shouts back, and the room explodes again. Everyone is yelling now, arms raised, fingertips bouncing onto chests or onto foreheads. It's all in dialect, a thuddy mixture of Ds and Us. There are sawn-off syllables – the last 're' of every verb is missing, as is the end of every name.

The argument somehow goes to the heart of everything: it's about who makes decisions and how, it's about unity and autonomy, it's about organization and respect, for the leaders and for the troops, it's about money and egos. But amidst the anarchic shouting, there's an order. Three or four people raise their arms, trying to catch the eye of Chill, who's standing behind the bar and roughly deciding who should speak.

Walking around the ring of chairs, inside and out, is U Mundatu ('Baldy' or 'Egg'). He's like an old-fashioned jester at a monarch's court: a clown and peacemaker. As everyone is growling, some storming out, he's interrupting courageously, telling home truths to whoever needs to hear them. He's a hardcore stoner, so offers a joint as a balm, bringing people back into the circle. He can flare up, too, but his big brown teeth are soon grinning again. And so between Chill and Egg, the meeting – in all its aggressive, chaotic but purposeful energy – goes on.

Tensions are high not just because it's the start of a new season but because of the split amongst the city's ultras. A man called Pietro left the Curva in 2015 to form his own group, the Anni Ottanta ('The 80s'). The group's title harks back to the glory days when Cosenza had the finest ultras in Italy. The move was about many things, including wheelchair access and opposition to the *Tessera* (the obligatory fan's 'loyalty card' needed to gain access to certain games), which the Curva had slowly started adopting. It was about egos, too, of course: about who should lead the singing and who had a direct link to the founding fathers. Although the Curva Sud called itself '1978', none of them were around back then, so Anni Ottanta claims to be the city's authentic ultra group. There's only one way to find out who is more ultra, says Vindov ('Window', a young lad missing a couple of front teeth): to 'come to the hands' and fight for the title.

All summer the tensions have been stoked. Insults fly on Facebook. The Curva Sud accuses Anni Ottanta of many things, mainly that they were never around when all the other groups stuck with Cosenza through relegations and bankruptcies. The

Anni Ottanta, they say, are being manipulated by the semi-retired leaders from those old days who disdain the lawlessness of the Curva. Sometimes the accusations are the same in both directions, that the rival group has accepted criminal elements to act as *spalle* ('shoulders') in the heat of battle. For its part, Anni Ottanta says the Curva is so anarchic that its singing and choreographies are embarrassing and that, most seriously in this profoundly anti-fascist city, there are now elements within it who aren't anti-fascists. The only thing both sides agree on is that no one from outside is supposed to stoke the divisions by talking about them.

So, Mouse and Chill and the other leaders of the Curva have a tough job. They know that they have to respect the dozens of smaller groups that come under the umbrella of the Curva Sud: the Alkool Group, Cosenza Vecchia, the 90s Gang (with their slogan, '*Zimeca*' – more or less 'shit-stirrers'), the Sciollati ('the messed up ones'), the Brigate (the 'Brigades'), and so on… There are dozens of groupings and 'currents', each with proud leaders and slightly different agendas and supporters. But at the same time, the Curva has to remain compact and united, not just at dangerous away games where fights are inevitable, but even on home turf.

Part of the Curva Sud's difficulty in its search for unity is that Cosentini (the inhabitants of this vibrant city) are viscerally opposed to the imposition of order. The Cosenza ultras proudly relate the criticism, voiced about them by a policeman on TV, that 'you never know how many they are, what time they're leaving, nor when they'll arrive, they appear out of nothing, and most of all they don't pay for their tickets'. That element of surprise isn't strategic. It's because they don't even know themselves when or where they're going to roll up. Appointments are as firm as butter in the sun.

Cosentini are proud of that anarchic streak. Some followers of the Wolves call themselves '*lupi spuri*' ('bastard wolves'), as if they're not even answerable to the pack. They relish the unnerving way they appear and disappear: one of their famous banners once boasted that 'Cosentini like playing hide-and-seek'. Getting everyone together, in one place, is a tough task. One poster about a protest promises 'a messy and disordered march'. That disorder is not a result of incompetence but of creative energy: the city is so small – just short of 70,000 souls – that you easily get side-tracked by a friend of a friend. It's so stimulating that you often find yourself enticed down a cobbled alley by a sudden impulse.

The banditry isn't just a pretence. In Calabria the scorn for authority is about something deeper. This is a part of the world where many of the citizens are convinced that nothing good will ever come from the state, from city hall or from the church. They have long distrusted the powerful, and judge each individual on their own merits, not their acquired grandeur. So here there are no titles, and often not even proper names or surnames but just nicknames instead: U Rimasto ('Left-Behind'), Mezzo-Chilo ('Half-a-Kilo'), U Fissato ('One-Track') and so on.

The city is way down on the big toe of the Italian boot and is a place of both compromise and intransigence. The name comes from the historic agreement, the 'consensus' of 356 BC, in which the warring Bruttii tribes recognized each other and made peace. The Pancrazio Hill, at the foot of which the Crati and Busento rivers unite, became the Bruttii's new capital, 'Cosentia'. Anyone who messed with the Bruttii usually came off badly. They were tough mountain people who lived on the high plains of the Silan mountains. In the fourth century BC, the Greek colonies of Magna Grecia – all along the Calabrian and Lucanian coasts – asked for assistance from home to suppress this war-like people.

Alexander I of Epirus (the uncle of Alexander the Great) was despatched but despite a peace accord with Rome, he was killed in 330 BC near the Acheron river, in the lost city of Pandosia Bruzia. Another attempted invader, Alaric (who sacked Rome in AD 410) is buried somewhere here.

In the nineteenth century, Cosenza was at the forefront of the insurrections against the Bourbon monarchy: the *carbonaro* Vincenzo Federico and the Bandiera brothers (actually from Venice) were put to death in Cosenza for fighting to unite Italy. And when that unification brought a brutal repression by Piedmont troops in the South, Calabria became famous for its brigandage. According to one historian, Vincenzo Cuoco, Cosenza was always 'a place of antique and ardent republicanism'.

But the city wasn't famous only for its rebellions. It was one of the most important cradles of modern philosophy, with the writings of the sixteenth-century Bernardino Telesio influencing Bacon, Bruno, Campanella and Descartes. Cosenza was even nicknamed the 'Athens of Calabria', and Norman Douglas wrote that 'the literary record of Cosenza is one of exceptional brilliance. For acute and original thought this town can hardly be surpassed by any other of its size on earth.'

Which is perhaps why this squatted ultra building in the deep South feels like the twenty-first-century equivalent of a gathering of brigands. In this shouty, egalitarian assembly, people are drinking and spliffing hard, while discussing strategy, enemies, evading capture and the conquest of new spaces. And when the business is over, people drink and smoke some more, and pump up the music – a mix of ska, punk and hip-hop.

Although it's anarchic here, there's actually a heartfelt organization at work. When the ultras moved into this building it was grim. Formally a school dining room – half a dozen rooms on the ground floor and a large basement – it had been used as a crack-and-smack den for as long as anyone could remember. Needles, excrement and broken glass littered the floor. Rubbish was piled high in the corners. Now it feels like a sparsely furnished flat: there are sofas, chairs, a bar, a toilet. They've got cardboard boxes of T-shirts and scarves. There are dozens of plaques and scarves from other ultra groups and memorials to dead comrades. The scarves on the walls all have a similar theme of generic outlawry: among them are the names 'Smoked Heads', 'Rebel Tendency', 'Clandestines' and 'Fedayeen Bronx'. But there's a house-proudness here too. There's no flush in the toilet, so you're supposed to fill a tupperware tub from the tap to flush it. There's a handwritten sign to remind everyone: 'An ultra always flushes the bog because he respects his territory and his brother who has cleaned it.'

The most striking element is the chromatic fundamentalism. Everything is painted in Cosenza's red-and-blue: the steps, the radiators, the doors, the window frames. You see something similar in the city itself: curtains, bonnets, hubcaps and shop shutters painted in the team colours.

It's the colours, you realize, that create the tribe. It's the colours that create the deep bonds. They're what you live and die for. As one of their songs goes: 'When I have to die, I want to bring my colours to paradise.' They're the totem. You defend them and impose them. Your colours aren't just simple hues, they're who you are. An insult to the red-and-blue is as intolerable as an insult to your mother or sister.

And yet no one mentions the football. There's never talk of any player. '*Cazzo*,' says one guy, 'I don't even know who we're playing on Saturday. I don't really give a fuck. The important thing is that we carry our colours there, that we make ourselves heard and make ourselves respected.' The real game is between the ultras.

Classical writers always knew that *agon* – the sporting 'struggle' – had an alchemic effect on the character of those watching. '*Effervescimus ad aliena certamina*,' wrote Seneca ('We get worked up at the struggles of others'). Tertullian, in his essay 'On Spectacles', wrote that 'there is no spectacle without disturbance of the spirit... For even if a man enjoys spectacles modestly and uprightly, as befits his status or age or even his natural disposition, his soul is not unstirred and he is not without a silent rousing of the spirit.'

But as well as being spiritually uplifting, sport could also open the gate to man's baser instincts, especially when the Greek *agon* gave way to the Roman *circensis*, the circus of gladiatorial fights and killings. Augustine writes of Alypius: '... he saw the blood, he drank in the savagery, and did not turn away but fixed his gaze on it. Unaware of what he was doing, he devoured the mayhem and was delighted by the wicked contest and drunk on its cruel pleasure... He looked, he shouted, he was fired up, and he carried away with him the madness that would goad him to return.'

Like the carnival, the circus was a place of ritualized licence, where rules went, briefly, into abeyance. The arena was a place of *parrhesia*, of speech without brakes, where the plebeians and the people could let off steam. There they could think and say things not permissible in the more ordered world outside. The moralists of the ancient world who saw what happened to fans in the arena used a language almost identical to the outraged commentators of our own day. Dio Chrysostum, in the second century, wrote of fans: '... they completely forget themselves, and without shame say and do the first thing that comes into their heads. It's as if they were under the effect of some exciting substance. They're unable to follow the game in a civil manner.'

The architecture of the arena – so similar to the stadiums of today – encouraged that contrast with the urbane, civilized world of the city as people abandoned their usual composure. As Elias Canetti wrote in his book on crowds:

> Outside, facing the city, the arena displays a lifeless wall; inside is a wall of people. The spectators turn their backs to the city. They have been lifted out of its structure of walls and streets and, for the duration of their time in the arena, they do not care about anything which happens there; they have left behind all their associations, rules and habits. Their remaining together in large numbers for a stated period of time is secure and their excitement has been promised them. But only under one definite condition: the discharge must take place inside the arena.

Violence was associated with these sporting contests long before the twentieth century. Football itself proved such an incendiary sport that, in 1580, the Governor of Bologna banned it in order to 'avoid fights, scandals and enmities'. The order was widely ignored, so another followed a year later, addressed to 'dishonest youths and boys, who with little respect and regard damage, ruin and break...'

Very often the violence was between rival suburbs or villages. Italy is a notoriously heterogenous country, fractured by wars between Barons, Dukes, Doges, Emperors and Popes as they fought for control of territory, tax revenue and obeisance. Emblematic of that incessant fighting was the Battle of Zappolino in 1325. It isn't remembered for the loss of over 3,000 lives but for the fact that, during the conflict between troops from Modena and Bologna, the Modenesi stole a wooden bucket from a well. Thanks to Alessandro Tassoni's famous poem, 'La Secchia Rapita', the fight is now simply known as 'the Battle of the Stolen Bucket'. Its theft was a symbol of disdain for the enemy; its retention a mark of martial prowess and civic pride. That hatred between neighbours meant that, once football was formalized as a sport in Italy in the late nineteenth century, it offered, in the words of Gianni Brera, 'magnificent pretexts for recurrent, collective feuds' between certain cities and towns. The symbolism of that bucket would be replaced by the ultras' herald, which bore the name of the group and was flaunted and fought over.

That formalization of football began in the early 1890s, when an English maritime doctor, James Spensley, introduced 'Association Football' to Italy. Since the opening of the Suez Canal in 1869, English crews had begun to dock in Genova on their way to and from India. Often, they only found time for informal kick-arounds on the hardstanding around Genova's port. But if they stayed longer, Spensley would take them up by the prison to play on the wet grass. In 1893, Spensley and various British consular officials formally constituted the Genoa Cricket and Football Club in an office in Via Palestro. On almost every scarf, shirt, sticker and website connected to Genoa (the club retains the English spelling) that iconic date is present.

As a city, Genova is famous for many things, including the green pesto of pine nuts and basil ('pesto' just means ground or crushed) and for the oily *focaccia ligure*. The mispronunciation of the city's name (or maybe the city's name in dialect, 'Zena') also gave the world the word 'jeans'. But the city was most renowned, at the turn of the last century, for its football team.

It was, by some way, the most successful club in Italy. It won nine *scudetti* ('little shields'), although the first championship in 1898 only lasted a day and featured just four teams. Doctor Spensley played in six of the scudetto-winning sides. The last time Genoa won a scudetto was almost a century ago, in 1924.

Some imagined that this English import would prove a civilizing influence, teaching a violent society how to compete peacefully according to rules and laws. But it didn't work out that way, either in England or abroad. Rather than sport replacing warfare, it often became an excuse for conflict, especially in Italy where the word for fan – *tifoso* – was coined because many over-excitable supporters were in such a sweat that they appeared to have typhoid fever.

There were many riots and fights because of the game, including infamous pitched battles in 1902 between Genoa and Andrea Doria (one half of the future Sampdoria) and in 1905 between Juventus and Genoa. In 1912, police had to save a referee from being stoned in a game between Andrea Doria and Inter. And in 1914, stones and revolvers were used in a match between Livorno and Pisa.

The first death in a game of Italian football occurred when a Viareggio fan was doubling as a linesman in 1920. Viareggio, a Tuscan coastal town, was playing its local rival, Lucca, and when the crowd became unruly, a *Carabiniere* (a member of the national militarized police) pulled out his gun and accidentally shot the linesman, Augusto Morganti. Three days of rioting ensued.

From 1920 until 1922, when the country appeared to be on the brink of revolution and chaos, rampaging fascist gangs called *Squadre d'Azione* ('Action Squads') were fighting workers, socialists and unionists. Their leader was a demagogic former journalist and war veteran called Benito Mussolini. The ranks of these squads were swelled by disaffected veterans from the First World War, who felt betrayed both by the Treaty of Versailles and by the scorn allegedly shown for their military valour. Many of the so-called *squadristi* were *Arditi* ('the bold' or 'the daring') – an elastic term that had stretched from a specific infantry regiment, founded in 1917 during the First World War, to include those men who in 1919 had occupied Fiume under the leadership of Gabriele D'Annunzio as a protest against the handing over of the city (in present-day Croatia) to the new state of Yugoslavia.

Youthfulness was a central characteristic of these gangs. They adopted a student song from Turin, which had been taken up by the Alpine troops, called *Giovinezza* ('Youthfulness'). In this, as in so much else, the black-shirted squads were eerily similar to the future ultra gangs. They had deliberately unsettling sobriquets – 'the Desperate', 'the Dauntless' – and carried macabre banners, often with a skull-and-cross-bones. There was a ludic element, too, revelling in stealing the symbols of their rivals, which they called *stracci* or 'rags'. The signboard of the socialist newspaper, *Avanti!*, was taken to Benito Mussolini's offices in Milan as a trophy. Very often, too, the *squadristi* were recreational drug users. Cocaine had become commonplace during the occupation of Fiume and was now fuel for aggression against the left. In Ferrara, the gang was called Celibano simply because it was the Italianization of the 'cherry brandy' they gulped before they went into action. Each squad had a boss called – using the Ethiopian term for a warlord – a *ras*. Many ultras (deliberately or by chance) now split the word 'ultras' in two on their banners, placing a symbol in the middle so as to make 'ras' a separate word, as if it were a nod to their ancestry.

Just as with the ultras fifty years later, the *squadristi* seemed to be recreating the factionalisms of the past. In his book, *Fascist Voices*, the late historian Christopher Duggan quotes an eighteen-year-old's shock at the bloodthirstiness of the spring of 1921: '… one act of vendetta follows another… people are pitted against each other as if the malign spirit of the Middle Ages had restored the old feelings of the Blacks and Whites [the two factions of the Guelphs that tore Florence apart in the time of Dante]. It's just the same now as it was then – only the colours of the parties have changed; but the ferocity is the same and an air of hatred swirls around our heads as if it were the very breath of life.'

The violence of the ultras was never on a par with that of the fascist squads (288 people were killed in public disorder in 1920 alone, only four of whom were fascists), but the symbolism was often identical: Mussolini wanted his black-shirted insurgency to appear like a 'war of religion', with its own liturgy and martyrs that would oblige Italians to recognize – as they hadn't, he felt, after the war – 'the holiness of the sacrifice of our dead'. There was a perverse religiosity to *squadrismo*, because the bloodshed sanctified the cause and made recanting akin to blasphemy. Faith was constantly invoked in fascist circles, partly because it papered over the cracks of ideological vacuity, but also because it enabled fascism, in Duggan's words, 'to map much of its value system onto the familiar landscape of Roman Catholicism'.

A few years later, after Mussolini had taken power, there was barely a match that wasn't accompanied by fights. In July 1925, shots were fired between fans of Bologna and Genoa who had encountered each other at Turin's Porta Nuova station. What's remarkable about the subsequent statement from the FIGC (the governing body of Italian football) is how the language used to describe the fans back then is almost identical to how it still labels ultras and their deeds: '… this deplorable streak which threatens to disrupt irredeemably the very life of football...' In the 1930s, Italy twice won the World Cup and the popularity of the sport, with all the surrounding passion and political exploitation, reached new heights.

Present Day: Cosenza v. Paganese (Serie C)

There's a sense of safety, even invincibility, when you're in a crowd. Everyone knows you're with them, and they're with you. You join up with a dozen, and then your dozen with dozens more. When there are two hundred of you, it's intoxicating. It's not just any crowd but your crowd, your crew. In the next two hours, nothing will come between you.

The view of the mountain behind the far end of the stadium, its crags kissed by the setting sun, elevates the mood. An unlikely victory would give you the excuse for another song, another beer. But the actual spectacle of blokes chasing a ball about – that seems a bit ridiculous. Singing in unison, with the same purpose, is the source of the buzz and the euphoria. Your voices unite, your chest vibrates. All the shouting is suddenly harmonic. You're making yourself heard at last but the words aren't yours, the rhythm isn't yours. You've become one with the group.

The unity doesn't come through words and music alone, but through actions too – the clapping and the jumping are tightly timed. It's all about fitting in. You're all facing one direction and you can see if the person in front claps their hands at the wrong moment, if someone isn't bouncing in time. There are also looser codes of reaction to the game: agony and astonishment, outrage and ecstasy. Everyone holds their head when a shot flays the post.

23

Yearning forearms stretch towards the ref when he gives a free kick to the other side. There's no space for neutrality. A T-shirt says: 'The strength of the pack is the wolf. The strength of the wolf is the pack.'

It's the first home game of the season. The previous match, at Monopoli, was a 3–1 disappointment. The Wolves had been 2–0 down within ten minutes and never looked like coming back. Now we're at the San Vito Stadium, in the Curva Bergamini. There's a passable portrait of Denis Bergamini, the Cosenza midfielder who was almost certainly murdered in 1989, on the back wall. Looming over the *curva* are two new high-rise buildings, both standing empty. 'The usual corruption,' sighs Boozy Suzy.

Only two thousand fans are here, so large sections of the stadium are empty. About a hundred ultras form the hardcore of the *curva*. There's no distinction between them and the ordinary fans, except for their noise and passion. Here, at least, it is raucous and contagious, the lyrics repetitive and basic. There's a lot about love and beauty and heart. For tough nuts, the ultras' songs are often pretty mawkish. If you think about the words, though, you miss the point. Like liturgies, they're repetitive for a reason. There are so many oh-ings – predictable rising and falling cadences with 'oh' as the only lyric – and a song is repeated for so long, again and again, that soon anyone can join the bandit roar. The wooden lyricism enjoys a brusque tempo. One-Track, the bearded pizza maker, gives everything a fast and booming undercurrent on the drum.

But nothing is spontaneous. If you burst into song of your own accord here, you will be shouted at and, somehow, persuaded to stop. Because on the railings, or 'irons', at the front are two or three men passing round a megaphone, their back to the pitch. These clerics lead the singing, furiously screaming at anyone who gives their throat a rest. The megaphone, covered with stickers from various groups, is in the hands of a hoarse and topless Elastic. 'Put away your fucking phones,' he screams angrily.

Now he's giving it full whack, and hundreds are linking arms and jumping as high as they dare, making the stadium vibrate a little underfoot: '*Che bello è, quando esco di casa,*' people are smiling, catching each others' eyes: 'How beautiful it is when I get out of the house, to go to the stadium, to support Cosenza. Oh-oh-oh-oh, oh-oh-oh-oh.'

Nowadays, many ultra groups dress almost identically. It reinforces the sense of the tribe, of belonging. Because of the drift to the far right, it's common for ultras to wear black shirts and have shaved heads. But any uniform would be too orderly for the Cosentini. 'All Colours are Beautiful' says one banner in English, which is partly a nod to this terrace's inclusivity but is really there because it makes the ACAB acronym ('all cops are bastards'). As ever in the ultra underworld, a noble impulse is mixed up with name-calling. But there's a sincerity about the wish for inclusion. Another banner, in the *tribuna* (the main stand), says 'Refugees Welcome'.

A few people have their eye on the game but many more are watching the spectacle of this terrace. This is the real theatre, the true festival. It's like an open-air club, full of bleary-eyed partygoers in the afternoon sun. That game over there on the grass is decidedly incidental. And even if you wanted to, you would struggle to see the action through all the flags. Many fans are hugging friends, looking back at the faces above us, staring down at their palms as they're skinning up. If you ask someone the name of a player, they look at you with annoyance – 'eh?' – like you had just asked them the time when they were in the midst of making love.

But then a goal goes in. For Paganese. Then a minute later, another. There are groans and shouts and insults. 'Our defence is as open as your mother's legs,' shouts Egg towards the manager.

'This is shit,' says Left-Behind. He's on the fringes of the singing, leaning on the horizontal metal poles. 'Shit, the only good thing that ever happened here,' he says, 'was the motorway to take us away.'

That sense of fatalism informs all of the festivity, because despite the fun, shit-ness is an integral part of this way of life. Shitty bars, shitty buses, shitty stadiums, shitty games. Apart from those moments of euphoria, being an ultra is a grim existence. The re-enchantment of grimness is part of the alchemy of this world. But often the spell is broken and you wonder why you're spending precious time and money on this crap. Many ask themselves: 'Who forces me to do this?'

But almost as if he can read the mood of his men, Elastic, with the megaphone, is heckling the crowd, screaming as if his voice alone could save a season. And suddenly everyone joins in the well-known song. 'Come on Cosenza, take us away from this shitty division.' It's an old favourite, sung by almost every group in the lower leagues: '*Forza Cosenza, portaci via, da questa merda di categoria.*' Suddenly, Left-Behind is brought to life, taken by the bouncing music and the vibrating concrete, and growls along. That song sums it up: the passion for the city but, at the same time, the longing that it might help you escape. Cosenza eventually lose the home game 0–2. No points after two games and, including a Coppa Italia disaster, a third defeat in a row.

———

1940s, Cosenza

There are two rivers in Cosenza. There's a legend that if you dip your hair, your morals or your silk in the Crati, they'll lighten and go fair. But try the Busento, they say, and they'll turn you and your cloth dark. The city grows at the confluence of these two rivers and their reputations. Their waters flow around the hilltop of the old city, Cosenza Vecchia, from whose summits and small squares you can glimpse the Silan mountains like sleeping rhinos on the horizon, black against the Ionian sunset.

In the mid-1940s Francesco spent most of his days hunting for treasure in those two rivers with his friends. There was a legend that Alaric had been buried with his riches in one of the two rivers. To keep the location secret, all the slaves who had dug the tomb were killed and buried along with their master.

The boys – Francesco and his friends – were only seven. They had shaved heads to keep them free of bugs. Hygiene was sometimes easier with scissors than with soaps. They knew the war was raging all around them. They had heard the bombs for months, first far off but now getting closer.

Because they were smart, they didn't look for treasure but for bones. They reckoned there would have been more slaves than gold, so the one would lead to the other. It added to the excitement too because every few metres by the edge of the water were chalky grey remains of birds and hares.

When they got bored of looking for bones, the boys paddled in the river, pretending to catch sight of gold in the water. It was normally just white stones, though once Francesco had put some tin down there and fooled everyone. His father was a cake-maker and Francesco knew how to make dull things glisten.

Born in November 1937, the oldest of four boys, there was a rough edge to Francesco. His mother had died when he was five. Once in a while, Francesco took a stick and pretended to be the executioner killing Alaric's slaves. He was like that when he was in the mood. He could only remember two things about his mother. The first was her white face in the coffin. It was all wrong: she was dressed up in finery, whereas in life she had only ever worn rough clothes. Any whiteness came from flour and wool, not lace and silk.

The other thing he remembered was that she used to kiss him after communion, as soon as she came back from that silent queue at the altar. She said she wanted to give him the flavour of Christ. All these bones in the riverbank reminded him of her, of what she must have become.

When they weren't in the rivers, the boys always played football. For the ball, they would creep up on the flock of sheep grazing outside the city. Francesco, the strongest, used to hold the ram by its horns as the other lads pulled wool off the animal. Often it had maggots and shit in it, but it didn't matter. They would steal socks from home and stuff them full of the wool. The balls eventually fell apart and, come the next spring, the boys began chasing the sheep again.

Francesco had three younger brothers. He played soldiers with them. They had a flag, some rag they had found in a stable. It was ripped apart in a fight, so now they had two halves of a flag. Without a mother to keep the peace, it was often a loud and melancholy house. Sometimes Francesco got into trouble for jumping into orchards and stealing the figs and mandarins. 'Every night,' he remembers, 'my father had to beat me for something.'

Once a week, Francesco's father brought home unsold pastries from his shop: *cannoli, sfogliatine, torrone, pignolate, susumelle* or *piparelle*. In their spartan home, those luxuries were a glimpse of another world where glistening cream oozed from soft pastries. The ones his father brought back had cream turning hard and yellow, so the children battled each other for the least stale offerings.

That year Francesco was sent to the orphanage. His father felt he needed direction and discipline, and the grand building – peach-coloured with wide, white vertical pillars over its three storeys – looked like the place to find it. Francesco still played with his friends but he missed his suburb, Laurignano, and the long, idle days with nothing to do. Now he had to practise handwriting and make his bed every morning. He escaped once, running back home, but his guilty, grieving father brought him back.

That summer, the war was getting closer. On 25 July 1943, two weeks after the Allies had landed in Sicily, Benito Mussolini was arrested. He was imprisoned on the Gran Sasso mountain in Abruzzo. On 8 September Italy announced that it was joining the Allied forces in the fight against Germany. Four days later, on 12 September, Mussolini was rescued from his mountain-top prison by an elite team of SS and parachute troops. As the Allies worked their way north up the Italian peninsula, Mussolini was installed by the Germans at Salò, a small town on the banks of Lake Garda. His regime there became known as the Repubblica di Salò, or RSI. For the next year and a half, until the end of the war on 25 April 1945, Italians fought a brutal civil war: German troops, and those fascists loyal to Mussolini and his Republic, battled the Allies and the Italian partisans. The furious debates in post-war Italy, which took place on the terraces as much as in academic circles, were about who could be considered the traitors in that civil war – the partisans or the fascists?

At the end of the war, there was no equivalent of Germany's denazification. Whether because of Catholic notions of mercy, or because of a conscious revulsion from the reprisals that took place in the immediate post-war years, Italy deliberately avoided any widespread prosecution of fascist war criminals, or even cleansing of its bureaucratic personnel. General Rodolfo Graziani, the Minister of War in the RSI, only served four months of a nineteen-year prison sentence. In *Mussolini's Italy*, R. J. B. Bosworth notes that out of 128,837 civil servants in Naples, only twenty-three ex-fascists were removed from their posts. The figure in Palermo was five out of 26,636. In 1950 only five German ex-soldiers were held in Italian prisons compared with 1,300 in France and 1,700 in Yugoslavia.

The problem was that almost everyone was compromised to some degree and the realists were, in Bosworth's words, 'appalled at the idea of a thorough-going critical legal examination of the relationship between Italian banking, business and law and their political masters under the dictatorship'. Better, it seemed, to look to the future than reopen the wounds of the past. One Italian sociologist, Paolo Treves, returned to Italy and wrote an essay called 'The Conspiracy of Silence' about this wilful amnesia. One young woman complained in her diary about this 'moment of chameleons'. The result was a post-war settlement that seemed, to idealists on both sides, founded on a squalid compromise. 'The Republic,' wrote Christopher Duggan, 'failed to define itself – and be defined by the outside world – clearly and openly in relation to fascism.' Both the fascists loyal to Benito Mussolini and the partisans loyal to anti-fascism felt betrayed.

The country's new constitution forbade the resurrection of

the Fascist Party 'in any form whatsoever'. But in December 1946, a new political party emerged: the Movimento Sociale Italiano. Its usual abbreviation – MSI – deliberately recalled the RSI, Mussolini's 'social republic'. The Western powers and the Vatican regarded the party as less dangerous than the much larger PCI (the Italian Communist Party) which sometimes appeared ambivalent towards parliamentary democracy. In 1952, the Scelba Law made the denigration of the 'values of the resistance', and the celebration of 'the exponents, principles, achievements or methods of fascism', illegal. That law was never applied to the MSI. The former general and war criminal, Rodolfo Graziani, became the party's Honorary President. The party's unofficial slogan was that old regime favourite, 'Boia Chi Molla' ('the executioner for quitters'). Soon the party had a newspaper, Il Secolo d'Italia, and youth wing, Giovane Italia (which later merged into the Fronte della Gioventù, the Youth Front). Every time an Italian government required the support of the MSI during the post-war years, small concessions were made to the rump of unrepentant followers of il Duce. The most symbolic, perhaps, was the burial of Mussolini's corpse in the family crypt in Predappio (on 1 September 1957), thereby making the small Romagna town a site of pilgrimage. The post-war settlement, however, was no more satisfactory for fascists than it was for partisans. They felt that men and women who had been courageous patriots were now being derided as traitors, and that they were the abiding loyalists in an era of hypocrisy and democratic cross-dressing.

The lingering bitterness, on both sides, about the compromises made by Italy's First Republic (1948–92) would find eloquent expression on the terraces. It was as if, a generation after the end of the war, the historical debates were revisited by extremist fans who chose ideological as much as sporting sides. Treves had written that there was a post-war 'conspiracy of silence', but the vociferous and countercultural ultras – loud loyalists, ever averse to fudging – would smash the conspiracy. They re-enacted that period of civil war in Italy's stadiums, taking inspiration from the names and emblems of those bloody years.

There's an extraordinary flexibility to an ultra group, almost as if – like a football team – it can change shape according to the situation. In one sense, it is very open and its boundaries extremely porous. If you're on the terraces, you'll be able to wander amongst its members and feel at one with them through the contagion of the choreographies and the songs. They don't merely welcome you, they scream at you, demanding more involvement and participation. But their headquarters in the suburbs are forbidding: a metal door, informal bouncers, access permitted only to an established in-group. The group is transformed from a very public to a very private organization.

That alteration is also structural. An ultra group invariably boasts about its egalitarianism and the fact that anyone is allowed to become a participant. It's true that there is a genuine and sincere inclusivity. And yet the group is profoundly hierarchical, structured like a company, with well-defined responsibilities and rewards. It's not unusual for the leader to call himself *Presidente* or *Capitano*. Often, in a large ultra group in a big club, it's harder to arrange an audience with that leader than a government minister. Much of the diction is similar to a political party: there is invariably a *direttivo* (the 'board'), the *tesserati* (the 'card-carriers' or 'members') and so on.

That mutability of the group is also evident in what it actually does. Being an ultra is both incessantly active but also eerily passive. There's non-stop singing during the game – a lot of hand-clapping and jumping and vocal straining – and the week is filled with meetings, bookings, choreographic preparations and uncomfortable journeys. But actually, the ultra is a largely static observer. The role is really about spectatorship of – and not participation in – the sport.

Because there's such an ambiguity about the group, an uncertainty about whether it is egalitarian or hierarchical, profoundly open or secretive, it seeks definition in other ways. There's a never-ending 'mirror-stage' in which the group studies itself and its moves: the incessant photographing of the terraces, and of each other dressed up in the colours, is an attempt to understand itself. And since the group is constantly changing – there are always retirees, those who are banned from stadiums by the authorities and then new recruits – that mirror-stage is actually not a passing phase but a constant.

What would be considered vanity or narcissism in an individual setting (plastering the walls of a bedroom with photographs of oneself) is instead an assertion of the tribe. Go into any ultra HQ and the walls are covered with snaps of the assembled masses on the streets and the terraces. In any game, there are hundreds of phones raised to take photographs but almost all are recording not the game, but the group's own moves, songs, banners and faces. It's a self-absorption that has reached new levels with the advent of social media.

And the same happens with rival ultra groups: we stand opposite them in the stadium, studying them, listening to them, imitating them, responding to them. It's remarkable that although every ultra group will boast about how unique they are, almost all do exactly the same things. The perception of the *curva* as a mirror is a common metaphor: 'Reflect yourselves in this marvel' the Catania ultras wrote on a banner to their rivals, Palermo, in April 2000. Often the notion of reflection is rather more coarse, like the time Inter ultras held up a banner to their Milan rivals just as the game started: 'the spectacle begins… look in the mirror', and thousands of fans turned round and dropped their trousers.

Talk to any older ultra and they will lovingly remember the childish excitement of trading photographs through the post with far-off fans from other groups, via the marketplace in the back-pages of sporting publication, *Guerin Sportivo*. Nowadays, they stalk social media accounts.

That mirroring doubtless takes place on an individual level too, as ultras, like Robert De Niro in *Taxi Driver*, practise their lines in the privacy of their bathrooms: 'You talkin' to me?' And it may be that the violence for which the ultras are so notorious is actually a symptom not of hatred at something superficially different (the rival city or colours) but something profoundly similar. Maybe the anger is aimed also at ourselves, our situation, and the failings we see in that mirror.

Torino

There are certain football teams that just seem to have more history: not in terms of trophies, but of tragedies that only make the fans more devoted.

In the 1940s Torino won five consecutive *scudetti*. At that time, ten of the eleven players in the Italian national team were from the club. But on 4 May 1949, a plane bringing the team back from a friendly match in Portugal crashed into the Basilica of Superga, the burial site of the House of Savoy, the former ruling dynasty of Italy. Thirty-one people lost their lives, including all but one of the 'Grande Torino' players (a single injured first-team player hadn't gone to Lisbon). Among the dead was an Englishman, the then-coach Lesley Lievesley.

At the funeral, Giorgio Tosatti remembers a city 'mute and dumb and breathing pain. I will never see again such a huge and quiet crowd, I will never see again a city suffer as much as Torino suffered that day.' The loss was so hugely felt not just because they were sensational players, capable of beating the mighty Roma 7–1. In the words of Franco Ossola, those players 'represented a series of values which the people had forgotten or lost along the way: dignity, honour, pride'.

Superga is now a place of pilgrimage, a shrine to loss and loyalty. There are scarves from all over Italy, and Europe, placed on the rails around the site. But far outnumbering all the others are the maroon ('*granata*') ones of Toro. There's a metal bull, the club's symbol, covered with stickers from fan groups. Photographs of players line the wall: large posters of all the victims, then a huge group shot.

The view from up here is magnificent. You can see the meeting of the two rivers, the Po and the Dora. You can see the long, straight boulevards, the white curves of the campus and the huge industrial warehouses. It's a city in which Juventus Football Club wins more medals but Toro embodies the deeper meaning of fandom. Fans of Toro suffer in ways that are almost uncanny. Gigi Meroni, their carefree sprite of a midfielder, used to move inside and outside defenders like a weaver's shuttle. He was killed at the age of 24, in 1967, when he was crossing the road. The coincidences between the Superga and Meroni tragedies were spooky: the basilica of Superga is where the members of the House of Savoy were buried and Meroni was killed on Corso Re [King] Umberto. The name of the pilot of the plane that crashed nineteen years before, in 1949, was also Meroni. The man who accidently killed the player as he was crossing the road was a teenage proto-ultra who had furiously protested against his hero's proposed sale to Juventus. That teenager, four decades later, became the President of the club, leading it to a near-fatal bankruptcy. The loss is still so deeply felt that when Torino wins, certain fans still go and pay homage to Meroni at the place where he died. There's a bronze shrine to him with a raffish photo. Above the photo is an angled football pitch with a huge football in the corner.

When thinking about fandom, it's impossible not to pause in Torino and ponder what it means to have martyrs. Their loss sacralizes a sporting cause. The melancholy around your team matches your personal sorrow, and therein lies the symmetry and satisfaction of fandom: you no longer feel alone in your state of bereavement. Your underdog team loses on the pitch, just as you do in life. Glory is evasive, but that in itself makes your commitment somehow glorious. In a secularized, rationalized, atomized world, that gathering around a single colour of loss, Toro's colour of blood, takes on an almost insane transcendentalism.

That explains what, to a non-ultra, is often incomprehensible: the sense of outrage when a player doesn't honour the *maglia*, the shirt, or the colours. Players are representing something far greater than themselves and will only understand how deep their mission is by listening to fans and hearing their stories. Sacralising the sport makes fans, and not footballers, the high priests of the lucrative game. As a Sampdoria banner once said:

'Sampdoria is a faith, her ultras its prophets.' A flier from Milan's Red-and-Black Brigades once boasted: 'We are the true moral masters of Milan.'

Even though it's a truism by now, it's especially clear in Italy that football has a religious dimension. The great Genovese singer-songwriter Fabrizio De André said fandom 'is a sort of lay faith'. Pier Paolo Pasolini said it was 'the last sacred representation of our time'. The stadium now seems a better place to ritualize and remember the dead, because while the church is supposedly universal, the cults initiated by the ultras are devoutly local. It's as if they have instinctively guessed that there's a profound link between a specific place and social bonds.

After the war, the frenzy common at football matches continued to spill over into insults and stone-throwing, punches and gunfire. In 1950 there was a pitch invasion in the game between Salernitana and Genoa. In February 1952, the referee of a Legnano–Bologna game was beaten up at Milano railway station. A few months later, seats were thrown onto the pitch in a game between Milan and Udinese. A year later, a referee disallowed a goal in the game between Pro Patria and Sampdoria, and fans pelted him with stones.

The violence was invariably aimed at the referee, who was the only non-partisan person in the stadium. Every year there were furious riots against refereeing decisions. In 1955, when Brescia won away at Salernitana 1–0, a thousand supporters heckled and threatened the referee. A penalty awarded by the referee in the Napoli–Bologna match of November 1955 led to a hundred people being wounded and eleven hospitalized amid 'shots fired between the crowd and the police'. All of those disturbances made the national papers, with photos of small mounted police units facing thousands of furious supporters. Sometimes the Sunday papers would publish charming panoramas of the riots as seen from above.

A sense of injustice was at the root of many of the riots after refereeing decisions. Provincial towns that felt ignored and over-looked suddenly exploded when they perceived that one man had been corrupted in order to penalize them yet further. There's a long history of referees accepting bribes, and many rioters – if they were anything like contemporary ultras – felt that they were defending local honour against corrupt outsiders.

Often the suspicion that the arbiters of the sport had been bought was well-founded. In 1955 Catania was relegated to Serie B because a referee called Scaramella had been paid 5,000 lire to give Catania a helping hand in their home game against Genoa (the final score was 2–0). The bribery was discovered when, on the ferry back to the mainland, a club official handed the referee the money but one of the notes flew into the sea and an argu-ment occurred about whose fault it was. The scuffle came to the attention of police and Catania paid the price.

Often, there was much more subtlety to the art of leaning on a referee. Back in the 1950s, trains didn't come all the way inland to Cosenza but stopped at Paola on the coast. A club official would often offer a lift to the ref, driving him the half-hour to the stadium. The lift back was, of course, dependent on the right sort of decisions having been made during the game. If it had gone well, the official would be escorted back with all the treats the club could afford.

An escort out of the ground was no small incentive for a ref. Half-a-Kilo, an ultra friend whose ironic nickname refers to his huge figure, tells me an apocryphal tale about the time his grandfather was goalkeeping for Cosenza. The referee gave a penalty against him, which he saved. The ref ordered it to be retaken and the keeper again saved it. When the ref saw another irregularity and ordered it taken a third time, Half-a-Kilo's grandfather ran up to him and bit off part of his ear. Although it's a tall tale (one hears many variants of it in Cosenza), its endurance in oral history does show how fans love to feel victimized by figures of authority and relish any redemption (even invented and imagined) through the infliction of violence.

There were often very real fatalities. In November 1958 the seventeen-year-old son of a former Inter player, Giordano Guarisco, was crushed to death when ticketless fans stormed into the stadium. Then in April 1963, on the day of the Italian Republic's fourth general election, Salernitana were playing Potenza in a play-off match for promotion to Serie B. Salernitana was losing 0–1 (the goal, fans thought, was offside). When in the dying minutes the referee failed to award a penalty to Salernitana, fans climbed over the fence separating them from the pitch. What happened next would be repeated many times over the years as police and fans engaged in brutal combat. One fan's shirt was turning red as police truncheoned him and he ran back to the stands to ask for help. Fans surged forwards, knocking down the fence that kept them off the pitch, and shots were fired. A forty-eight-year-old Salernitana fan, Giuseppe Plaitano, was still in the stands, standing next to his son, Umberto. He died almost instantly. The police maintained that there was no order to shoot and that the sounds of firing were simply the explosions of tear gas canisters. But the autopsy showed that Plaitano died from a 7.65 calibre bullet, the same round used by the police. That day sixty-seven people were also wounded: thirty-seven civilians and twenty-four security officials, three *Carabinieri* and three firemen. One sporting almanac, in 1968, wrote about a riot at a Livorno–Monza match: '... if we continue in this vein the archaeologists of the fourth millennium will find in Ardenza [a Livorno suburb] the bones of referees and linesmen.'

The killing of Giuseppe Plaitano, like the shooting of Augusto Morganti in 1920, was the result of trigger-happy policing. It meant that the hatred between fans and authority was no longer confined simply to the corrupt referee. Now, above all, it was focused on the police and *Carabinieri*. One of the main Salerno ultra groups is now called Ultras Plaitano. In that decade of mounting social unrest and rebellion, a prelude to the revolutionary 1960s, there was growing cynicism towards the *celerini* (the riot police) who, with tear gas, truncheons and pistols tried to maintain order at Italian football matches.

In those years, various football teams started to encourage what were called, in English, 'clubs' for their supporters. These fan associations were often created and financed by the football club proper: they were given help with transport to away games, with tickets and finding an empty bar to use as an office. Many people credit the great Argentinian coach, Helenio Herrera, with the creation of supporters' clubs (he wanted to have an away support to encourage his Inter players in the 1960s) but in reality there were much earlier precedents: Lazio had its Aquilotti ('Eagles') in the 1930s, and later, its Circolo Biancoceleste. Torino had been followed by its Fedelissimi Granata ever since 1951. Fiorentina had its own Club Vieusseux and Club Settebello.

Occasionally those supporters' clubs did favours for players and team officials. Carlo Petrini, the former player who, after retirement, blew the lid on the game with a few tell-all books about the shadier side of the sport, recalled how certain supporters would provide flats for players to meet their mistresses.

Supporters' clubs were also, sometimes, channels of political propaganda: the Inter groups were organized by Franco Servello, who was on the Inter board and also a parliamentarian for the neo-fascist MSI party. Supporters' clubs of the biggest teams often had hundreds of offices (and hundreds of thousands of members) throughout the country, making them powerful political and financial lobbies.

By 1964, Cosenza's little football stadium, the Emilio Morrone (named after a twenty-three-year-old goalkeeper who died during a game in the 1940s) had been replaced by a new stadium, the San Vito, a mile or two to the east. The walk there had become a procession every Sunday afternoon. A man nicknamed 'the Baron', Giacomo Gigliotti, used to pick up the orphans from Piazza dei Bruzi and walk them to the stadium after lunch. On the way they would all sing 'Dove Sta Zazà?', a Neapolitan song from 1944 about a man who had lost his love.

Present Day: Matera v. Cosenza

Stadio XXI Settembre. The singing has been off for a while. When it peters out, you can hear a few shouts. There is something about the fury in those sounds that makes it clear that they aren't the usual insults aimed at the players. A few people turn around to see what is happening, and that makes more take a look. The voices are raw now and suddenly it is kicking off: feet flashing in faces, the windmilling arms of unprofessional fighters. Others start piling in and above the shouts you can hear the muffled thud of knuckles on skulls. It's mean now, people being dragged across the steps by their collars, others being twatted on the

41

ground, two on one. This is Cosenza fighting its own – it's the Curva Sud against Anni Ottanta. Those on the wrong end of it limp out of the ground.

Everyone has a different idea of what the row was about. Some say it's about who is true to the faith and who is a heretic. It's about who has always been present and who has been absent. It's about who has the right to lead the singing at away games and, therefore, who is the top dog back home too. It's about who pulls in the most supporters. Since in this ultra world the weapon of choice is that blunt but brilliantly effective one of sheer force of numbers, whoever has more 'hands' is likely to be the toughest defender of the honour of Cosenza.

The game finishes 0–0 – Cosenza's first point (one point is awarded for a draw) of a possible nine – but no one is talking about that afterwards. Within hours, one of the main groups from the Curva Sud, the Old Drunkards of Cosenza Vecchia, publishes an online communiqué: 'Fistfights are part of the ultra world, and in thirty years of history we've given, taken and given blows. Many of us have paid the price of being ultras, with stadium bans, arrests and repression.' Then it got to the real issue: '… we believe that what's left of the Anni Ottanta should dissolve itself with a bit of dignity. The time for chats and wars on Facebook is finished. Now the historic figures above all must take a step backwards… to turn a new page for the organized fans of Cosenza…'

That, it seemed, was key to the disagreement. Here was one group claiming to be the radical, youthful wing (despite the name 'Old Drunkards') and asking the older generation to clear off. Later that week there was another communiqué, once again from the Curva Sud, announcing a fan strike:

On the occasion of Saturday's game against Fidelis Andria,

the ultras of the Curva Sud will stand alongside our banned brothers on the little hill and will therefore desert the stadium. No banner will be present... this is the emptiness they want. All this to protest against repressive and disproportionate measures which have seen Daspos [stadium bans] of up to five years... because of a simple if nervous protest against the club and the team...

By now, such press releases were easy. You could post them online in a flash. There are millions of them from ultra groups up and down the peninsula: long, eloquent, verbose explanations and justifications. What they reveal is how much group creation and retention is now political and public: calling for the resignation of a rival leader or the dissolution of his group, announcing a strike, denouncing repression, expressing an ideology. It is – and this is where hooliganism receives its unexpected, Italian twist – extremely well-organized.

1960s, Acri and Montagnola (Cosenza)

By the 1960s, Francesco, the motherless boy from Cosenza, had entered the seminary in Acri. Acri was a remote, hill-top town 25 kilometres northeast of Cosenza, halfway between the Tyrrhenian and Ionian seas. A journey that now takes half an hour from Cosenza used to take half a day.

The Franciscans had a sports association called Gioventù Francescana, and Francesco played as much football as he could. He always wanted to play up front because with his robust frame, and the odd elbow, he could bounce defenders off him. He was

43

always screaming for the ball, swearing that he couldn't miss if they would just give him the thing. He counted his goals and told everyone all about them. Maybe his boastfulness came from loneliness: his siblings and father had by then emigrated to America, and in the cool corridors of the seminary, the only approval he could come by was his own.

His other passion mixed vanity with goodness: he wanted to make a name for himself, following in the footsteps of the saints and the apostles. He studied the New Testament every day but also raced through books about contemporary holy men like Raoul Follereau, the French 'friend of lepers'. Even during his novitiate, he would stand underneath trees in the parks and preach loudly. He went to Napoli to finish his theological studies and, in 1964, took orders and a new name: Padre Fedele.

He was sent to Rome and then to Milano. He devoured books and imagined he would become a theologian. 'I thought,' he says, 'I was always going to live amongst books.' But for his first posting, in November 1969, he was sent back south, to a dirt-poor suburb called Montagnola, just down the hill from Acri. Quite a few people there were illiterate. The houses didn't have running water or electricity. 'There was nothing,' he says, 'not even a church.' They used a schoolroom for services.

This was a part of the world where a young, enthusiastic priest on his first posting was mocked to his face. Many of the old men of the town were openly anticlerical or so used to the Church's broken promises that they just ignored him. But Padre Fedele wasn't the sort to be ignored. He was what they call a nut-cracker. When he saw men playing cards in a bar shortly before Mass, he sat down to play with them, saying they would compete for a bottle of wine. Padre Fedele wanted another bet too: he would give them 10,000 lire if he lost, but if he won they had to come to church. He won: 'I drank the whole bottle myself,' he laughs, 'and the next Sunday they came to Mass.'

In 1970 he organized a protest march against the authorities for failing to provide basic utilities. People thought it was a religious procession and took off their hats as the march passed, but Padre Fedele kept shouting about there being no lights and no running water. He threatened to go on hunger strike unless everything was sorted out within ten days. 'I made,' he says with typical modesty, 'an unforgettable speech.' Nine days later – in a land where nothing ever seemed to change – the telegraph poles and pipes arrived.

The old men playing cards started saying hello to him. They weren't exactly warming to him but they weren't hostile any more. He was a lad who made things happen. Padre Fedele carved out a football pitch on a rare bit of horizontal waste ground and set up a team. He played centre-forward, still screaming for the ball as he had done ten years before. He was a pain in the neck but great fun to be around. 'The only thing bigger than his ego,' one mother said, 'was his heart.'

The Birth of the Ultras

Groups of ultras existed before the actual name came into being. Tradition has it that the first group was Milan's Fossa dei Leoni ('the pit of lions' was the name of an old training pitch used by the team). Founded in 1968, it had emerged – like another Milan ultra group, the Commandos Tigre – from one of the formal Milan supporters' clubs. Even then, the habit of splinter and division was evident: although both groups were supporting the same team, AC Milan, they were divided zoologically into 'tigers' and 'lions'.

A year later, in 1969, other groups were founded: the Ultras Tito Cucchiaroni of Sampdoria, the Commandos Fedelissimi of Torino, and the Boys (with their subtitle 'the black-blue furies') of Inter. The Commandos and Boys, too, had emerged from their teams' official clubs.

There's much debate about when the word 'ultra' entered the lexicon: its first recorded use was as a description of the diehard monarchists of restoration France in the 1820s, but the Sampdoria group liked to believe they had invented the word 'ultras' as an acronym of '*Uniti legneremo tutti i rossoblù a sangue*' ('united we will beat up the red-blues [Genoa] till they bleed'). In 1970 there was a rollercoaster game between Torino and Vicenza. Two penalties awarded in the last five minutes allowed Vicenza to win the game after going 2–1 down. Furious Toro fans followed the referee all the way to the airport, smashing as much property as they could on the way. When a journalist later called them 'ultras', the name stuck and the hottest heads of the Commandos Fedelissimi became the 'Maratona Club Torino Ultras Granata'.

By then, it was becoming a trend. Two teenagers in Verona founded, in 1971, the iconic Yellow-Blue Brigades. In 1972, Gennaro Montuori, known by his nickname Palummella, created the Commando Ultrà Curva B in Naples. In 1973, Genoa's Fossa dei Grifoni ('pit of griphons') was born and, in the same year, the Ultras of Fiorentina.

In the beginning it was hard to understand quite what these new groups were. In many ways, they were just youthful splinters from those formal supporters clubs, the product of yet another schism. But very soon it was clear that the ultras were different. They stood behind the goals inventing new songs and choreographies, and were so loud that often the other supporters on the terraces complained. The unruly exuberance of British fans was always a point of reference. One Inter fan returned from Anfield in Liverpool to say that the waving scarves made him feel seasick. He meant it as a compliment, implying that the fans were – and it wouldn't be a bad adjective for the ultras – choppy.

Emerging at the very beginning of Italy's *anni di piombo*, its 'years of lead' of political violence and assassinations, the ultras borrowed the language and imagery of the armed struggle. Ever since the Piazza Fontana bomb of 1969, which killed seventeen people in a bank in Milano, the country had suffered a series of slaughters and assassinations. The 1970s was a decade in which the Red Brigades and other guerrilla groups killed numerous industrialists, policemen and politicians, leading to the arrests of thousands of far-left activists. Neo-fascist terrorist groups, meanwhile, set off bombs that killed dozens and contributed to a feverish suspicion of conspiracies and coup plots by shadowy far-right forces. Many early ultra groups had names like Brigades, Commandos, Fedayeen, Red Army, Tupamaros, Vigilantes, Armada, Fronte, Phalanx and so on. The slogans of the terraces were borrowed from the political struggle: 'better red than dead' (an inversion of the usual, anti-communist line) or 'Boys [instead of fascists] get back in the sewers'. The aping of the political insurgency was evident from the gestures of the *curva*: raised left fists or Roman salutes or the two forefingers of the right hand waving a flat pistol in the face of the bourgeoisie. Often balaclavas, and scarves pulled up to the eyes, lent anonymity to the menace.

From their very inception, then, ultra groups reflected the violence of the 'years of lead'. The late sociologist Valerio Marchi wrote that the movement was made up both of 'people having experimented with mass violence in the political field' as well as by 'people having experimented with violence in the fulfilment of everyday needs'. The bloodthirstiness of the early chants (constantly invoking the death of the enemy) reminded many of the *sangue, sangue* chant of the ancient Roman arenas. 'We are the pit of the lions,' sang the Milan fans. 'Blood. Violence.' The symbols held aloft to the opposing fans – coffins, skeletons, skulls and so on – created a charade that this would be a fight to the death. *'Devi morire'* – 'you must die' – was a recurrent chant. Most of the big teams, of course, played each other at least twice a season (and more if there were cup games), so the fans had plenty of time to observe and envy rival ultras. The competition between teams was, in their minds, now a competition between terraces to decide who had the best names, moves, songs, banners, flares, drums and muscle.

Like all subcultures, the ultras relished their bad-boy status. The self-portraits of ultras often combined both a parody of what the *bien pensant* commentators said about them, but also a pride in recounting that disdain, in listing all the reasons that the ultras were beyond the pale: 'The ultras are evil,' wrote one, 'they are the dark side of the football, the horrid obscenity of civilization... the open sewer of the stadiums. The icon of blind and irrational violence. The worst, if not the only evil, of the football system which otherwise appears as candid and immaculate as a virgin... we are thugs, misfits, sons of a violent and unhealthy society. We are everything you don't want us to be, but we continue our lives in the ghetto of stadium violence... we're ultras and we don't give a fuck about anything else. We're ultras and we love the *'tifo'*, the chaos, the struggle, the fights, and urban violence.'

In many ways, the ultras seemed to be defining themselves against Nietzsche's *Letzter Mensch*, the 'last man' in *Thus Spoke Zarathustra*. The apathetic, pacifist and decadent bourgeois was the opposite of what they aspired to be. In a bloodless, atonal world they yearned for action. Life in Italy is very often described as *farraginosa*, muddled or confused. It derives from the spelt ('*farro*') mulch fed to cattle, and implies the sticky gloop of compromise or bureaucratic complication that creates inertia. The ultras – like the futurists before them – wanted to slice through that stodgy morass. They were, they repeatedly said, opposed to the meekness of the comfortable life, they were rebels who refused to compromise, they were crusaders who saw little valour in lonely, modern existence that offered no causes and no battles.

But at the same time, the *curva* was a parody of the violence unleashed by political terrorists. It seemed a *son-et-lumière* satire of that world, a teenage imitation of violence. To many it was little different to the way young boys pretend to be great centre-forwards when they're having a kick-around in the streets. Paradoxically, the ultra world actually seemed like a safe retreat from the political extremism of the time. Against that backdrop, the ultras' folkloristic recreation of a medieval *contrada* seemed almost innocent, as removed from political assassinations as a Punch-and-Judy show is from domestic violence: related, but imitative, a warning as much as an incitement.

In fact, one of the earliest tenets of ultra faith was that politics should be banned from the terraces. The curved terrace was – the paradoxes in this world quickly pile high – a place both of political extremism but also of neutrality, of violence but also of pacification. In the sacred space of the terraces, all divisions were supposed to be healed. Adherence to different political hues – invariably red or black, communist or fascist – was surpassed by attachment to the colours of the *maglia*, the football shirt. So, for example, an ultra from the far left like Pompa in Florence (a huge man who would defend his brothers to the last) could work side-by-side with an ultra from the far right with a strangely similar nickname, Pampa, because for both the violet of Fiorentina was the colour that transcended all others.

The ultras' scorn for society was, inevitably, reciprocated. The early ultras were described – in language still replicated almost fifty years later – as a 'primal horde' or 'mob', the infernal result of a deindividuation in which human reason is submerged by collective, animalistic instincts. Stanley Cohen, in his book *Folk Devils and Moral Panics*, wrote that society's scapegoats are like 'Rorschach blots onto which reactions are projected...' It was the same with ultras, who were quickly interpreted according to the prejudices of the mainstream. An ultra seemed, to some, a twentieth-century 'homo sacer', that accursed man of Roman times who was expelled from society and considered so worthless that he could be killed by anybody without incurring guilt. Alberto Arbasino's criticism typifies such disgust, describing a 'spontaneous, collective, very violent crowd without aim. I have never seen such ridicule, never seen such a numerous crowd so out of control... an immense, biological outburst, like the dark, disordered Mediterranean carnivals, like the sad Mexican fiestas, like the apocalyptical saturnalias of the Roman slaves...'

The great critic Umberto Eco was characteristically subtler. He wondered if these outlaws weren't just Italianate Larrikins (mischievous, but good-hearted) or Beagle Boys (the cartoon criminals from Donald Duck): '... a cheating rabble, true, but with a certain charge of crazy amiability because they stole, to the tunes of proletarian confiscation, from the stingy, egotistical capitalist.' Since the inception of the ultra phenomenon, the question has been posed whether they are scallywags or hardcore criminals, countercultural Robin Hoods or just violent hoods.

The ultras seemed so youthful, energetic and mercurial that every label seemed to slide off them. Valerio Marchi drew comparisons between the ultras and all those historical inversions of the social order, from the Feast of Fools (promoting revelry and humility in the church when the lowly clerics briefly took power) to the Charivari (noisy, symbolic processions) and the Soties (when fools dispensed wisdom).

Back in the early 1970s, the terraces often looked surprisingly unthreatening, rather like a low-budget carnival. The choreographies were performed with loo rolls and paper plates, with cardboard, Sellotape and bedsheets. In the same way that the players, in the 1970s, appeared a bit rough-and-ready, far less pampered than their successors, so too did the ultras. Paint was slapped on banners without worrying too much about the type font (nowadays there's a specific font called Ultras Liberi ['free the ultras']). Drums were often nothing more than upturned paint tins. One Lazio ultra remembers that the first drums they had were empty kegs of Dash detergent. A cut bottle was used as a megaphone. Flare effects were frequently provided by stolen fire extinguishers because it was easier to get hold of them than naval flares. It was a time in which football was affordable: one Lazio ultra remembers that the return ticket for the bus to Bologna cost 500 lire (under £4 or $5 in today's money). Even for a Juventus game, tickets behind the goal only cost 300 lire. In most stadiums it was easy enough to sneak your way in without paying. One ultra from Ancona happily recalls that 'the capacity of the stadium was a pretty elastic concept'. Smaller clubs often didn't have more than one stand of seats, so the ultras gathered on the highest grass, eating pumpkin seeds and learning new songs.

Away games were often even better. Relying on force of numbers, many ultra groups didn't bother paying for rail tickets or food. They just burst into a carriage or café and rode, or ate, for free. There was plenty of theft, too, but the 'bounty' wasn't always the obvious (a stolen car or motorbike, say) but a train emptied of paper towels for a choreography, or coins prised from a phone booth to throw at rival ultras. You would see them on the train tracks filling their pockets with stones from the sidings for the same purpose. Many returned from away games with pockets still bulging, this time with banknotes from who-knows-where.

Coming back with a good story was almost as important. The more brazen the theft appeared, the better. Torino ultras told each other about the time that their mate, Margaro, nicked a watch in Zurich, realized he didn't have the winding key and went back to the shop to ask for it and to get the watch wrapped too. Staff at these places were often so weary or scared that they didn't even challenge the notoriously volatile ultras. It was rare for these groups to stop at motorway service stations – the Auto-grill – or in railway bars without overwhelming the place and taking whatever they wanted. Railway and service stations were also the scene of many a pitched battle.

The founder of Bologna's Vecchia Guardia, Bebo, once called the ultras the '*schiuma dei quartieri*' ('the froth of the suburbs'). The description nods to the effervescence of the movement, the bubbling energy and dirt emerging from the less refined urban spaces. Petty criminality bled into hedonism because the terraces were a sort of *zona franca* where anything was allowed. As cannabis became commonplace throughout Europe, it was inevitable that rebellious youths got high as they sang their hearts out. The terraces were where you could score and skin up with impunity. There were pushers, pick-pockets and entrepreneurs. It was all part of the carnival.

If you were on one of those famous terraces of the big clubs in the early 1970s, it went dark as the teams came out onto the pitch because of the smoke from so many flares and fire extinguishers being let off. The handkerchiefs over the faces and the balaclavas were not just to render the wearers masked and edgy, but because you couldn't breathe the toxic air. When the smoke cleared, you could see the team colours still flying on pillow cases and bedsheets: red and blue (Genoa, Catania and Cosenza), or cherry red (Torino), or red and yellow (Roma) or light blue and white (Lazio) or the barcode strip of Juventus.

In the huge old stadiums of the big teams, with up to 10,000 on one terrace alone, there might have been a few hundred flags. Some were not much larger than a sheet of A4 paper, while others were as big as sixteen square metres, the inch-thick plastic poles bent like nail-clippings as the huge heralds were worked against the wind in a figure of eight. Thousands of scarves were rotated above heads or held in horizontal lines, stretched by yearning arms. Drums were beaten. The primary aim, in the early years of the ultras, was the creation of pageantry and spectacle.

The terraces also offered many youths an alternative to organized crime. In an era in which career choices were decidedly limited, especially in the South, there was a constant temptation to make quick money by working for criminals. Although Michele Spampinato, founder of Catania's Decisi ultra group in Sicily, was writing about the 1990s, his recollection of that temptation is echoed in many ultra memoirs from different decades. '... the possibility of being recruited by a Mafia clan as muscle presented itself every day,' he said. 'We didn't have a lira in our pockets and they offered you the chance to make a lot of money. Dealing drugs, doing acts of revenge. You started like that and who knows where you could end up.' Far from being quasi-criminal gangs (which is now the default reading of the ultras), these groups were also an alternative to organized crime, perhaps the only alternative for toughs in search of camaraderie and excitement.

But for those gentrified fans watching from the *tribuna* there was something sinister in all this, something reminiscent of *The Lord of the Flies*. The first statistical analysis of the ultras, conducted by the sociologists Alessandro Dal Lago and Roberto Moscati, showed that 57.2 per cent of ultras were under twenty-one (and 11.2 per cent were female). When those researchers cross-referenced their research with another study from Pisa, the figures were even higher: 62 per cent were under twenty-one and 13 per cent female. Often the more genteel fans expressed their dislike of this new phenomenon, singing '*curva fè schifo, fè un po' de tifo*' ('Curva, you're disgusting, do a bit of supporting').

The late 1960s and early 1970s were years in which sons customarily rebelled against fathers, in which the bequest of parental wisdom was scorned by impatient and angry children. The move from the tranquil *tribuna* to the chaos of the *curva* was a symbolic enactment of that rebellion. The *curva* was perhaps the only place in the whole country where kids felt in charge. It was an open, public place where they could finally stick it, in every way, to those pompous old men inclined to long soliloquies on the technicalities of football, all delivered in a dull, professorial drawl.

But in common with many rebellions, it was also a strange gesture of emulation: an angry shout to the father saying, 'I'm more passionate than you; this is how to do it properly.' Often, the ultras weren't renouncing their ancestral roles but reinventing them. One of the mottos used by Lazio fans was 'from father to son', a notion that following the white-and-light-blue shirt was an act of familial loyalty.

The ultras took all these paradoxical strands – fidelity to

tradition combined with teenage rebellion, tacit violence but also an escape from it, rejection of organized crime but embracing of petty criminals, fixation on football but also on each other, rootedness in the local and yet casting an admiring eye at other clubs and countries – and wove them into the colourful theatre of the *curva*. These paradoxes were present because of the immense variety of those drawn to the terraces. It's very clear that the vast majority of terraces are inclusive spaces, with no entry requirements other than your attachment to the same colours. 'When I become a fan,' one says, 'no one asks me what I do in life. I have a scarf, a flag, a banner and the rest doesn't count. At the stadium you never have that feeling of being surplus or out of place.' The result was that, as Pierluigi Spagnolo wrote in his book, *I Ribelli degli stadi*, 'you find a graduate next to the kid who lives on his wits, the dentist and the mechanic, the schoolteacher and the unemployed, the son of a banker and the son of a smuggler, the health-freak and the drug addict, the scion of the well-to-do families and criminal recruits...' The egalitarianism of that space was so profound that Grinta ('Grit' – later founder of Lazio's Irriducibili) remembers the men who gave his father the formal 'lei' address in his office would, on the terraces, give him the 'tu' and use his first name.

The variety of people gathering behind the goals was reflected in the astonishing array of dress codes. There's a livery to rebellion, it is often said, an orderliness and uniformity. But perhaps because Italy is a country in which fashion is often uniform, in which there's an instantaneous, chameleonic imitation of the latest trend, the ultras' stylistic rebellion – at least in the 1970s – was about randomness. There wasn't one look, but thousands of them.

In the photos from that decade, there's a great hotchpotch of

Wrangler T-shirts and the curly, three-lined lettering of the Adidas insignia, of berets and balaclava caps, of parkas and jackets with team badges, of sideburns and long hair and no hair. There was no iconic livery that united the ultras, and almost nothing in their dress that would have astonished or frightened the well-to-do. There's a photo of Geppo, one of Roma's most idealistic, if doomed, ultras, with long hair and topless but for his denim dungarees. He looks benign, not shocking.

Therein lay the romance of being an ultra: it was crazily, zanily, unfathomably various. 'The *curva* was the only place where you could be whoever you were,' explains one man now the wrong side of middle-age. 'It was where you seemed, briefly, in control of your own life.' And it seemed revolutionary because the *curva* was sucking in the soul of the streets. Suddenly, the same man continues, 'the lad with two-inch shoe soles who limped around town was shouting his heart out... the damaged girl who everyone knew had been treated very badly was now protected by a few thousand friends.' The *curva* became places of genuine companionship for thousands of young men and women with psychiatric illnesses. Their numbers swelled in late 1978 when the country's asylums were closed. Of course, quite a few people with mental conditions could be handy in a fight, and it's doubtful that their exploitation by others had ceased. But many terraces became spaces that celebrated their insanity and exclusion. There was even a Cremona ultra group called Sanitorium and one in Ragusa called Manicomio ('asylum'). The words of the Roman ultra, Geppo, sound almost scriptural: 'I am in the streets, in the protests, in the schools, in unemployment, in the syringe: I am in the rejected.'

Many anthropologists talk about choreographic rituals through which primitive groups reintegrate a sick member into a community. In the Mediterranean basin, it was called Maenadism or Tarantism, and in Latino-African cultures Candomblé or Shango. The ultras always bang on about choreographies (the organized displays of banners and flags) but perhaps their most important choreography is the unconscious one of welcoming disturbed minds into their midst, into what one Cosenza fanzine memorably called *mamma curva*, the mother who loves you whoever you are. During the drugged, frenzied and furious singing, during all the dancing and shouting and hugging, outcasts became part of a fellowship. One of the common slogans was 'last in society, first on the terraces'.

Antonio Bongi decided he wanted to start an ultra group when he went to the old Stadio Comunale in Turin and saw the Ultras Granata (the 'maroon ultras') incessantly hammering their kettle drums. He was fascinated by the noise and the energy, by the roar of distant voices in unison, and he yearned to create something similar for Roma.

Antonio had only lived in Rome, on and off, for a few years. His real name was Anthony. He had been born in Santa Monica, California, and was the grandchild of Herbert Stothart, the Hollywood composer known for *The Wizard of Oz* underscore and the song made famous by Marilyn Monroe, 'I wanna be loved by you'. His father, a Tuscan architect, had fallen in love with Stothart's daughter in his home city of Florence and the couple moved to California.

Anthony was their oldest boy. He grew up speaking Italian and English at the same time. He wasn't always sure where he was from and became uncannily good at imitating those around him, doing accents, picking up songs and aping pompous adults. With his dark hair and dark eyes, he was immediately recognizable in those proud family photos in the Californian sun of the late 1950s.

From the age of six he started spending more time in Rome, where his father had found a job in an architect's studio. Anthony reinvented himself as Antonio. He was living in the posh part of town, on Via Cassia, where many of his neighbours were Laziali. But Antonio was fixated on the red-and-yellow of Roma. The stadium became a way for him to integrate, to be accepted as a local. He found a world where nicknames emerged from surnames or faces or habits. One guy with an ear ripped off was called Tazza ('Tea-Cup'). Another slurped bottles of pop all the time and ended up being called, for the rest of his life, Coca-Cola. There were hardcore left-wingers like Roberto Rulli and Valerio Verbano, but also figures from the far right, like Mario Corsi and Francesco Storace. They were all just teenagers, many of them from the rougher suburbs to the south.

It was demographically appropriate (and imitative of Inter's Boys), that Antonio Bongi's new ultra group was called 'Boys'. Their full name was 'the Red-and-Yellow Furies'. They had a spot in the north terrace and various leaders were given free entry by the Roma management. Their first away game was to Bologna, on 15 October 1972. Bongi, the leader, was only fourteen and suddenly found himself having to defend the honour of Roma, his herald and his foot soldiers. It was always a good sign if the team won the game when you first hung out your herald on foreign soil, and that day Roma triumphed, scoring three goals. In the early to mid-1970s, Roma was supported by various other ultra groups as well as the Bongi's Boys: the 'Guerrillas', the 'Panthers', 'the Pit of Wolves' and the 'Fedayeen'.

The team in those years was often a disappointment. Although fans called it *la Magica*, it was also called *Rometta*, 'little Roma'. It could never hope to compete with the rich teams of Italy's North. The only *scudetto* the team had ever won was way back in 1941–42. Roma had a few decent players but not enough class to challenge for the title. A twenty-one-year-old Claudio Ranieri (later a much-travelled manager) was amongst the reserves. There was a tall, quiet teenager – a box-to-box midfielder – called Agostino Di Bartolomei who was breaking into the team. But sporting highs were hard to come by. In an Anglo-Italian Cup match in the spring of 1973, Roma was beaten by Newcastle United, Oxford United and Blackpool.

Roma's great rivals, Lazio, were much closer to sporting glory. In 1971 the club had appointed a manager, Tommaso Maestrelli, who had taken them straight back into Serie A. With his salt-and-pepper hair and mild manners (he was nicknamed 'tissue paper'), he seemed a father figure. He invited players to his house for meals. But tactically he was revolutionary. He was one of the first exponents of 'total football', persuading all his players – bar two central defenders and the goalkeeper – that they could be attackers. Dutch scouts working on similar tactics in the early 1970s asked to watch some of his training sessions. What was extraordinary about him was his taciturnity, which disguised profound values. In his first speech to the Lazio players, he apparently said: 'I will speak little and that little will be seen to be a lot... We will love one another and avoid any misunderstanding. I consider loyalty the best gift given on this planet. We will grow together.'

Those character traits had already brought Maestrelli much success. He had managed Reggina to promotion from Serie C to B in 1965 and, five years later, took lowly Foggia into Serie A. In the 1972–73 season, Lazio had come within two points of winning the *scudetto*. Like many great managers, Maestrelli managed to put together a team of players who had hitherto been mostly scorned or ignored: Mario Frustalupi was in his thirties, a reject from Inter who critics felt was over the hill. Luciano Re Cecconi was a blond midfielder who had played under Maestrelli in Foggia. Maestrelli also brought in Renzo Garlaschelli, an attacker who had only scored twelve goals in over a hundred games for small clubs. But the main man was a tall striker who had grown up in South Wales: Giorgio Chinaglia.

Maestrelli's exciting new brand of football caught the imagination of fans and, by the mid-1970s, there were various ultra groups following Lazio: the Tupamaros (named after the left-wing Uruguayan guerrilla group), Vigilantes, Aquile, Ultras, Folgore, Cast, Marines and, the largest group, Commandos Monteverde Lazio. Many ultras wore military fatigues, partly to exude an air of menace but also because in many stadiums, as in Italian brothels, there was a discount for soldiers.

Weaponry was often paramilitary, too. One of the young fans from those days remembers how the ultras went to away games:

> … as if going on great military manoeuvres, with camouflaged clothing, parachutists' helmets, military boots, dark glasses and handkerchiefs to cover the face. In the luggage of the coach, other than banners, were bags containing pick-axe handles, iron bars, chains, slingshots and iron ball-bearings. There were those who also brought flare-guns and someone who sometimes turned up with axes, knives and real pistols.

In the hyper-politicized 1970s, territoriality wasn't just a charming attachment to your own turf but a defence against real enemies: there were certain squares in the capital – Piazza Euclide or Piazzale delle Muse, in the heart of the Parioli district – that were known to 'belong' to the neo-fascists and, by extension, to the Laziali. Even your clothing was part of a political livery. The Lazio fans wore El Charro Camperos, the knee-high Tex-Mex cowboy boots, and either long green Austrian-style loden coats or bomber jackets. They called left-wingers (with longer hair, All Star trainers, check shirts, and kefiahs) *zecche* ('ticks'). They listened to their own singers too. Lucio Battisti was a favourite of the Lazio fans, partly because his song, '*La Collina dei Ciliegi*' ('The hill of cherry trees') spoke of 'forests with straight arms', a hint that his own political persuasion was the same as theirs.

Every *curva* seemed to create and then cherish folkloric characters from those sporting Sunday afternoons. Lazio had Leonida, a man who dressed as a Roman emperor – with a white sheet and laurel wreath – and blessed the terraces. Luciano, meanwhile, was a character who shouted out the formations, adding sarcastic Latin – '*ora pro nobis*' or 'pray for us' – after the names of opposition players. There was a tubby, abrasive man called Goffredo Lucarelli, better known as 'er Tassinaro' (the 'Taxi-Driver'). He was unable to pronounce his 'r's and seemed a parody of a Roman yokel. He constantly played tricks on people, lighting firecrackers between the fingers of ultras asleep on the bus.

Other groups were always on the look-out for him, hoping to give him a beating. Once, at Inter, he had to hide in the first-aid room and put on a nurse's outfit to get out unharmed. His taxi licence was eventually rescinded because he argued with a Roma fan and then left him stranded halfway to the airport. So, he got work driving a hearse and deliberately lined up jobs which took him to the same parts of the country as Lazio. One time, taking a corpse to Siracusa, he parked his hearse outside Catania's stadium to watch the game. Told that he would have to move, he refused: 'It's only for a couple of hours and this guy isn't in a rush.'

Having come so close to the title in 1972–73, there was a fear that the following season Lazio wouldn't be able to regain such heights. But Maestrelli's team was renowned for being everything he wasn't. It was a rough, bullish, street fighter's team with more than a hint of madness about it. Various players did parachute jumps from military planes. The defender Sergio Petrelli didn't play cards but persuaded a few other players to join a firing range instead. Soon, half the team collected pistols, firing them off in the woods and in hotel car parks. There was even a story of two teammates lying in their hotel room, each trying to persuade the other to get out of bed to switch off the light. Neither would move, so in the end one got out his pistol and shot out the bulb.

Giorgio Chinaglia was taller than everyone else on the pitch, and recognizable by his thick hair and sideburns. He was powerful but, more than just muscle, he was extraordinarily stubborn, determined that nothing was going to stop him putting the ball in the back of the net. He seemed to take his many penalties with the meanness of someone kicking over a kid's sandcastle, more anger and speed to the kick than accuracy. He once scored a goal against Napoli as the shirt was being literally ripped off his back. That season there were plenty of goals scored by Chinaglia that seemed to owe more to willpower than anything else. In one game, the ball came into the crowded box and Chinaglia barged it in, leaving opposition players lying on the floor wondering what had hit them.

And always the manager, Maestrelli, was holding everything together. In one home game, against Verona, Lazio were 2–1 down at half-time. Maestrelli stood in front of the changing room door, refusing to let anyone in. He sent the players back out onto the pitch, as if the shame and embarrassment of standing out there alone for the whole of half-time might make them buck up their ideas. The crowd were perplexed to begin with, not sure what was happening. But then they began to sing loudly and the players stood rigidly in their positions, staring angrily ahead. 'We had blood in our eyes,' one Lazio player remembered. They stood there, waiting for the opposition, desperate to put things right.

Within four minutes of the restart, they had equalized. The next goal was the best – a midfielder running from the halfway to the goal-line and pulling it back to Chinaglia. Never one with the silkiest touch, Chinaglia tried to trap the ball but it rose above his waistline. So, he smacked it in with a high left boot. The image of those eleven players standing on the pitch during the interval became a sign of a team that refused to succumb.

The footballing fates meant that Lazio had the chance to win the *scudetto* at home, in the penultimate game of the season, against Maestrelli and Re Ceccone's former team, Foggia. It was the same day as the referendum on whether Italy's 1970 divorce law should be repealed (59.3 per cent voted against repeal). It wasn't a great game but Lazio won 1–0 thanks to yet another Chinaglia penalty thumped into the back of the net. As the crowd flooded onto the pitch, Maestrelli just put his head in his hands.

It was an extraordinary *scudetto* because the team was made up of mavericks and rough diamonds who were often at each others' throats. In contemporary football's era of uber-professionalism, in which everything is made safe and predictable, fans look back on that swashbuckling team with profound warmth. The baggy and unsponsored cotton kits, the angled plywood advertising boards, the long hair and the simplicity of goal celebrations (a brief hug between two or three players near the goal) make that season seem from another age, as do the tales of pistols, parachutes and all-night poker with litres of whisky.

With the passing of the years, that *scudetto* became for Lazio's ultras a source of great nostalgia. 1974 wasn't seen as an age of innocence but perhaps the opposite: an era in which players could be reckless. The players seemed then as raucous and as impassioned as the ultras themselves. That rare affinity between the ultras and Lazio players was cemented by Chinaglia. They sung his name, rhyming it with *battaglia* ('battle') in a chant borrowed from the MSI's youth movement. Chinaglia was nicknamed 'Long John', and the Taxi-Driver once said that 'Long John was for Laziali like the giant Gulliver for the Lilliputians.'

Present Day: Reggina v. Cosenza

The squatted building, the Casa degli Ultrà, is still bare, so the excited singing reverberates. People are smacking flagpoles on the metal bars of the window, keeping time. Everyone is dressed up for tonight's away game: hoodies, scarves, sweatshirts naming the town or suburb they're from. It's a riotous party, lots of drinking and smoking. Chill grabs the megaphone and puts on the siren so it sounds like the police are about to crash the gathering, which only serves to increase the exuberance.

'Oh, *pezzo di merda*,' someone shouts at the imaginary police charge. Drinks are being passed round: straw-bottomed flasks of wine, local brews, Silan liqueurs. All the usual crew are here. Elastic, as tense and well-sprung as ever. He looks you over, asks you a few questions to make sure you're not a flake. Mouse, short and pugnacious, cracks jokes and seems livid at the same time. His anger is all part of the act, until he really starts steaming. Half-a-Kilo is in his usual shell suit, starting a new song whenever it goes quiet and teaching people new variations on the lyrics which make them laugh. One-Track is on the drum, getting a roll going like a breaker at the seaside, keeping everything frothy. Left-Behind is quietly watching everything, cradling his herbs in his palm. Skinny Monica, the lean lawyer, has her right fist in the air, keeping time to the song. She's wearing a black T-shirt that says: 'a woman in the stadium is like an away-goal: worth double'.

People drift outside, getting ready to go. It's now dusk and others are rolling up on foot, on scooters, in cars. Many are waving flags or scarves out of windows and making as much noise as possible. They pretend to crash into mates, braking at the last minute, and there's more fake outrage and laughter. Half a dozen hired minibuses are parked in convoy by the river.

Given the precarious position of the club, the high spirits are surprising. In the first six games of the league season, Cosenza has lost four times and drawn twice. Those results were bad enough, but it was the way they had lost which felt insulting. Cosenza had let in four goals against Siracusa. Attendances are dropping below two thousand.

Before September was out, the club sacked the manager, Gaetano Fontana, and replaced him with a Tuscan called Piero Braglia. With his grey hair and measured tones, he seemed more like a teacher than a manager. Three days later, Cosenza lost at home to Catania 0–1. They seemed to have a bit more about them in that game but even so it was now October and the team still hadn't won a game. Cosenza was second from bottom of Serie C, one of three third division tiers (Serie C is split into North, Centre and South).

Tonight's game is hardly likely to be a breeze. It's away against Reggio Calabria, where Cosenza hasn't won for fifty-eight years. To add to the gloom, many of the lads here know that – because of the fighting in Matera a month ago – they're bound to be given a stadium ban and forced to sign in at the police station during all games. It's like becoming a prisoner in your own city. So, this game might just be their last hurrah for many years.

Everyone is playing tough. 'Keep your scarves on tight,' goes the command, because any filthy Reggiano might try to nick it, if not actually cut it off your neck. It's a derby with a political edge. The Reggina ultras have sometimes toyed with fascistic slogans and paraded their racism. One year, the notoriously tolerant Cosenza ultras taunted their Reggina counterparts with a banner suggesting they had little cause to be upset by non-white people: 'what an ugly joke nature played on you, you fascist with dark skin'.

But whilst there's a lot of tough talk about defending ourselves, no one is packing anything serious. There are huge lumps of cheese but no one has a knife, so it sits sweating in the evening sun. Occasionally, someone takes a bite as if it were an apple. Disorganization is part of the package: PinoNero screams at his brother Left-Behind for ripping up his ticket and rolling it into a roach. He had torn up the barcode that, in twenty-first-century football, produces the green arrow that clicks you through the turnstiles.

'No, fuckwit, that's last week's ticket,' shouts Left-Behind as smoke comes out between his teeth. 'It says Reggio.'

'That's where we're going tonight, you twat,' PinoNero screams back.

'We're not playing Reggio.' Left-Behind is in a bit of a haze now.

'Of course we fucking are,' shouts SkinnyMon.

Everyone laughs, and once the spliff has been smoked they begin taping the ticket back together again.

It's almost 200 kilometres to Reggio, at the very end of the big toe of the Italian boot. Kick-off is only two hours away but people are milling around still, taking photos of each other. Nearby are the city's unfinished projects: the wooden pedestrian footbridge over the river, which is boarded up and rotting, and just beyond it the Jolly Hotel, standing like a tombstone.

Suddenly, everyone piles into cars and minibuses and the convoy is off, honking horns and waving flags and scarves out of windows as it snakes through the city towards the motorway. Men standing outside bars shake their fists in encouragement for the colours.

Much of the motorway is on concrete stilts over canyons. The convoy careers along at top speed, the ska at full whack. Vindov is our racing driver. He's arguing with the bloke in the middle seat next to him. To make his point he takes both hands off the wheel. Other times, as another minibus overtakes at 150 kph, Vindov swerves close to shout an insult out of the window. Boozy Suzy spills rum down her top. Everyone is singing and laughing.

We get close to Reggio but as half the minibuses pull off at one exit, the others overshoot. They're getting into the bowels of the suburbs now, which is not a good place to be out on their own. Vindov is speaking on the phone at the same time as driving and continuing his argument with Dino. Another ten minutes and the convoy is back together. It's four minutes to kick-off and we've only now seen the floodlights. 'Better that way,' says Half-a-Kilo, pointing at rotating blue lights, 'keeps this lot waiting.'

And there, having waited since half-past six, are four police cars and two police vans. They go in front and behind our dozen minibuses, their sirens clearing the roads. Vindov keeps trying to overtake the escort, which only makes them go faster. And now it's about being noisy. Telling this shit-hole city that you're on their turf. A moped is coming up on the outside. Vindov swerves hard and blocks the moped driver, who brakes and honks, raising his hand in hatred for the Cosentini. Left-Behind puts our megaphone outside the window, its siren blasting to mock the escort.

Outside the ground, it's tense. The match has already kicked off and everyone wants to get inside. One-Track and Mouse are telling the riot police that one or two lads don't have tickets. In truth, it's much more than one or two, more like a dozen: Vindov, Egg and another ten or so. Those without a ticket say it's a protest against the hated supporter's card, the *tessera,* which, in theory, all travelling fans now have to acquire. Those refuseniks are respected by the group: they've taken a stand against an authoritarian state. They've refused to supply all their details, to get barcoded, to be filed and stamped as 'trusted' by a system they don't trust themselves. But now there's a stand-off. The riot police don't want the un-ticketed 10 per cent outside the stadium, roaming angry in a city that hates them. An agreement is reached and those purest, and most idealistic, of ticketless ultras slip into the stadium too.

Barcodes, turnstiles, dust-downs. Getting into a stadium is a soulless exercise. You can feel the scorn as you're kettled into the latest grim arena. There's a plainclothes plod with a small camcorder, holding it a foot from everyone's face. And this for a low-key game in one of the three third divisions. The battle with the authorities is partly a question of who can be more in your face without provoking a fight. The authorities tend to be keener to avoid a scuffle, so try to appear emollient. But this silent cop with the camcorder seems particularly wrong, provocatively putting the lens in Mouse's face, who leers forwards and tries to butt it, screaming 'oh' at the cop dressed like a banker. Suddenly everyone is getting in on the action, screaming 'oh' at the police. There's a bit of a surge and the police close ranks, pushing us all towards the steps to the *curva*. It's play-acting, mostly, but feels like it could kick off into more serious aggression at any moment.

The game is ten minutes in by the time we get into the stand, high up in one corner. The bright lights, the shaved grass, the shiny kit: it all feels so tidy and removed from us caged animals. Already inside are a few Cosenza fans standing together in twos and threes. The Reggiani chant 'fuck off'. The Cosentini return the compliment. But the stadium is only about one-tenth full. After all the arguments, the pain, the danger and the disorientation of the journey, we're here, in a concrete shit-hole of a stadium where the football is as exciting as a stale biscuit.

A few look over at what's happening on the grass but most are busily cable-tying all the banners on the metal rails or Sellotaping them onto Perspex screens. Flags are unfurled, drums twatted hard, and suddenly Elastic, on the megaphone, screams one syllable, arcing the sound across the heads of the hundred or so fans. 'Co.' The crowd shout it back to him: 'Co.' Then silence. 'Se!' he screams. 'Se!' repeated. Long silence. 'Nza.' Then: 'Cosenza, Cosenza, Cosenza' again and again.

Then we sing. It sounds uncannily like that old cowboy standard, 'Red River Valley': 'The flags will flutter, the drums will return to sound...' The singing goes on and on until you're almost mesmerized, not conscious that you're singing at all. You even forget quite how surreal it is to sing an American country song on the southernmost tip of Calabria. Being on the terraces with ultras is a bit like a crash course in popular and classical music: you end up singing Ettore Petrolini's 'Tanto pe' canta' or Patty Pravo's 'Il Paradiso' (with the adapted lyrics 'you don't realize that we die for you...'). Then suddenly you'll be eulogizing a team to the tune of 'Libiamo' from Verdi's *La Traviata* or 'Va, Pensiero' from *Nabucco*, then a protest song before sliding into some cartoon theme tune (usually 'Popeye').

Ten minutes into the second half, right in front of us, there's a cross from the left. One Cosenza attacker dummies to play the ball but lets it bounce between his legs, so it comes to Ettore Mendicino with his back to goal. He flicks it up with his right leg, turns and, as he's falling backwards, volleys the ball into the net. We away supporters go berserk: hugging, screaming, jumping. It's the first time anyone has really noticed what's happening on the field. 0–1 to Cosenza. Vindov is shouting in my ear: 'You can write whatever the fuck you want about us, but you have to write this: "Cosenza is beautiful and Vindov loves Cosenza."'

'Lupi, Lupi, Lupi,' we scream, arms over each others' shoulders, facing the grass now. 'Wolves, wolves, wolves.' No other goals are scored and it is, finally, Cosenza's first victory of the season, the first time in more than half a century that the team has won here. The police herd the Cosenza ultras underneath the steps as the home crowd shuffles off. For an hour we're kept there, singing and taunting.

In a world where political and religious adhesion was on the wane, the terraces gave rootless youths that enchanting sense of being able to call somewhere home. The ultras seemed to be looking for that vanishing grail of modern life: belonging. In Catania, for example, there is an ultra group called Estrema Appartenenza ('Extreme belonging'). It's a concept equally treasured by hooligans, at least as portrayed in film. At the conclusion of Alan Clarke's film about violent English fans, *The Firm*, one character repeats 'It's about belonging' three times.

That sense of rootedness encouraged ultras to believe that they were the infantry of their *borgo* ('hamlet' or 'borough') or *contrada* ('district'). In later decades, this aggressive adherence would become a blast against both modern football with its rootless stars and against the 'whereverism' of globalization. But in the 1970s, the folkloric use of flags and pennants had something playful about it. Very early on, the aim of the ultra performance was the defence of the group's ensign or herald and the attempt to snatch the enemy's one. It was not unlike the English Boy Scouts' 'wide game', in which young lads raced round trying to capture the rivals' flag. The greatest shame that could befall an ultra group was for its herald to fall into enemy hands. The unwritten code of ultra honour said that if a group's herald was ever taken, it should immediately dissolve. That was why the object was, without exaggeration, considered sacred. Without it, that beloved sense of belonging could go up in smoke. The group would disintegrate or else lose face for breaking the unwritten rules. It was a symbol of continuity with the past, a representation of the colours of your city or suburb, and of your presence. It was often hung upside down if members of the group were in prison or banned from matches (a phenomenon so common now that most are displayed the wrong way up).

They were bulky though – imagine 30 square metres of linen or plastic rolled up – and so on away trips there's usually someone with a massive backpack, guarded by other foot soldiers. If you want to steal another group's ensign, you looked out for their backpack. There might be many decoys, of course: other ultras carry holdalls full of booze, flares, megaphones, scarves and drums.

The battle over the heralds was the central pretext for the violence of the movement. Even though only 0.3 per cent of Serie A and Serie B games in the 1970–71 season saw any violence, it was clear that fights were an integral part of being an ultra. The lexicon of the subculture was littered with phrases like *spranghe* ('bars'), *chiavi inglesi* ('English keys' or 'spanners'), *bastoni* ('sticks'), *agguato* ('ambush'), *bombe carta* ('paper bombs') and *legnate* ('woodenings', as it were, usually with a baseball bat). Doubtless, boasting about the fights meant that their size, danger and frequency were greatly exaggerated (one loses count of the number of times one hears that someone was so badly beaten up that 'the suture cotton ran out'). And many first-generation ultras romanticize those early years as times of healthy fisticuffs, which they portray as part of a consensual scrap between teenagers, and nothing more.

The ultras have always been very frank about the centrality of violence. It was part of the founding vision of this world. One of the stickers of the Ancona ultras said bluntly '*La nostra vita è violenza*' ('Our life is violence'). In Gianluca Marcon's short documentary, *E Noi Ve Lo Diciamo*, Frank (from the Ultras Avellino) says that fighting 'is part of my way of being… it's an essential part of my being an ultra'. Michele, from the Vigilantes Vicenza, says something very similar, that fighting is 'the element that closes the circle of being an ultra. It's something that whoever is inside [the ultra world] wants to be there.' Imagining an ultra without physical violence, some of them say, would be like cooking without salt. That tiny element informs and flavours everything.

Bocia is the eccentric leader of the Atalanta ultras in Bergamo and he has no hypocrisy when it comes to discussing fights. 'Violence is in the very essence of being an ultra,' he once claimed in a newspaper interview. 'Fighting is our drug, all ultras look for a fight. It's something you have inside you, that increases as the game gets closer. When you have to make yourself respected in a city which isn't yours… or else when the enemy arrives on an away game, and at 10 a.m. you're already there, in the *piazzale* in front of the stadium… It's a defence of your territory to make the enemy understand that here you're in charge.'

Often the language used about such events downplayed the violence and turned it into something softer or more slapstick: 'a few buttons flew off the shirt', and so on. There was a tradition in many grounds that the turnstiles would be opened for the last fifteen minutes of the match to allow those who couldn't afford a ticket to come in. For the ultras, however, it was an excuse to leave the ground and go hunting for their rivals. It was what they ironically called the '*passeggiata*' – the 'stroll'.

Many of the memoirs of those early years offer little more than descriptions of one battle after another. In *Una Vita Da Molosso*, Aniello Califano wrote 'when we lost, whether it was against Livorno, Latina or whoever, when we went out there were slaps for everyone we met along the street… even though we were a small provincial city, no one was able to move in a mass as we were, whether it was for numbers or turbulence… All the Adriatic,' he wrote, 'was our blackboard.'

Often, the fights are all ultras want to talk about. When you listen to them, they all sound fairly similar: the prelude was almost always a brief dance at distance, a chance to big up your group and to belittle the enemy. You circled and studied, shouting insults. The fear gave you an unbelievable energy and focus. Until at a certain point contact became inevitable – a leader shouted '*carica*' ('charge') – and the distance disappeared. You picked out your man and saw nothing else, rushing towards each other like lost lovers.

For ultras, those fights had an almost sacred quality. They talk about the sensual intensity of them, an absolute clarity to life all of a sudden. The greater the danger and fear, the greater the adrenalin rush which makes you feel somehow superhuman. For once in life, you're absolutely present. All other places and time zones have been obliterated, and now – as the enemy howls back, arms raised, and rushes your brothers – you have complete focus, a concentration which is merely instinctive. Compared to this, everything else was false or ephemeral. But you felt nothing. Not even the blows. You saw blood, you heard bodies being pounded, the crack of metal on skulls, but you fought through it, focussed only on defending your brothers and attacking theirs. Because suddenly you're a pack animal once more, speedy and brutal. It was a buzz you could get nowhere else, and for many it became as addictive as the finest pharmaceutical, something to be sought at all costs and at all games.

It's possible to watch thousands of hours of footage online from those fights. Often filmed from the stadium stands, or from high-rise buildings, the ultra groups look like shoals of fish, moving as one body. The anonymity of the fighters – hooded, scarves over the face, just dots in the distance – is matched by the blue helmets of the police, like bubbles, which move into the midst of the shoal. There is a bizarre beauty to it, just as captivating as watching a murmuration of starlings: the group is suddenly dark and dense, then pulls apart, dispersing so much you can see individual dots before it quickly regroups.

The ultras claimed to have an ethical code. Fights took place, so they said, only between ultras, not with ordinary 'scarfers' and run-of-the-mill fans. Numbers would be more or less even. No one ever reported anything to the police. There weren't supposed to be blades or other weaponry. When someone asked for mercy, you were supposed to give it. Il Bocia fondly calls the code '*genuino*', true or honest, and in some cases the fights were strangely stylized: one ultra from the 1980s says 'the encounter was very beautiful and correct, like a nineteenth-century duel.'

It's a language echoed by many others who portray the fighting as something knightly. '… first comes the group,' wrote one Brescia ultra, 'the colours which represent the history of the city, of our territory and the traditions of our people… a medieval or chivalrous concept.' He, like all ultras, felt that the fights were part of the values 'which should represent the dignity of every man: loyalty, solidarity, confrontation, seriousness, humility, transparency, sincerity, territoriality and tradition.'

There was rarely anything overtly political about the fights. If a notoriously left-wing *curva* came up against a right-wing one, it added a nice edge to proceedings but it was never the ignition. Yet it was inevitable that the regularity of these fights attracted those who were prone to violence, and the groups – needing as many fighters as they could find – actively sought to recruit through both charm and intimidation. Those who glimpsed something 'spiritual' in the fights were often from the same wing of extremist thought.

If there was, as they said, a 'code', it was often broken. One ultra memoir remembers how an Opinel blade was a ubiquitous accessory: 'all the lads of the group went around armed with knives, more than anything to cut hash, but also to have a psychological guarantee.' That was in the 1980s but it's the same today. Carrying a knife is the street version of a nuclear arsenal: a deterrent for the good guys in your crew. It was a grey area that many ultras bluntly acknowledge. As Massimo, from the Ultras Cremona, says, 'there is a limit, but where is it written? You don't get yourself killed to say "I'm honest".' Another ultra memoir talks incessantly of knifings without, eerily, any agency: '... in the struggle two Atalantini were reached by knives...' The use of knives in fights was, he writes, 'spreading like an oil slick'. The Inter ultras once even held up a banner saying, 'In fights the only rule is that there are no rules.'

Despite the rhetoric, then, it was rare for fights to be merely with fists. Many ultra memoirs give loving accounts of encounters with iron bars, rods, flagpoles and screwdrivers. Flagpoles and women were used to smuggle in weapons. One ultra calls the preparation of weapons before a fight 'laying the table'. Maybe the songs were just taunts and boasts but they were also hymns to weaponry. 'Hidden amongst my school books,' one song went, 'I'll bring a pistol.' By the mid-1970s, many ultra groups were already playing with flare pistols. The stab in the buttocks was common, and even those stabbings had a code: the backside was so far from the vital organs that in the unlikely event anyone was arrested for it, they would never be done for attempted murder. The fact that the stab was in the backside had the added advantage of suggesting that the rival was running away and thus a coward.

Many older ultras are nostalgic for those old days in which the fights were even creative, like a violent version of upcycling in which anything to hand – coins, stones, pipes, bricks – could come in handy. At least in the retellings, there was a strange playfulness to the encounters, as if most didn't want to take it too far. 'He asked me if I could swim,' remembers Beppe, 'before chucking me off the bridge.' On one occasion, the leader of Bologna's Total Chaos group, il Giustiziere ('the Executioner') lost a tooth in a fight with Cosentini, and they all stopped to look for it. Another ultra recalls the early days in which rivals were humiliated rather than wounded by having dried cod placed in their clothes and mouths. Juventus ultras once placed manure on the Torino terrace, having gained access by bribing the stadium custodian with two chickens.

Often it was more serious, however. In December 1973 a seventeen-year-old Neapolitan fan, Alfredo Della Corte, was celebrating his team's away victory over Roma in what was called 'the derby of the South'. He was waving a large flag and shouting 'Forza Napoli' at a Roma fan. The man pulled out a gun and shot him twice in the face. The bullets knocked out nine teeth and it was only his molars that saved Della Corte's life. That same year, the fifteen-year-old *capo-ultra* of Roma's Boys, Antonio Bongi, remembers the Torino ultras storming the *curva* ten minutes from the end of a game. Wearing motorbike helmets and armed with chains and baseball bats, they duly captured the Giuliano Taccola Primavalle banner. 'That was the first time I had contact,' says Bongi. 'Until then I didn't know football could be so violent.' There was often, though, a strange graciousness to the ultras too. The Torino ultras knew that Giuliano Taccola was the Roma player who had died aged only twenty-five so they cut the painting of Taccola's face from the captured banner and sent it to the Roma ultras via mutual acquaintances as a sign of respect.

Everyone agreed that it was in the metaphysical furnace of a fight that a group truly became brothers. In Giuseppe Scandurra's *Tifo Estremo*, twenty-five-year-old Minos says: 'When you have beside you twenty or thirty people who, in that moment, you trust more than anything else in the world, you're greatly united... It's something which reinforces evermore the bonds which link you to the group and the people who are a part of it.' The bonds forged in a mass brawl were profound. You saved each others' lives, or else – tender as well as tough – you visited mates in prison or hospital. Perhaps it was attractive because, in an increasingly bloodless, relativist world, men finally felt like warriors again.

That's not how the ultras see it, though. Most are very weary of questions about violence. It's all people ask about, they complain. 'It's just there,' they say, 'it's what this life is.' Often, they'll offer a street version of that Brechtian line: 'The rushing river they call violent, but no one calls the banks that channel it violent.' In other words, we're violent because society is restrictive, pressing in on all sides. *Gruppo d'Azione*, one of the best books on the ultras and concentrating on one gang from Spal, speculated that 'violence was the only reply to give to personalities like Andreotti, Craxi [considered corrupt politicians] and all the putrescence that was flowering around'. It was a response to existential pessimism.

Critics always said that the violence was pointless but that, say the participants, is precisely why it is so pure. As one of the characters in Nanni Balestrini's sensational novella, *I Furiosi*, says: 'Violence is beautiful because we have it in our blood and there's beauty when you smash everything. It's an exultant moment when you see the flames or the police running away or when the armoured vehicles arrive and you're in the middle of a merry-go-round, when you hear falling glass, the smell of teargas, the flames of the Molotovs, people who are running, the shouts… stadium violence is more of a drug than political violence because it doesn't have any objective. It's an end in itself.'

Many couldn't, of course, accept this meaninglessness and sought to understand what one ultra calls the 'demented aggression'. Sociologists guessed that it reflected despair about unemployment, or that modern rootlessness was creating an exaggerated need to belong. Hannah Arendt, talking about violence in post-war society, believed that it was caused by the bureaucratization of modern life: 'In a fully developed bureaucracy there is nobody left with whom one can argue, to whom one can present grievances.' We never manage to face-off with those who appear to have power over us.

But most ultras, like the hooligans, found such intellectual speculation faintly ridiculous. In the Alan Clarke film, *The Firm*, Bex's crew are watching some pompous presenter attempt an analysis of the hooligan phenomenon. One of the lads cuts through the guff by turning to his mates and asking: 'Why don't he just tell 'em we like hitting people?'

Anyone who has studied progressive radicalization, however, would notice that many of the ingredients for an escalation were present: a group of people often without hope or direction but finding profound meaning in each other had developed a concept of the sacred. The representation of that sacredness was to be defended at all costs if the affections and bonds of that group were to survive. Just as the footballers were representing the colours of the city, so too were these ultras. They had a sense of sacrificing themselves for the cause. And it wouldn't be long before the blood of martyrs was creating a longing for revenge.

There's often a screaming intensity to the ultra world. One memoir is written entirely in block capitals. But in the Cosenza fanzine, there's a short piece about how future meetings of the Curva Sud would be organized. 'We know that our assemblies need to be improved,' wrote Tubby. Having come through recovery, he understands group meetings and offers his advice: 'Know how to listen' and 'don't interrupt'.

He explains to me how he will line the chairs up like a classroom until, when the group regains maturity, it can go back to a circle. 'This way we're trying to give still more force to our non-hierarchical chaos.' In case the planned seminar about how to organize an assembly sounded too heavy, it would be followed, he said, 'by that joyful and bohemian sociality which has always distinguished us'. It's hard to imagine a few sentences that better encapsulate Cosenza's terraces: anarchic, addicted, recovering, chaotic but – most revolutionary of all, especially for Italy and the ultras – learning how to listen.

Mid-1970s, Turin

Turin is an august city of wide boulevards and stately palaces. The perpendicular grid is ribboned by two rivers – the Po and the Dora Riparia – that merge near the city's monumental cemetery where many of the players of the 'Great Torino' are buried. The basilica of Superga dominates the skyline, reminding Torinesi of past glories and of mortality. Beyond, but still close, are the whipped-cream peaks of the Alps.

The first capital of a united Italy, Turin has always felt grand. With its large Jewish and Protestant communities, it feels less obviously Roman Catholic than many Italian cities, and its trams, chocolates and Frankish dialect give it a decidedly Central European air. It's a region of *bon-viveurs* who have produced glorious concoctions: not just fine wines like Barbera and Barolo, but all those aromatic drinks like Cinzano, Vermouth and Martini. The city is, most importantly, home to both Juventus and Torino football teams.

In the years of economic boom throughout the 1960s, Turin had changed radically. The car manufacturer Fiat had brought tens of thousands of workers from the South to its Mirafiori factory. Most were Juventus supporters and if they weren't, their kids soon became fans. Juventus supporters and the club's ultra groups have always been unlike all the others. Whereas ultra groups were usually expressions of an organic territorial attachment, that was rarely the case with Juventus. Because of its monotonous success, the club's fan base wasn't Turin, or even Piedmont, but the whole of Italy. It's been estimated that as many as 14 million people in the country support the 'old lady' of Italian football, which is why it's also nicknamed 'the girlfriend of Italy'. In Turin they called the supporters and players the 'rigatìn' ('the lined ones') or the 'gobbi' ('the hunchbacks'). Often, the insignia of Juventus ultra groups wasn't simply the team's black-and-white (inspired by Notts County's colours) but also Italy's tricolour of red, white and green. The colours of the Italian flag suggested not just that the team was constantly winning the *scudetto* (and in 1971–72, 1972–73 and 1974–75, Juventus won its fourteenth, fifteenth and sixteenth *scudetti*) but also that it was a national team.

As happened almost everywhere, Juventus ultra groups emerged from within the formal fan clubs like Primo Amore ('First love') and Juventus Club Filadelfia. The first Juventus ultras had been inspired by the far left and had names like Venceremos (echoing the rallying cry of the Latin American left). One famous left-wing slogan – 'power has to belong to the workers' – was transmuted to 'power has to be black-and-white'. But very soon, other political forces came to the fore. The Panthers dressed like their far-right Lazio counterparts: '… camouflage jacket, jeans stuck into the para-boots, bandana on the forehead like the Apaches, the flag as a pretext for the flagpole which was a truncheon…' There were many political allegiances amongst the thousands of Juventus ultras but there was a rump of Mussolini lovers who were ever-present and who would, as the decades passed, slowly take control of the *curva*.

Another of Juventus's early groups was called Fossa Dei Campioni ('the Pit of champions'). Its symbol was a winged helmet and, of course, a tricolour on the cuirass. Its leader, Antonio Marinaro, had been born in Melfi, in Basilicata on the instep of the Italian boot. Nobody quite knows why Antonio Marinaro was nicknamed 'Jackie the Ultra'. Some say it was a simplification of Jekyll, because this hulking man with a Freddy Mercury moustache had two sides – kind and aggressive, gentle and bellowing. Like so many others, he was one of the *capo-ultras* who found belonging not in his roots, but in his new surroundings. Being an ultra was a way to assert himself despite being an immigrant. It was the same for Pino Fridd n'Pitt ('Pino Coldheart'), a young tough who had been born in Foggia, in far-off Puglia. In the first game he saw, at the start of the 1977 season, Juventus beat Foggia 6–0 and he decided then to put down roots with the winners.

The Fossa slowly morphed into a new group called the Fighters. Their iconic leader was Beppe Rossi. With his thick hair, hook nose and winning smile, he was what they call in dialect a '*baccaglione*', a smooth-talker. The Fighters kept the helmet as a symbol, adding spanners crossed like bones in a pirate flag. (Spanners were one of the preferred weapons of ultras, forceful but rarely lethal.) Rossi, like so many, was slightly obsessed with creating an 'English' form of fandom: doing away with the kettle drums and using only hands, voices and scarves. He loved Pink Floyd and the Liverpool anthem, 'You'll Never Walk Alone'.

The Juventus choreographies back then were basic. Rossi's grandmother used to keep spare wood she picked up so he could nail together coffins to symbolize the death of the opposition. One time, an ultra came across hundreds of unused posters of the pop-star Bobby Solo, so they used them in a choreography. It was all fairly naïve compared to what came later and there was no money in it, no incentive other than passion for the team and one's ultra siblings.

It was, according to Beppe Franzo – a lifelong Juventus ultra – a 'spiritual vision of existence'. But this alleged spirituality was often similar to that of those early twentieth-century Mussolinian black shirts who found transcendence in violence. Franzo talks very frankly about what the ultra code has always been: 'Never step backwards, never abandon your neighbour in the fight, hit hard… The old nature of men through all the ages resurfaces, uncontrolled and uncontrollable.'

Unlike their Juventus rivals, Torino fans were used to failure. 'We are,' wrote two fans, 'massacred by destiny… we're trapeze artists of weeping, adept at being ripped off, acrobats of the art of enjoying little…' One Toro player, quoting something he once heard, put it more bluntly: 'Supporting Toro is like masturbating with sand.'

Legends grew up as much around Toro ultras as their underachieving team. 'Strega' – the 'Witch' – was a hard-as-nails leader who began a tradition of dressing up as a priest and offering the last rites to Juventus before derby games. Sogliola ('Sole', as in the fish) had been to prison so many times that he used to bore people on away trips by describing each prison he saw on the way to the game. Il Pittore ('the Painter') made striscioni (banners) so long that he had to sit with his sewing machine by the window, the material flowing from one flat to another, linking people to his maroon creations. People often told the story about him being so nervous during a game that he gripped the icy tubes of the terraces and his hands got stuck. The only way to free him was by using the old-fashioned 'Alpine solvent' of urine.

What keeps all these characters in the collective memory is the fact that, like Lazio two years before, they were the ultra leaders at a time of sporting glory. After decades of suffering, the Torino team began not only to reflect the passion of its fans but its completely unexpected success lent sudden prestige to them.

Many of the players at the start of the 1975–76 season had been at the club almost all their careers. Paolo Pulici would spend fifteen years at Torino, while the team's leader was a recently retired player, Giorgio Ferrini, now serving as the assistant manager. He wasn't exactly ugly but he looked mean: a bit of acne scarring, a pointed nose, limp hair. In his career, he had used his elbows to such good effect that no one ever got past him and he was nicknamed 'la Diga' ('the dam'). The team now had a defender whose actual surname meant Corporal. The coach was Gigi Radice, called 'the German' for his icy eyes and chilly manner. Like Maestrelli before him, he was a coach who brought in players, like Patrizio Sala, that he knew and trusted from his days managing elsewhere. What endeared so many of those players to the ultras was their stubbornness and honesty. One player, Francesco Graziani, was once being courted by the Napoli president but he wouldn't be wooed by money: 'I'm sorry, Mr President, I've given my word and I only have one.'

The players had many superstitions and, as they accumulated victories, the more those little actions became entrenched. Paolo Pulici – nicknamed 'Pupi' – insisted on leaving the changing room last and the players always sat on the same seats in the bus. The connection with the fans was embodied by a girl who always came out onto her balcony to wave on the team as their coach went to the stadium. If she didn't appear, they had to stop the bus and wait. The players nicknamed her *bagna cauda* after the piping, anchovy-flavoured hot-pot prepared by all self-respecting Piedmontese. The ultra world was often male-dominated but amongst Toro ultras, as everywhere, there was a contingent of female ultras who became objects of all the usual male imaginations: goddesses, sisters, mothers, lovers. As one impassioned Toro fan wrote in quasi-erotic prose, those female fans were 'the priestesses who fed the fire of passion'.

It was a sensational season because Toro didn't just win the *scudetto*, they did so having been six points behind Juventus in an era when only two points were awarded for a win. By late autumn it had seemed that it would be the usual stroll for the hated rivals. But then, on 7 December, Toro won 2–0 against Juventus. They beat Milan at the San Siro and swatted Verona 4–2. It was when they beat Juventus again, in the return match on 28 March, that people began to believe. Toro scored nine goals in two games – against Fiorentina and Cagliari – and sealed the title in a suitably Torino style by drawing the last game of the season in which Toro players scored both goals (one for themselves and one for the opposition).

The ecstasy wasn't understated. 'The Painter' stuck 5,000 tri-colour stickers all over the city. Horns honked long through the night. Many ultras went to stand by the lamppost where Gigi Meroni had lost his life. Almost everyone that emotional summer made the trek up to the Superga Basilica to cry in happiness and pain. And this being Torino, the pain wasn't over. Within months of that *scudetto*, 'the Dam' – Giorgio Ferrini – suffered two brain aneurysms and died at the age of thirty-seven.

———

Present Day, Hotel Centrale, Cosenza

It is shaped like a boat, the prow nudging close to the dual carriageway. Its facade is glinting white marble and a mosaic of
tiny tiles that sparkle in the evening neon. Up top, a glitzy sign
announces its name: Hotel Centrale.

A few men in hoodies are putting a ladder to the side of a glass-
fronted atrium that was supposed to become a spa. It's night
but all the lights are off because the hotel was never finished.
It was confiscated by magistrates investigating financial crimes
during its construction. 'Mafia association' and 'fraudulent bankruptcy' are the accusations. It's thought the man building the
hotel also embezzled large sums from something called the Field
Foundation.

The men smash a window and crawl into that large greenhouse
of an unfinished spa. They're astonished by the luxury. The tubs,
radiators, tiles – everything looks designed and costly. The name
of the spa suite, 'Thala Tepee', has been carved into the oak door.

They move away from the glass and pull up the ladder, so
that no one from outside knows what's going on. They are from
a loose organization called 'PrendoCasa' – literally, 'I take a
house'. They have chosen this date carefully. It's 30 December,
a time of year when police have other priorities. The figurehead of the movement is a lawyer called Ferdinando. He's a
tall man, so unflappable that he seems permanently deadpan.
'We're a popular movement which defends those who need
housing,' he says. 'There are a thousand evictions in Cosenza
every year, and that's only counting the regular, registered ren-
tal contracts.'

There are so many overlaps between PrendoCasa and Cosenza's ultras that it's hard to draw any lines between them. Both occupy spaces and defend them, sharing their squats with those in need. And there's a large overlap of personnel. Both, they say, move in and fight for rights. The squat sign (a zig-zag arrow in a circle) is a regular symbol of the Cosenza *curva*, and someone has painted 'Squat the World' in jazzy lettering outside the Casa Degli Ultrà.

'There's always been an ultra soul among us,' says Ferdinando. 'The first to come to our squats are always people from the terraces. Our squats have become the offices for various ultra groups. There's not much need for political debate,' he says. 'For us it's normal that if you've grown up in the ultra world, you have a certain mentality. Not because of politics as such, but because you're used to debates about creating a different city.'

'We come from the teachings of the Nuclei Sconvolti [the main ultra group from the 1980s],' says Vindov. 'It's an automatic thing for us to do politics from below.' Vindov is active in both the ultras and PrendoCasa. He says Cosenza is 'a welcoming city of solidarity that has maintained the wild and rebel spirit of the Bruttii [the pre-Roman tribes who inhabited the hills and mountains surrounding the city]. Housing occupations are a patrimony for our city, they can usher in a true social innovation from the margins.'

The men spread out and go through the floors, opening the rooms and seeing more luxurious fittings. There are eight rooms on each of the six floors. The whole hotel seems built deliberately to waste money. 'This happens all the time,' says one weary lad. 'It's a constant cementification of our city. It suits politicians and constructors to throw up new buildings and vanity projects. Huge sums are chucked at them, the contractors make a mint and disappear before the job is finished, and we're left with this...' He throws an arm around a dark, half-finished bathroom with brushed steel towel rails.

It often seems as if every quango intended to improve housing for Calabrians suffers from corruption, as if the millions on offer are too hard for greedy suits to resist. Millions went missing from Gescal (the 'GEStione Case per i Lavoratori' or 'Workers' Housing Organization'). Other money ring-fenced for social housing was slipped into a fund to pay for a white bridge over the river that contrasts with the wooden, rotting one a few hundred metres away.

Because there's such widespread corruption in city hall, the outlaws of PrendoCasa believe they're not felons but virtuous activists, and the buildings they occupy are strategically targeted for the message the occupation will send. In November 2016, they moved into an empty building that had once belonged to Aterp, the regional agency for social housing where €100 million had gone missing. There are now fifty-five people living in the former offices, including thirteen kids.

The plan for this hotel is, as always, to open it up to anyone in need. Ferdinando knows it will be months, if not years, before the Hotel Centrale is auctioned off on behalf of creditors. Until then, the authorities would almost rather have his group there – repairing, heating and fixing – than leave it empty and open to vandals. Within days posters go up around town, urging people to come along to a 'painting and planting' day.

By the following morning, they have sorted out security on the door. They've hung a banner over the name of the hotel. 'Decorate the Centrale in defiance of corruption,' it says. As people hear about what has happened, they begin to roll up, hoping for a bed. Many are immigrants, often with children.

Within days they have repaired a few basins. They've got

electricity in ways that they won't explain, but which they admit aren't legal. 'An occupation is illegal,' Vindov says, 'but that's the only way to give these people a house.'

1977–78

Throughout the mid-1970s ultra groups proliferated. In 1974 Bologna's Forever Ultras were founded, as were the Ultras Fiorentina. Vicenza's Vigilantes came together in 1975 and a year later, the Brigate Neroazzure of Atalanta, the Rangers of Empoli and Ultras Livorno came into being. Every year brought new groups: 1977 saw the creation of the Panthers of Salerno, the Boys of Parma, the Ultras Ghetto of Reggio Emilia and so on. Very often those groups were just formal titles given to dozens of fans who had been singing and fighting it out for years.

That process of consolidation in so many *curve* wasn't simply an attempt to deal with political violence but also to bring order to the chaos. Back then, the price of entrance to the stadium was so low that even the poorest in the city could go along. To the teenagers in the vast suburbs of growing cities, the Sunday afternoon behind the goalmouth was a weekly carnival in which the most anonymous could be seen, admired, heard and spoken about. New flags and banners appeared each Sunday. Spontaneous slogans, gestures, songs and all sorts of political positions were trialled in the bear-pit.

The ultra movement was only one of many Italian insurgencies in the late 1970s and much the least threatening. Mafia turf wars were scarring Sicily and political terrorism was escalating. In 1977 the armed struggle brought new kinds of violence every week, often culminating in shoot-outs between the police, the far right and the far left. Nothing made much sense any more: Francesco Lorusso, a member of Lotta Continua (a leading ultra-left group) was shot dead in March that year. The next day, in seeming revenge, a police officer was shot dead in Turin by a Prima Linea militant (Prima Linea was a terrorist group that had split from Lotta Continua). The following month, again in Turin, a lawyer defending one of the Red Brigades was shot dead. In September, Walter Rossi was killed in Rome whilst distributing fliers protesting fascist violence. As always, many were killed who seemed absurd or irrelevant targets – among them, the deputy editor of Turin's *La Stampa* newspaper and a bystander, Roberto Crescenzio.

It was also the year that Luciano Re Cecconi, the title-winning Lazio midfielder, was shot dead in a jewellers when, allegedly, a pretend robbery went wrong. For Lazio ultras, Re Cecconi was one of the first martyrs. On 24 April 1977, the Taxi-Driver and his troops got the night train to Milano for a match the next day. When the train arrived at dawn, the Taxi-Driver walked all the ultras to the cemetery where the blond Lazio legend, originally from Milano, was buried. It was a walk of 20 kilometres but no one questioned his command, with songs and beer fuelling the march.

At the start of that bloody year, Bongi – the smart Italo-American in Rome – sensed which way the wind was blowing. Perhaps because he still saw things with an outsider's eye (he had moved back to the States for a year when his parents divorced), he kept talking to his mates about the need to make the terraces apolitical. Many of his friends were from the far right, many from the far left. 'Outside the stadium there were people who were killing each other,' he remembers. 'It was tough. I said, "We're not going to do politics here so lay down your arms".'

He and his mates from the chaotic Roma *curva* agreed to come together behind one banner. So, on 9 January 1977, a new name was unfurled at the Stadio Olimpico: Commando Ultrà Curva Sud. It came to be known as CUCS. Bongi achieved what most *capo-ultras* could only dream of in this endlessly schismatic country: something approaching unity. He particularly liked the acronym because it seemed to him a remote echo of those American universities like UCLA.

The game itself that day was a good omen. Roma won 3–0 against Sampdoria with that promising teenager from a few years back, Agostino Di Bartolomei, scoring twice. Bongi and Geppo led the singing: 'Oh, Agostino, Ago Ago Agostino gol!' The player had become the beating heart of a red-and-yellow revival. But even he carried a pistol outside the ground, just for self-defence he said.

A few months later, on 25 May, Bongi went to the Stadio Olimpico to watch the European Cup Final between Liverpool and Borussia Mönchengladbach. He took a tape recorder so that he and his friends could learn some of the English chants. By the beginning of the next season, they had Italianized 'Oh when the saints go marching in' in honour of the prolific striker, Roberto Pruzzo.

Many Lazio ultras had gone to that cup final to support the German side. Grit remembers that they took a black banner with yellow writing: 'Sieg Heil'. 'The Germans looked at us as if we were Martians,' he recalls. The politics of the Lazio terraces were very clear. The flag of Mussolini's 'Social Republic' of Salò was common and the ultras once played a joke on legendary striker Paolo Rossi, walking onto the pitch to give him a pretend pennant that actually turned out to be a black flier for the MSI, complete with its flaming tricolour. The 'Lazio, Lazio' chant was invariably accompanied by Roman salutes and, according to Grit, 'even the many lads who couldn't care less about the ideology automatically did the salute'. Much of the extremism was imitative.

They were years in which the choreographies, as well as the violence, became increasingly sophisticated. The use of flare guns was near ubiquitous. One, aimed at the Perugia striker Walter Novellino, actually hit the Lazio player, Lionello Manfredonia. Grit recalls Lazio ultras firing ten flare guns at their Fiorentina counterparts.

The Lazio solution to political terrorism was the opposite of Roma's. Where Bongi was trying to impose an absence of politics, the Laziali – after heated debate – chose a side. The main umbrella organization, GABA (the 'Associated Sky-Blue-and-White Groups'), morphed into something different. On 1 October 1978 the Eagles Supporters announced themselves with a banner that had in the middle of its logo the eagle of the Wehrmacht. From now on, the majority (though by no means all) of Lazio ultras – already closely twinned with the far-right ultras in Verona – were standing behind a long banner that suggested they were proudly *nostalgici*, longing for the return of fascism.

Many of the Lazio ultras were militants in the Fronte della Gioventù, the youth wing of the MSI. (The party seemed stronger than ever in the 1970s, winning as much as 8.7 per cent of the ballot – 2.7 million votes – in 1972). The esoteric fascist philosopher, Julius Evola, was hugely influential on that generation of Lazio ultras. In his book, *Men Among the Ruins*, Evola consoled those who suddenly seemed on the wrong side of history. He created a pseudo-spirituality in which the fascist faithful, like Christian apostles, awaited the return of the saviour (many, in fact, called themselves the 'children of the sun', believing that the dark night would soon be replaced by the rising star).

In 1977 it certainly seemed as if the new dawn had arrived. The first 'Hobbit Camp' was organized in Benevento that summer. It was to become an annual festival for those eager to soak up the culture of fascism. (Tolkien had long inspired Italian neo-fascists who liked to quote Bilbo Baggins' line that 'deep roots don't freeze'.) There was a popular left-wing slur that fascists belonged in the 'sewers' and so a magazine called *La Voce della Fogna* ('The Voice of the Sewer') was launched. The Celtic cross (an encircled plus sign) borrowed from the OAS (the French terrorist paramilitaries who raged against Algerian independence and tried to assassinate De Gaulle) became the default symbol of this resurgent fascism. It was adopted as the official emblem of FUAN (the MSI's student organization) and hinted that the far right – as well as being influenced by Evola's wafty paganism – was now toying with Catholic fundamentalism.

There was also a tension in that world between debate and deed (the A of FUAN stood for 'Action'). The poster advertising that first Hobbit Camp had a straight arm pointing a finger that looked, deliberately, like a pistol. Evola, as well as counselling patient quietism, had theorized about a martial and racial elite in *The Aryan Doctrine of Battle and Victory*, mirroring the tension in post-war fascism between biding one's time and taking immediate action, between being a part of the democratic process and being implacably, even militarily, opposed to it.

Pino Rauti and Stefano delle Chiaie, the co-founders of Ordine Nuovo and Avanguardia Nazionale respectively, were two of those who favoured action. Both left the MSI, frustrated by its collusion with the musical chairs of parliamentary politics. Both organizations were paramilitary. Rauti's Ordine Nuovo (though nominally called a 'study centre') was repeatedly suspected of involvement in terrorist atrocities, from the Piazza Fontana bombing in 1969 to the killing of investigative magistrates like Vittorio Occorsio. Nonetheless, from 1972 to 1992 Rauti was an elected member of the Chamber of Deputies, even becoming, later, the leader of the MSI. Meanwhile, Delle Chiaie – moving first to Spain and then Chile – became a confidant of Nazi-fascist fugitives throughout the Hispanic world.

The overlap between that not-quite underworld of far-right sympathizers and the Lazio terraces was obvious. Pierluigi Concutelli was part of Ordine Nuovo and described himself as a 'Lazifascista' – a play on words, echoing 'nazi-fascista'. Whilst in prison for the murder of Vittorio Occorsio – an examining magistrate whom he blamed for the prosecution of far-right terrorists – Concutelli committed another two murders, strangling two far-right terrorists who were about to grass. When he emerged from prison after thirty-four years, he was given the shirt of the then Lazio midfielder, Pavel Nedved.

Many of the mainstream Lazio fans, those who simply loved the white-and-light-blue of Lazio, were unaware how much the terraces were being politicized. After all, the eagle had been a symbol of the team ever since 1900. A trained eagle flew from the stands to the pitch at each game, and the club's anthem was 'Fly, Lazio, Fly'. So, many didn't realize or else turned a blind eye to the Nazi associations of the new ultra group.

The Eagle's new banner, like that of Roma, seemed blessed by the sporting result of Lazio–Juventus on 1 October 1978, with Bruno Giordano scoring two sensational goals. In the first, he was on the edge of the area when the ball came to him. He was almost falling over, leaning backwards on his right foot as he swung his left, hitting a volley so hard that Dino Zoff in the Juventus goal didn't even see it. But it was his second goal, Lazio's third, that stuck in the mind. In an almost identical position, he received the ball from a left-wing cross and with his first touch, on the instep of his right foot, dinked it over the Juventus defender. He looked up, saw Zoff rushing towards him, and calmly put the ball in the far corner of the net as two Juventini rushed back in vain. The whole action took all of two seconds.

1978 was as violent as the previous year, marked by more tit-for-tat killings. Both factions had their martyrs. On 7 January two far-right militants were shot outside the offices of the MSI in Acca Larentia, in Rome. That evening, when a journalist allegedly disrespected the victims by flicking a cigarette butt in a pool of blood, a riot began in which a third young man was killed by a police officer. Other deaths followed. The father of one of the murdered young men committed suicide. Then, on the first anniversary of Acca Larentia, another militant, Alberto Giaquinto, was killed by police.

That slaying of three *camerati* (the fascist equivalent of 'comrades') represented a decisive break for the far right. Youthful militants no longer trusted either the MSI or police to protect them. Some renounced extremism altogether but others became even more radical. A far-right terrorist organization, NAR (the 'Nuclei of Armed Revolutionaries'), was founded and became involved in various executions and the bombing of Bologna railway station in which eighty-five people were killed in 1980. One of NAR's leaders was the Laziale Alessandro Alibrandi, known as Ali Babà. Another nascent neo-fascist movement, called Terza Posizione ('Third Position') attempted with much ideological gymnastics to create an alternative fascism, siding neither with capitalism nor communism.

The killings continued. Two left-wing radicals, Fausto Tinelli and Lorenzo Iannucci, were murdered in a Milanese social centre. Valerio Verbano, an activist in the far-left group, Autonomia Operaia, was killed in his home in Rome, probably because he was compiling a list of neo-fascist activists. Angelo Mancia – known as 'Manciokan' amongst his Lazio mates – was shot dead as revenge.

The motivations for those killings were political, but the perpetrators and victims were often regulars on the terraces. The murders of Tinelli and Iannucci were linked to a huge, curly-haired lad who was part of Roma's Boys. Verbano, meanwhile, had been a member of Roma's Fedayn. Verbano's murder was, like the deaths of the two men in Milan, thought to be the work of the NAR.

There were still many ultras who hoped that their youthful movement could resist the escalation of violence. Geppo was the poet of Roma's *curva*. He had long hair and wrote stirring songs, like the doctored Marseillaise: 'When the hymn is raised, all the earth will tremble, we will sing until death, raising our colours...' He was often the first to run onto the pitch to hug the goal-scorer.

In 1978, a magazine called *Guerin Sportivo* published an optimistic letter from Geppo. 'The yellow-red support is civilizing,' he wrote. 'With violence put aside, our only thought is to make the support more beautiful and folkloristic. We have decided to eliminate violence... we try and teach our kids that we don't go to away games like gypsies, that robbing in service stations means dishonouring the name of Rome... politics, political parties, ideologies – they're all things which create divisions on the terraces. What the fuck do they have to do with the Magic? One goes to the stadium to sing, to sing and to sing again for Roma. What's the rest got to do with it?'

1977–78, Cosenza

Everyone knew Luigi Palermo as 'Zorro'. He had earned the nickname when he cut a Z into the cheek of an enemy. He was a crime boss but in the old-fashioned sense. He made money through contraband cigarettes, protection rackets and prostitution. He was opposed to dealing what he considered the dirt of drugs.

But rival gangs and even his underlings fancied making more money by dealing heroin in the small Calabrian city. On 14 December 1977, whilst Zorro was driving home in his Mercedes, another car ran into him just outside the Cinema Garden. Two men got out and fired four shots, killing him instantly.

So began a war between the Pino and Perna families for control of the territory. Over the next eight years, there were twenty-seven murders, including the killing of a twelve-year-old boy. In those years, Cosenza had an unofficial curfew after dark. Not that there was much to do anyway. There was just one bar open in the evening, in Piazza 11 Settembre. Every few months there was another shooting and slowly heroin began to be slung in the side alleys.

Like every other football ground, Cosenza saw some serious disturbances in those years. In December 1970, during a Cosenza–Internapoli match, fans ran onto the pitch, hitting and kicking the referee. Eventually the hunted official managed to reach the changing rooms but the fans kicked down the door. The beating continued and a linesman's wallet was stolen.

There were plenty of supporters' clubs. The Fede Rossoblù, an informal gathering of committed fans, was run by a thin seventeen-year-old with longish hair called Piero. He lived on

97

the main drag, Corso Mazzini, and had a red-and-blue flag on his balcony. He loved the football team but, much more, he loved all the misfits who found meaning in following those colours. Years later someone would say about him, 'Piero Romeo gathers all the madmen.'

There was something both gentle and slightly insane about Piero. He was impatient with the pompous and stuck-up, but he always had time for the local characters and lost souls. With his endless pranks, he was quickly becoming one of them himself. There were stories of him picking up the free little cards of Saint Francis from the sanctuary at Paola and selling them outside the stadium to raise money for his ticket to the game. Once, when working on a campsite with a friend, he dressed as a monk and administered communion to all the campers, slowly getting them drunk as he insisted they take the chalice again and again.

Opposite his family flat, with its balcony overlooking the main street, lived a friend of his father, a headmaster. The head-master's son, Claudio, was a decade younger than Piero but they often used to chat. Seven-year-old Claudio, with his thick black hair, would hold onto the railings outside his father's office as he tried to impress that impish seventeen-year-old across the street with his knowledge of football.

What changed their world was the return of a young Cosentino who had been working in Rome. Lello's family had found him a dream job in the capital working for SIP, the telephone monopoly. It was comfortable, permanent employment. But there he had discovered the Stadio Olimpico and its Roma ultras. He loved that crazy mass of humanity – all the singing, screaming and drug-using. In Rome, Lello took every substance he could lay his hands on. He liked gambling and had the whole array of human vices. His attendance at the SIP offices was erratic and he was eventually sacked when someone phoned in enquiring for the number of Lazio football club and Lello, with his love of Roma, replied 'Lazio doesn't exist', before hanging up.

When he arrived back in small, provincial Cosenza, Lello seemed almost an alien. With his shades, swagger and insatiable appetite, he looked like John Belushi in *The Blues Brothers*. He started talking to everyone about how the city needed to up its game. He hung out in the bars – the Gatto Nero and the Taormina – where the fans gathered and spoke incessantly about how every other club in the country had an ultra group. Piero was one of the first who became enthused.

The name they decided on was Commando Ultrà Prima Linea. Prima Linea means 'front line' and was the name of an extremist left-wing organization founded in 1976 that had emerged from Lotta Continua ('Continuing Struggle'). Like the Red Brigades, Prima Linea was fighting a war, killing its political enemies. The ideological leanings of Cosenza's first ultra group were clear. The group made its first appearance in 1978, when the stadium ban for that attack on a referee was over. Lello, Piero and a dozen or so others stood slightly apart from the ordinary fans in the main stand. They had a banner emblazoned with the name of the group. They sang incessantly, with Lello on the megaphone repeating as many of the songs from Rome as he could remember.

One of the lads watching them, sitting with his father, was Ciccio Conforti. Short, thirteen years-old with a curly black mullet, Ciccio was from a well-heeled family in Corso d'Italia. His father worked in the food industry and his mother was a piano teacher. Ciccio was a pianist too. He had drifted towards the Fronte della Gioventù, the youth wing of the fascist party. He sold their magazine, *Dissenso*, in Piazza Kennedy – just beneath Piero and Claudio's balconies – and sprayed the then fascist slogan – 'Europa Nazione' – on the walls of the city. 'But the stadium put me on the right track,' he says, smiling.

As soon as Ciccio saw the Commando Ultrà Prima Linea, he wanted to be a part of it. He and his school-mate, Nunzio, scratched 'Commando Ultrà' onto their school desks. They used to hang around Piazza Kennedy, not to sell *Dissenso* now but to be close to Lello, Piero and the others who had open-air gatherings.

The group listened to The Clash on big tape decks, playing 'White Riot' again and again to try and understand the shouted lyrics: 'I want to riot... are you taking over, or are you taking orders?' They loved the thrashy energy of punk and everything it stood for. They passed round bottles of cheap wine and got pissed together. Soon someone brought some burgundy buds of marijuana down from the hills to the east, from Rovito, and they started smoking weed. Everyone smoked except Piero, who made up for it by polishing off the wine.

But it was a strangely innocent time, too. Ciccio used to go to the printers at the end of the working week to pick up all the loose off-cuts of paper. He would pile them in boxes with Nunzio and then cut the thin columns into postage stamp pieces, ready to use as confetti to be thrown from the stands on Sunday. They blagged coins from anyone they could and bought toilet rolls in bulk, which they chucked onto the pitch to create white ribbons between the ultras and the turf.

In the 1970s there was no separation of opposing fans. Visiting ultra groups rolled up *en masse* to buy tickets and then huddle together in the same *tribuna* or *curva* as the home fans. There were no police escorts or stadium security. You could bring almost anything into the stadium and compliant club staff would often open up gates from one sector to another if the home fans wanted to impel 'respect' from the visitors.

By 1979, Cosenza's Commando Ultrà Prima Linea had quite a following for home games at the San Vito Stadium. Lello and Piero gathered an unruly crowd that made incessant noise through the games. Any insult to the honour of Cosenza was punished. In March that year – in a match against Calabrian rivals, Vigor Lamezia – the visiting fans taunted the Cosentini with the chant '*ripescati, ripescati*' ('fished out, fished out' – Cosenza was only in the division because it had been 'fished' from a lower league by a bureaucratic procedure). The Cosenza ultras charged, using their flagpoles and fists to persuade visiting fans to leave the stadium.

Despite the dangers, there was something magical about away games. Ciccio and Nunzio, just thirteen, found themselves in the company of tough, older men as if they were part of an army. Blokes they might have been scared of in Cosenza were now slapping them on the back and passing them a flask of wine or a joint. (Years later, one of the favourite songs of Ciccio's group would start: 'I was thirteen and was smoking weed…')

It was the first time, apart from summers by the sea, that those young men had gone so far from home. Every other Sunday they would leave the city behind on long train journeys across the South and it made them feel like old-fashioned adventurers. All the arguments and personality clashes in the group were forgotten when you were singing and fighting side by side. Far from home and outnumbered, the brotherhood and the bonds just seemed to deepen. And every Sunday night, the dishevelled gang returned to Cosenza with black eyes, bruises, and stitches, as well as stolen food, scarves and sometimes wallets. Their stories would race round the city and more people would want to join the group.

That year, a film directed by Walter Hill called *The Warriors* was released. Adapted from Sol Yurick's novel, itself based on

Xenophon's *Anabasis*, it was the story of a street-fighting gang crossing New York to get back to their own neighbourhood. It entranced Italian ultras. More than one group now called themselves 'Warriors'. The Cosenza crew went to see it at the cinema again and again. Several tried to copy some of the looks, the slang and the insults. Ciccio was growing up fast and school seemed suddenly somewhere that just taught you – as The Clash song went – 'how to be thick'. One night, Ciccio and Nunzio broke into their school, stole all the registers and burnt them. It didn't take much to work out who was responsible and the two youngsters were expelled.

28 October 1979: Roma v. Lazio

As often happened in the *curva*, no one knew his real name. He was simply known as Lo Zigano – 'the Gypsy' – because of his rag-like clothes. He was eighteen and had been going to watch Rome at the Stadio Olimpico since he was eight.

Zigano was from one of those struggling Roman families eking out a living any way it could. His father was an unemployed welder who sometimes sold fruit in Piazza Vittorio Emanuele, where the family lived. Zigano had dropped out of school and was helping to support his family with odd-jobs as a waiter, mechanic and, sometimes, as a mugger.

Roma football team was the only thing that gave his life much meaning. 'In whom or in what should a youngster of eighteen believe?' he once asked. 'What goal are adults holding up for the new generations? My ideal is Roma.'

One of his friends from Roma's red-and-yellow terrace was

Geppo, the long-haired poet who wrote songs for the ultras. A few months before, in March 1978, the two boys had stormed into the offices of a Roman newspaper, *Il Messaggero*, because they were angry at the depiction of the ultras. There, Geppo and Zigano explained what ultras were: 'We're the true fans… we give blows and we receive blows.' The boys explained the escalation of hatred between Romanisti and Laziali. In a previous derby, the Laziali had unveiled a banner saying that the rival Roma ultras would 'end up the same as Taccola' (the player who had died aged twenty-five). The Romanisti replied with a banner hoping for 'tens, hundreds, thousands' of Re Cecconi (the Lazio player who had been shot dead in 1977). They revelled in that death with another banner: 'Tabocchini [the jeweller who accidentally shot Re Cecconi] has taught us that killing a Laziale isn't a crime.' The Stadio Olimpico was the first stadium to have a players' tunnel to protect them as they jogged onto the grass and, in October 1977, CCTV was introduced too.

Given all this, the atmosphere for the Roma–Lazio derby of October 1979 was tense. The walls of the capital were sprayed with death wishes for the opposing side. 'It wasn't just rhetoric,' one aged ultra insists to me. 'We really did want to read about our enemies being knifed or shot.'

The day before the game, Zigano bought three high-powered nautical flares in a shop in Piazza Emporio. They cost 15,000 lire each. He, Geppo and their mates smuggled them into the ground, along with an aluminium pipe to act as a launcher for the flares, inside a rolled-up banner. Tensions increased when the Laziali realized that the Romanisti had somehow broken into their lock-up in the stadium, taking all their flares. The Romanisti, in turn, were aggravated when the Laziali unveiled an insult to the Roman captain who was struggling to come back from injury: 'Slobbering Rocca', it said. 'The dead don't resuscitate'. Another banner said 'red-yellow holocaust'.

At half-past one, Zigano loaded one of the naval flares into the tubing and let it off. It flew over the Curva Nord, where all the Laziali were gathered, and out of the stadium. Everyone around him applauded and cheered. It was one of best flares they had seen. Zigano loaded up another and let it off. This time it flew across the whole stadium, landing directly in the crowds on the Curva Nord.

Vincenzo Paparelli, a thirty-three-year-old mechanic, wasn't even supposed to be there. The season ticket belonged to his brother but he had given it to Vincenzo for this big match. He was sitting there eating pumpkin and sunflower seeds with his wife, Vanda, and their two young children. Vanda suddenly heard a thud.

'Did you hear that?' she asked, turning to her husband. The flare was sticking out of his left eye and he was collapsing away from her. Instinctively she tried to pull it out, but burnt her hand. He slipped to the ground. People all around stood up, screaming for the emergency services, but Paparelli was already dead.

On the Curva Sud, the Romanisti didn't even know what had happened. They saw some movement on the far *curva* but nothing more. Encouraged by the others, who were allegedly singing '*Morirete tutti*' ('You're all going to die'), Zigano let off the third flare but it banana-ed this time and ended up on the empty athletics track around the pitch.

The Lazio fans – many in their hand-knitted blue-and-white beanies – took down their banners. A lot left the stadium to confront the Roma fans on the other side. Some screamed at Pino Wilson, the Anglo-Italian Lazio captain, that the game should be called off (it wasn't). By then, even the Romanisti realized something had happened. Zigano heard the shouts of 'assassins' from the remaining Lazio fans and slipped out of the stadium, hoping not to be recognized.

He was on the run for the next fifteen months, moving between Bergamo, Milano, Brescia, Pescara and even Switzerland. He occasionally took trains but normally hitch-hiked and found odd jobs where he could. Zigano had been literally playing with fire without any real understanding of the consequences. Whilst on the run, he phoned Paparelli's brother to express his horror at what had happened and saying that he would turn himself in. He was even interviewed in Switzerland by two journalists, telling them: 'I've ruined my life with that junk... that tragic man has died but I'm a wretch too because I continue to live with this weight on my conscience.' On 25 January 1981 he did hand himself in. He was tried, found guilty of manslaughter and sentenced to seven years and eight months.

There were many other consequences of that grim killing. Lazio's Eagles decided, after much argument, that they should now move permanently to the Curva Nord (until then, they had only stood there during the Rome derby, when the southern end was taken by Romanisti). It felt, to them, like a sacred place now. They first assembled there on 9 December 1979 for a Lazio–Udinese match. The Laziali started singing a song, to the tune of the 'Fanfara dei Bersaglieri' (the 'Riflemans' Fanfare', the song of an elite Italian infantry corps) about their desire to 'avenge the death of Vincenzo Paparelli'.

That match was the first real darkening of the ultra world. 'Before that day,' remembered Grit in his memoir, 'it was a game, a fashion, a phenomenon of youth, whereas now for me and so many of my friends it wasn't a game any more but a daily battle... everyone had the same hatred as me inside them.'

For years there continued to be cruel graffiti in the capital invoking the hope that there would be 'ten, a hundred, a thousand Paparellis', or else taunting the Laziali with memories of 'flares in the face'. Well into the 1990s, Vincenzo Paparelli's son Gabriele had a brush and bucket of paint in the boot of his car to cover up the taunts in case his mother saw them.

The Roma fans, meanwhile, were banned from using the CUCS banner, with its mention of 'Commando'. Kettle drums and any mildly military paraphernalia were banned. Yet because of that, one of the most evocative songs of the ultra movement was born, now sung in almost every terrace in one form or another. It's the same 'Red River Valley' adaptation that the Cosenza ultras sing. With its musical triplets and wistful hope that one day the flags will again fly and the drums return, it sounds like the rousing hymn of a revivalist awaiting the return of the Lord and the Promised Land. The tempo changes as the lines are repeated again and again, suddenly slowing right down so you relish every beat and become hypnotized into a kind of blissed-out reverie: 'When to the sky the flags are lifted / the kettle drums will return to sound / only one shout will be raised, /Roma win again for the ultras.'

What was notable by now wasn't the yearning diction but the way in which the word 'ultra' itself was creeping into the songs. Worship often slips from one idol to another and even before that first decade of the ultra movement was over, it was clear that they were beginning to sing not only about the team but about themselves. Their secular god of the shirt had been replaced by a god incarnated in the group itself (called demotheism). Like so many cultish movements in which the congregation replaces the numinous with something much closer to home – themselves and their own leader – so some ultras began to insist that their group, not the team, was now an entity that couldn't be insulted, teased or touched.

Present Day, Cosenza

There are seven *striscioni*, each about eight metres long and made of blank wallpaper. We're waterproofing them with Sellotape, running it across the width of the banner to protect them against rain. The tape is only five centimetres wide, which means a lot of runs to do eight metres, seven times.

All the crew are singing songs as they work, short bursts that last two or three seconds. Others join in and laugh. Then it goes silent until the next one begins. Mouse pulls the Sellotape so fast that it roars. He stabs his blade into one end to break it, paws it round the back of the banner and then pulls again, passing me the loose end.

It looks like he's let himself go a bit. His beard is scratchy and his moustache is long. It makes him look the wrong side of rogue. He's put on a paunch and his flies are broken. But he's constantly shouting, arguing, joking, pretending to be furious.

Each person who turns up brings a few rolls of Sellotape. 'All in order?' they ask as they come in. They cock their heads to read the banners: 'No to expensive tickets' one says in huge, red-and-blue letters. Another pleads with the club president to offer cheaper tickets. In a way, it's part of the ongoing battle with the *tribuna*. At the moment the *curva* costs 10 euros and the *tribuna* 12, so many families go for the calm, safe second option where you also see the game better. That means that the rival ultra group – Anni Ottanta – has an easier job packing the seats. Mouse wants to attract troops back to the 'peoples' option' by getting prices dropped in the area behind the goal. The *curva* has, after all, always been the place of cheap standing – the only seating is flat concrete steps – and the greater the price difference with the *tribuna*, the more foot soldiers roll up in the *curva*.

It takes a long time to tape up eight metres. Once one banner is done, there's another to get on with. People decide we need a break and we pile upstairs where's there's now a fridge illuminating the darkness. We pull out beers, throwing coins into the empty fag packet acting as a till. 'It's been a strange season,' says SkinnyMon. 'But we're always here. That's what counts.'

After the brief hope provided by that away victory at Reggio Calabria, things went downhill again for Cosenza. They lost to Monopoli and, worse, to Catanzaro. But in the January transfer window, Braglia, the new coach, did some smart business. He got a Nigerian on loan from Spezia, David Okereke, and bought an attacker from Ascoli, Leonardo Perez (who had a habit of celebrating goals by giving his fascist fans a Roman salute). The excitement and suspicion about these new signings is so great that anyone in the city with a foreign accent is thought to be another new player for the Wolves. *'Ma voi,'* someone asks me, using the second person plural, *'siete qui per giocà?'* ('Are you here to play?')

That winter Cosenza won five games in a row. A bald Frenchman called Baclet scored a double. The brilliant striker on loan from Napoli, Gennaro Tutino, also scored a few. There was something of a family feel to the club when it was winning. Kevin, the son of the late club legend, Gigi Marulla, was part of the staff, while the manager's son, Thomas Braglia, had joined the squad.

The stadium is opened before lunch so we can hang out all the banners. Police and club officials watch on from afar: *Cosenza Siamo Noi* ('We are Cosenza', with the subtext that no one else is), *Lo Sballo Continua* ('The buzz [or trip] continues'), *Quote Rosa Cosenza* ('The Pink Quota', a gathering of female ultras). The white paint is cracking off the cloth on a lot of them but that adds to the sense that this is a place that treasures tradition. As it says around the smiling face of Denis Bergamini, 'Our Curva, Our History.'

We go to hunt for lunch but it's Sunday and everywhere is closed. It takes half an hour of jovial shouting to decide that we'll go to the supermarket. The check-out girl sees a crew of ultras and asks us all to hand in our bags since, she charmingly says, 'there might be more of you'. Then they quickly decide to close, so we grab our bags and traipse out. Dozens of others are rolling up now but a disconsolate Mouse says wearily, 'It's closed, it's closed.' An argument starts about which idiot decided we should come here.

We drive around trying to find a bar foolish enough to take us in. The convoy goes on and on, laughing out of the windows at mates and old men. We end up in a pizzeria at three. By now everyone is hungry and only Egg is keeping the crew going, singing, shouting, banging. He breaks a glass and a few of the Sunday diners clear out pretty quickly once we get settled in.

We drink and eat and drink and sing. By the time we get back to the stadium, the winter sun is clipping the sandy hillock behind the empty north end. In a corner pen are eighty or so *Aretusei*, which is what erudite papers call the fans from Syracuse. Their section, from this far end, is a small triangle with blue-and-white flags. On the left is the *tribuna*, the Anni Ottanta and the ordinary fans, the rump of Cosenza's support.

The game kicks off. Men chase a ball. We sing 'Cosenza' to the tune of 'Volare'. Nothing happens on the pitch except that Half-a-Kilo is out there on the track, his green bib and camera showing his professional side. 'Half-a-Kilo is one of us,' the chant goes, telling everyone that the press photographer down there is an ultra too.

It's rare for Italian pitches not to have an athletics track around the rectangle. For an English fan, it makes the game seem distant. Maybe that distance from the action is a metaphor for the distance between Italians and their government. But those athletics tracks make you feel like you're watching the game the wrong way through binoculars, and so in the end it's more fun to watch Egg screaming in the winter dusk.

You'll always meet someone you know in the *curva* and some-one you don't. You'll usually know all the songs, although this Sunday there's a different one. At one point, bored by a game that is drifting towards a dull nil–nil, we start singing 'We are children of Telesio'. There, in one unexpected chant, is another aspect of the ultra world – just when it looks utterly thuggish, it'll surprise you with its learnedness. Probably few of these ultras will have read the sixteenth-century philosopher but he is one of the sources of their pride in Cosenza. Their boast isn't just that they're tougher than the Sicilians from Syracuse, but more cultured. It reminds me of another chant from a few months ago, when Torino ultras sang at the managing director of Juventus not that he was a son-of-a-bitch, but that he was a son of Polyphemus, the one-eyed monster with giant sheep from the *Odyssey*. It's hard to imagine English hooligans name-checking David Hume or Greek mythological figures in their insults.

Early 1980s, Cosenza

In the 1979–80 season, Cosenza won Serie C2. The football itself wasn't exactly gripping. The Italian game back then was all about *catenaccio*, 'chaining' shut the defence. At one point, the team played out five nil–nils in a row (a result that the great sports-writer, Gianni Brera, once called the perfect game of football). But the promotion to Serie C1 meant that the club was now facing some serious teams, and its ultras were up against some major-league ultras from Reggina, Salernitana, Nocerina and the rest. 'We definitely never went anywhere to break anyone's balls,' remembers Ciccio. 'But we weren't non-violent. If we had to defend ourselves, we did, and pretty well too.'

One of the ultras' recurring metaphors for the *curva* is that it is 'a gymnasium for life', that it trains you for all life's eventualities. Sometimes the most important lesson wasn't about survival in a fight but about avoiding them. You needed to be so threatening that no one would start a row; so united that no individual would peel off and do something stupid. It was always a balance between appearing foreboding but also organized, between not starting anything but, if it did start, throwing the first punch. As they say in Cosenza, 'Who hits first, hits for three.'

That strange balance made those away-days to the big cities tense but exciting. The smallest misplaced insult could bring down on the group the wrath of an entire city, so there was a fragile restraint to the antics of the visiting ultras. As well as endless tales of mass brawls, many of their favourite reminis-cences from the late 1970s are about passing rival gangs *without* it kicking off: in silence, with scowls, but with strange respect. The fact that every city had its own dialect, unfathomable to cities only 50 kilometres away, helped maintain the distance. You could give orders and not be understood. Some say that the lack of separated sections for away fans, and the lack of a police presence, actually made the ultras more, not less, restrained. 'In away games,' remembers one, 'you were shitting yourself.'

But often Cosenza's Commando Ultrà Prima Linea was too

exuberant. The release from a week of work, of nagging at home or at school, meant that the away-days were times of epic drinking and smoking and singing, and people often picked fights before they had weighed the odds. There was the time when Cosenza, having been relegated back to Serie C2, was playing against Turris in late March. Three coaches had taken 150 Cosentini the 300 kilometres to Torre del Greco, squeezed between the Gulf of Naples and Mount Vesuvius. Most were thoroughly pissed or stoned by the time they entered the empty stadium, and they started singing and shouting and insulting the natives. Suddenly a few hundred locals stormed in with chains, metal bars and wooden poles. The old lady serving in the bar at the back of the stadium was even handing out empty bottles to the Turris fans, who smashed them into jagged daggers and charged the Cosentini. After the assault, the group huddled together in silence, checking cuts and bruised ribs, and watched their team lose 3–0.

That was partly how vendettas grew. If an ultra group gave you a beating on their turf, you made them pay when they came to yours. Until recently, all Italian number plates revealed, in the first two letters, the provenance of the car. It was common on a match day to hunt for the vehicles of the enemy, slashing their tyres, smashing windows and spraying 'merda' on the dented metal. Which only meant that the next time you went there, the atmosphere would be even more tense.

In the 1981–82 season, Cosenza came second in the division and was promoted back to Serie C1. More and more local lads were attracted to Cosenza's ultras. Sergio was well over six foot, a lanky lad, the youngest of seven kids. His father was from Sicily and both his parents were school caretakers. He had grown up in Via Popilia, the long road at the foot of the old town centre that ran parallel to the River Crati and the railway tracks. He was a good-looking tough, a convinced communist who had 'Prima Linea' tattooed on his right forearm. Nunzio, always quick with labels that stuck a lifetime, quickly gave Sergio the nickname 'Canaletta' ('Drainpipe').

Paride was almost as tall, but more angular and with bird-of-prey eyes. He was something of a punk, always trying out odd clothes and colours. He was, along with Luca, the brains of the group, coming up with ideas and connections. Vincenzo, a chubby lad with thick hair, was the least mischievous of them all in some ways. He was the only one, other than Piero, who didn't smoke. He was mollycoddled by his mum, who always sent him off to away games with trays of *lasagne* that he guarded more closely than his wallet. When Nunzio gave him the nickname of 'Pastachina' – evoking a loveable, rotund home-boy who loved his food – everyone knew who he was talking about without having to ask.

Piero was like an older brother to all of them. Lello, the dude who had come back from Rome, was often away – no one knew quite where. So, Piero had become the leader of the rabble. He was somehow irreverent and wise at the same time. Many of those kids were having constant bust-ups with their parents. Ciccio, expelled from school and always fighting with his strict father, had run away from home. The only things he took with him were a change of clothes and his collection of photos from the terraces. He went to Rome for two days but quickly regretted it and went back. Piero was there for him, able not only to listen but also to talk to his parents. But Piero insisted he was never a *capo*. It was the opposite of everything he believed in. As he used to say, in tight dialect, '*Nua sim'i' Cusenza e capi unni vulimu.*' ('We're Cosenza, and we do not want bosses.')

Many of the teenage ultras were little more than lost boys

looking for a cause. They felt the world around them was dangerous and bent. The Red Brigades, the NAR and the Mafia were still assassinating people across the country. In the summer of 1980 a passenger aircraft was shot down over the island of Ustica, while near Cosenza a crashed Libyan Mig23 was found in the Silan mountains – another Italian mystery that was never solved.

To many young men, the world seemed rotten. The dream of a workers' revolt had died with the previous decade, and 1980 was the beginning of a counter-revolution. In the autumn of that year almost 25,000 workers were laid off by FIAT but the so-called 'silent majority' marched against the unions. Corruption and hidden networks seemed to dominate the country. A masonic lodge, P2, was exposed, showing that the cream of Italian politics and business were enrolled in a secretive society with decidedly authoritarian aims. Even football wasn't immune from graft, with revelations that great teams including Milan and Lazio had been involved in match-fixing. The fights were getting ever more serious too: in a tournament in June 1981 between Inter, Milan, Feyenoord, Peñarol and Santos, there was a brawl between rival Milan and Inter ultras involving knives and pistols. Many were badly injured and one Inter fan, Vittore Palmieri, died in hospital. (A peace accord, which still holds, was agreed between ultras from two Milanese teams in 1983.)

By comparison, the ultras of this small Calabrian city seemed like idealists. The group was often experimenting with its name. The Commando Ultrà Prima Linea had become Ultrà Cosenza, but Ciccio called the inner circle, in English, the 'Mad Band'. There were heated arguments. There were discussions about money and transport and players, and about new faces. But the group was a sort of brotherhood, which meant that an insult to one of them was an insult to all. They fought for each other and that loyalty – not blind, but born of affection – inevitably attracted even more youngsters. Claudio, the young lad with a balcony opposite Piero's, was eleven now. Cheeky, bright, eloquent and still with a shock of curly hair, he hung out with the young men who gathered below his house in Piazza Kennedy and longed for the day when he could go away on the trains with them to faraway cities and come back with stories of his own.

Back in those days there were no barriers between the terraces and the turf. Cosenza's cheerleaders, Piero and Ciccio and various others, could stand on the grass behind the goal to conduct the orchestra. When Pastachina joined Piero at the front, the *curva* started another jokey song, to the tune of '*Alouette, gentille alouette*': 'Pastachina, cocaine, heroin', the joke being that he was addicted to his mum's *lasagne*.

Vincenzo – Pastachina – both loved and was embarrassed by the attention. He had become, in some ways, the group's mascot, the good-natured lad who people could tease because he was obsessional in his red-and-blue faith. Sometimes during a game that was going well, he was so overwhelmed that he would ball his fists and roll them both against his forehead as if he couldn't believe it. Once or twice he was so overcome that they had to call an ambulance because he was laid out. Blood pressure, he said.

Then, in 1982, a man appeared on the terraces who would change their lives forever. The terraces of Italy were, by then, full of eccentrics and odd-balls, of characters and petty criminals. But no one had ever seen anything like this man. It was he, more than any of them, who turned Cosenza's *curva* into a national phenomenon and opened up a debate about what exactly it meant to be an ultra and to live 'beyond' the norms.

―――――

1982: Violence

In 1982 Geppo – the long-haired poet of the Roma terraces – sent another letter to *Guerin Sportivo*. A few years before, he had urged pacificism among all football supporters. He had been holding out for solidarity amongst the excluded, an allegiance between the ultras even if they had different colours. It was exactly the same hope expressed by the character Cyrus in *The Warriors* movie, when he urges the gangs to unite against the police: 'Nobody is wasting nobody and that is a miracle. And miracles is the way things ought to be.' But now Geppo's tone was resigned. 'If I go to Turin, they beat me up, the same happens in Milano, Florence, Avellino, Catanzaro… by now it's done, I am at last a thug. The scarf I bought I will use to cover my face… Who knows if one day instead of beating each other we will be united…'

Geppo was writing shortly after one of the most frightening experiences of his life. On 22 November 1981 Roma was playing Inter in Milano. As usual, the Inter ultras had hung their banners all around the stadium and gone off for lunch. Somehow, Geppo – wearing a railway blanket borrowed from the overnight train – broke in with friends and stole, burnt and shredded those *striscioni*. It was the most galling thing that could befall an ultra group and when the Interisti realized what had happened they stormed the Roma section of the terrace.

The game itself was fraught, with five goals and a sending-off. But it was nothing compared to what happened on the stands. The SAN suffix of the Inter ultras, the Boys, stood for 'Squadre d'Azione Nerazzure', the Black and Blue Action Squads, a deliberate echo of the Duce's SAM, 'Squadre d'Azione Mussolini'. The

Interisti knifed any Roma supporter they could find. Eleven people were stabbed.

That sort of escalation turned even the pacifists into knife-carriers. Bongi took the decision to hit back hard. 'For the return match,' he says, 'even I, a peaceful guy, said "it's their fucking lookout", you know what I mean? I went after the Interisti. It was one of the few times I was stopped by the police and my dad kicked the shit out of me.'

Geppo's admission that he, too, was now a thug went to the paradoxical heart of the ultra world. Like many anarchists and socialists, some ultras longed for a form of fandom that was not prey to patriotism and *campanilismo*, but that could unite the oppressed. Yet Geppo and those ultras like him were accused of making a category error. Being an ultra implied not just a tight brotherhood, but also allegiance to specific colours. A rainbow was a heresy against chromatic fundamentalism.

Geppo's wistful tone was seized upon as apostasy and the magazine received hundreds of replies ridiculing his hope for a rainbow ultra world. A Juventus Fighter wrote that 'reading Geppo's letter I was left so ill that, if I had had him in front of me, I would have spat in his face. He maintains that he's a thuggish fan, I say that he's a chicken.' An Inter Boy wrote that 'if we step on each others' toes, if we are mightily provoked, we can't stand by and watch. We react, and in that case, there's no quarter for anyone.'

That allusion to provocation underlines how similar the ultra world was to that of the Hells Angels described by Hunter S. Thompson: '… their idea of provocation is dangerously broad, and one of their main difficulties is that almost nobody else seems to understand it.' One suspects that many ultras wanted it that way. If you never knew when someone was going to take offence and fly off the handle, you walked daintily around them.

Geppo's reply to the debate was moving. 'None of us know why our Sunday work is thuggishness, we just do it. All of you have called me a penitent: I'm not, I'm just trying to understand why we have all this anger inside us and why we dirty a clean day like Sunday, why we ruin the party of a game of football.'

Geppo's regret showed that the ultra world, so often considered mindless, was perhaps sometimes the opposite, and that violence wasn't a consequence of thoughtlessness but of despairing analysis. Geppo was daring to hint that football was a charade, that players' attachment to the *maglia* ('the shirt') was delusional: '... when I see Roberto-gol [the nickname of Roberto Pruzzo] under the Curva Sud I hug him and I deceive myself that he has scored for Roma and for us. But afterwards I start thinking and, as usual, thinking hurts. Maybe I'm a thug because I think too much.'

The more violent they became, the more the ultras were scorned. Like many marginalized groups, they turned the insults to their advantage. They seemed to relish being rejects, as being always 'beyond': beyond hope, beyond the pale, beyond civilization. They were the untouchables in the caste sense – dirty, disinherited and dangerous. As things hotted up, they were untouchables in other ways too. The names of different groups reflected that identity. An ultra group in Teramo is called *Zezza*, a dialect word for 'filthy'. Other teams had 'Dreadful Elements', 'Incorrigibles', 'Lost Minds', 'Extraneous to the Masses' and 'the Unfortunates'. As usual, it prompts a comparison with punks, who had group names like 'Unwanted', 'Rejects' and 'the Worst'.

It was, at least, safely predictable. They were rebelling against rejection by doing everything they could to ensure that they would be rejected. They obliged people to pay attention to them, even if the timbre of that attention was disdain. The more the ultras detected that disdain – and it wasn't hard – the more they attempted to offend society's sensibilities.

21 March 1982, Rome

Andrea was thirteen years old in the spring of 1982. Most people called him Puccino simply because his older brother was nick-named 'Pucci'. The boys' parents were originally from Puglia. Their mother worked for the petroleum giant Eni, and their father worked as an engraver. They lived in Via Livorno, a road that ran from Piazza Bologna towards the ring road and the railway lines. The first floor of their block of flats housed the offices of the MSI and its youth wing, the Fronte della Gioventù.

Pucci was twenty-one. He worked as a lighting engineer and was listened to when he spoke, partly because he was normally so quiet and introverted but also because he could flare up when needed. He was close to the far right but actually dressed like a left-wing hippy, wearing Pakistani shirts and sandals and rings on his fingers. He was one of the leaders of the Fedayn, an outfit founded by Roberto Rulli and associated with the left. Everything got mixed up in the ranks of Roma supporters. In the bar where the ultras gathered, politics dissolved in the face of the Roma faith.

Andrea looked up to his older brother and was always trying to emulate him: playing billiards, messing around with mopeds and motorbikes, going to the Stadio Olimpico. Andrea wasn't particularly good at school – he had been held back a year, and one teacher said he spent most of his time drawing motorbikes and engines and putting up Roma stickers high on the walls where the caretaker struggled to remove them. He often skipped school on a Monday to sleep off the excesses of an away game the day before.

21 March 1982 was one of those days, up north in Bologna. Someone was supposed to give the brothers a lift but it fell through, so they got the train along with Pucci's girlfriend, Giovanna. Not everyone getting on the train was a Roma fan. Some just went along for a riotous day out, like the short lad with thick, curly hair nicknamed Marmot. He was a Lazio fan really but followed the crowd. He was the sort of person who did daft things to try to be popular. Still only fifteen, he lived with his grandmother in Tor Bella Monica, a rough area of high-rise buildings to the east of the ring road. Marmot's dad had left home years ago and his mother was in a psychiatric unit.

The game that Sunday was disappointing: Roma lost 2–0 and the match would mainly be remembered for the goal scored by a promising seventeen-year-old in the Bologna ranks, Roberto Mancini. It was Roma's third successive defeat. Angry fans traipsed back towards the railway station, hundreds of them piling into the carriages of the 17.16 express, singing and shouting. Most had been drinking and smoking for hours. Pucci lost sight of his younger brother but reckoned he could look after himself.

The train was just outside Orte, on the Lazio-Umbria borders, when someone shouted 'cursed referee' and set light to a curtain. Soon afterwards, another hand pulled the red emergency handle and the train screeched to a halt. By now, black smoke was gushing out of the open windows of the carriage near the back of the train.

The fans piled out onto the grass by the tracks and watched

the flames. A couple of them – Marmot and a man known as Geronimo – were proud of the chaos they had caused and boasted that they had taught the authorities a lesson. Other fans were rotating their scarves in the air as if they were in the stadium, only this time shouting 'burn olé' instead of 'Roma, olé'.

Pucci was walking up and down the carriages, looking for his younger brother. 'Have you seen Andrea?' he kept shouting. 'Where's Puccino?' The back three carriages were uncoupled to stop the fire from spreading. The fire brigade arrived but the train was on an embankment and the hoses weren't long enough. By the time they were able to douse the fire, the carriage was reduced to a metallic skeleton.

Eventually everyone was ordered back onto the front carriages and the train restarted its journey to the capital. It was a squeeze and Pucci still hadn't found his brother. Maybe he hadn't got on the train in Bologna after all. Or maybe he was here somewhere amidst the chaos and they had just missed each other.

The train pulled in to Termini station four hours later than expected. Pucci told the transport police that his brother was missing, and then he went home. It was the middle of the night but when he got back to Via Livorno, his parents' lights were still on. He knew they would be worried. His mother rushed up to him when she heard the door open.

'There was a fire on the train,' Pucci said by way of explanation.

'And Andrea?'

'I lost sight of him.'

'What do you mean, "lost sight"?'

His father came into the corridor. 'You were supposed to keep an eye on him.'

'There were three or four hundred of us. It was chaos. He'll be fine. He'll be along in a minute.'

That night they stayed up waiting. Pucci kept trying to reassure his parents that it would all be fine but the longer they were waiting, the more nervous they became. There were accusations and recriminations. Finally, just as the sun was coming up, the phone rang. They were invited to a morgue to identify a body 'which might be a relative of yours'. His brother's carbonized body had been found on the floor of the train lavatory.

Andrea's funeral took place two days later in Lucera. Pucci was a broken man, immobilized by guilt and disbelief. He became even more withdrawn than usual. He felt his younger brother's death was his fault and that he had returned home like a coward. His only way to deal with his guilt was to blame those who he felt were even more responsible than himself. His closest friends heard him say that he would find those who had set fire to the carriage and light them up 'like a Christmas tree'.

In the following weeks he began using again – not just smoking joints but taking anything that was offered to him: uppers, downers, powders. He was a mess, a violent mess, one desperate to avenge his brother in the hope that it would erase his own guilt. His substance use was part of that erasure but he needed more.

Marmot, who everyone knew had started the fire, had gone to ground. He used to hang around Piazza Bologna with all the teenage fans but since Andrea's death, he had disappeared from the scene. For weeks Pucci tried to find him but without success. So, he approached one of his closest friends, a far-right activist with a long scar across his neck: Paolo Dominici. Dominici knew Marmot, and Marmot and his friends were more likely to trust him than Pucci. By then it was July. For weeks Italy, and Paolo Rossi, had been thrilling everyone with their successful World Cup campaign.

Dominici finally got hold of the young boy and he followed Pucci's instructions. He invited Marmot to a *fungaia* (a mushroom-growing cavern) in Via Tiburtina with the excuse of showing him some stolen radios. Dominici and Marmot met at Piazza Bologna late on the evening of 10 July, the eve of the World Cup Final in which Italy would beat West Germany 3–1. They got on the 61 bus to Via dei Monti Tiburtini, the other side of the railway lines. When Marmot arrived, Pucci was waiting for him.

A few months later, on 7 October 1982, Geronimo got a phone call from Zigano, the same guy who in 1979 had let off the nautical flare that killed Papparelli. Zigano was doing his military service and had obtained leave for a night. He wanted to invite Geronimo out for a pizza.

Like Marmot, Geronimo was never seen again. Neither body has ever been found, even though there are various urban legends about where they might be. Revenge had been served but it didn't remove Pucci's sense of guilt, which if anything was exacerbated. He could only see the worst side of himself, unbrotherly and murderous. Everything seemed pointless. He stopped going to the stadium and to the bar. Over the next few months, Pucci began injecting every day. It was a slow, hedonistic form of suicide.

The full story only came out a few years later when Dominici was in a drug treatment programme in Calabria. In 1989 he was, as they say in the recovery community, 'making amends' and confessed his part in Marmot's disappearance to his drugs counsellor. Police took up the case but by then Pucci was dead. He had died of an overdose – or 'in his sleep' as it's euphemistically called – in 1986, aged twenty five.

———

1982, Cosenza

To begin with, they thought the strange man in their midst was in fancy dress. He had a tidy beard and wore a brown habit and white rope belt. The rope was knotted, like he was the real thing, but the *curva* in those years was full of eccentrics and attention-seekers. No one thought he was actually a monk.

The fans ignored him to begin with but he wasn't a man who liked being ignored. He started shouting advice to players and ultras alike. He rubbed kids' hair.

'Why are you dressed like that?' one of the boys asked him.

He told the lad that he was a Franciscan friar.

'Really?'

'Really.' The man didn't take his eyes off the pitch. 'But I could have been a footballer if I'd wanted to be.'

The monk was deadly serious. He told the boy about the best goals he had scored, the games he had won single-handedly for various teams, winning them promotions. His boasting came naturally, as easily as those goals.

'Father,' shouted one of the fans, 'you'll bring us all bad luck coming here. Stick to your church.'

'There's no such thing as luck,' the monk shot back, 'only providence and prayer.'

'What did he say?'

It was unsettling having this ecclesiastical figure in the midst of their bacchanalian afternoon. They weren't sure they wanted him around, but the more jibes and jokes they sent his way, the faster his replies. He wasn't even one of those well-spoken priests that they had all seen in dark, staid churches. This man yelled in dialect and swore like a builder. And he never went to the *tribuna*, always the *curva*.

One Sunday a boy brought some red-and-blue felt tips to the game, and whilst the monk was singing along with the crowd, he coloured his white rope blue-and-red. But the monk noticed him, slipped off the rope and twirled it around his head like a scarf while singing 'Maracanà'.

The monk rolled up to games with some of the children from the orphanage – young boys who were still in single figures, real tykes with shaved heads and lumpy faces. Some of the ultras asked the orphans about this strange man, still half-convinced he was a joker dressed up for the day. But the boys just shrugged and said, 'He's Padre Fedele.' He was, they said, obsessed by only two things: football and the Gospels. 'That's all he talks about,' they said, smiling. 'That and himself.'

At the next game Padre Fedele was introduced to the inner circle of Cosenza's ultras. When someone was on the fringes of the group, it was usual to bring them in and present them to the man with the megaphone so that the arriviste could be checked out. But the monk wasn't as humble as other fans. He turned towards the lads and proclaimed with a guffaw, 'You reprobates are the brothers of Christ.'

Many cheered, more at the recognition that they were reprobates than at the idea that they were siblings of this man's saviour. Plenty of others raised their arms sharply and told him where to go. But he gave as good as he got, and he could always hold his own in the quick-fire banter.

Over the next few months they got used to the loud presence of the man they simply called U Monaco ('the Monk'). He could be a real pain. At half-time, when many were skinning-up, he would brush past them and accidentally-on-purpose overturn their spliffs, spilling the weed all over the concrete. They would shout at him and he would shout back, telling them to give it up. When he heard that some of the lads were going to a brothel, he went to find the lads' girlfriends and told them about it. Many said he was nothing other than a fucking ball-breaker. Any time the *curva* went quiet, he would start a song of his own, and even if people didn't join in, he would stick at it, enjoying the limelight. He quickly became one of the many eccentrics you looked forward to seeing on a Sunday afternoon.

But beneath his buffoonery and moralizing, he was also doing something subtle. He was talking to these loud, lost young men and changing the way they saw themselves. That aspect of being an ultra that they so celebrated – being excluded, angry, forgotten, despised – was precisely what made them precious, he said. Here was a man of the cloth who genuinely seemed to value them. You, he said, understand the poor, the lame, the broken. You can be the foot soldiers of a new solidarity in this city.

Many of the ultras thought it was baloney. None of them, except Pastachina, were church-goers and they were instinctively suspicious of anything and anyone that came out of what they considered the corrupt and cosy world of Catholicism. But Piero, as always, was listening. He was thinking about what this loud and lovable monk was saying. The Monk kept saying that being an ultra was so important that they needed to get even more radical.

There was something in that message that sunk a hook in Piero. It wasn't that he wanted to lose focus on the red-and-blue. That had always been his obsession. But that focus, the intensity of the ultra life, was deepening. Being an anarchist, Piero was sceptical of anything that came from the state. He believed in living at ground level, which was part of the humility of being an ultra. But now this Monk had come along and was telling them that being an ultra wasn't just about brotherhood with the lost boys of the terraces, but solidarity with the homeless and hungry of the city.

At the same time, a new ultra group had come into being. On 9 October 1983, the Cosenza ultras revealed the new group in the home game against Salernitana. The banner was long, the top half completely red, the bottom all blue, with almost playful yellow letters spelling out the name: Nuclei Sconvolti ('Deranged Nuclei'), with a large marijuana leaf between the two words. The name was perfect. That plurality had an inclusivity to it. And no one had ever heard of an ultra group called Sconvolti before. The word also means 'messed up', 'dishevelled', 'upset' or 'freaked out'. In time, the name was often abbreviated to NS.

But it was, perhaps, the iconic leaf that gave clarity to the identity of Ciccio's group. There was something sacramental in their use of the weed. Although it seemed banal to non-stoners, and heretical to believers, the ultras felt there was something of the communion chalice about the passage of a spliff from one brother to another. As Andrea Ferreri wrote in *Ultras*, 'smoking spliff in the *curve*, like passing a bottle, is a rite which unites people, it's the glue which, with the passage from hand to hand, from mouth to mouth, enlarges the circle, makes it into a single body...' He called the use of cannabis 'a collective rite which unites and sacralizes everything'.

The Cosenza ultras were instinctively anti-prohibitionist. It seemed typically hypocritical to them that a natural substance which grew so healthily in the hills of Calabria should be illegal, when organized crime was flooding the city with heroin. Weed only added to their self-perception that they were bandits, rebels and smugglers. The industrial quantities they smoked also enforced or exaggerated many aspects of their group: on the one hand, zany humour, oneiric creativity and impetuous pranks, and on the other hand, unpredictability, sometimes even mental instability.

In the ultra world 'madness' was invariably celebrated. The ultras wanted to be seen as psychotic. It wasn't just that the *curva* was occasionally a repository, or sanatorium, for people with psychiatric issues. They revelled in playing on society's fear of their craziness. There would eventually be a splinter group of Juventus ultras called Insani ('The Insane') and Salernitana had a gang called 'Upset Minds'.

Ostentatious drug use was part of that self-presentation as scary, crazed and unpredictable. The Lazio ultras sang 'We start Monday with LSD / We take amphetamines until Wednesday...' One of the early slogans of the Nuclei Sconvolti was equally calculated to send shivers down the bourgeois spine: '*Pipe ai vecchi, acidi ai bambini, Nuclei Sconvolti clandestini*' ('Pipes for the elderly, acid for babies, [we are the] deranged clandestine nuclei').

But in Cosenza there was a distinction between hard and soft drugs. One of their banners, years later, announced: 'No smack, no coke, but roll [a play on words of their favourite player, Marulla] a spliff.' Another time, they wrote; 'Heroin? No – we are ultra', which implied that they were both beyond and over heroin.

Luca was, by then, one of the brains of the Cosenza *curva*. Looking back, he sees the use of the marijuana leaf not as a stoner's fixation but as part of the group's campaign 'against both the police and organized crime that was spreading heroin everywhere. It wasn't a hymn to the buzz, but part of a war against heroin.'

1982–83, Roma

Many fans spoke of the 'magic' of those Sunday afternoons. That usage hinted at the transformation that happened when team and fans came together. By some unfathomable alchemy, those ultras who were lonely or lost found themselves in the midst of a riotous, gleeful group. And – even more miraculous – a team that had seemed perennially disappointing, Roma, was reflecting that alchemy, becoming a serious contender for the Serie A title. The magic words that made it all happen were, according to the ultras, the lyrics of their songs. 'We felt,' says one veteran of CUCS, 'as if the game couldn't start without us.'

Romans have always enjoyed bar songs. Taking those bawdy, ironic ballads from the bars to the terraces created a sense of continuity with the past. It meant that the terraces, too, now spoke to Romans about who they were and where they came from. Those songs wove in many of the myths of Rome: the empire, the grandeur, the circuses. The club symbol was a wolf suckling Romulus and Remus, and that notorious legend – of royal brothers reduced to orphans living in a cave and working as shepherds – was powerful because it echoed what all fans feel: we're better than this, our ancestors were mighty and it's only a matter of time before we avenge this injustice. The ballads weren't necessarily heroic but the oompah celebration of boozy idleness in a song like 'The Society of Pimps' was relished by many ultras who felt they, too, were the outcasts of the *zozza società* ('mucky society').

The songs were tributes to the ultras' dogged determination to be always at Roma's side: We're going to 'grind out the kilometres, overcome the obstacles...' they sang. Roma didn't just have some of the best choreographies, blazing red-and-yellow, but they had a fine choir. 'Tell me what it is that makes us feel friends even if we don't know each other,' they sang along to the Antonello Venditti song, 'Tell me what it is that makes us united even if we're far apart, thank you, Roma, that you make us cry and hug each other still.' If you weren't moved by a love for Roma, it all sounded dreadfully sentimental – what they call in Italy *strappacuore* (literally 'heart tuggers'). But if you were a Romanista, those songs simply gave you goosebumps and, as they say, 'polished eyes'.

The change in Roma's fortunes was, in large part, down to a new ruling that, from the 1980–81 season, allowed every Italian team to sign one foreigner. Roma bought a Brazilian midfielder, Paulo Roberto Falcão. With his light, curly hair and upright, elegant style, he seemed to control the game at both ends, scoring goals but also making interceptions and goal-line clearances. He could pass with a back-heel, a shoulder punch, a cushioned header.

He had endured plenty of disappointments in recent years. Roma came second in 1981 and third in 1982. Worse for Falcão, his Brazilian side were outplayed by Italy in that 1982 World Cup. But there was a sense in the 1982–83 season that things were looking up. 'Come on Roma, come on wolves, the dark times are over,' said one banner. As with the Torino championship victory a few years before, there seemed to be a profound connection between the team – including a young Carlo Ancelotti and prolific strikers like Bruno Conti and Roberto Pruzzo – and its ultras. In the days before internet statistics, players used to phone up the Italo-American ultra, Antonio Bongi, a fanatical memorialist, and ask him to describe their goals again. Franco

Tancredi, the goalkeeper, said he longed to hear all those Roman anthems that gave him courage between the sticks. Players hugged ultras, as they did on that joyous 1 May 1983. With the title in touching distance, Falcão scored a free kick against Avellino and instinctively ran towards Geppo and Er Mortadella behind the goal and embraced them. (Er Mortadella was supposed to be doing military service and had bunked off from the barracks for the day; when he was spotted on TV, he was duly punished for absence without leave.) On the day the title was won, on the last day of the season against Torino, the CUCS banner was finally allowed to return to the stadium.

8 February 1984, Trieste

It was the first leg of a cup-tie, a local derby between Triestina and Udinese, both teams from the northeast corner of Italy. After the goalless game, scuffles broke out between opposing fans. There were reports of cars with number plates from Udine being upturned, sometimes even with people inside them.

A twenty-year-old boy with black, curly hair and a half-shut left eye was walking back to his car, a Fiat 128, in Via dei Macelli. Stefano Furlan was an only child. He had just left school and was doing odd-jobs, working in a florist and at a hospital. Eye-witnesses saw three policeman grab him. He was apparently punched and truncheoned and, held by his hair, his head was smashed against a wall. He was taken to the police station, where there were more beatings. He was released at 8 p.m. and got home about an hour later.

His mother remembers the precise scene when she saw him.

'When I opened the door he was staring and pallid. His jacket and puffer were in pieces. He had tears in his eyes. "Mum, I've been beaten up. A policeman truncheoned me on my head, and then in the station slaps, punches, kicks."'

He was feeling so nauseous that he went to bed almost immediately, at 9.30. The next day he didn't go into work because he had a headache and dizziness. By the afternoon his mother was so worried she took him to the hospital. There he fainted and fell into a coma. Doctors discovered a fracture of the side of his skull and behind it was a blood clot. For almost three weeks his mother sat by his bedside. Stefano never opened his eyes again. He sometimes seemed to squeeze her hand but she was unsure if that was just a reflex. After a respiratory crisis, he eventually died at 10.30 p.m. on 1 March.

'Stefano,' his mother said, 'was the only focus of my life... I had only him.' In pursuing a legal case against the policemen who had beaten him up, she received threats, including one written on her son's tomb. She was offered money to drop the case but fought on even though justice was illusory. The one policeman found guilty was given a one-year suspended sentence. He left the force to become a body-builder and fitness trainer.

The familiar face of Stefano Furlan – with his long hair and half-shut eye – has become emblematic in the ultras' denunciation of police violence. His is a name always used when the ultras complain that the forces of order are just as violent as they are, and yet enjoy impunity. The Curva Nord of Triestina's new stadium, the Nereo Rocco, is named after Furlan.

In those years, the ultras' hatred for the 'forces of order' began to surpass their loathing for rival fans. The disparaging slang – *i blu* ('the blue'), *la sbirraglia* ('the cops') – was a sign that the ultras, for all their differences and mutual animosity, could unite around insulting police and *Carabinieri*. It was now a three-way fight, but the third element – uniformed, armed with tear gas and truncheons – had an unfair advantage. The ultras hated the impunity of the police. Their righteous anger was often understandable, but the continual de-legitimization of the police encouraged overlaps between organized crime and certain ultras. Their outlaw insistence on *omertà* towards all authority meant that there were now anthropological similarities between teenage rebels and professional criminals. 'When one ended up in the clink,' one young Juventus ultra remembers, 'the only thought was *omertà*.'

Later that year another death revealed how violent the inter-club rivalries were becoming. In September 1984 Marco Fonghessi, from Cremona, was stabbed to death by a man from Milan's Red-and-Black Brigades.

The Romanisti were convinced that 1984 was the year they would win the European Cup. They had Agostino Di Bartolomei, Falcão, Pruzzo... and the final was being played against Liverpool in their own city. Legend has it that, after Roma lost 2–0 against Dundee United in Scotland, officials from Roma tried to bribe the referee, Michel Vautrot, in order to win the return leg. Roma won 3–0. (The son of the club's president, years later, admitted the truth of the accusation.)

There were such serious fights between Roma supporters at the offices selling tickets to the final with Liverpool in May 1984 that police were called in. Pitched battles followed. Cobbles were ripped up and thrown, knives flashed, batons used.

One of the Roman lads, Alessio, used to go on holiday to Calabria and knew Ciccio, Luca and Paride. He sold them his spare tickets. There had always been links between Cosenza and Roma. Lello had started it and then many of the Calabrians had gone to support Roma against their hated Calabrian cousins, Catanzaro, the year before (a game abandoned because of disturbances). At Catanzaro they had met Geppo.

When the Cosenza boys arrived in the capital it was covered with red-and-yellow. Balconies, shop windows, statues – everything was given a scarf, a sticker, a flag. It felt like you were making history just being there. In Piazza del Popolo there were fights with Liverpool supporters. The Scousers chanted in favour of Roma's hated rivals Lazio, so the Romanisti sang for Everton, Liverpool's local nemesis. There were punches but it was too beery for the fights to be more than a few windmills, and the police soon pulled them apart. Ambulances and police trucks raced in all directions.

The fact that the game was against Liverpool made it even more meaningful for the ultras. The torch of fanaticism had been passed from Liverpool to Roma, with Bongi and his mates borrowing 'Yellow Submarine' and 'You'll Never Walk Alone' and 'When the Saints…' That torch had in turn been passed to Cosenza. So, for nineteen-year-old Ciccio and his 'mad band' to see both sets of fanatics up against each other was exhilarating. It didn't disappoint. The English pulled their scarves taut and sang 'You'll Never Walk Alone', and in return the Romans gave them the whole arsenal: 'Ahi, ahi, ahi, ahi, magic Roma, my heart is sad when it's far from you', to the tune of 'Cielito Lindo'. Then the usual one about raising the flags to the heavens to the tune of Gene Autrey's 'That Silver-haired Daddy of Mine'. For hours before the game it was, as well as a series of fights, a giant sing-off.

The Romanisti were convinced that they couldn't lose, least of all on the pitch. But it ended in a draw and went to penalties.

In front of a nervous south end, the Liverpool goalkeeper Bruce Grobelaar did his famous wobbly legs routine, pretending to be nervous, and two Roma penalty-takers fluffed it. Liverpool had won. As Liverpool players lifted the cup and their fans celebrated and sang, the Curva Sud was silent. Many didn't move for an hour or more. Most were crying. Lorenzo – then only eighteen and now a lawyer busy defending ultras in court – says he didn't speak a full sentence for a month.

That final, though, was equally notable for what happened on the fringes of the game. Agostino Di Bartolomei was incandescent with rage, allegedly throwing a shoe in the changing rooms at Falcão because the Brazilian hadn't stepped up to take a penalty. Their bust-up would eventually lead to Di Bartolomei being sold to Milan. Also in that famous match, the banner of the Boys made its reappearance. Various young toughs were longing to bring a bit of discipline and warrior spirit back to the Curva Sud. That night, dozens of Liverpool supporters were knifed, creating amongst them a hatred of Italians that would cause carnage at the following year's European Cup Final at Heysel.

By then, it was becoming clear that the attempt to maintain the Curva Sud as an apolitical zone was failing. Old and new groups were breaking the consensus, with the Guerillas bleeding into another group called Opposing Faction. They were meeting in the basement of a church in Via Gallia under the leadership of a man called Rommel. It wasn't long before many Roma ultras were singing that their team was 'the pride of Roman youth' to the tune of the old fascist favourite, 'Little Black Face' (a 1935 song about a black Ethiopian girl rescued by Italian colonizers in Ethiopia).

———

Drugs and ultras were becoming increasingly interconnected. Throughout the 1970s a large proportion of ultras had enjoyed smoking *canne* ('canes'). On the terraces, balsamic gusts of weed mixed with smoke flares and cigarettes. The names chosen for new groups now came not from political engagement or even from martial prowess but from defiant substance abuse. It was all about, they said, the 'buzz'.

One ultra memoir, written by two members of Spal's Gruppo d'Azione, wearily remembers an away game as 'the usual delirious journey involving alcohol and various drugs'. On trains, they would often nick the little red hammers meant for smashing windows in an emergency in order to raid chemists for various pharmaceuticals: Valium, Darkene, Rohypnol.

By the mid-1980s the roles and the drugs were changing. Care-free bohemianism was getting darker and ultras were no longer just consumers but dealers too. The *zona franca* of the *curve* was the ideal location to sling. It was almost impossible to get busted in that mass of hostile humanity. Often on the terraces you would have a man with a bulging money belt, taking notes from fans in return for wraps of green or white. It's still the same today.

For many ultras, drug use was becoming habitual rather than recreational. Many became dealers to pay for their hits. Nino was one of the leaders of Inter's Vikings group. He had a cheeky-boy face and front teeth so short that most of his smile came out at the sides. But you could tell he lived on the edge: he had a boxer's nose, a short zig-zag scar from the left corner of his mouth and another scar across the bottom of his rib cage, as if a sad-face symbol had been carved on his paunch. The symbol of his group was the *labrys*, the two-headed axe that had always been an icon for the far right.

Nino had become a coke fiend and was buying the gear

wholesale to sell on street corners. Much of the ultra way of life was about territorial conquest. It was the same, Nino found, in dealing: you had to conquer your corner and defend it fiercely. The fact that many of the rival dealers were black immigrants only made the fight, for Nino – with his 'honour and loyalty' T-shirts – more compelling.

Once, he needed to conquer the park in Baranzate, in the northwest of Milan. He went there on his motorbike with an ultra friend. Approaching the Liberian dealers without taking off his helmet, he shot one in both legs and, placing the warm gun on his neck, said he would kill him if he ever saw him dealing there again. That shooting put a few more ivy leaf tattoos on Nino's left arm, each one representing a year spent in prison. But at least people knew not to mess with him.

One of the cities most affected by the flood of heroin was Verona. The wealthy city was at a crossroads of motorways, the A4 and A22, so it became a nexus for wholesale deals and was nicknamed 'the Bangkok of Italy'. Amongst the ultras of Hellas Verona, there was also a rather British attitude towards alcohol abuse. As one writer put it, they enjoyed 'an excessive use of every type of alcohol: wine, beer, digestifs, grappa…' The Verona ultras liked their players as tough and uncompromising as they were. Their hero was Gianfranco Zigoni, a feisty, fearless player known as much for his sendings-off as his goals.

Verona's main ultra group was the Brigate Gialloblù, founded in November 1971. Its motif had a three-runged yellow ladder between the two words (the team were known as the 'scaligeri' because the Scala family had ruled the city in the Middle Ages). There were also many other satellite groups: Verona Front, Rude Boys, Provos and, naturally, Hellas Alcool. The Veronesi were, more than any other curva, considered very Anglophile, partly because there was a 'London Shop' in the city but also because a Scot, Joe Jordan, signed for the club in the 1983–84 season. There was even an ultra group called the Tartan Army. Many other groups had English names, like The Deadly Sinners Club. At most Hellas Verona games, Union Jacks were waved. The 'Butei' – dialect for 'lads' – were even twinned with notorious Chelsea hooligans and followed the English practice of leaving calling cards on rival ultras they had beaten up: 'Well done,' said the card, 'you've just met the yellow-blue brigades.' Typical of this irreverent, violent form of fandom was the ASU group, the 'Association of Humans of the Barn'. They had violent initiation ceremonies, enjoyed headbutt challenges and sang, 'If you don't know us, get out of the way, we dirty everywhere' or 'We are evils'. (The English deployed by the ultras was often deliberately pidgin, almost as if they wanted to point up their own illiteracy or provincialism.)

The Veronesi were grudgingly respected throughout the ultra world not only because they always went looking for violence, but because they incarnated something called *goliardia*. It's a term repeatedly used by ultras to describe the bohemian, slap-stick silliness of the ultra way of life. The Veronesi took parasols or beach mats to games to suggest it would be as relaxing as the beach. They wore quartered yellow-and-blue suits, or tuxedos, or yellow building-site helmets. One time, against Udinese when they won 5–3, they threw carrots instead of stones, singing '*buon appetito*'.

That playfulness was reflected in their songs. 'We are afflicted by a violent mentality,' they sang. The football was important to some but usually incidental to the fights before or after the games: 'We don't give a fuck about this game' said one banner. When it came to those fights, however, the Veronesi prepared with military precision. During a game against Milan, when the fog was so thick that visibility was reduced to a few metres, two thousand Veronesi managed to creep up on the Milanese ultras in complete silence. But it was rarely playful. In 1977 a hand grenade was thrown onto the side of the pitch and the Italian press started comparing the city less to Bangkok than to Beirut (then consumed by a vicious civil war). Every Verona game was accompanied by urban warfare: shops smashed up, cars rolled, rival ultras battered, fires started.

Sometimes the hatred was mixed with irony. 'Don't be racist,' said one sticker, 'hate everyone.' And often the disdain was aimed not at foreigners but at anyone from the South: 'From the Po downward, there's no more Italy.' But it was getting less amusing every year and younger elements were moving in with a more extreme agenda. Celtic crosses – a perennial symbol of Italy's far right – were combined with 'Sieg Heil' chants. One of the major ultra groups in the mid-1980s was the Verona Front (created by adherents of the MSI party's youth wing). Bananas were thrown at black players and, in May 1983, the first of many swastikas appeared amongst the other banners.

Some felt the first appearance of a swastika in the *curva* wasn't dissimilar to the way English punks occasionally used them. When, in December 1977, *Time Out* asked a punk why she wore a swastika, she replied that 'punks just like to be hated'. And there was, after all, a Verona group called the 'Punk Brigade'. A generous observer might have hoped that there was as much self-hatred as hatred towards others in that grim gesture on the Verona terraces.

But it was very clear that Verona's ultras were becoming ever more right-wing. It was a city often unrepentantly loyal to Mussolini. During the Second World War it had been the base for the Gestapo's General Command and it repeatedly produced extremist groups in the post-war era, like Rosa dei Venti, Fronte Nazionale and Ludwig (the latter a label for two Nazi-inspired serial killers, Marco Furlan and Wolfgang Abel, who are thought to have killed more than two dozen people. 'Our faith is Nazism,' they once said, 'our justice is death.').

Verona football club was slowly becoming a dark place. Even one of the admiring chroniclers of the *curva* wrote that 'with deplorable cynicism players or managers hit by misfortune or personal tragedies were targeted; those who had separated from their wives or who had physical defects. With the arrival of the first black players in the Italian championships, the fury and bad taste became greater...' Often the Veronesi laughed off the outrage at their Nazi iconographies. Like most ultras, they wanted to provoke and outrage, and knew that the swastika was the ideal emblem for that purpose. But for some of them it was a genuine political creed and one that was spreading through many terraces. Long gone were the days in which most ultra groups were inspired by the far left. By the mid-1980s it seemed much more radical and extremist – always ultra obsessions – to align with the far right.

But in 1985 no one cared too much about a few cretins flaunting Nazi symbolism on the Verona terraces because football had produced another miracle. On 11 May Hellas Verona won the Serie A championship. It was one of those rare occasions in which an absolute underdog not only came out on top but added to the folklore of the national sport. The icon of that Verona team was a Dane, Preben Elkjær Larsen. Of his many nicknames – 'Mayor', 'Mad Horse', 'Buffalo' – the one that stuck recalled his goal against Juventus when he ran half the length of the pitch with only one boot: 'Cinderello'.

That month, though, also showed the horror that football can cause. Fifty-six people died in a fire at Bradford City's Valley Parade stadium. A few weeks later, in the European Cup Final between Liverpool and Juventus at Heysel, in Belgium, thirty-nine people lost their lives, thirty-four of them Italian. A charge by Liverpool hooligans caused the Juventus fans to rush away, creating such a dense crush that a wall collapsed. In an act of both practicality and devotion, many of the dead were covered, and carried away, wrapped in Juventus flags. 'It was a shame that had to be washed, in ultra ethics, with blood,' wrote one Juventus ultra.

Beppe Rossi, the leader of the Juventus Fighters, was never the same after Heysel. His whole career on the terraces had been based on admiration for and imitation of the English fans, especially those of Liverpool. Now, in creating the panic that caused the deaths of so many fans, they were responsible for slaughtering his brothers. Many Juventus ultras felt guilty that they were far from the action when it kicked off (they had requested seats in the opposite terrace to increase their allocation) and were unable to defend the ordinary members of the public in the infamous Sector Z.

Rossi, like so many on the terraces, began to find consolation in the needle. But Heysel also marked one of the first occasions in which the ethics of the ultras, paradoxically, appeared more noble than that of the sportsmen. The idea that a game could be played immediately after so many deaths appalled those on the terraces. Certain fans had talked to the players, even going to the changing rooms to clarify exactly what had happened, but the show had to go on. The Juventus players' celebrations at their victory were even more galling. That dark night in Belgium marked the beginning of a cleaving apart of players and ultras, not just amongst Juventus fans but across the country. Players were no longer considered heroic or representative of their fans in any meaningful way. If that profound role – of heroically representing the people – no longer belonged to the players, it was one that the ultras would claim for themselves.

There was another regrettable but understandable consequence of Heysel: a return to the fascist-era hatred of the English. An old Mussolini maxim – 'God curse the English' – was now endlessly repeated and surpassed by far stronger insults. The tragedy was still an excuse to insult Juventini ('minus thirty-nine' was a regular chant by their rivals) but it was also a pretext to Italianize fandom. For Juventus – the most popular team in Italy – Heysel closed the door on supporters' cosmopolitanism, with the result that the tricolour, and the far right, were nudged towards the frontline there and on many terraces.

But the creep towards the far right was also happening because new groups were emerging from within the same terraces. If one major group had dominated the terraces of each club in the 1970s, throughout the 1980s a rival one usually emerged. In Turin a group calling itself the Granata Korps came to the fore. (The use of Korps – a German military unit and usually associated, in the minds of the ultras, with Rommel's Afrika Korps – left few in any doubt as to their political leanings.) In 1982 Bologna's Mods were created, largely by dissidents from the city's Forever Ultras. There were many reasons for the emergence of these new groups – personality clashes, different notions of what being an ultra implied – but many major groups founded in the 1980s emerged in opposition to the generally far-left ethos of those that had emerged in the 1970s.

————

1985, Cosenza

By 1985 the Nuclei Sconvolti were holding their weekly meetings in Padre Fedele's convent. Over the previous few years the Monk had become a well-known figure. He would sometimes lead the pre-match singing on the stadium's PA system, or climb one of the floodlight poles and lead the chants from 30 metres above the *curva*. 'I had become the king of Cosenza,' he remembers.

He would be photographed kissing the turf or, in the midst of the fans, wearing a red-and-blue hat and spinning a scarf over his head. On the morning of Sunday match days, he would even go, with Pastachina, to say mass for the players. His notoriety was such that Reggina, local rivals to Cosenza, once displayed a banner saying: 'Tuo Padre Fedele, Tua Madre Mignotta': 'Your father is faithful [Fedele], your mother's a whore.'

The space in that convent meant that the Nuclei Sconvolti were able to store more material. Padre Fedele helped them with logistics too, lending them his van or his kitchen. It was an era in which ultras across the country were competing to perform the most memorable choreography. Ciccio and Piero wanted to create a red-and-blue flag that covered the whole of the main stand. They ordered 1,200 metres of material from a factory in Prato, 750 kilometres away. Tonino drove all the way to pick it up, piling the stuff in cardboard boxes. Piero's mother was a seamstress, and he was good with a sewing machine too. He spent every spare minute in the convent, laboriously stitching the red to the blue, then the blue to the red.

All week people dropped in, taking photos. Others helped lay the sewn stripes out flat, or went to find a sandwich for Piero.

Someone found a couple of shopping trollies to pile it all into, as it was so heavy that no one could really carry it. The whole city knew about the *bandierone*, the 'huge flag'. On the morning of Sunday 6 April 1985, all the lads laid the flag out flat in a car park. As they unrolled it, they couldn't believe how big it was: 100 metres long and 20 wide. 'It looks,' said Paride, always the intellectual of the group, 'like Gulliver's scarf.'

Once it was laid out flat, a gust of wind lifted up a corner and travelled obliquely all the way through the material like a wave, on and on through red-and-blue. The stoned ultras watched it in awe. The flag was alive. They rolled it up again, twenty of them carrying it to the back of Padre Fedele's battered blue van.

The ultras sat in the main stand that Sunday. It was a match against Catanzaro, the local rivals. Unevenly, the flag was pulled down over peoples' heads, from the top of the *tribuna* to the bottom. As lads jumped in excitement underneath it, it seemed as if it was bouncing. Then those in the top row fired white confetti all over it, and it looked snow-frosted. Even though Cosenza won that derby 1–0, with a left-foot strike from a tight angle by Alberto Aita, people only spoke about the flag, about how an entire sector of the stadium had been turned red-and-blue.

Two months later, on 5 June 1985, the Cosenza ultras opened up a soup kitchen for the poor. A local lawyer offered the Monk a ground-floor building on Via Mazzini, only a few metres from where Piero and Claudio lived. Although some of the ultras thought it was a waste of time, most were drawn to the idea, Piero especially. He was soon thinking about the menus, the seating, where to get the food. The *curva* and the foodbank seemed, to him, one and the same. Cooking food for those who were hungry was an irresistible madness, just like ultra fandom.

He was a good cook, too. He loved mooching around the

shops, trying to find ingredients and jovially knocking down their prices, bumping into friends in those shops and going for an early glass of wine. He enjoyed the dexterity required in the kitchen, the chance to listen to his favourite music – still The Clash, but also The Sound, Depeche Mode and U2 – as he rolled out the pastry.

When the Nuclei Sconvolti first opened their soup kitchen, only three punters rolled up. But the next week there were seventeen. The additional volume of food wasn't a problem – Padre Fedele could always press-gang people into giving. It was just that everyone came with a story that they were desperate to tell. Once food had been eaten, tools were downed and many ultras shot off back to their families or jobs. It was always Piero who hung around listening to people's stories. He sat there until evening, inviting those homeless men and women into the kitchen to munch on leftovers as they told him their woes. Invariably he would persuade them to come to the stadium on Sunday, telling them that the terrace was the route to salvation.

That summer, Padre Fedele and the Cosenza ultras organized the first national meeting of ultras. Through word-of-mouth, the ultras from Genoa, Atalanta, Reggio, Bari and beyond heard about the meeting. A debate was held in the Cinema Italia with the title 'Leave the ghetto to create an ultra counterculture'. But more than merely being countercultural, the meeting was an attempt by Padre Fedele to publicize the fact that ultras were able to come together in peace. He had a slogan he repeated continuously: 'Fandom yes, violence no. Peace.' By coincidence, a journalist for *La Repubblica* was on holiday at a beach near Fuscaldo, and came over to see what the ultra gathering was about. His article gave it publicity and soon many other journalists came to interview the odd monk and his band of countercultural, charitable ultras.

The photos from that gathering show just how young the ultras were. In the sunshine of the Silan mountains, those gathered around Padre Fedele are mostly in their late teens or early twenties. Those young men had begun to glimpse a different way of being ultras. 'We were saying,' remembers Luca, 'lads, be careful of a war between us. The real enemy isn't the person who is like you in another city but the institutions.' The Cosenza ultras were, in their way, every bit as uncompromising as their counterparts in Verona, only their fury wasn't aimed at outsiders but at overlords.

1986

Despite Padre Fedele's best efforts, the violence continued. On 13 April 1986 a seventeen-year-old Roma supporter was burnt alive in a train carriage. Paolo Zappavigna, of the Roma Boys, had let off a smoke flare in the aftermath of Roma's 4–2 away victory at Pisa but the flames caught the curtains. A gust of air from an open window meant that, within minutes, the whole carriage was ablaze. The fire extinguishers had already been robbed.

A month later, in May, Geppo was arrested in Sardinia. He was accused of killing a German tourist in a hippie encampment called the Valle Della Luna. He was in prison for nearly a year, something he called an 'insufferable hell'. He didn't mix much with the other prisoners partly because most were Sardinians who spoke a dialect he barely understood.

By the time Geppo came out it was as if his spark had gone. Now, you only got flashes of his optimism and enthusiasm. His heroin habit had turned him skeletal. He still had charm but he used it mostly to blag a few thousand lire from old friends like Bongi or Mortadella. He had turned inward, focussing on the needle and nothing else.

When he finally got back to Rome, he discovered that the great unity of CUCS – bringing together all the Roma ultras under one banner – was disintegrating. The club had signed a former Lazio midfielder and the CUCS was bitterly divided over the issue. Things were on the slide. Roma – captained by Carlo Ancelotti and coached by Sven-Goran Eriksson – had just missed out on another *scudetto*, pipped to first place by Juventus.

December 1986, Central African Republic

Paride's legs kept shaking. His forehead was resting on the hot glass of the bus but he was sweating so much that his head kept sliding down, his chin bouncing on his chest as he woke up. The bus was overcrowded, and it smelt of sweat and woodsmoke. There were people sitting in the aisles, some trying to lie down to sleep.

Padre Fedele brusquely barged people out of the way as he brought a nun over to Paride. She looked at him, held his forehead and took his pulse. 'He's probably got malaria.'

Paride smiled wearily. He had guessed as much. He tried to bring his knees up to his chest but there was no space. Everyone else was wearing T-shirts and he was covered in all the clothes he had but was still shivering. The nun said he needed Chloroquine and he went back to staring out of the window.

Paride had seen death close up now. In the last week he had witnessed the effects of leprosy and AIDS. Just the day before, Padre Fedele was weighing a tiny baby on the scales, so thin it looked like she would break. She just died there in that metal basin. And now he was ill, too, and the whole trip was becoming a blur: the flight from Lamezia to Zurich, and from Zurich to Bangui. In the airport he had seen well-dressed diamond merchants and missionaries. And then all those sheet-metal shacks for miles and miles. The only actual buildings were the ministerial palaces.

It was Padre Fedele, of course, who had suggested this trip. He needed some strong men to load and unload clothes, shoes and provisions for the missionary stations in Bangassou and beyond. The Monk knew, too, that once the young men had seen this poor and archaic world, they would be affected by it. The Central African Republic in 1986 was so corrupt that there was no postal service because people stole the stamps. They had only 200 TV sets in the whole country. And yet it was also so devout that church services would go on all day, with people coming and going between those wooden pillars, bringing food and clapping, and raising their voices to the skies.

Paride remembers on that first visit taking breakfast to one of the primary schools. As Piero was unloading the food, he had said to his mates: 'This is worth more than one hundred Cosenza victories.'

'What did you say?' asked Drainpipe, appalled that there might be anything more important than that.

Piero repeated it again, as he gave some bread to a little kid in a torn yellow T-shirt. Drainpipe and Paride nodded, knowing he was right. In these strange weeks, Padre Fedele was showing them what it meant to be ultra, to go beyond everything. Here they had the same long and uncomfortable journeys, bouncing along the dirt tracks, but when they arrived, they weren't defending their scarves but giving them away.

'This,' Drainpipe had said, giving his red-and-blue scarf to a kid, 'is very precious. You understand?' And Drainpipe held it above his head, and the three ultras burst into song, making the kids all laugh.

On that trip they saw another side to Padre Fedele too. They already knew he could be volcanic and he was true to form. When their bus ran out of petrol and the shrewd businessmen with containers by the side of the road tried to charge the Monk three times the usual rate, he screamed at them in his most vulgar Cosentino, lamenting their lack of support for his charitable mission. When people kept him waiting for hours, he would explode again, shouting in fury and frustration. But, like much of his behaviour, it was a bit of an act. He got wound up for effect and he calmed down as quickly as he heated up. But they saw how canny he could be. He had packed dozens of little calendars with photographs of himself with Pope John Paul II. Other than Diego Maradona and Bob Marley, John Paul II was the most famous man in Africa. The stone-faced soldiers at all the roadblocks always let them through when Padre Fedele showed them the photograph of himself smiling next to the Pope. He would point to his chest proudly, saying 'that's me', and as he gave them the calendars they would drop their guns and raise the barriers.

Those boys weren't the same when they got home. It was as if they had discovered an aspect of being an ultra that went far deeper than football. It was still full of folly and risk, it was still a battle and an expedition onto foreign soil, but now it was real. They weren't merely screaming encouragement to others but giving out food and clothes. Paride, once he had recovered from his illness, no longer felt like a provincial punk, an orphaned kid who liked to be provocative. He believed in something. Nothing religious – all three of the boys were full of scorn for

149

the bourgeois Catholicism that surrounded them. But there was a new sense of awareness, of purpose. 'I felt things,' Paride says, 'a calling which wasn't born of nothing. And that solidarity was a profound, integral part of the ultra world.'

'It had nothing to do with being an ultra' – Drainpipe smiles at the memory, three decades on – 'and everything to do with it.'

1987, Drughi and Irriducibili

Ultra groups were strangely like Italian political parties: they seemed to be constantly breaking up, reforming, finding new leaders and labels. In Bologna there were now the Forever Ultras, but also the Mods and Total Chaos. Fiorentina's Forever Ultras had dissolved and now various groups were fighting for ascendency: Giovani della Fiesole, L'Alcool Campi and the Collettivo. Underneath and in between all those main groups were dozens more, all splintering, fighting, making up and coming back together (I once counted thirty-two different groups underwriting a communication from the overarching 'Brescia 1911' group).

The reasons for splits were various. An Italian preponderance for *scissionismo* ('schismatism') was certainly one cause, as was the uncompromising nature of being an ultra. If your founding philosophy goes counter to conciliation and concession, it is inevitable that there will be internal disagreements. 'You were constantly having to have an argument,' one leader from the 1980s remembers. Although they were defined by *lo scontro* ('the fight'), *capo-ultras* were also *scontrosi* ('argumentative' or, really, 'looking for it'). The way of life was about being *contro*, permanently 'against' as well as beyond. So, after a dozen years on the frontline, it wasn't surprising that a few of the founders were weary. They were close to thirty and many had settled down or descended into addiction or prison. Under incessant pressure from the police (now using helicopters, CCTV, intelligence and informants), many decided to semi-retire, often creating in time their own Vecchia Guardia group (the 'old guard').

By the mid- to late 1980s a new generation of young radicals were fighting their own ultras for control of the centre of the *curva*. That fight for ascendancy wasn't only because of clashing egos. Often rival groups had different political positions but the fight was also about money. Many groups had more than a thousand formal adherents. Control of the terraces implied control, also, of certain suburbs. It meant your group would have the monopoly in those quarters – on the dealing of tickets, memorabilia and, in some cases, narcotics. By then many clubs were giving ultra groups help with tickets, transport and storage. But various ultras began to see a business opening and, during the economic boom of the 1980s, the public had the spare cash to snap up inflated, touted tickets or imported powders.

One teacher in Rome remembers asking all the children in her class what the students' parents did for a living and one replied, 'My father is an ultra.' It had become, for the top echelons, a profession. One man who arranged a conference of ultras in the late 1980s was amazed to see that all the *capo-ultras* carried mobile phones (an absolute rarity then), which were constantly ringing. Those tough men had become go-to fixers.

All sorts of fringe benefits were associated with dominance in the *curva*: the concessions to sell burgers, scarves or become a stadium parking attendant were often in the gift of ultras, who were becoming adept at exerting subtle pressure on the clubs. As ticket prices slowly increased, the ultras realized that a fan strike could cost the club millions of lire in lost revenue. For men who were so easily provoked into fights, finding a pretext for that protest was never difficult. Urban riots, too, were becoming so common that damage to the cars or businesses of club presidents was easy enough to arrange.

The terraces of Juventus and Lazio led the way in this commercialization. By 1987, a decade after its foundation, the Fighters were on the wane. Beppe Rossi was by then battling a drug habit and his group had been caught up in violent clashes against Fiorentina fans. The group decided to fold.

Then, on 27 September 1987, in a game between Juventus and Pescara, a new banner appeared. In white letters on a black background, it said 'Arancia Meccanica' ('A Clockwork Orange'). The police objected to the implication of violence in the title and tried to ban it. But at the next game the ultras cut the letters out, sewed zips on, stuffed one letter down each of their pants, then smuggled the banner into the stadium and zipped it back together.

To save the hassle, they decided to change the name to Droogs, the raping-and-killing characters from Anthony Burgess's novel. But in the aftermath of Heysel, even that invented word sounded too English to the Juventus ultras, so they turned it into Drughi. Their symbol was a tricolour circle containing the silhouettes of four bowler-hatted brutes with batons. The head of the Drughi, and the man who insisted on the Italianization of the group's name, was the Juventus ultra from Foggia, Pino Coldheart.

Something similar happened at Lazio. The 1980s had been dark years for Lazio. They had been relegated to Serie B in the aftermath of a betting scandal. The beloved Giorgio Chinaglia had returned from America – where he had played with Pelé and Franz Beckenbauer for the New York Cosmos – to become

President of the club, full of promise and hope. His tenure was embarrassingly chaotic and the club only avoided relegation on the last day of the season against Pisa. Giorgio Chinaglia fled back to the States.

Whilst Roma had been winning the *scudetto* and reaching European Cup finals, Lazio had been playing provincial teams. It was a club that seemed, according to fan and writer Maurizio Martucci, 'cursed and melancholic'. Every ultra, though, knows that sporting failure hones the terraces: relegation and disappointment clears away the fair-weather supporters, leaving only the loyal rump of purists.

By then there were dozens of ultra groups on the Lazio terraces: Falange, Hell's Eagles Destroyers, Eagles Korps, Gruppo Sconvolti, the Deranged Group and Eagles Girls. As well as the Eagles, there were the Vikings, which had always been a more explicitly far-right outfit. The Nazis' double-edged axe was one of its symbols, as was the old Mussolinian motto, '*molti nemici, molto onore*' ('many enemies, much honour').

Grit was a short, chain-smoking man who owned a print shop. He had grown weary of what he considered the cosy world of the Eagles – those middle-aged men with close links to the Lazio hierarchy who rode on comfortable coaches to the away games. He knew many of the teenage tearaways and stragglers who took the trains and wanted to bring them together to create something very different: a militarized group that could march to the stadium all together, all wearing the same outfits. Toffolo, one of those teenagers who gathered around Grit, remembered years later: 'We maintained that their [the Eagles'] mentality was dated. We considered ourselves more "ultra", more ready to attack if attacked.'

The group announced itself on 18 October 1987, in a game

between Lazio and Padova, with a 9.8 metre *striscione* surrounded by blue-and-white chess boards. The Irriducibili (the 'Irreducibles' or 'Die-Hards') were unlike any ultra cabal before them. Often, they did daft stunts. They went to Bologna all dressed up in Zorro masks because it was carnival, or wore giant glasses in the *curva*, which perplexed onlookers until a huge banner was unwound: 'I see only blue and white.'

In an interview with Gianremo Armeni in the pages of *Limes*, Toffolo – later one of the group's leaders – was refreshingly blunt about how they got by. 'We left Rome without even 100 lire in our pocket because we didn't have it, and I stained myself with little robberies to find money.' If the ticket collector ever checked for tickets, 'We scared him and he went away. We always found some way to get into [the stadium]. There was never a problem for food because we raided some service station or bar.'

Like most gangs, they were frightening not just to enemies but to those who wanted to become members. Those aspiring to join were subjected to the same sort of hazing that exists in many close-knit criminal groups. The Irriducibili travelled in one train compartment and you had to be brave just to enter it. The aspiring recruit would have their shoes thrown out of the train window as they were forced to sing famous songs. If the singing was no good, they were beaten up. Or else the gang would shout 'doors and lights', and everything would go dark and the Irriducibili would set upon the aspiring member, thumping and kicking them. Only the toughest, who fought back and showed their valour, would be allowed to join. And if you joined, you would all become mates as together you smashed the windows of a shoe shop on the way to the ground for a pair of replacement boots.

Many ultra gangs had similar initiation ceremonies. The degree to which you accepted the humiliation demonstrated how much you wanted to join the gang. It created solidarity because membership acquired through effort, pain and even blood was more highly prized than something not, literally, fought for. The belittling guaranteed servitude, humility and loyalty, because it showed the new recruit that – outside the confines of the group – they were nothing. And loyalty was the most highly prized asset. It was the first rule of the streets. Yuri was one of the leaders of the Irriducibili: '... the first thing was that [the new recruit] shouldn't ever abandon us. We left armed with pick-axe handles and billiard balls. We were those twenty to thirty who repeated "We're compact and united and now what happens has to happen." I knew that once off the train there was going to be a battle and that you had to demonstrate that you weren't scared.'

There was a prankish exuberance to the Irriducibili. As a protest against police escorts to the stadium, they would, on command, all start running, or equally suddenly stop walking at a red traffic light. Playing on the notion that the ultras were the twelfth man in the team (and many clubs, as a fawning gesture of appreciation, 'retired' their number-twelve shirt), the Irriducibili held up a banner saying *Mister, Facce Entrà* (effectively 'Manager, give us a game'). They took the mickey out of Roma fans by using dialect to suggest that Laziali were far more rooted in 'Romanity': *'Da dove sei sortito, dar bagajo de quarche salumaio?'* ('Where did you come from, the luggage of some salami seller?'). They sang the word *'Irr-i-du-ci-bili'* to the tune of 'God Save the Queen'.

Like the Drughi of Juventus, the Irriducibili had as their symbol a man in a bowler hat, this time swinging a kick whilst holding a flag. They called the figure – taken from one of Grit's brother's drawings – Mr Enrich (Grit pretended, to give it cosmopolitan heft, that it had come from an English comic strip).

When one newspaper accused the Irriducibili of being 'stray dogs', they replied the following Sunday with a banner saying: 'We're not dogs because we don't have owners. We're not strays because the Irriducibili unites us.'

That sense of unity came across in their dress code. Grit and his boys had begun to dress alike. To begin with, it was casual gear – baseball caps, Fred Perry shirts, Reeboks and so on. But soon they were wearing bovver boots, tight jeans and green bomber jackets. One of their banners said *Blousons Noires* ('Black blouses'). Very often the Irriducibili marched with right arms erect, singing *Avanti Ragazzi di Buda* – 'Forward Youths of Buda' – an anti-Communist song about the Hungarian uprising of 1956.

The group met every Thursday night in their headquarters in Via Ozanam or in Piazza Ottovilla, to the west of Rome. As well as planning choreographies, fights and songs, those meetings were also about fashion. The Irriducibili had begun to make serious money selling scarves, flags and shirts across the capital. For Grit, it was simply a way to finance the extravagant displays but he had attracted into his new group some uncompromising characters who saw a real commercial opportunity for themselves. One young man, nicknamed Diabolik, was mesmerized as he watched the notes changing hands. He had never seen so much cash and, now that the Irriducibili controlled the Lazio terraces, he made up his mind to take over the firm and the finances.

1987–88, Cosenza

Many older ultras talk about the late 1980s as the glory years of the movement. In an era before televised games and the internet, the number of ultras at away games was so huge that those human migrations every Sunday were called – the same adjective is always used – 'oceanic'. The stadiums, they say, were always *gremiti* ('packed').

In Cosenza, a new group was emerging, Nuova Guardia. Claudio, the young, curly-haired boy whose apartment balcony faced Piero's, had gathered a group of young men: Pietro, Gianfranco, Roberto, Manolo and 'Arancino' (Nunzio had given him the nickname 'Rice ball' because he was a bit round and red-haired). Claudio's father had died of cancer and, he remembers, he 'didn't have any brakes any more'. His fury and bewilderment were vented in the stands.

It was the same for many of those young men. Paride had lost both of his parents and was more or less living with Luca, whose father had also died and whose mother was often away in Milan. Luca and Paride started producing fanzines, first 'Rebel Voice' then 'Paper Shout'. There were many fatherless young men on the terraces who were suddenly both bereft and free, grieving and yet energetic. They found new fathers in the *curva*, veering between Piero and Padre Fedele.

The Nuova Guardia group had absorbed both the idealism and irreverence of the Cosenza *curva*. 'On all occasions, break balls' said their banner. Their politics were the same as the older generation of the Nuclei Sconvolti: they admired the 'autonomous' left. Gianfranco was a teenage boxer who dreamt of opening a gym for kids with problems 'to teach this sick society a way of giving dignity to everyone'. All of them felt that the society they were growing up in was rotten: 'With the institutions of this city having such high levels of corruption,' Gianfranco recalls, 'we had to give something back to the disinherited.' Claudio imagined Nuova Guardia standing with 'the mad, the invisible, the babies, the ultras, the rebels, the artists...'

But combined with that idealism was the frenzied hedonism of ultra life: 'those Ulyssean journeys, drunk, trains being stopped, the monotony of your week replaced by the danger of the away game.' They held their own in-fights and, everywhere, defended the honour and colours of Cosenza.

It was an exciting time to follow the team, which now had a tidy midfielder called Donato Bergamini. From Ferrara, in the North, he was nicknamed 'Denis'. He was good-looking, with blond hair, deep-set eyes and a determined stare. He was only twenty-two when he arrived in the deep South, and in many ways he seemed a lot more innocent than his teammates. The fact that he didn't know how to play cards was just one example of his unworldliness. He described himself as *schivo* ('shy'). He had no hobbies other than football and fast cars. As a player he was the sort of tidy grafter a coach often appreciates as much as the fans.

It was a tight-knit and efficient team. Alberto Urban was an attacking midfielder with whom the coach, Franco Liguori, had worked at Cavese. The goalkeeper was a big youngster called Luigi Simoni. The team had a charismatic, fast-living attacker called Michele Padovano. 'Padovano, score for us,' the ultras sang to the tune of Bob Marley's 'Buffalo Soldier'.

In thirty-four league matches during the season, Cosenza kept twenty-two clean sheets. Not that they scored a huge number of goals either. There were three draws in a row in December and January, then, later that spring, another four successive nil–nils. But there was something almost inevitable about that season. Ever since that first fixture, when Cosenza had won 2–1 at Cagliari and the ultras had held up a banner saying 'Cosenza

Rise Again for Us', there was a feeling that this might be the year that the team, after twenty-three lean years, would get promoted back to Serie B.

Towards the end of the season, on 17 April 1988, Cosenza was away at Salernitana. For years, the rival ultras of both cities had fought furious battles, and the Cosenza players were escorted to the ground by police. There were brawls between ultras, and the game itself was dirty. Cosenza players were hacked down, scythed from behind, elbowed in the face. Then it all changed. From a long free kick, from well inside the Cosenza half, the ball bounced twice and suddenly Padovano was in on goal. He smacked it past the keeper with his left. More fights broke out immediately, even in the press box. The atmosphere was so tense that the ecstatic Cosenza commentator, Federico Bria, had to whisper into his radio microphone. 'Cosenza has scored. Excuse me if I don't shout but the situation here is a little bit ugly. You can exult,' he said as quietly as possible. 'Padovano has scored in the twenty-fifth minute of the first half.' Cosenza held on to win the game 1–0.

After all those no-score-draws, Cosenza won six out of its last nine games. The momentum and excitement grew with every victory. The last home game of that season was against Nocerina. Red-and-blue banners were hung between the narrow lanes of the *centro storico*. Cars and garage doors were painted red-and-blue, while balconies were draped in the same colours. Cars drove around with speakers on the roof, honking incessantly. *'Forza Lupi'* – 'Come on, Wolves' – was written on scarves and bedsheets. Any flags that had the same colours as Cosenza were good enough: the Norwegian flag, the Confederacy's stars-and-bars.

At the game, the stadium announcer was so drowned out

that he had to start reading the formations from the top again and again. There was no players' tunnel back then so the teams walked onto the pitch from a dense mass of physios, subs and journalists on the flat grass at the far side of the pitch, as if they had just strolled in from the car park. Red-and-blue smoke flares rendered half the crowd briefly invisible. 'Never again prisoners of a dream', said the banner.

The game was an easy enough 2–0 victory for Cosenza. Alberto Urban scored from a cut-back and then Maurizio Lucchetti smashed home a powerful lob from outside the area. But it wasn't enough. Other results meant that the team still needed one more point for promotion to Serie B.

The last game of the season was on 5 June 1988 at Monopoli, on the Adriatic coast between Bari and Lecce. Eight thousand Cosentini went along. It was a red-and-blue invasion. Someone opened a gate onto the pitch and the Cosenza ultras stole banners, taking some home but immediately burning others. The start of the game was delayed and Padre Fedele had to go on the loudspeaker to plead with the crowd to calm down. The game ended in a draw, and Cosenza was finally promoted.

Fans ran onto the pitch and hugged the players. Everyone had to dodge vases and plates that the locals threw at the celebrating fans as they walked back to their cars and the train station. One man walked into a shop and joined the train back to Calabria holding an entire cash till. The celebrations continued all that summer. Cosenza was, by its standards at least, back in the big time.

At Inter (the other team in Milano), Paolo 'the Armourer' had created a new ultra group called Skins. Their joy in bloodshed took fights to a new low. In October 1988 an Ascoli fan had been beaten to death a week before his wedding. The Skins were the first to imagine that they were insulting their Milanista enemies by writing on a banner 'Milanisti Jews – same race – same end'. Something eerily familiar was happening. The inebriated hatred reminded observers that the far right had never really gone away. Teasing and taunting had, over the years, turned into overt anti-semitism and racism.

But the more scandalized the media, the more publicity these groups received. In July 1989 Udinese (in Friuli, in the far northeast of the country) was on the verge of signing the Israeli midfielder Ronny Rosenthal from Standard Liege. But that summer the city's walls were spray-painted with antisemitic slogans by various ultras: 'Rosenthal Go Home' and 'Jews out of Friuli'. Wary of going against its own ultras, the club decided not to sign him. (Within a few months, he was playing for Liverpool, scoring a hat-trick against Charlton Athletic and winning the league title).

28 January 1989

The postal van travelled the same route each week through the rice-growing plains halfway between Turin and Milano. It journeyed north up the provincial road 594, which ran parallel to the Sesia river, taking cheques and cash up to the rural post offices in Gattinara, Borgosesia and Varallo. The vehicle always had a *Carabiniere* escort travelling behind.

It was still dark and foggy when, shortly after 6 a.m., a white Fiat Golf with Turin plates drew alongside the two-vehicle convoy. The Fiat Golf had been stolen two days before by the Drugo Pino Coldheart, one of three masked men in the car. Before the *Carabinieri* realized what was happening, a pump action Franchi shotgun had shot out two tyres and their car was in the ditch. They radioed for support.

With the escort out of the way, the Golf revved after the postal van. Two shots were fired into the air and the driver of the van pulled over. He and his colleague were bound with rubber strips. Duct tape was placed over their eyes. They were roughly shoved into the back of the Golf. The three men took off their masks. Pino took the wheel of the hijacked van and sped off in the dark with the Golf behind. The vehicles turned left and left again, so that they were heading south. Within minutes they came to the dirt track near the Cavour canal in Greggio where, the night before, the three men had hidden an off-road Toyota and a Peugeot 405.

Two early-morning hunters saw what happened next. The three men started cutting open the postal bags, one cutting his hand badly and swearing. In one of those bags were various jute sacks with cash and cheques. The man with the cut hand threw them in the back of the Peugeot and the men drove off. The hunters went and raised the alarm.

The armed robbers were tense now. Pino was in the Peugeot with Alessandro; Maurizio was behind driving the Toyota. All three had pistols down the side of their seats. They could already see one or two anglers along the canals and rivers, and knew that the police and *Carabinieri* would have sent search vehicles to the countryside around Vercelli.

They were on the road north to San Giacomo Vercellese when a road block stopped them. The *Carabinieri* were immediately suspicious of the two cars containing three men, driving fast at dawn. But when they approached the vehicles, they saw that two of the three suspects were colleagues: Maurizio Incaudo and Alessandro Chieppa were both *Carabinieri*. Antonio Scino, one of the on-duty *Carabinieri*, noticed that Alessandro's hand was bleeding.

'What are you doing here?' Salvatore Vinci asked his colleague, Maurizio. As he posed the question, he looked inside the Toyota. 'You know there's been a robbery?'

The first shot knocked Vinci to the ground. He was hit in the abdomen but returned fire. Maurizio Incaudo got out of the car and fired again, at point blank range. Further up the road, Pino and Alessandro were firing at the other *Carabiniere,* who was now running into the rice-fields, returning fire as he splashed and screamed, the bullets creating geysers all around him.

Scino didn't see the cars speed off, but the shots had stopped. He couldn't hear anything except the thudding of his own blood. He stood up in the rice-field and only now did he realize how cold the water was. He waded up the bank. 'Salvatò', he shouted, looking for his colleague. 'Salvatò.' Then, as he ran, dripping, along the road, he saw the crimson clothes and lifeless body of his colleague.

By then, the two cars were a few kilometres north, in Ravasenda. They had found an old military warehouse in the woods and had forced the lock. Inside, they counted the money. It came to just over 200 million lire. They sat on the ground, reliving what had happened, the excitement soon giving way to anxiety. They waited for a few hours, arguing about what to do next. Maurizio Incaudo was shaking and weeping. 'I'm fucked up,' he repeated. He wasn't only a *Carabiniere* himself, but was the son of a *Carabiniere*, and he had killed one of his own. 'It's all fucked up,' he kept saying.

He told the others he was going to end his life and went up to the first floor of the warehouse. The other two, Pino and Alessandro, joined him there when they heard cars approaching. There were helicopters overhead too. The only way out was to jump from the back window, a drop of 20 feet. They urged Maurizio to join them but he refused. As they ran off into the woods, they heard a shot. Maurizio had taken his own life.

The other two were picked up later that night. Like Maurizio Incaudo, one was also a *Carabiniere*. The other was twenty-six and already had a colourful curriculum vitae. Expelled from a police academy in Trieste in 1982 for violence, he had been arrested repeatedly for affray and GBH. He had attacked Inter fans and *Carabinieri* and was, until his arrest, the leader of Juventus's top ultra group, the Drughi.

Present Day, Sambenedettese

The June sun is setting over the main *tribuna* now and there are bats flitting in the floodlights. Men, stripped off to the waist, pump their fists in time to the music. People are bumping into old mates they haven't seen for months or years. Left-Behind is here, as are Vindov, Mouse, Boozy Suzy, Chill and all the rest. San Benedetto del Tronto is halfway down Italy on the Adriatic coast. Its team is called Sambenettese or, simply, la Samba. '*Lasciate ogni speranza voi ch'entrate*' says the banner as you come into the stadium ('Leave all hope, you who enter').

It's a club with loyal ultras, partly because they have many martyrs. Two young women lost their lives in a fire in the old stadium, the Ballarìn, in 1981. In 1986 a Samba fan, Peppino

Tomassetti was knifed to death outside a nightclub by rival fans from Ascoli. But most of all, the Samba fans mourn Cioffi. In 1977 he had co-founded the Onda D'Urto ('Shockwave') ultra group. Tall and thin, with receding hair and round glasses, he worked as a parking attendant at the local railway station. He always perched on the 'irons' at the front of the *curva*, inciting the other ultras with a megaphone. But on 4 May 2003, he was shifting position when he fell seven metres onto the asphalt below. He was in a coma for the next eighteen months until his death. The north stand of the new stadium, the Riviera delle Palme, is now named after him. 'Curva Nord Massimo Cioffi', it says in large white letters on a red-and-blue background. The Cosenza ultras, who know their history, applaud as the rival ultras sing the name of their late leader.

Ever since March Cosenza had been climbing the league table. The team had scraped into the knock-out competition for promotion to Serie B, and had already beaten Sicula Leonzio, Casertana and Trapani. The same players – Baclet, Okereke and Tutino – just kept scoring. This evening is the return leg of the quarter-final. The home game in Cosenza ended 2–1, so a draw would be enough to send Cosenza into the semis. There are about a thousand Cosentini at the ground. The team's warring ultra groups – the Anni Ottanta and the Curva Sud – have been separated into the ground level and first tier of the south stand. Cosenza are playing in white and there's no contest. We're singing trills of 'Come on, come on, come on, come on… score us a goal.' And they do: 1–0 with a clean strike from Domenico Mungo.

'We're going to win,' the ultras keep singing. *'La vinciamo noi'*. It's strange how little nervousness there is. 'We're not going to lose this,' says Half-a-Kilo happily. The flaps of his red-and-blue shell suit are rattling in the seaside breeze. Left-Behind is singing so hard that the vein on his forehead looks like a scar. Baclet scores and it's 2–0 with only a few minutes left. And then we're all densely packed again, singing the Popeye tune to the opposition: *'Che siete venute a fà?'* ('What did you come here for?'). Vindov, now worse for wear, grabs me and screams in my ear: 'Cosenza is beautiful and Vindov loves Cosenza.'

1989, Genoa

Genoa's main ultra group was called the Fossa dei Grifoni ('The Pit of Griffons'). It had made its first appearance at Monza on 3 June 1973, when some fans wore parachute regiment berets and T-Shirts with 'FG' on them. In many ways the Genoani were more English than other ultras. They gave Italian the word 'mister' for a football manager (because of their great interwar manager, Mr William Garbutt). They also screamed English words during games: 'hands', 'corner' and 'offside'. The fact that the stadium, too, is rectangular rather than oval, and without an athletic track, makes it feel more English and the noise booms off the vertical walls, rather than dissipating in the air.

Through their early years, the Genoa ultras had had the usual problems: fights, arrests and addictions. A man known as 'Onion' was shot dead in April 1982 over a drug debt. Another, Scotto, went to prison for dealing. But as always, the openness of the *curva* made the ultras admirably non-judgemental. His friend, Nico Ruello, wrote about Onion, '... for the group he wasn't a drug addict but a companion of many, many battles.' Other friendships were cemented too. A twinning was created with Napoli when Genoa unexpectedly equalized there in the dying minutes at the end of the 1981–82 season, and the whole San Paolo stadium celebrated Milan going down instead. The Genoani were twinned, too, with the anarchic ultras of Cosenza, having met them at Padre Fedele's ultra conference.

Luca had left Cosenza to live in Milan to be closer to his mother during his father's illness. But at every opportunity he took the train to Genova. 'There I rediscovered that human warmth and passion for life,' he remembers. 'At the end of the 1980s and in the early 1990s, the Fossa was a splendid community for those without a community, permeated by a passion for the team and a love for the city.'

It's intriguing how ultra groups reflect the cities from which they emerge. Genova is a rough, steep, crowded city. It's not dirty as such, but gritty. There's graffiti all over the narrow lanes near the seafront. As you walk those lanes there's only a ribbon of light six floors up, and you feel like you're in the bottom of a canyon that cuts left and right below the laundry floating in the salty air. There's something rebellious about the place, a sense of energetic defiance. Nicknamed 'La Superba' ('the Proud'), it's a heady mix of mountaineers and seafarers, of provincials and internationalists. Because it's always been a port, it feels Portuguese and North African and English too.

The Genovese poet Eugenio Montale called it a 'land of iron-work and mast forests in the evening dust'. There are flat, spacious *piazze* and steep, narrow lanes. The geometric contrasts of dazzling sunshine and shady recesses make the city feel, according to Antonio Tabucchi, like a chessboard with 'stains of shade and glare'. Like many ports, it's also infected with something of the Portuguese *saudade*, the melancholic sense of the passing of a place or person.

That melancholia wasn't often lightened by sporting glory,

which only seemed to make the Genoan ultras more fanatical. 'Only those who suffer learn to love,' said one of their banners in 1988. 'We suffer, we love you and with you will we return to greatness.' They also did a good line in insulting humour. Since they gathered in the *gradinata nord* (the north terrace) and their derby rivals, Sampdoria, in the south (*sud*), the banner for one derby read: '*Noi nordici, voi sudici*' ('*sudici*' meant 'filthy', but sounds like 'Southerners' too). Sampdoria was created by the fusion of two other Genovese teams, Andrea Doria and Sampierdarenese in 1946 and was thus considered by fans of Genoa – a club dating from 1893 – decidedly *arriviste*.

By the time he came out of prison, Scotto had learnt to read. He was a much-loved figure around the city who had been running with the ultras ever since he was twelve. By then his parents had divorced and he used to pretend to each that he was with the other as he rode around the city on a moped. He was already over six foot tall by then and going to away games. 'You beat each other up,' he says. 'It was like a classical medieval tournament, just trying to capture their flag.'

With his pear-shaped face and stars tattooed around his left ear, Scotto was, by the late 1980s, one of the leaders of the terraces. The other was a man called Puffer. The oldest son of a Sicilian father and Genovese mother, Puffer had first been taken to the stadium by a schoolteacher. He had joined the neo-fascist organization Terza Posizione, that 'third position' between fascism and communism that never seemed far from Nazism, but he was soon expelled. He called himself a 'right-wing anarchist' or, sometimes, a 'red fascist'. By the late 1980s, he was, he told me, 'using cocaine in abundance'. In many ways, Scotto and Puffer were opposites: one huge and anti-fascist, the other diminutive and elegant, and far to the right. But 'we're like brothers', Scotto says. 'Never had a political argument.' Genoa was one of the places where politics never seemed to overshadow the colours.

The group always met in Via Armenia 5r, a cul-de-sac off Piazza Alimondi near where Puffer lived. It had been rented to the ultras by Pippo Spagnolo, the grandfather of Genoa fans. He called the ultras, in dialect, his *figgieu*, his 'sons'. It was Spagnolo who had once organized, along with the ultras, a boat to take Fabrizio De André and a thousand other fans (the legend sounds eerily similar to Garibaldi's thousand patriots) to a game in Sardinia. When it looked like the club might go bust in the 1969–70 season, Spagnolo inspired fans to become shareholders in the club they loved, organizing 18,000 investors to stave off bankruptcy.

At the end of the 1988–89 season, Genoa won the Serie B championship to earn promotion to Serie A. The main reason for their success was the team's manager, Franco Scoglio. Born on Lipari, one of the tiny Aeolian islands off the north coast of Sicily, Scoglio's surname meant 'rock'. Straight-backed, balding, forthright but gracious, he was a maverick, having learnt his trade the hard way in the lower leagues of Calabria and Sicily. In Messina, Scoglio had nurtured a raw talent called Totò Schillaci, the Sicilian with the blazing eyes who would illuminate Italian football for the next decade.

Scoglio was the sort of man who left goodwill wherever he went. Journalists nicknamed him 'the Professor' because of his intellectual delivery. Almost everything he said in his calm, deadpan way was quotable. Players knew that his obsessive attention to detail – positioning, preparation, diet – would improve them. He came out with gnomic comments that subtly changed one's understanding of what football was. 'Bellopede [a Messina defender] mustn't pass the ball to Orati [a Messina midfielder],' he said when coaching the Sicilian side. 'Bellopede must put the ball in an area of the pitch where Orati has to be. Pay attention, they're not the same thing.' Credited with having invented the 'rhombus midfield', Scoglio spoke about spatial dimensions and zonal occupations, and created teams whose passing and movement were often mesmerizing. 'I'm not a football coach,' he said proudly. 'I'm a teacher of football.' He went even further: 'I'm coaching the fans, the club, the city.'

Scoglio felt at home in Genoa. He found something there that he hadn't felt since he had left the little island of Lipari. It was partly to do with the sea. 'The sea is civilization,' he said once, 'sentiment, passion, storms, love, landings, leavings, the sea is everything... madness walks with the sea.' There's no doubt that he liked the sound of his own voice ('I will die talking about Genoa,' he once said) but then so did everyone else.

Scoglio's first stint at Genoa, resulting in promotion to the promised land of Serie A, might not have been high-scoring but it was exciting in other ways. Marco Nappi was nicknamed 'the Seal' because he invented a form of dribbling in which he bounced the ball repeatedly on his forehead whilst running at full pace past bemused opposition players. In one game he ran all the way from penalty box to halfway line with the ball pinging off his forehead, tiny bounces as he ran fifteen paces until at one point he was running so fast the ball seemed to stay there, and so he nodded it down and sprinted onto it, taking him past the opposition midfield.

There was a symbiosis between Scoglio and the ultras. Scoglio seemed as passionate as they were. He celebrated goals with pumped fists, facing the fans in an era in which many 'technical commissaries' were more cold-blooded. He wore the Genoa scarf around his neck. When he won a big game, he would hug his players and smack their backs ten or twenty times. It was partly him charming them, as he charmed everyone, but he said, 'I want to remain at Genoa exclusively because of its fans, for its ancient Fossa... The history of this city is the history of this ancient fan base.'

But in the summer of 1989 it turned nasty in the city. On 10 May that year it was the final of what was then called the Cup Winners' Cup in Bern. The Catalonian club Barcelona were playing Sampdoria. The Dutch master Johann Cruyff was in the Barcelona dug-out, chain-smoking in his beige trench coat. The Sampdoria coach was the legendary Serbian manager Vujadin Boškov.

It was a one-sided game. Barcelona scored early with a tap-in header and then scored on the break, near the end, when Luis María López Rekarte broke through and, from just inside the area, slid the ball past the advancing Sampdoria goalkeeper, Gianluca Pagliuca. It was a defeat celebrated wildly by Genoa fans. Whilst their team had been labouring in Serie B, Sampdoria had been exciting Serie A with its great attackers, Roberto Mancini and Gianluca Vialli. That Wednesday evening, with 20,000 Sampdoria fans at the game in Switzerland, thousands of Genoa fans, all wearing their red-and-blue tops and scarves, partied in the streets. Convoys of cars, with flags pointed out of their windows, drove through the suburbs. They spray-painted slogans on walls like 'You're in Bern, we're in the armchair, the Cup to Barcelona', or deliberately sang songs in 'Samp' areas of the city.

It wasn't just young men but whole sections of the population. There were (so newspapers from the time say) old ladies shouting obscenities, schoolchildren imitating the adults, flicking the finger to any evidence of the rival creed. It was an opportunity for chromatic aggression, spray-painting walls red-and-blue in suburbs that were on the front line between the two teams.

There was nothing new about goading rivals by revelling in their misfortune. When Genoa had been relegated after a defeat in Florence, Sampdoria fans met the Genoani at the train station and sang insults and slurs. In the past they had organized processions of coffins, with donkeys wearing red-and-blue helmets, and even processions of sheep to symbolize how far the 'Griffons' had fallen. In 1988 the Sampdoria fans had gone to Modena to support the local team as Genoa tried to avoid another relegation, and for the end of the 1989 season they had planned to hire a helicopter – decked-out in Samp colours – to drop excrement in the stadium during Genoa's last match of the season. The *sfottò* – barbed insults – were all part of the ultra game.

But there was something about those celebrations in 1989 that infuriated the Sampdoria ultras. They had been so close to one of the greatest prizes in club football and the disappointment was already sickening before the Genoani rubbed their faces in it. There were isolated incidents of individuals getting beaten up and Samp ultras trashed a Genoa bar. Tensions were also high because the city was suffering the consequences of a contracting economy. With heavy industry in decline in the late 1980s, the city's port and petrol industries were badly hit and 60,000 Genovesi had lost their jobs.

Everyone was ready for a fight. In the ultra mentality there was no other way for the Samp ultras to redress the insults they had received. If they didn't react, it would be a sign of submission and an invitation for more ridicule. There would be no retreat, they said, but counter-attack instead. Their leaders contacted the Genoani of the Fossa dei Grifoni and told them the date and place for the fight: Tuesday 16 May, at 10 p.m. in Piazza Galileo Ferraris, one hundred on each side.

For days leading up to the encounter, people hid bars, spanners, baseball bats and chains nearby, in skips, lorries, lock-ups and garages. The ultras were excited by the military planning, looking at maps and lanes, where to ambush and where to block escape routes. This was no longer about football or fandom. This at last was action, what they called a 'coming to the hands'. There was a lot of macho bravado that afternoon, young men describing what they were going to do and to whom. As much as anxiety, there was relief: at last they wouldn't just be exhorters, but actually on the pitch, performing for the honour of their colours. This was the war they longed for.

The Samp ultras had been waiting in the piazza behind the stadium for almost an hour when a hundred ultras from the Fossa dei Grifoni rolled up, all in motorcycle helmets and carrying metal bars and chains. They started running towards the Samp ultras, yelling incoherently and ignoring the two police units trying to keep them apart. It was, witnesses said later, like watching a film of troops rushing towards each other. Some in the front line were knocked to the floor immediately as others ran on, rampaging through the ranks, swinging the weapons in their hands.

The noise was intense. The police fired fifty-eight shots in the air, whilst metal hit metal and bone. Seven cars were burnt, six policemen were knocked to the ground, stamped on, kicked. Spanners smacked skulls, elbows broke cheekbones. The city was shocked by the violence. But in truth there wasn't that much unusual about it. That season at least one game in ten saw violence of some kind.

What was unusual, however, was the response. The city had

an alternative councillor, a young Communist called Mario Tullo. He had spent years on the terraces and understood the fans. Rather than demonize them, he started phoning and visiting both sides. He spoke to the police, to fellow councillors and friends. He wanted to bring the ultras together into a cooperative, called tentatively Genova Point.

It seemed, to many, a ridiculous idea. Christian Democrats and Socialists pontificated that it was the usual Commie nonsense of giving a hand to idiots who should be locked up. The many parents of law-abiding but unemployed children were angry that the ultras might jump the work queue and start getting decent contracts from the city council. But Scotto, the self-educated bear of the terraces, got it immediately. 'One way to make everyone calm,' he said, 'is to entrust the most agitated with responsibility.'

The ultras began to talk to each other. Many were bored of prison or of being nagged by their wives to go straight. Others were simply desperate for any kind of wage. The Samp ultras invested as a group in the start-up, and elements of the Fossa dei Grifoni invested individually. The name was changed to Genova Insieme, 'Genova Together'. They decided that 30 per cent of the cooperative's employees should be people who were 'socially excluded'.

That year the 500-million-lire contract for cleaning the stadium was up for renewal. It seemed natural to give the contract to the ultras who made most of the mess. It wasn't plain sailing. Rather than pay a VAT bill, the first president pocketed 120 million lire, so Scotto took over the accounts. When he went to pitch for jobs for his band of merry men, businesses, for some reason, seemed to trust him. He was – like most people in Genova – blunt and straightforward. If he didn't like the smell of somewhere or someone he walked away. But if he took on a job, he got it done. The ultras began cleaning swimming pools and the juvenile prison. They took over parking lots and won the cleaning contract for the city's aquarium.

The Guardia di Finanza were constantly on their case, checking on bank balances and sub-contracts. But they found nothing amiss. Scotto was simply doing what he said he was doing. As the head of Ikea said of the ultras, who worked as delivery men also putting the furniture together, 'They've always shown simplicity, humility and responsibility.'

Part of the cooperative's strength was that oldest weapon of the ultras: force of numbers. When the legendary singer-songwriter Fabrizio De André's guitar was auctioned to raise money for the medical charity, Emergency, Mario Tullo put in a call to the ultras. Within a few hours 8 million lire had been raised. They raised a further 50 million when a hospital needed medical equipment. 'It's important to consider young ultras,' said Tullo, 'not as a mass of delinquents but as lads who are living in a particularly uneasy situation, and to begin a dialogue with them and, in the case of the cooperative, help them to grow through a project.' It wasn't rocket science. As Luca, from Cosenza, says: 'People want to do good. All you need to do is put them together.'

4 June 1989, Milan

Many of the Roma ultras had taken the overnight train. At the first few stops they hung out of the windows singing, banging on the metal exterior and waving flags. The carriages were full of dope smoke and happy shouting. Other than yellow-and-red everywhere, there was a lot of light denim and curly mullets.

Antonio De Falchi loved these away games. He was a quiet lad of eighteen and often used his long, straight hair as a curtain against the world. He was such a gentle kid that he once went to a game without his belt so that the police wouldn't hassle him, and his mates teased him as he held up his trousers with one hand. He was loosely part of a group called Impero Continua, the 'On-Going Empire'. The exuberance of away days made him feel less timid, like he had a gang around him at last and permission to be noisy.

Part of his quietness was the confusion of grief. His father had committed suicide three years before and he still couldn't understand it. That was another reason he loved these trips: the chance to be with men who seemed so noisy and strong. He was the youngest of eight children growing up in Torre Maura, a suburb in the far southeast of the city just inside the ring road. His most precious possessions were his moped and the shirt that Sebino Nela, the great Roma defender, had thrown him after a game at Cremona back in April.

The train arrived in Milan at half-past eight the following morning. There was more singing and flag-waving but Antonio peeled off with three of his mates. He wanted to see the city a bit and to buy postcards. It must have felt, to Antonio, like an efficient city: clean but oddly cold. The boys hid their scarves as they wandered around. Everywhere they saw the blue-and-black of Inter, since Giovanni Trapattoni's team had won the *scudetto* that year with great players like Lothar Matthäus, Aldo Serena and Walter Zenga. The red-and-black of Milan, too, was in every other bar and shop. Just eleven days before that Sunday, they had won the European Cup 4–0 with Carlo Ancelotti in midfield and two goals apiece from Ruud Gullit and Marco Van Basten.

At midday Antonio and his friends wandered towards the

stadium to buy their tickets. The San Siro was a building site. Like many other Italian stadiums, it was being enlarged for the World Cup, which was to be held in Italy the following year. The boys were in front of Gate 16 when a man came up to them and asked for a cigarette. Then he asked for the time. It was an old tactic to tell if someone had the wrong accent. One of the boys tried to fake a Milanese accent but it didn't wash. The Milanista whistled and motioned to his friends to run over. It was an ambush. Antonio and his mates sprinted away but a kick caught his heels and he fell over. He took more kicks and punches on the ground but the police were quickly there. Antonio tried to get up but fell to the ground again. He was struggling to breathe and then wasn't breathing at all. One of the policemen tried to resuscitate him but he died there, in the shadow of the stadium.

The three men arrested for Antonio De Falchi's death were all from the Gruppo Brasato ('the Braised Group', maybe so named because they were stewed in alcohol; their symbol was a Halloween pumpkin holding an axe and a tin of beer). One of the men was even part of Milan's official security detail. At the trial, two of the three were acquitted and, on appeal, the third was also acquitted. De Falchi, the defence said, had a heart defect which affected the oxygenation of the blood and made him appear cyanosed (meaning blueish, rather than pinkish, skin). It was another crime without punishment.

For Romanisti, De Falchi became a martyr, a name to be sprayed on city walls as a reminder of his sacrifice for the cause. One famous banner, addressed to Roma players, said: 'Antonio died for that shirt. Honour it.' In the 2003–04 season an ultra group was formed in his honour, Brigata De Falchi. But for the other side, it was a death to be turned into a taunt. The Italian for a heart attack is a 'heart arrest', so when Milan next played

Rome, the Milan ultras unfurled a banner saying, 'Your arrest is of the heart'.

A few days later a train was taking Bologna fans to Florence for the so-called 'Derby of the Apennines'. Ivan Dell'Olio had just turned fourteen. It was his first away game. The train had stopped at a station, Rifredi, when ultras from Fiorentina began throwing stones at it. One of the ultras had a Molotov cocktail that he hurled through an open carriage window. The flames spread everywhere, rising up from the puddle of fuel and engulf-ing the carriage. Dell'Olio survived but suffered 75 per cent burns. In Genova, Scotto put an extra thousand lire onto the price of the ticket (worth about 80 pence in 1989) and sent the funds to Dell'Olio's family.

One Bologna fan, Armando, said, 'That's when we understood the game was finished. There had always been a violence similar to courtyard wars. It had been a game with roles, you had an enemy and you took his scarves. But this was something more serious. People were crying, people were annihilated. You felt that that episode had killed your innocence.'

18 November 1989, Cosenza

During its first season back in Serie B, Cosenza nearly made it into Serie A, finishing in sixth place. The ultras were now on the national stage – going to big cities in the North like Udine, Brescia and Genova – but they still most relished going up against their hated rivals, Catanzaro.

That winter the team's quietly efficient midfielder, Denis Bergamini, broke his fibula in training and missed the rest of the season. By then Bergamini looked older than the innocent, blond boy from the North who joined Cosenza aged twenty-two. He hair was cut much shorter on top and he had a mini-mullet behind. He was still good-looking but he had lived a bit.

In the summer of 1989 the club had hired a new coach, Gigi Simoni, and invested in a Calabrian attacker who would become a club legend, Gigi Marulla. There were high hopes that this season the club could go one better and actually reach the promised land of Serie A. But after a dozen games Cosenza found itself penultimate in the league table. The Lupi had drawn seven games, lost four and won only once. Their next game was at home to Messina, and the team was staying in the usual Motel Agip in Rende, a suburb of the city.

At training that morning, Bergamini seemed fired up. 'We have to win,' he urged his colleagues. 'We have to get out of this wretched position in the league.' He was sufficiently light-hearted, though, to play a trick on one of the players, cutting off the ends of his woollen socks. When Simoni, the coach, invited everyone to a post-match barbeque at his house, Bergamini said to everyone that it would be a celebration of their victory.

After training that morning Bergamini rushed off. Nobody knew where he was going. He was back for lunch with the rest of the team at 12.30, then slept in the room that he shared with Michele Padovano until around three. He then drove in his Maserati to the Garden Cinema in the city, where he was due to watch a film with teammates. During the screening he asked his friend, the team masseur, where the toilet was and left his seat.

From having been a carefree young man, Bergamini now seemed weighed down by worries. His injury that January hadn't helped. It was the first serious stoppage of his career, and for someone who had few interests outside football, he was clearly bored. He was also pensive: he had arranged for his on-off girlfriend to go to London for an abortion, and he worried that her traditionalist family would be infuriated if they found out.

But there was something that his family didn't understand about his behaviour. That summer Bergamini had been on the brink of joining Parma, much closer to his home in Emilia-Romagna. Despite the deal being seemingly done, he had received a call from Calabria and suddenly cancelled everything. It appeared to his family that he was under some mysterious pressure from down South, as if he were being controlled in some way. 'I even thought that he was being blackmailed,' his father said years later.

On the Monday before that Messina game, Bergamini received another phone call, at his parents' house, after which they saw him red-faced and sweating profusely. Bergamini even confided to an ex-girlfriend that someone in Cosenza intended to harm him. When she laughed it off he became very angry – the only time, she said, he had ever lost his temper with her. The Friday before the match, when he was in his hotel room that afternoon, another phone call had clearly spooked him. Afterwards he was, according to his room-mate Michele Padovano, 'extremely worried, he was scared'.

It's probable that Bergamini was slowly learning what a dirty game football could be. As Padovano (who would go on to play for Juventus and also spend time in jail) once said: 'In football the cleanest person has scabies.' It is highly likely that Bergamini's salary was being topped up in cash. He had bought his Maserati for far more money than he had withdrawn from his account but that didn't surprise anyone. Back in the 1980s, cash was the main currency in the shadowy world of Calabrian football.

Match-fixing had always dogged Italian football, and to cynics it seemed odd that a team that had performed so well last year was now losing so many games, despite reinforcements like the big-hearted Marulla and Berga's return to fitness. Years later one player admitted that games were being chucked. Only a handful of players were involved but Bergamini was allegedly furious with their attitude and led the opposition to the scam, screaming at teammates during games and presumably berating them, too, in the changing rooms. Bergamini's father was so disgusted by what he saw in the last game his son ever played, a 1–1 draw at Monza, that he said he would never watch the team again. 'This is the last time I'm coming to watch Cosenza because you played shamefully,' he told his son. A theory emerged that young women had been used to befriend players, providing them with carnal fun and cash in return for throwing the odd game. It was a sordid theory but it didn't seem improbable.

That evening before the Messina game, Bergamini – normally the most punctual in the team – didn't arrive for dinner in the hotel. At 7.30 p.m., when the team was sat at table, a phone call arrived for Gigi Simoni, the manager. At first the receptionist didn't interrupt the meal, because those were orders, but the phone rang again. On the other end was the same young girl called Isabella. She said that she was Bergamini's girlfriend and that Denis had just committed suicide by throwing himself under a lorry. The manager thought it was a bad joke so the girl passed the phone to a man 'with a rueful voice' who confirmed the story.

Nothing about the suicide added up. Denis's family were convinced he had been murdered. 'I felt,' his father said, 'that they had killed him.' None of the players believed in the suicide either. Denis's room-mate and best friend used identical words to his father. 'They've killed him,' said Michele Padovano. 'There's no other logical explanation.'

Isabella Internò – the young girl with whom Bergamini had had a torrid, on-off relationship – claimed he was fed up with football and wanted to escape to the Amazon or Hawaii. That was why they were driving to Taranto's port. But Bergamini didn't have a passport and his allegedly suicidal thoughts didn't match the determination he had shown just that morning in training. In his last interview he had even said, 'I like living.'

Internò alleged that she and Bergamini had spoken for a long time on a muddy plateau by the side of the main road, and that he had then thrown himself in front of a lorry as if 'diving into a swimming pool'. His body was apparently dragged a long way before the truck came to a halt.

As the team's unofficial chaplain, Padre Fedele went to the morgue. He took along Drainpipe, one of the leaders of the Cosenza ultras, who remembers the shock of seeing the hero of the Cosenza midfield laid out on the zinc. The shock wasn't only at the dead body but at the state of him. 'They said he had been dragged along the ground by a lorry for seventy metres,' Drainpipe remembers, 'but his face was clean, not a scratch on it.' There were no grazes or abrasions on Bergamini's body. His watch was intact, his gold necklace unscratched, his face unmarked. Not even his shoes showed signs of the impact or of the muddy lay-by. 'We never had any doubt that he had been killed,' says Drainpipe. Nor did Bergamini's family. 'Nobody,' Donata Bergamini, his sister, told me, 'ever believed that version of events.'

For the ultras it was an unprecedented bereavement. Fans of many teams had mourned the loss of players in the past but rarely had they ever had to fight, along with that player's family, to prove that one had been murdered. The fact that it was Bergamini, too, made the grief particularly acute. During his convalescence from injury he had often stood in the stands with the Cosenza ultras, enjoying their unruly chaos.

'It was they,' says Donata, 'who immediately after the killing of my brother continued to shout his name and to wave a flag with his face on it. They had so much anger inside about what had happened to Denis.'

'Something just broke the day they whacked Denis,' one ultra told me. 'Our trust in the whole football fairy-tale was over. Something we loved was snatched away, not just Denis, but our belief that what we were watching, what we were being told, was in any way trustworthy.' Being an ultra had always been about never accepting bullshit from above, and for the hardcore on the Cosenza *curva* 'that was a moment that we, as a group of a few hundred, knew we were being lied to. It stank.'

As weeks went by, questions around the suicide story only increased. It emerged from subsequent witness statements that Isabella Internò had met one player, Francesco Marino, before Bergamini's death and phoned him afterwards. No explanation was ever given for that contact. She was in a relationship with a policeman, who she later married. Others alleged that there were links between the top echelons of the club and organized criminals, since one club official had married the sister of a crime boss.

Then, at the very end of that dark season, something happened which – to the conspiracy-theorist ultras – only confirmed that there was a cover-up. Two men who were at the bottom of the club ladder – they were fixers who helped with the kit, the travel arrangements and the bookings – contacted the Bergamini family. One, Domenico Corrente, delivered Bergamini's shoes to his father, possibly as a humane gesture since the player's clothing had been so hastily incinerated, or maybe to underline to the family how improbable the suicide story was. The other fixer, Alfredo Rende, promised Bergamini's father that at the end of the season he would come and talk to him, to give him additional information about the death of his son.

After the last game of that fateful 1989–90 season – in Trieste (another nil–nil draw which aroused suspicions, since both teams needed just a point to be safe) – Corrente and Rende were travelling back to Cosenza in an Alfa 75. It was only as they approached Cosenza, after driving 950 kilometres, that the accident happened. It was on the same stretch of road where Bergamini had died, on the Statale 106 Jonica. The car flew into the opposite carriageway where it was hit by a lorry. Both men in the car died instantly.

Present Day, Sud-Tirol

After that victory against Sambenettese, Cosenza's opponents in the semi-finals of the play-off hailed from the south Tyrol, in the far north of country. It feels (and often is) very Austrian. The residents speak Italian with a Germanic accent. They live in pine chalets with low, well-ordered log-piles stretching the length of the houses. The team in Bolzano even has a Germanic name: Fussball Südtirol.

The first game of the two-legged tie was in the north. Not many ultras made the 1,134-kilometre journey, and just as well. Although the Lupi played well, opening up the home defence on frequent occasions, they never found the back of the net. Shots flew wide, were blocked or skewed high. Frequently, a Cosenza shot rebounded off the advertising hoardings and bulged the net from behind, convincing the distant fans that a goal had been scored.

But in the ninety-first minute, a local lad – substitute Michael Cia – saw his first shot bounce back to him and he swung his right leg, smashing the ball into the net. A team that had hardly threatened for an hour and a half suddenly stole the game, 1–0. The next day the Cosenza press called the result *beffa acerba*, a 'sour mockery'.

The return game was only a few days later, on 10 June. The teams came out as the Cosenza fans were singing along to what had become their anthem, that old Bahamian folk song made popular by the Beach Boys, 'Sloop John B' (as reimagined by a Cosenza punk band, Lumpen) – 'I feel so broken, I want to go home.' The match was similar to the first leg. Almost from the start, Südtirol were defending their narrow lead. Cosenza were piling on the pressure but the tall, blond defenders from the North were solid. But then, halfway through the second half, in the twenty-fourth minute, the Cosenza player Alain Baclet dived onto a free kick and guided the ball the far side of the keeper. The tie was now level but the momentum was all with the home team. The injustice of that first leg was going to be avenged. In the ninety-fourth minute, a Südtirol defender rose to head away a corner but the ball skimmed off the top of his head and into the goal. The place went berserk. After all the hugging and shouting, many tough ultras sat down, for the first time all match, and wept. Cosenza was going to the final of Serie C.

The ultra world was very different after the World Cup of Italia 1990. Dozens of historic stadiums were renovated or replaced. The ultras' end of the oval, the *curva*, had always been sacred ground and the 'irons' were the altar of their temple. It's true that groups had very occasionally swapped ends, moving from the Curva Nord to Curva Sud or vice versa for reasons of allegiance or animosity with other ultras. But that was almost always on their own terms. Now, in the name of an international tournament that was a foretaste of the globalizing game, their homes were being bulldozed. Juventus and Turin both left the Stadio Comunale, Bari moved into Renzo Piano's Stadio San Nicola, Cagliari's Sant'Elia was restructured, a third 'ring' was added to the San Siro.

There were other reasons for the rebuilding. After the horrors of Heysel, Hillsborough, Bradford and the rest, stadium security was seen as essential to avoid atrocities and tragedies. It was easier to whisk fans in and out of those stadiums if they were located a few stops from the city centre, constructed in wastelands between railways and dual carriageways. On those scrublands, far from the bars and boutiques of a town centre, the ultras couldn't do too much damage. Money, too, was a motive: the larger the ground, the larger the possible profit.

For those who had been in the ultra ranks for twenty years, it was melancholic to see small grounds disappear. Rickety, romantic stands from the suburbs were suddenly empty. Walking to the new ground was often no longer possible, and when you got there you felt no connection. Not all the stadium changes occurred because of 'Italia 90' but that rebuilding set a trend that was followed for years afterwards: Ancona had played at 'the Doric' since 1931. It wasn't even a stadium, more a field squeezed between housing blocks and a stone ticket office with 'Doric Sports Pitch' written above the lintel. It was a place bathed in memories but in 1992 the team moved to the Stadio del Conero, half a dozen kilometres away. New stadiums often had wide concrete ditches around the pitches so that the ultras could now never touch the grass. One, the Mapei in Reggio Emilia, even had a ditch with water and fish, with the result that animals were closer to the action than the fans (and were often more fun to watch than the football).

In Abruzzo, Teramo upgraded its ground, moving a few stops away on the local train line. But the old ground was untouched because of the obstructionism of the ultras. To them, developing the old ground would be like building a casino on top of a cemetery. One of the ultra groups took on the name '13 Steps' in memory of the number of stairs in their old *curva*. The faces of dead comrades were spray-painted on the walls, reminding citizens that their memories were cherished in this specific place.

Italy usually lets ruins stay as ruins. Chancing upon a forgotten amphitheatre or forum has always been the charm of wandering its towns. These twentieth-century stadiums were also mostly left where they were, weeds sprouting through the cracks, saplings getting taller on the pitch. Sometimes their disuse was a result of council paralysis or fan pressure but often it was nothing more calculated than laissez-faire. The Torino ultras still meet in the 'Bar Sweet' opposite the crumbling remains of the old stadium. The longevity of these relics is remarkable. One of Roma's first pitches, in Testaccio, still stands empty despite not being used since 1940.

The face of the ultra world, too, was changing. The list of ultras who died of overdoses in the early 1990s was long: Geppo, the young man who had written the idealistic ultra manifesto... Zigano, who had gone on the run after Papparelli's death... Beppe Rossi, the Juventus Fighter who had suffered so much after Heysel – all passed away after succumbing to their addictions. In a milieu in which *gaudeamus igitur* – 'let's party therefore' –

was the motto, it wasn't surprising that excessive celebrations of freedom led to premature deaths.

But in the early 1990s many surviving, die-hard ultras left the front-line and some of the famous groups of the first two decades dissolved. In Genoa, in the summer of 1993, the Fossa dei Grifoni folded, amid claims that 'we don't recognize this football any more'. Often groups dissolved because arrests or knifings had already decimated the ranks and ruined their reputation. Verona's infamous Brigate Gialloblù dissolved in November 1991, a few days after four 'brigadeers' had been knifed in a Coppa Italia game against Milan. The dissolution of formal groupings was also strategic: an accusation previously only used against mafiosi, 'delinquent association', was now being trialled against ultras, and the less evidence of formal association the better. Perhaps many no longer felt the adolescent fury that energized those Manichean fights. Those easy labels of 'faith', 'honour' and 'revenge' seemed a bit embarrassing when emotional maturity brought an appreciation of subtlety and difference. For those who had just loved the singing and folklore, it didn't make sense to beat up kids simply because they lived in another part of Italy.

Sporting disappointments also played a part in the exodus. Cosenza only just stayed in Serie B in 1991. They had been in a relegation play-off against Salernitana. In the sixth minute Gigi Marulla ran between two defenders and headed the ball in with his thinning hairline. Cosenza won 1–0 and avoided relegation to Serie C. Afterwards, Marulla revealed that the day before the game four fans had boarded the players' bus. Marulla remembered that they knelt before the players, saying: 'Calabria is a bitter land, present us this joy tomorrow.' Marulla (himself Calabrian) felt 'like I was on a mission for a people'. He, at least, understood the ancient notion of championing a cause.

But the following year there was more disappointment. Lecce, on the spur of the Italian boot, was often the graveyard of hope. It was there that Roma had, a few years before, failed to clinch another title and a distraught Bongi decided to withdraw from the ultra front-line. Something similar happened to Cosenza in 1992. The team was within touching distance, for the first time in its history, of Serie A. Ciccio had organized 10,000 flags for the occasion. Some said that as many as 15,000 Cosentini went to the seaside stadium in Salento.

With only ten minutes to go, Giampiero Maini scored the game's only goal for Lecce. Udinese had won 2–0 at Ancona and so Cosenza's hope of reaching Italy's top division disappeared. The trudge back to cars and trains was, remembers one observer, a *via crucis*: 'The Leccesi were burning brushwood and creating fires which accompanied us all the way to the station and creating a red-hot climate…'

Ciccio wanted to quit. 'After that disappointment I wanted to do away with all the banners, leave off for a year.' He had an idea to gather all the disparate groups behind one single banner: '*Vivere ultrà per vivere*' ('Live as an ultra to live'). Soon there were other sadnesses. On 27 September 1992 the Cosenza midfielder Massimiliano Catena scored a sensational goal. The ball was closer to the halfway line than the penalty area but he hit it so hard that it flew into the net. Everyone knew his father was dying and the fans and players stood to applaud him. Just a few days later, driving back from seeing his father in Rome, Catena – aged twenty-three – died in a car crash. The Curva Nord took his name.

Many of the most politically committed ultras had begun to spread their focus outwards. Claudio and the Nuova Guardia boys in Cosenza occupied a building just outside the city. They called it Granma, the name of Castro's boat, but someone mangled the name and it became known as Gramn. 'The struggle isn't at the stadium any more' was the slogan. In the early 1990s there was a flurry of new projects emerging from the Cosenza *curva*, including a radio station (called Ciroma, or 'Chaos') and a publishing house (called 'Coessenza'). Paride even stood for mayor. Elias Canetti had once written about the ancient arenas forming 'a closed ring from which nothing can escape', meaning that all the fury and rebellion was tolerated if it stayed only there, contained in that space. Many of the Cosenza ultras were trying to break that ring, to allow the idealism of the stadiums to energize the streets.

Other ultras gave up because they glimpsed the impotence central to the experience of being a fan. All that exhortation – the sweary invective and derision – was partly a result of an awareness that the fate of the fan was, really, to do nothing. Whilst watching twenty-two men run you're rooted in one spot. You can make as much noise as you want, but it's like a prayer in the face of an earthquake. You are a voyeur, watching, rather than making, love. Punks at least made music or, as Johnny Rotten called it, 'chaos'. The Hell's Angels had bikes to ride and repair. But the ultras, once they had choreographed and sung and done the usual *battimani* (the rhythmic handclaps), were really just spectators, static and passive. Because most stadiums in Italy are elliptical, the position of greatest power for an ultra – the very centre of the *curva* – is precisely the point most distant from the ludic cauldron. It seemed a confirmation of exclusion or irrelevance. That, perhaps, was one of the sources of the ultras' fury: the fretting that they're not really needed. Maybe that's the cause of the vein-popping screams of the *capo-coro* – the man with the megaphone – as he tries desperately to keep his troops active, scowling at anyone who dares to stand near him and not sing. And hence, one assumes, the genuine delight of the ultras when the chance arises to get a bit of action themselves.

There was, too, a growing awareness that the ludic was linked to illusion ('in lusio': being mocked or 'played with'). As in so many temples, some of the participants no longer believed in the conjuring trick, or in the rhetoric that their presence affected the action. Whether because of match-fixing, or rising ticket prices, or impersonal stadiums, the ultras were increasingly aware that they, as much as the ball, were being played with. One sociologist, Osvaldo Pieroni, had moved to Cosenza and had been drawn to the red-and-blue faith. Having followed both the team and the accounting trail (this was back in the 1993–94 season), he wrote a disenchanted monograph claiming that the game had become 'a kind of self-deception... everyone pretending that they don't know that Italian football is, in effect, one huge rip-off masked as a party'. He compared the club to a prostitute, 'faking reciprocal attraction and spontaneous availability, pretending there were no profit incentives or intermediaries...' From a dedicated football fan it was melancholic, albeit understandable, prose: the Cosenza president had used the club to boost his failed bid to be elected to parliament, had run up huge debts and was then imprisoned for forgery.

But the mystery of football is that, just as you're about to give up on it because it seems fictitious, it gives voice to the fans' sense of futility. It was, perhaps inevitably, Torino that reiterated why people kept coming back for more. Emiliano Mondonico was the team's manager in the early 1990s. In 1992 he took the team to a Uefa Cup Final against Ajax. Torino repeatedly hit the woodwork but failed to score. When what he thought was a clear penalty wasn't given, he picked up a chair from pitchside and raised it above his head, shaking it with rage. It was, he said years later, 'the symbol of the person who supports against everything and against everyone. It was a symbol of the person who won't put up with it any more and who reacts with any means at his disposal. It's a symbol of Torino because a chair isn't a rifle, it's a weapon of the hostelry.' Torino, said Mondonico, was 'the hope of a better world'. Torino lost the final but their supporters felt someone had understood their sense of futility and impotence. Meaning emerged, as ever, from loss. When Mondonico was dying of cancer decades later, Toro ultras marched with chairs, raising them to the gods. There was no violence, only rage and sadness.

If many were leaving the *curva*, others were moving in. On 30 January 1992, at the Hotel Universo in Rome, a conference was organized by two politicians from the MSI party. Entitled 'A Fatherland Called the Terraces', and with invitations issued to the notoriously right-wing fans of Lazio, Juventus, Inter and Roma's Boys, it was an attempt to harness the energy and radicalism of the ultras for electoral politics. Within a year the Lazio ultras were chanting that 'We want Fini [the MSI leader] for mayor'. Many ultras scorned the flagrant attempt at exploitation but the conference was evidence that reemergent right-wing political parties saw the ultras as the foot soldiers of a new movement.

Given what was happening on certain terraces, it was natural that neo-fascist politicians sought political support there. When Hellas Verona was on the verge of signing Maickel Ferrier, the Dutch midfielder from Suriname, a black mannequin was hanged from the stands by supporters wearing Ku Klux Klan outfits. There were also racist chants and banners ('Give him the stadium to clean'). Bowing to ultra pressure, the club decided not to sign him. Another Dutch player from Suriname, Aron Winter, was bought by Lazio in 1992 and immediately, on the white marble walls on the way to the Stadio Olimpico, antisemitic slogans appeared. One read 'Winter Dirty Jew Out', accompanied by a swastika.

Ever since the end of the war, anti-fascism had been the foundation stone of the Italian Republic. But the collapse of the Soviet Union had gutted the credibility of Italian communism and by 1992 the other pillar of Italian post-war politics, the Christian Democrats, had been decimated by corruption scandals. These events represented the collapse of Italy's First Republic and a political and ideological vacuum opened up.

Many of those who stepped into that vacuum conflated footballing populism with a fondness for the authoritarian strand of Italian history. When the owner of A.C. Milan, Silvio Berlusconi, burst into politics by creating his Forza Italia party out of Milan supporters' clubs and Publitalia, he made anti-communism the centrepiece of his slick sloganeering. He identified the MSI and the anti-southerner, anti-foreigner Northern League as his ideal political partners. With a huge media empire to ram home his message, Berlusconi made sure that fascism was *sdoganato*, 'cleared through customs'. Everyone could see what was happening. It was an assiduous but subtle rehabilitation of a political extremism that had been shunned by the mainstream for five decades. Berlusconi rarely missed an opportunity to express his admiration for Mussolini and pointedly avoided the traditional 25 April celebrations marking the country's liberation from Nazi-Fascism. By 1994 many neo-fascists who had been imprisoned as militants in the 1970s and 1980s found themselves in mainstream politics, if not in the upper echelons of government.

The danger was sufficiently acute that in 1993, a law was passed (the Legge Mancino) outlawing fascist slogans, salutes and ideologies. It was an updating of the 1952 Scelba Law, which prohibited the recreation of the Fascist Party in post-war Italy. But that legislation was so rarely enforced that it enabled the resurgent fascists in Italy to butter their bread on both sides. They were able to present themselves both as persecuted underdogs and martyrs, while at the same time enjoy impunity for their proselytizing.

Present Day: Siena v. Cosenza (Lega-Pro Final)

It's still 2–1 with ten minutes to go. Marotta, the bearded Siena striker, is toiling away. It's tense now and we're singing as it's the only thing to do: 'Take us away from this shitty division.' They call it *sgolarsi*, doing your throat in.

Alain Baclet has come on as a substitute. All through the run to this final, he has come on and scored so there is an expectation that it will happen again. He's a tall, completely bald Frenchman, able to lunge for crosses with his head or toes. It seems as if everyone is tired except for him. Suddenly a long, looping cross comes in and Baclet runs in front of everyone and buries it in off the post with his right. The place explodes. 3–1.

Chill, behind us, is hugging SkinnyMon. 'It's OK,' he is weeping, 'it's OK, it's OK.'

People are jumping up and down, falling off the ergonomic seats with their annoying plastic edges. Vindov races around, slapping his forehead. Boozy Suzy is taking endless photos to prove, in decades to come, that she was here. A team that was second from bottom in October has just won the play-off between three different Serie C divisions (North, Central and South).

When that third goal went in everyone in the stadium knew that Cosenza were back in Serie B. Siena had fought all through the second half and now – minutes before the end – had conceded a third. There was no way back.

Superficially, the communal ecstasy of that *curva* was about promotion: not just this team's, but this terrace's re-entrance onto the national stage. But that was only the surface meaning of this emotional excess. It was a collective triumph that brought people back together, even the warring ultra groups. And for the thousands of Cosentini living in the North, it meant that next season – with the team in a national league at last – they would see their friends at many more matches. Looking around as the dazed fans walked out, you could see all the familiar older figures of this fan base: Paride and Claudio and Ciccio and Padre Fedele… And like all comings-together, it was also a reminder of all those who weren't here. Not just Drainpipe (on a personal strike in protest at the team hiring a player, Leonardo Perez, who is a declared fascist with a twitchy right arm) but all the other absentees – dead parents, Piero, Denis Bergamini, Ettarù and all the others, the victims of the earthquakes and overdoses, of car crashes and cancer. Fandom is another way of remembering the old days and the dead.

What united these people wasn't their passion for football, as such, but the markers it puts down in their lives. There was something political in that incredible victory too. Perhaps it shouldn't be surprising that the vast majority of terraces today are in the control of leaders of the far right. The ultras' longing for absolutism, for something on which they'll never compromise, their desperation for unity when they're told there's disintegration all around them, their defence of territory and the conquest of another's, the identity expressed through colours and clothing, the delight in order in a country that is often chaotic – all are perfectly aligned with the makeshift philosophy spun by an ex-Socialist from Predappio in the aftermath of the First World War. But Cosenza's victory in that final seemed to offer a distant, maybe naïve, hope: that the definition of those extremist words – ultra, oltre, outré, other – couldn't be hijacked by extremists from one side alone. These anarchic, devoutly anti-fascist Cosenza ultras offer the solace that, perhaps, there's more than just a mythical order and racial intolerance on the terraces. And a victory for this almost unknown Calabrian city, against a stunning Tuscan town that was once instrumental in the founding of capitalist banking, suggests that sometimes football is able to invert the established hierarchies and give succour to the underdog.

As we're walking out of the ground, there is a T-shirt in front of us that says in dialect: '*Tu insisti, io persisto, u vu capì ca risistu!*' 'You insist, I persist, don't you understand that I resist!'

PART TWO

7 July 2016, Stura di Demonte

Ciccio Bucci pulled his Jeep Renegade onto the hard shoulder of the viaduct. The dual carriageway here was forty-five metres above the flood plain of the Stura di Demonte river. It was known as the 'viaduct of suicides'. This was where Edoardo, only son of Gianni Agnelli (the late owner of Fiat and Juventus), ended his life in 2000.

Bucci had always been obsessed with Juventus. Born in 1976, the oldest of three boys, he had grown up in San Severo, an ancient trading town in Puglia, on the spur of the Italian boot. He had spent his childhood watching the greats of Juventus – Michel Platini, Roberto Baggio, Fabrizio Ravanelli and Gianluca Vialli – and had been hypnotized by the black-and-white stripes of the club. They seemed, somehow, a symbol of the efficiency and decisiveness of the North, of a world where there were more than just shades of grey. Bucci had become an obsessive supporter.

He took off his trademark shades and rubbed his face. Below his gelled black hair, his right eye was heavily bruised and his forehead was cut. His throat still hurt and he massaged it with his fingers to test the pain. He tried to think how he had got here, so far from home and so close to the end. Things hadn't been the same since his mother had died. She had always believed in him and with her gone, he had lost his self-belief.

He looked at the swank inside of the Jeep. Jeep was Juventus's sponsor and he was working for the club he loved. He kept telling friends that, for the first time in his life, he was 'official'. The club had given him this chunky car as part of his role as an SLO, a 'supporter liaison officer' (even though, officially, he was an employee of a security company called Telecontrol). He was a go-between, trying to smooth out issues between the club and its intransigent ultras. That was why his dream job had turned sour. You couldn't win. He was always being threatened and, like last night, beaten up.

Bucci got out of the car and took in the view. In the distance he could see the first of the mighty mountains of the Alps. In the foreground were rectangles of industrial units and corn fields. Somewhere there was Beinette, the village where he had once lived with Gabriella, his ex, and their son Fabio. He had just been back there to water her plants as she was on holiday.

Fabio, his son, was the only thing he loved more than Juventus. That thought started the tears. Bucci felt he had to do this to make Fabio safe, to keep the thugs away from his family. There was nothing else he could do now. Everything was inevitable and logical. He heard a couple of workmen shouting at him as he climbed over the metal railing. He stood on the other side. Only his heels could fit on the edge and his knees were bent by the bulging railing. He looked up to the sky, then down to the concrete and scrub below. He closed his eyes, thinking of his mother and of Fabio, and stepped off.

Present Day: Cosenza v. Verona

It was Cosenza's first home game in Serie B. As luck would have it, it was against the team that, apart from Catanzaro, their ultras hated more than any other: Hellas Verona. Almost thirty years ago, the Cosentini had held up a famous banner deriding the

Veronesi: 'The culture of our land against the stupidity of your minds. Verona is first only for heroin.' The differences were largely cultural. The Northern city was nationalistic to put it lightly, whereas the Cosentini were so anti-nationalist that they chanted 'Zaire' after the African country had beaten Italy 4–0 in the Seoul Olympics in 1988. All manner of flags are present in the Cosenza stadium, but never the Italian tricolour. Another famous Cosenza banner, held up to Verona fans, said simply: 'Get the Nazis out of the Terraces'.

But nothing in Italian football is simple. The San Vito stadium had been used for concerts through the summer, and then in the hours before the game there was heavy rain. When the pitch was inspected the turf peeled off as easily as skin from an onion. Cosenza had waited decades to face Verona in Serie B and now the match was called off. Verona was awarded a 3–0 victory by the bureaucrats of Italian football.

That was the least of the problems for Serie B at the start of the season. During the summer three teams from the division – Cesena, Bari and Avellino – had gone bankrupt, meaning that there were now only nineteen teams left. Everyone knows that a division has to have an even number of competitors so that each has a match to play. But it was impossible to ascertain who should take those three vacant places: those who had been relegated from Serie B the previous season, or the teams who had missed out on promotion from the three Serie Cs? Trying to make that decision when the season was already underway was a bit like trying to replace a puncture when you're already riding the bicycle. One team, Entella, even found itself without a league. Having hoped to have its relegation rescinded, it was excluded from Serie C but then not admitted to Serie B, meaning that it was in limbo. A former foreign minister, Franco Frattini (who was by then the President of the Collegio di Garanzia per lo Sport, the country's top sporting tribunal), said, 'It's easier to organize a G7 summit than Serie B.'

Something very similar happens every summer in Italian football. There's uncertainty about which division many teams will play in. There's even confusion, often, about how many teams a league will have, since the numbers constantly change. That chaos is partly the result of the fact that, given the understandable desperation for justice, there are many levels of sporting tribunals. There's an almost pathological inability to take a binding decision and uncertainty drifts into the autumn. The same happens in ultras' legal trials. You never hear them say that they were found guilty or innocent. Instead they'll list their trials (for the same crime) like results in the football season: 'I won, then lost, then won again.'

The bigger teams are usually bounced up the leagues at the expense of the smaller ones. The effect all these shenanigans have on the ultras is intriguing. It gives them a role in the summer, as they threaten protests or public disorder. But it also gives cachet to their rhetoric that modern football is corrupt and that they – far from being the evil of the sport – are the guardians of its soul.

Early 1990s: Diabolik

'I realized watching the [1990] World Cup,' wrote Grit in his memoir, *Anni Buttati* ('wasted years'), 'that football was changing and was becoming a way to publicize oneself.' Being a graphic designer, Grit was clever at creating eye-catching choreographies. Lazio's Irriducibili were even noticed when they weren't there. In the first season after that World Cup, the Irriducibili led a fan's strike for the first half of every match, leaving only a banner in the empty stand saying '12th man on the pitch only when we want'. It was a way of urging the club not to take them for granted. Another display – 'prisoners of a faith' with the lettering behind bars – identified the ultras with prisoners of conscience.

The group also had a brilliant artist, nicknamed Disegnello ('the little designer'). And so, much as the Irriducibili criticized the spectacularization of the sport through television, they were also the beneficiaries of it. Banners were no longer just strips of cloth but flags that covered the entirety of the terrace, one quarter of the stadium. The more pharaonic the display, the more likely that the group and its message would be picked up by TV cameras and, in later years, the internet.

It was a world that was becoming increasingly self-conscious about appearances. All rebellions are acts of style as well as substance, and the ultras had always been poseurs. The Lazio ultras, in particular, prided themselves on their stylishness. 'Dress well, behave badly' was one of their mottoes. But now the fixation on appearances was almost pathologically self-reflexive. One member of the Irriducibili in the early 1990s remembers selling photographs of the terraces to individual ultras on match days to fund the next choreography, which would then be photographed and the images sold and so on.

Gone was the spontaneity of the 1970s, with all its revelry in individual expression. Now one dominant group would obscure your view of the pitch in order that thousands of square metres of material could briefly be beamed into living rooms around the world. The uniformity was acoustic as well as visual. At the start of the 1991 season the Irriducibili had erected four huge speakers on the Curva Nord and now one man with a microphone could make more noise than thousands of unamplified individuals. The Irriducibili bosses called it '*coerenza*' – 'consistency' – but to many insurgents on the terraces it seemed creepily totalitarian.

Most importantly, as the terraces' displays became more grandiose, so the need for income streams increased. The costs of a one-off choreography were increasing and it was perhaps inevitable that ultra groups started looking for innovative ways to meet those costs. Every match day the terraces became like an open-air souk and the money paid not just for gargantuan displays, but also for the legal expenses of an ultra on trial, for their family if in prison, and for the rent of a group's HQ.

The marketplace in Lazio's Curva Nord was particularly busy. It was partly because in the early 1990s football suddenly became fashionable amongst not just the masses, but also the monied. Fans on the terraces had disposable income and Lazio was, for once, considered cool. The club had a new owner, the food entrepreneur Sergio Cragnotti, and he had invested in Paul Gascoigne and Beppe Signori. Signori, a diminutive striker who barely seemed to fill his shirt, consistently scored spectacular goals. For the first time in almost two decades, it was exciting to be a Lazio supporter, and in a world of chromatic conformism, it was hard for supply to keep up with demand for the white-and-light-blue of Lazio. Club merchandising is notoriously weak in Italy (it's often hard to find any official strip), and the Eagles group, after plenty of scraps with the Irriducibili, had folded in 1992. The Irriducibili now had a near monopoly on merchandise and, in that huge terrace, thousands of customers.

There was a young man in Grit's ever-growing band called Fabrizio Piscitelli. He was nicknamed Diabolik after the cartoon character thief and assassin. Diabolik looked a bit like Quentin Tarantino, with a big chin and an unsettling grin. He invariably wore a baseball cap and rimless glasses or shades. He was an avid drugs-user but his main high came from fighting, which, he said, made him 'feel alive in a world of the dead'.

He especially liked fighting the police. 'You feel even more alive when you fight the guards,' he once said. 'You know from the outset that they're stronger than you, when you are armed only with a belt, and they're armed from head to toe. But when they try and come on the terrace, and everyone runs away and only twenty madmen remain to take them on, without fear in front of security cameras, knowing that only one of you will be left standing… that's like playing football for us.' Diabolik could be pally or brutal, depending on the situation. 'For the good of Lazio we were looking to injure people on the other side, for the good of Lazio we wanted to go onto the terraces and kill them. We wanted to show how much we were prepared to do for Lazio, with blood.'

But Diabolik had a good head for figures too. With a friend, Toffolo, he had crunched the numbers. Friends of friends introduced Diabolik to various contacts in Naples. He started meeting men who called themselves 'textile merchants' – businessmen trading in counterfeit shirts and scarves that they imported from Asia. The mark-up, he realized, could be huge. The difference between the purchase and sales price was between thirty and sixty thousand lire (roughly £10–20). On a match day Diabolik reckoned he could shift a few hundred units in half an hour, probably a few thousand week-to-week. And shirts and scarves was just one of the possible income streams. His friends in Naples, the Senese family, had other, less legal products on offer if Diabolik was willing to shift them as well.

Nobody knows exactly how Grit was forced out of the iconic group he had founded. One Lazio ultra told me simply that

Diabolik and his mates were 'a Rotary Club of evil'. One senses, speaking to him, that Grit still yearns to be an 'ex officio' member of the gang. He refuses to divulge what happened for fear of riling his replacements. But by the mid-1990s Diabolik had taken charge of Lazio's Curva Nord and was soon living up to his nickname.

12 September 1993, Cosenza

Even in Cosenza, where Padre Fedele had fought for pacificism, there had been an escalation in violence with other fan groups. In one Lecce–Cosenza game, on 14 March 1993, homemade hand grenades had been thrown and one Lecce fan lost his hand. Another Lecce fan threw one of the bombs back and it exploded next to the foot of a Cosentino, whose mobility was so diminished that he later took his own life. In that violent match, Padre Fedele was waving his hands up and down, furiously shouting at his boys to stop being stupid.

But everyone, it seemed, had lost control. Someone lost an eye when a lighter was thrown in a Brescia game... another broke his leg jumping from the top ring of Verona's Bentegodi stadium, where he had gone to rescue a 50-metre banner saying 'Come On Wolves'. Surrounded by Veronese skinheads, he had to jump onto the concrete steps far below. From above, the Veronese showered him with flares and urine and so the Cosentini had ripped up the seats and used them as frisbees, aiming at those Aryan thugs.

Even between the Cosenza crews there were arguments. It came to a head on 12 September 1993, in a game that should have been remembered for Pietro Maiellaro's Maradona-like dribble, running around half a team and half a pitch before scoring for Cosenza. But on the terraces there was a furious brawl between rival ultra crews from Cosenza. There were as many reasons for the fight as there were people involved. Some said it was part of a turf war between rival criminal clans. Others said it was about personality clashes and leadership. But that was the day that the unity of the Cosenza *curva* ended. As ultras often do when they've attracted the wrong attention, the groups went quiet. The Nuclei Sconvolti dissolved. 'All guilty,' said one banner at the next game, 'all in silence.' The Amantea group held up a banner announcing that it was going to snooze: *'Amantea S'Abbiocca.'*

By then Padre Fedele was becoming something of a star in the Italian media. He had gone to Messina, in Sicily, to study medicine and had his own slot on a TV show. Every Christmas he put up a tent in the main square, as he had in Cosenza, to gather funds for his charitable trips to Africa. He organized twinnings between Cosenza and other teams that hadn't been sanctioned by Cosenza ultras. He was trying to bring people together who, perhaps, didn't want to be. He tried to unite the supporters clubs with ultra groups. A biography, written by Paride, was published.

Then, at a conference in Lecco against stadium violence, Padre Fedele had met a porn star called Luana Borgia. There was an immediate chemistry between them. They both craved the limelight and were curious about the other's extreme life choices. Over the next few months a flirtatious dance began as they tried to bring the other round to their position: carnal libertinism or the confession of Christ, or maybe both at once.

The two were spotted in the stadium together, which only increased the gossip. Always a volcanic fundraiser, brow-beating sinners into putting cash in his coffers, Padre Fedele hung out at Bologna's 'erotica fair' next to Borgia. (She said they raised enough to finance an ambulance and an operating theatre in Rwanda.) For rival ultras, the target was too good to miss. The Fiorentina ultras dedicated a banner to Padre Fedele, complete with an erotic drawing: 'Padre Fedele, Faith divides us. Desire unites us.'

The Monk had always been unmonkish – he could shout and swear as well as anyone – and he had often joked about how red-blooded he was. He wasn't pious, but a commoner. As if to underline that comparison, he had once quipped while holding the knots that represented his vows: 'These two [poverty and obedience] are knotted tight, but this one [celibacy] is coming loose.' The ultras weren't moralists and didn't really care if a man who had been so loving was, occasionally, loved in return. It might make him a bad monk but to the largely atheist ultras it definitely didn't make him a bad man. But Paride and Luca were alarmed. By then Padre Fedele's convent had become a precious place of cultural insurgency. There was a walk-in surgery, the soup kitchen and rooms for the homeless, for the impoverished and, increasingly, for immigrants. The ultras held their weekly meetings there, paying 300,000 lire a month (just shy of a hundred pounds) for the space. It was an exciting ferment of new initiatives and ideas, and Paride and Luca were concerned that Padre Fedele was playing with fire. His flirtation with a lusty woman wasn't the problem. It was more that he was so vocal about injustice that he had made enemies who could use his weaknesses to bring down not just him, the revolutionary Monk, but the whole countercultural movement that surrounded him.

Because of its deliberately devil-may-care culture, the ultra world had always been dangerous. But invariably the loss of life had seemed incidental rather than deliberately intended. It was just that, in the reckless chaos of fights and smashing Molotovs and flashing knives, there were victims along the way. In some ways, it was almost surprising that so few people died. But something changed in the mid-1990s. Now certain ultras seemed to be actually taking aim. On 30 January 1994 a twenty-two-year-old man called Salvatore Moschella was bundled out of (or allegedly jumped from) the window of a moving train after threats and beatings by ultras from Messina. The Messina club president said of his ultras, 'For me they will always remain good lads.'

Three years later, in the summer of 1997, Abdellah Doumi was hanging around Turin's *murazzi*, the walls and wharfs on the western bank of Turin's section of the river Po. Doumi was a twenty-four-year-old Moroccan immigrant from Casablanca. He had learnt enough Italian to break the ice with passers-by. But certain drinkers didn't want ice broken by foreigners. Various men from Toro's Granata Korps – including a man nicknamed Yeti, with a dog called Adolf – surrounded Doumi. The water was there, right next to them, silent and dark. It seemed almost unavoidable now. The men formed a line instead of a circle, just like they did in terrace rucks, raising their hands and insulting the enemy. Doumi was splashing in the water now. Bosh had opened up the store room of the bar and, with instinctive speed, empty bottles were passed from hand to hand. Soon they were being thrown at the Moroccan who, to avoid being hit, was heading further from the bank. He tried to get closer to the steps further downstream but someone threw a hoover at him and now he was in trouble: dazed, terrified, drunk, drowning.

Four men were later tried and sentenced for manslaughter. The judge, in his sentencing, wrote that 'there's no doubt that there was an elevated component of racial hatred'. But the ultras were inevitably defended by the brotherhood. The Granata Korps hung up a banner after the sentence denouncing 'Communist justice'. Because his son had been found guilty, Yeti's father – in a bizarre twist of logic – said, 'I'm ashamed to be Italian.'

The same year, in a match between Salernitana and Brescia, a fight broke out amongst the fifty or so Brescia ultras who had made the long journey south. A twenty-eight-year-old welder, Roberto Bani, was knocked out and, never emerging from his coma, died six days later.

19 November 1994: Brescia v. Roma

It was the middle of the night and something didn't look right. Amongst the Roma fans in the railway station, heading north to Brescia for the game, there were unfamiliar faces. There were Lazio fans like Corrado Ovidi and many of the scarves were black, not red-and-yellow. Maurizio Boccacci, a man with a thin face and heavy eyelids, was giving the orders. He was the founder of the Movimento Politico Occidentale (MPO) and wasn't a football fan. The MPO had recently been outlawed, accused of recreating the Fascist Party.

Many of the Roma fans were from an ultra group called Opposta Fazione ('The Opposing Faction'). Its slogan was *'meno calcio, più calci'* ('less football, more kickings'). Its leader, nick-named Rommel, had recently been arrested and sentenced for a bank job in which his accomplice, Kapplerino (a diminutive version of the name of the Nazi commander in Rome during the Second World War), and a security guard had been killed.

Two of the other leaders of Opposta Fazione, nicknamed la Rana ('the Frog') and Er Polpetta ('Meatball'), were also on the train. The former was a local councillor in the MSI, the latter an acolyte of Boccacci in the MPO. A burly man called Daniele De Santis was also there, as was a Roma youth player, Daniele Betti, who was suspended for the weekend's game and had decided to travel with the fans. The Roman police at the station realized something was amiss and phoned the Brescia *Questura* (police station) to warn them of trouble.

The men carried onto the train bags containing flags and banners, but also axes, knives, firecrackers, flares and home-made bombs. The train pulled out at 3.30 that morning, arriving at Brescia at midday on Sunday, 20 November. The men were herded onto buses and escorted to the stadium. As they left the buses, they shouted old fascist slogans like '*boia chi molla*' – 'the executioner for quitters' – and attacked the police.

For hours it was street warfare. Smoke from the flares mixed with police tear gas. Homemade bombs were thrown. Truncheons and axes clashed. The city's Deputy Commissioner, Giovanni Selmin, was stabbed in the abdomen and rushed to hospital. Another officer was injured by one of the rudimentary bombs. Cobbles and lampposts were ripped up and thrown at the *Carabinieri*.

Inside the stadium it was hardly more tranquil. Flares were thrown onto the pitch and into the home fans' stands. Fascist salutes were given in all directions, the straight arms forming a forest of flat erections. The game was goalless but no one was watching the game. During the hours of fighting, the apparent commander, the fascist Boccacci, repeatedly changed jackets to make it harder to recognize him.

There had, of course, been plenty of scuffles and fights in the past. They were an almost weekly occurrence. But this was very different. It was a ferocious and planned attack on the police by neo-fascists from both the Lazio and Roma fan groups. It was a show of strength, a declaration that from now on the terraces were the territory of the extreme right.

The investigation that followed tried to unravel the reasons behind the insurrection. It was partly, the investigators concluded, motivated by a change of ownership of Roma itself. The previous president, Giuseppe Ciarrapico, was politically sympathetic to the right and had gifted ultras tickets that they could then tout at a profit. The new president, Franco Sensi, broke the tradition and the riot was, perhaps, partly an attempt to threaten him into submission. But investigators also believed that the riot was a defiant response by Boccacci and his associates to the forced dissolution of both his MPO and a comparable organization, the Base Autonoma. It was a form of retribution against what they perceived to be a repressive state. There were other theories, too. That neo-fascists had deliberately chosen to stage a show of nationalist strength in the heartlands of the separatist Northern League. Others believed it was nothing more complicated than nihilistic violence.

Whatever the causes, the violence in Brescia in 1994 was one of the first warnings that the ultra movement was evolving. All movements shift and slide into something else, something which bears a clear relation to – but also a subtle rejection of – their former selves. With a movement as fractured and chaotic as that of the ultras, it was inevitable that, decades after the first group had been founded, the phenomenon would be altered. 'Alter', after all, was an etymological cousin of the word ultra. That subtle, slow mutation was also occurring because in some ways the ultras had, by 1994, slightly lost their *raison d'être*. The

1. Antonio Bongi (*right*) and Agostino Di Bartolomei at the Coppa Italia final, 1984

2. Cosenza from the Summit of the Pancrazio Hill

3. Cosenza support, 1980–81 season

4. Cosenza Vecchia

5. The extremist wing of Lazio support

6. Geppo

7. Matteo Salvini with the boss of the Milan Curva Sud

8. Nuclei Sconvolti – Luca (*far left*), Ciccio (*second left*), Piero (*white jacket*), Paride (*white hairband*), Padre Fedele (*red and blue hat*), Drainpipe (*far left front*)

9. Pastachina with Bergamini, Padre Fedele behind

10. Piero, Drainpipe and Paride in Africa

overleaf:

11. Police and ultras clash again

12. Juventus Curva Sud*

13. The Irriducibili give Roman salute to honour Mussolini

14. "You Haven't Done Anything to Us"

transgressions of the ultras – bingeing on banned substances, dressing up and dressing down, travelling to far-off cities – had become normalized within society by the late twentieth century. You no longer needed the support of the pack to transgress and to travel. What Umberto Eco wrote about the carnival could equally apply to that other carnival location, the *curva*: 'Carnival comic, the moment of transgression, can exist only if a background of unquestioned observance exists.'

The conundrum of how to remain outlaws in an indulgent world was answered loudly and eloquently by ultras from the far right. The 'gestures, actions and slogans' of fascism were still nominally illegal under the 1993 Mancino Law. The law was rarely applied but its existence persuaded neo-fascist ultras that they were now the only outsiders, and the guaranteed scorn of mainstream society when those gestures were photographed, filmed and publicized only reinforced that perception. Only amongst fascist ultra groups, they said, could you remain beyond the bourgeois. As the Western world appeared to enter the 'end of ideologies', this new generation of ultras would become ever more ideological. In a period of profound political confusion, many terraces began to offer the opposite: certainty and the absolute. If the mainstream was globalizing, with nations mixing and secularizing, these ultras would be the opposite: regional patriots, faithful to their long-lost cause.

Toying with the symbols of Nazi-fascism had long been used by contrarian rebels as a way to spite society or – as Hunter S. Thompson said of the Hells Angels' swastika fetish – as a 'gimmick to bug the squares'. The widespread sucking of teeth in the media every time certain ultra groups sang fascist songs or performed the straight-arm salute meant that they were both vilified and publicized, which is what they wanted. Many of the eloquent sociologists of Italian stadiums, like Giorgio Triani, felt that the fascist symbols were more a pose than a belief, used 'for their shock effect, for their terrorizing power, for their capacity to evoke cruel and bloody scenes'. Many ultras used an almost identical reasoning: it was a flicking of the finger to the system, nothing else. The ultra world, said the apologists, had always been full of *bricoleurs*, mixing-and-matching symbols from across the globe. Nothing was off-limits, they said, and never had been. Now there were simply more Roman salutes and images of the man they called 'Mascellone' (the 'big jaw').

Even the far-left ultras were sometimes slow to stop the drift. Many spoke of the *curva* as a *conca*, a 'bowl', so accommodating that it took in all the outcasts, even extremists from the right. If there were the odd grim symbol here and there, once a month, it was a sign not of the terraces' intolerance but the opposite. Many were slow to see that the movement was, by the mid-1990s, being deliberately hijacked by a very determined far right uninterested in tolerance.

That early insouciance, however, was soon replaced by alarm. Alessandro Dal Lago was one of the most perceptive observers of the Italian ultras. In 1990 he had published a book called *Description of a Battle*, in which, counter to the received wisdom, he suggested that the ultras' violence was largely ritualized, not real. Now, though, he admitted to perceiving something far darker: '... the exploitation by extreme right-wing groups... using the ultras as an electoral basin. We're talking about a leaden atmosphere, incarnated in runes, swastikas, Roman salutes, belligerence, racist banners and so on which have largely marginalized both the original ritualism, but also whatever remained or remains of left-wing symbology.'

The error had been to equate ritual with the superficial and assume, condescendingly, that ultras were so thick that they didn't really know what they were doing. In reality, in the quasi-religious world of the ultras, ritual was the opposite of superficial. It was a consequence of deep roots. Anyone who has participated in ultra meetings knows that the iconography of the terraces is never inadvertent or casual, but rather the result of fierce debate and argument. A central part of the Sunday ceremony at the stadium was the revelation of, and reverence towards, a group's symbols. So began a feedback loop in which the segregation of the 'deviant' group led to more radicalization, stigmatization and isolation, which in turn increased the deviancy. Societal scorn affirmed neo-fascists in their convictions and they upped the production of more fascist graffiti, banners and slogans, which only created more scorn and attracted recruits who saw in those symbols and slogans a reflection of their own politics.

For those on the right, however, it was as if the ultra world had finally found its true self. One of the new generation of Torino ultras, Roberto LoSpinosa, once said (in a documentary called *Ultras for Better or Worse*): '... the phenomenon itself is right-wing, as an idea it's right-wing.' One Hellas Verona ultra said that 'to be an ultra means to be right-wing. An ultra group is certainly right-wing, certainly fascist. It's the actual group which demands it. We are fascists and the terraces aren't places for democrats. The terrace is a place where you recognize leaders, where there are sergeants, lieutenants and captains. It's organized in a military way and the ultras are militarized.'

Having once offered a teenager-ish rejection of elders, this new generation of extremists positioned themselves as treasurers of the past, or at least their version of it. The names of ultra groups had always offered eloquent hints about how the movement saw itself and now many started calling themselves 'Tradition' or (as with the Roma group) 'Tradizione Distinzione'. There were other key words which spoke of their affiliations – 'honour' and 'loyalty' – and new songs whose lyrics described 'straight arms to the sky'. Paramilitary clothing became more common as did dressing identically: often black hoodies or green bomber jackets, partly because homogeneity made identification by the police far harder, but more because it lent a military appearance of foreboding unity. As Italy began to witness, for the first time in living memory, mass immigration (first from Albania and Eastern Europe, and then from all over the globe), a movement that seemed predicated on disdain for the other was appealing to a new generation.

The extremism of the terraces was given resonance because, after the stable, anti-fascist certainties of the First Republic, Italy was now grappling with historical debates dating back to the Second World War. The Establishment view that partisans were morally superior to those Italians who had remained loyal to Mussolini was being challenged by revisionist historians and right-wing politicians. The arrest of a German war criminal brought the debate suddenly to the fore. In 1994 an American TV station tracked down a former SS captain who had been living in Argentina for almost half a century. Erich Priebke had been stationed in Rome in the Second World War and was considered one of the officers responsible for one of the worst atrocities of the war on Italian soil, the execution of 335 Italians in the Fosse Ardeatine caves on the outskirts of Rome on 24 March 1944.

The killings were revenge for a partisan attack on German troops in Via Rasella in Rome, in which thirty-three soldiers had lost their lives. Adolf Hitler had ordered that thirty Italians (later reduced to ten) be executed for every single German killed. A Gestapo officer, Priebke was in charge of selecting the 330 Italians and he added an extra five, personally shooting at least two of them. He escaped from a prisoner-of-war camp in Rimini in 1946 and with the help of various priests had emigrated to Argentina.

In 1995 Priebke was extradited to Italy and stood trial for war crimes. The legal case continued for three years and Priebke's cause was enthusiastically taken up by those who saw the trial as a chance to rewrite Italian history. Priebke was depicted, by these revisionists, as a loyal soldier and the Italian partisans as murderous terrorists. Many of the ultras who had been in Brescia in 1994 were at the forefront of the campaign. In January 1996 they put up memorials in Via Rasella in honour of the dead German soldiers ('... victims of an anti-fascist and partisan slaughter perpetrated by vile assassins...'). In April 1996 they defaced the memorials to the victims of the Fosse Ardeatine murders. Surviving partisans and witnesses were threatened. In many ways the neo-fascists' position was absurd: their ideology twisted patriotism to the point at which they were defending a German war criminal and belittling the memories of hundreds of Italians. But it wasn't only mavericks and isolated eccentrics defending Priebke. His defence lawyer, Carlo Taormina, was a prominent politician in Berlusconi's Forza Italia party.

Throughout 1995 there were repeated and seemingly random attacks on foreigners in Rome – a Bengali man at Portonaccio, a Russian wearing a kippah in the Primavalle gardens – and ever-increasing antisemitic graffiti in cemeteries. In 1996, after Bologna had gained promotion to Serie A, there were anti-immigrant lynchings across the city, with eight North Africans hospitalized, one having been stabbed in the kidneys. It was very clear that the political wind had radically altered.

Even though he had been present at the Brescia–Roma match, Maurizio Boccacci wasn't an ultra, and it would be absurd to suggest that the rise of the far right was merely down to the ultras. But many extremist political movements – first Movimento Politico, Meridiano Zero and Base Autonoma, and later Forza Nuova and CasaPound – found fertile soil amongst the tough nuts of the terraces. In 1999, on 25 April – the day celebrating Italy's liberation from fascism – a banner held up by Roma ultras at the Roma–Parma match read: '25 April 1945 – when cowards proclaimed themselves heroes.'

Left-wing observers had often worried that football, more than religion, was Sunday's opium of the people, and that the two hours of contained fury depleted the energies and opportunities for real insurrection or liberation. But many felt that the left-wing intellectuals' scorn for the terraces in some ways created a vacuum that was filled by the far right. '... if today many terraces are orientated towards the extreme right,' wrote Andrea Ferreri, 'part of the responsibility lies with the indifference and criminalization that the political forces of the left have expressed towards the ultra world.' Whereas right-wing politicians had seen an electoral base, and a propaganda cauldron, in the terraces, the left had been strangely elitist towards those in the cheap seats.

29 January 1995, Genova

Simone Barbaglia was a troubled eighteen-year-old. He didn't really know where to call home. After his parents had separated, he lived with grandmother near the San Siro in Via Primaticcio. Later he moved back in with his mother, her new partner and their son. He had been excluded from school trips for bad behaviour and was often failed at the end of a school year. He had quit education in his mid-teens and eventually got a job mowing lawns for a maintenance firm.

Even as a fan, he didn't know where he belonged. In his youth he had followed Juventus but as Milan had recently supplanted Juventus as the most exciting side in Italy, Simone had switched and become a Milanista. He had drifted towards a splinter group of the famous Brigate Rossonere, Brigate 2, which was much further to the right. He was an informal member of a sub-group of that splinter called Gruppo del Barbour, because of the jackets they wore. The leader of the Brigate 2 splinter group was nicknamed '*il Chirurgo*' ('the surgeon'). He was an accountant with a history of football-related knife crime throughout the 1980s.

Milan used to give out hundreds of free and discounted tickets to ultra groups, and the Surgeon would sell his batch to aspiring ultras every Thursday in a bar called Il Sorriso ('The Smile') in Bovisa, to the north of the city. Simone went along and bought his ticket for Sunday's game against Genoa for 30,000 lire (about eight pounds).

The next day Simone asked to borrow a butterfly-knife from a mate. 'I want to cut up a Genoano,' he said. Milan and Genoa had once been twinned, partly because both sets of fans were traditionally left-wing, but that twinning had ended and there were often fights between the two sets of fans, most recently in September 1993. Simone took his friend's knife home with him that night and practised flicking it open.

On the Sunday morning, the Surgeon and his crew didn't get the 'special' train laid on for Milan fans. They wanted to go under the radar and got the 11.50 instead. There was the usual boasting and boozing on the way, and by the time the splinter group got out at Genova Brignole, they were excited and singing loudly. It was a five-minute walk along the Bisagno river to the famous stadium.

Claudio Spagnolo, known as 'Spagna', was hanging outside the famous *gradinata nord*. Here, on Via Spensley, everyone was wearing the red-and-blue of Genoa. Spagna was twenty-four and during the summer had worked with his aunt in an estate agents in Porto Rotondo, in Sardinia. He liked reggae and hung out in the Zapata social centre in the city.

At 1.40 p.m. the splinter group – under the command of the 'Surgeon' – moved in. It wasn't a well-organized charge. Simone rushed forwards with his hands in his pockets. He pulled out the knife and opened it up. Simone later described what he was thinking: 'The idea of being seen running away by Carlo [the 'Surgeon'], and showing him that I lacked courage, was unbearable. If I pulled out a knife I would have given to Carlo a demonstration of my courage. I cared what he thought about me...'

Simone jabbed his blade at Spagna, who was off-balance having tried to disarm him with a kick. Spagna fell to the ground, bleeding profusely. Within minutes he was dead.

The disgust at that killing was unprecedented. As soon as word got around, the Genoa ultras removed all their banners. Fabio Fazio, hosting a live programme about football, abandoned the studio. The match between Genoa and Milan was postponed.

The Milan fans were kept inside the stadium. Simone and friends swapped jackets and scarves. One of them chucked his knife in the toilet. Having identified and photographed everyone, the police decided to let them get their coaches home to avoid reprisals within Genova. They arrested Simone at dawn the following day.

In place of the postponed matches a week later, a summit took place that Sunday, 5 February 1995, between various ultra groups in Genova. The slogan was 'Basta Lame, Basta Infami' ('Enough of knives, enough of villains'). But the statement released to coincide with that conference, and published in the *Gazzetta dello Sport*, offered as much defiance as it did contrition. The ultras condemned 'these villains' and 'this vile behaviour'. 'We shout enough,' they said, renouncing 'the fashion for twenty against two or three with Molotovs and knives.' But at the same time they wrote that 'if living as an ultra is truly a way to live, let's get our balls out'. They warned that 'the police will be waiting only to see us finished. Let's unite against those who want to kill the entirety of the ultra world, a world free and true despite all its contradictions.'

Barbaglia was sentenced to fourteen and a half years for the killing. Outside the stadium there's now a column of eleven massive blocks of white stone remembering the Genoa fan. Nearby, a plaque uses the same words as a Genoa banner after the killing: 'To live in the hearts of who remains is not to die. Bye Spagna.'

1996, Catania

Michele Spampinato was as skinny and tense as a piano wire. He had sharp elbows and fast feet, though his face was wider: big ears, a wide nose and a blink-and-you-miss-it smile.

He had grown up in the Catania suburb of San Cristoforo. It was a suburb close to the centre but completely different: instead of the Roman ruins and Vincenzo Bellini's grand baroque architecture, here there were narrow alleys, crumbling balconies and aluminium shacks. Wires and pipes were strung haphazardly from one block to the next. It smelt of fish, fruit and tobacco. But there was a grass-roots panache to the place. '*La Moda alle Puttane*,' said one spray-painted wall, '*Lo Stile agli Ultras*' ('[Leave] fashion to the whores, and the style to the ultras').

The umbrella ultra organization in Catania was called the Falange d'Assalto Rossoazzurra, the 'Red-and-Blue Assault Phalanx'. It had been founded in 1979 by a short fascist called Ciccio. Everyone called him Ciccio Fascista or else Ciccio Falange. The group had a red-and-blue drawbridge for a door just next to Castello Ursino. Ciccio Fascista liked the fact that Catania's terrace had always been politically black. Catania football club had originally been called the 'Associazione Fascista Calcio Catania'.

But Spampinato was beginning to peel away from that historic group. He wanted to do things differently. He had gathered a small crew of people from the tough suburbs who followed him because he was so decisive and he made them love where they lived. 'How can you not love a city,' he says in his double-quick manner, 'which allows you to ski around a volcano, where one side there's an eruption, and the other side the sea?' All the kids from other tough suburbs liked hanging around him.

Spampinato wasn't fixated on the name of his emerging group. That refusal to get attached to a name was part of his attempt to avoid a Mafia-ization of the terraces. 'There's a great wound here,' he says, 'which is the Mafia. There's no point pretending it doesn't exist. It's rooted in the suburbs and every suburb is the representation of its family. You've grown up with that. You live your suburb as if it's a group, with that name, and in another there's another name, and you bring that mentality into the terraces.'

Spampinato wanted to avoid labels that divided the red-and-blue faithful. If you concentrated only on the purity of the

Catania cause, he felt, there would be no divisions. 'Ever since the 1990s,' he remembers, 'we've tried to do away with banners.' It was almost as if this tense man, then in his early twenties, was a puritan, smashing the images and icons that got in the way of the true object of adoration.

Soon, he and his men were meeting up not in Castel Ursino, but in Piazza Dante, in the open air under the oak tree by the wall of the monastery. There you could get a bottle of beer for less than a pound and if you didn't have the dosh, someone else would pay or you could put it on a tab. Spampinato bossed those weekly meetings. He had a stringy energy about him that could whip people who were offside. He would roam around while talking, stare at the troops with disdain, or pick a fight with someone and make an example of them. He would seem to sulk, going silent and brooding. But then suddenly he would tell someone to shut up, and tell them why. If the guy kept inter-rupting, Spampinato would take him outside the circle and teach him how to behave. That was the only time you could take your eyes off him.

Once Spampinato decided the line, discussion was over. He would make up his mind in a split second, interrupting one cause and ruling for another. (The group was eventually dubbed 'The Decisives'.) His voice was what settled it. When he said 'this is an order', there was silence.

Spampinato had grown up on the legend of a team punished and pimped by sporting authorities on the mainland. But there were moments of glory too, like the time Catania unexpectedly beat Inter 2–0 in 1961, denying them the *scudetto*. The com-mentator screamed '*clamoroso al Cibali*' ('sensational news' from Catania's ground), a phrase now used any time there's an astonishing shock.

Back then, the stadium's custodian was a gruff man called Angelo Grasso. He was there for thirty years, and every year the insults he put up with got worse. People broke his windows and urinated on his little house from the stand above. In 1983 he lost it, loading up a shotgun and firing as fast as he could into the Curva Sud. He injured thirty-two fans and killed one.

Catanesi have always felt a bit like underdogs. They think their city should be the capital of Sicily (as it used to be under the Aragons). But there's only ever been bad luck. Catania has been destroyed nine times, either by earthquake or by the lava of the mighty Mount Etna, whose snowy peak comes into view on every corner. After each disaster, the Catanesi reconstructed their city, trying to rebuild it in the same place, with the same squares. In the little fort at the end of the long hill away from the main square, there's a phoenix with the inscription '*Melior de Cinere Surgo*' – 'I will arise better from the ashes'.

Perhaps that's why Catania has an obsessional support for the team. It's a way to identify with this beautiful, scarred city. The older fans will tell you that the club was co-founded by a baron, Gaetano Ventimiglia, who went on to work with Alfred Hitchcock… or that, like the Great Torino of the 1940s, Catania too had had a Hungarian coach, Géza Kertész. He had died in the Second World War and was remembered as the 'Schindler of Catania', having tried to rescue various Jewish families. It's a support which always bleeds into superstition: a hole has been smashed into the Perspex of the players' tunnel so that salt can be thrown on the players to bring good luck.

Spampinato became furious when he saw people supporting other teams. There was only one way to change that. 'A sort of repression' – he doesn't miss a beat – 'an imposition that helps people never forget that here you don't support Milan or

Juventus. Here there's only Catania. You do that by numbers, gathering people, saying "here there won't be a party [for a Milan or Juventus *scudetto*] because otherwise we'll give it to you".' 'Those who aren't with us,' Spampinato liked saying, 'are automatically our enemies.' If you wanted to become the top dog of the terrace – the person to lead the singing and stand at the centre – you had to fight the other local groups too. And you had to prove you were somehow more ultra than they were: harder, more extreme, more radical. Spampinato loved the adrenalin of hand-to-hand fights and the effect it could have on the loser: 'We expected respect, and if we didn't get it, we imposed it.'

That attachment to the shirt meant that the Catanesi ultras were amongst the first to refuse to chant the names of individual players. After the 'Bosman ruling' of 1995, footballers were allowed to leave clubs when their contracts expired, meaning that many became far more itinerant than before or, according to fans, increasingly disloyal. Spampinato decided that no individual should be applauded or eulogized. 'Sporting behaviour doesn't inhabit our latitudes,' he says. 'Zola once scored a goal here and people were clapping, and we got up en masse and were practically about to chuck them off the balcony.'

Spampinato was always fretting about betrayal. He said he loved the city like the murdered anti-Mafia journalist Giuseppe Fava loved it: '... like a whore who uses all her charms to drive you mad, but who has betrayed you thousands of times.' Being an ultra was nothing to do with sport. 'I really don't love football,' he told me once. 'If you ask me about Serie A, I just don't know. Juventus will be top, because it's always top, but I limit myself to the division where Catania plays.' And the team was for him a representation of what he really loved: this city where, he said, 'You're always in contact with people. You're at home in any home.'

He was worried that outside players would betray the city. The greatest honour for those on the terraces came once, in Messina, when Catania's away-strip was the same white as the home team, so the Catania players had to borrow red-and-blue shirts from the fans. 'The players,' wrote Spampinato in his decent memoir, *Quando Saremo Tutti Nella Nord*, must 'be aware of the breath on their neck... They must memorize our faces and think that they will find us in front of them every time their effort is insufficient.'

Sometimes the targets were worryingly precise. One banner was held up saying that a particular city councillor was 'in the cross-hairs'. But often the banners were surprisingly erudite, like the long Latin warning they held up (repeating words spoken to Frederick II): *'Noli Offendere Patriam Agathae Quia Ultrix Iniurarium Est'* ('Don't offend the land of Agatha [their patron saint] because she is the avenger of every injustice').

For all their attachment to the sacred *maglia*, the shirt, Spampinato's crew were casuals. They didn't wear football tops, but everyday clothes. Many ultra groups, from the mid-1990s onwards, were camouflaging themselves amongst the masses in this way. It was partly fashion but also a strategic decision. Wearing mufti made it harder for police, and opposition ultras, to identify them.

Spampinato's crew began to get a reputation as one of the toughest in Italy. It was partly because to get to any game outside Sicily, the Catanesi had to get a ferry in Messina and that sort of bottle-neck was always good for a ruck. Amongst all the minibuses and cars queueing in one crowded loading area, the Catanesi always knew exactly which teams were going where. They weren't happy with chance meetings. The Decisi deliberately turned up five or six hours before an away game, waiting outside the stadium for the rival firm to show up. 'It was a swagger,' he remembers. 'You step into a city not yours and say "We're here, we're Catania in your house" – he's jabbing two fingers onto the beer mat – "we're strolling around so if you want to confront us, here we are…"'

They had look-outs in stations and airports, ready to warn Spampinato of a rival's approach. They printed fake tickets to allow people into games, thus forcing the police to accommodate them in sections reserved for the opposition, who were then attacked. They wore balaclavas: 'We became an army without a face,' remembers Spampinato. In a match against Messina, the throwing of stones, paper bombs and flares was so incessant that a Messina fan, Antonino Currò, died.

One summer Spampinato and his mates attacked the Juventus ultras who, awaiting a pre-season friendly, were eating and drinking under the Catania terraces. Spampinato smashed a beer bottle over the head of one of them and the rest attacked hard, capturing the Fighters' banner. In ultra lore, if your herald is taken, the group should dissolve but what happened next – according to Spampinato – was that the Fighters paid €20,000 to a mafioso in order to have their herald returned. Spampinato gave it back at a tense meeting but only once his group had cut it up and defecated all over it.

The Decisi wasn't the only group in those years. Catania had the Sostenitori, the ANR (the 'Non-Recognized Association'), Irriducibili, Falange, Ultras Ghetto, Gioventù, Indians, Drunks, Club Angelo Massimino, Pazzi, Zafferana Rossazzurra, and so on… But Spampinato was now at the head, leading the charge. His troops united under a banner saying 'A Sostegno di una Fede' ('Supporting a faith'). Once a decision was taken by the Decisi directorate, the line was imposed. Yet, at the same time, there was such energy and spontaneity that it was almost impossible to give direction to the crowd. 'The group doesn't exist any more,' Spampinato wrote of those years. 'The mob dominates, and it's the mob which dominates itself.'

Present Day, Carpi v. Cosenza

We're supposed to leave at midnight, so people start rolling up at the squatted HQ an hour or two before. There are a few new women here tonight, one successfully winning at pool as the men are paying more attention to her body than the blue baize. She keeps changing the rules but they don't seem to mind as long as she hangs around.

The megaphone is out and we're warming up our voices. Mouse is drinking rum so fast he's already sunk half a bottle. He's up and singing, smashing a chair on the ground so that it rattles the rhythm: 'How beautiful it is, when I get out of the house...'

As usual, there are lots of quiet, sober people on the fringes, smiling on. Those with stadium bans pass by to wish everyone good luck on the long journey north. A good-natured shouting match takes place over money, as we realize we haven't got half the dosh we need to get to Emilia and back. The plan is to drive through the night, cut across to the east coast via Basilicata and maybe have breakfast in Ancona. Then head further north, towards Bologna and beyond.

'Be at the ground by ten,' says Half-a-Kilo.

A couple of people slap the back of his neck, laughing. 'We won't get there until half-time. Not with Rosario driving.'

There's an argument about who should go in which minibus, and you can see people manoeuvring to get in the one with the pool hustler. Those arguments overlap with the money arguments until there's absolute confusion. Chill is driving Skinny Monica in his BMW – that's all he cares about – so he refs the discussion.

We leave at half-midnight but can't find Left-Behind. He's not answering his phone, so we drive around the city looking for him. On every other block, Rosario sees a mate and shouts out the window: 'Where's Left-Behind?'

We park up and wait in one place. An hour goes by. Then we move on and wait somewhere else. Finally, he shows up. Rosario shouts at him but Left-Behind says something quietly and we go and look for Egg. We eventually hit the motorway after two in the morning.

Rosario drives fast but doesn't wear a seatbelt, so for the next twelve hours there's a beeping in the van. Rosario gets to choose the music, too, and the only station he can pick up in the mountains plays cheese-tastic pop interspersed with late-night loners trying to chat-up other loners live on radio. The tunnels are just long enough for you to fall asleep when the radio loses reception, but as you emerge from that tunnel the cheese is back in your right lobe. He's slappy with the pedals too, so that you're thrown around the bus like rizlas in the wind and pretty soon we all give up any idea of sleep. Boozy Suzy passes round what's left of the second bottle of rum. Left-Behind scrunches up his buds in a spiked grinder and chain-smokes.

It's mid-morning by the time we reach Ancona, that kink halfway up the Adriatic ('*ankón*' is the Greek for elbow). No one has slept but exhaustion is strangely inebriating. Most of us have been drinking all the way north, so can't tell the difference between tired and tipsy, but even the straights seem red-eyed and wired, ready to have fun when they pile out of their vans.

The woman in the bar looks nervous as thirty Calabrians pile in. But she sells all her pastries in five minutes and relaxes once she's seen the cash. We loaf around on chairs, wondering whether the city's famous white monument to the fallen – a circle of columns and steps – should be bulldozed because it was built during the *ventennio*, the Mussolini years.

By then we're refuelled and start warming up our voices. Within a couple of hours we're in Carpi. It's supposed to be one of the Italy's prettiest towns but we see only the police. They're waiting by the motorway toll-booths, and pull us over. They insist we wait until all the other minibuses are here. 'It's just us,' says Rosario, playing dumb. The police don't move, knowing others are on their way. 'We want to get to the game,' whine the troops. It's almost kick-off. The police are standing around ignoring us. We hang around another twenty minutes. We've travelled through the night to miss most of the first half.

As the other minibuses arrive, the police finally let us move out. The sirens are loud as they escort us to the ground. Those near the windows lean out, leering at the smart signoras in their fur coats. As we're singing, people bang out the rhythm, bouncing empties together so hard that the bottom drops off one bottle and sends glass across the road.

It's only when you finally get inside the ground – we're on a thin ribbon above what looks like a velodrome ramp – that you see how many Cosentini there are. Many of those who live in the North have rolled up. There are toughs, young kids, families, friends. Donata Bergamini, the sister of the murdered midfielder from the 1980s, is here being hugged by fans. We've come together far from home and it feels defiant. We're the away fans, the underdogs, the scorned Southern 'peasants' – but here we are, singing loud and raising the red-and-blue flags in a foreign land. It feels like a conquest – contained and caged but a daring trespass nonetheless.

The game finishes 1–1. Cosenza equalize in the dying minutes of the match so it feels almost like a victory. We're still singing as we walk through the car park. As we drive past the station we can see Cosentini singing on the platforms, other passengers smiling at them as the police rush in to stop the noise.

It's a dizzying, exhausting experience. It's euphoric when you're in the midst of it but then, the weariness and head-aches kick in. All the rhetoric is about defiance but perhaps there's no rebellion to it at all. Maybe we're nothing more than caged birds.

Ciccio Bucci's upbringing in San Severo, in Puglia, had been unpretentious. His father was a school caretaker, his mother a housewife. He had two brothers, and the house was noisy. Bucci was always on the look-out for an opening and his parents seemed indulgent of his impish ways. They knew he was a bit of a rogue but he was always cheerful and fun. And he wasn't a bad boy. He was in the scouts and attended a technical secondary school to study book-keeping.

His friends called him a '*trascinatore*', an 'inspirer' or 'insti-gator', and he was always coming up with a plan. Tall, thin and dressed smartly in cheap clothes, Bucci tried to be friends with everyone. He was elected college representative but also hung out with teachers, betting on football results in the bar. He was popular and persuasive, even if you were never quite sure what plan he was hatching next. The one certainty was that any time Juventus was playing somewhere in the South, Bucci would find a ticket and go and see them. He sometimes travelled north, to watch them in Turin with one of his brothers.

Every time he stood on the terraces, he made friends. He had that salesman's ability to make people think he was being generous to them. Soon the people he met were being generous back, offering Bucci a bed in Turin for the night or a lift to the stadium for next Sunday.

After a few years of travelling to Turin for games, Bucci decided to move there permanently. But that first winter was tough. After the steep, cobbled alleys of the South, he found the flat, perpendicular boulevards of Turin dull. The Piedmontese seemed cold and up-tight to him. They didn't have the easy-going good humour of his mates from San Severo. He felt they looked down on him, not just because he was a Southerner but because he had become something of a hustler.

He hadn't found a job as an accountant and so used his energy and imagination to make ends meet. He set up market stalls, standing on the back of trucks with a wrap-around mike, extolling the virtues of a plastic kitchen gadget or a revolutionary cleaning cloth. Soon he got into counterfeit merchandise, selling Juventus shirts and scarves sourced cheaply outside the city. He became another character on the streets and the terraces just trying to get by.

Sourcing and selling tickets to his friends down South, and to friends of friends, was another little earner. He became a fixer to his mates from San Severo who wanted to see a game at the Delle Alpi stadium. He was an amateur travel agent, too, organizing buses and trains and cheap hotels. His reputation grew. If you wanted a ticket, everyone knew that Bucci was your man. He made friends because he was more a fun chancer than a cut-throat tout. He had started to make good money and over the years learnt to become a *bon viveur* in a city renowned for its fine wines, chocolates and aromatic drinks.

Because he was trying to source tickets, he became friends with a group that always seemed to have a few to sell: the Drughi. Soon he was doing the same as many others, getting tickets in bulk and selling them on at a profit wherever he could. He started hanging in their club, three bus stops beyond the end of the metro in Mirafiori, a poor suburb to the south of the city. He loved it in there. Even the ceiling was tiled black-and-white. Everywhere, there were photos of players in black-and-white. There were fist-high piles of tickets and bank notes, a dog called Snatch and a huge poster of Benito Mussolini. The more of their tickets he sold, the more friendly they became. For the first time since moving north, he felt like he had found a family. Many of the men were from the South and all, like him, loved the 'old lady' of Italian football.

There was a power vacuum within the Drughi in the late 1990s. The group's leader, Pino Coldheart, was in prison after his botched armed robbery and so Bucci rose through the ranks fast, quickly earning himself a gold star on the beam of the group's HQ for ticket sales. In many ways this ultra gang was akin to a sales force, with each member selling as many tickets as they were able and adding to the public, and private, coffers.

Quite soon Bucci was living the high life. He was always on his phone – he had 3,000 contacts stored in it – and the thing would ring all hours of day and night with people begging him for tickets. He could almost name his price. He had settled down, too, outside the city, with a woman called Gabriella. They had a son called Fabio, and lived in a flat in Beinette opposite a metal recycling depot.

———

9 January 1998

Nobody called him Claudio. Hardly anyone even knew his surname was Marsili. Everyone knew him just as Cupido.

The police knew his real name though. In over fifteen years of 'militancy' on the terraces, he had been arrested for theft, public disorder and drug-dealing. His rooms were covered with far-right symbols, including Celtic crosses and swastikas.

By 1998 he was thirty-two. He had never worked but had got by doing jobs for Diabolik's Irriducibili. He had become one of the leading figures in that firm. But he always had his own income streams too. On 9 January he arrived with a mate on a stolen white moped outside the Cariplo Bank in Largo Boccea, a main road in the west of Rome. His aim was the same as always: disarm the guard, take him hostage, bring him inside the bank and get him to open up the safe. Cupido pulled down his balaclava, took out his Smith & Wesson .38 and walked quickly up to the guard.

This time the guard, from the Mondialpol security firm, was quicker on the draw. He fired his Beretta repeatedly. Cupido fell onto a car and slid to the pavement. He was pronounced dead at the hospital shortly afterwards.

At the next Lazio game a large banner was unfurled: 'Claudio always in our hearts.' '*Sangue paga sangue*' was sprayed on the wall outside the bank: 'blood pays for blood.' As usual, the elevated rhetoric of the ultras seemed to suggest that the criminal was the victim. At Cupido's funeral a banner read: 'Three villainous shots have taken away our friend.'

Over the years a number of ultras – like Il Drago – had been involved in bank jobs. What was surprising was less the fact that there were armed robbers amongst the ranks of the football fans on the terraces, than the ability of those terraces to invert everything you thought you knew about right and wrong. The thief was legitimized and the institution demonized, so that, like Bertolt Brecht, they seemed to ask 'What is the robbery of a bank compared to the founding of a bank?' 'I believe,' the ultra-defending lawyer, Lorenzo Contucci, once wrote, 'that the number of those with criminal records is higher in parliament than amongst those who frequent the terraces.'

24 May 1999: Piacenza v. Salernitana

It was the last day of the Serie A championship. Piacenza only needed a draw to avoid relegation, whereas Salernitana needed to win. It ended in a 1–1 draw, with the players fighting as they came off the pitch, and the ultras smashing up toilets, cars and coaches. Fifteen hundred Salernitana fans were herded onto a special train, escorted by only ten police officers. It left at 8 p.m. but it was a tortuous journey because the emergency brake was repeatedly pulled. At various stations people piled out to smash windows. A fire extinguisher was thrown at another train. By 8 a.m. the following day the train was south of Naples, entering a 10-kilometre-long tunnel. Someone lit a fire and the wind of the tunnel, coming through the broken windows, fanned it. Suddenly, the fifth carriage was ablaze. A twenty-one-year-old firefighter, Simone Vitale, went in and dragged out a few people but the last time he went in, he was overwhelmed by the fumes. One eye-witness said that the tunnel 'seemed like an enormous cigar vomiting smoke'. Vitale and three other men – another twenty-one-year-old and two teenagers – died. Following the tragedy, a new 'observatory' was established: the Osservatorio Nazionale sulle Manifestazioni Sportive (National Observatory on Sporting Events). It was intended to gather intelligence and advice in order to avert any future tragedies.

The timing of a spiritual ceremony is an integral part of its meaning. A monastic day is divided by the liturgy of the hours. The rise and fall of the religious year is measured by saints' days and feast days, each marking time, reminding us of the passage of seasons and of lives.

Kick-off for Serie A games had always been Sunday afternoon. That was the ritual for decades, as much a part of the weekly rhythm as work, meals and, maybe, Mass. But around the turn of the millennium it felt to many football fans as if the hands had been ripped from the footballing clock. Because of the advent of pay-per-view TV in the late 1990s, games were played at ridiculous times and places.

Two broadcasting companies paved the way: Tele+ (a French company in which Silvio Berlusconi's Fininvest had shares) and Stream (set up by four of the most powerful club presidents). Then, in 2003, Rupert Murdoch bought both companies to found Sky Italia. To maximize viewing figures, and thus advertising revenue, Sky Italia needed a big game every evening, not all happening at the same time on the same day. Matches were now spread across the week like butter across toast. It suited everyone. Money was flooding into the game from TV deals, attracting better players, giving fans the hope of promotion or even trophies, and increasing the salaries of the suits who had once put money into clubs rather than take it out.

Like all fundamentalists, the ultras were constantly on the lookout for heresy. They felt that their liturgical calendar had been sold to the highest bidder. It seemed as if their absolutism – presence at every game – had been relativized. You could now claim a presence, of sorts, watching the match from your armchair. You could certainly see the game better in your slippers. The old way of being a spectator – as participant in, even a rival to, the event – was being replaced by a static, stay-at-home zapper. Between 1990 and 1999 the average attendance in Serie A games had been 31,000. By the 2006–07 season it had plummeted to below 20,000. In the 1988–89 season ticket sales had accounted for 50 per cent of the income of Cosenza football club; by 1990–91 it was only 20 per cent.

The staggered games are called, in Italian, a 'broken calendar' (the same word is used to describe the meat in a casserole – *spezzatino*). It is an eloquent description of the rupture that television created. Staggered games meant that the league tables rarely spoke clearly any more. There were now asterisks and double asterisks to explain which club had played one, or two, games fewer. The excitement of contemporaneity had disappeared, as games were brought forward (the *anticipo*) and deferred (the *posticipo*).

For ultras, television's ability to slot games where they wanted had many disadvantages. They were less likely to bump into rival ultras in service and railway stations, all heading across the peninsula at the same times. They were forced to travel thousands of kilometres on work days, meaning that 'presence' became harder for those with regular jobs and that the 'oceanic' away-days were a thing of the past. As numbers dwindled, it was only the radical rump that remained.

The televising of so many games, however, had the advantage

of publicizing the banners. Now one could disseminate a message not just to a half-empty stadium but to a whole nation. The Teramo ultras made their feelings clear with a banner to the footballing superpowers who moved matches with mathematical calculation: 'Anticipate your death, postpone your funeral.' Catania urged 'boycott Sky to reinforce a way of thinking'. The Bologna ultras had a banner saying: 'Football: for us passion, for you television.'

Matches weren't just sloshed across the week. Absurdly, the Italian Supercoppa was once played in Tripoli, in Libya, for reasons of commercial expansion. Quite often games were moved for reasons of public order. The most exciting matches – the heated derbies and grudge games between enemies – were now deliberately timetabled to make it hard for fans to be present. On 9 April 2001 the match between Fiorentina and Roma was moved – by the Prefect – from the weekend to a Monday in order to avoid the usual street fights between fans. (In Italy only hairdressers have Mondays off.) The rearranging of that match was, for the ultras, the umpteenth example of Establishment scorn. But the response was humorous. In the stadium the 8,000 Romanisti who managed to take a day off work to support the red-and-yellow of their team unfurled a large *striscone* saying, in dialect: 'We're all hairdressers.'

One of the best banners not only lamented the shredding of the liturgical calendar of football, but also celebrated the Cosenza ultras' notoriously erratic, rebellious timekeeping: 'We arrived late... or maybe too early. Either way, our time doesn't resemble yours.' The Reggiani wrote '*Questo calcio ci fa sky-fo*', a play on words that suggested that they found this new football 'disgusting', misspelling it to include Sky. The ever-eloquent Atalantini wrote plaintively: 'Give us back our Sundays.'

It was as if those fans who believed in presence were suddenly replaced as the customer of choice. The share of a club's income from ticket sales plummeted as that from television deals, and thus advertising, increased. The organized fans who had always been faithful felt, understandably, cheated. They were reduced to being a colourful and noisy relish to add to the televisual offering. So it wasn't, perhaps, surprising that in 1999 an ultra manifesto was agreed by many groups and published on the excellent ASRomaUltras website. It made many demands, most of which would appear eminently sensible to even the most mild-mannered fan: transfers should take place only in summer; games should all be played on the same day, at the same time; football owners should only be allowed to own one team; shirts should be numbered from one to eleven, and so on.

The trouble was that the ultras were often both the resistance to, but also a reflection of, the sport around which they gathered. Theorists have often spoken about the 'deludification' of football, about the ways in which play (hard-fought but fun, beautiful because pointless) can be transformed into something nastily serious (desperation for points and all sorts of secondary gains). The ultras followed a similar trajectory: the early years had been characterized by – their favourite word – *goliardia*. It was a playful, Bacchanalian party. Even the violence was (it was this which, they said, endowed it with 'purity') meaningless. But the ultra world, too, became 'deludified'. Violence was increasingly serving the purposes it more usually does (power and money).

Many ultras are adamant that they have never made money out of their faith. 'Here', they all say, 'there's no tripe for the cats' – a saying that implies chronic poverty. It's undeniably true that the vast majority lose, rather than rake in, cash. But with the industrialization of the game certain ultras realized that para-military gangs could turn a tidy profit. Over the years many businesses like 'Punto Roma' or 'An Infinite Love' would pop up offering 'services' – tickets, tour packages and merchandising – to fans. In Milano, having sealed a non-aggression pact, the two leaders of the rival terraces – Franco Caravita and 'the Baron' – opened a clothing shop together, 'Mondo Ultrà', in Via Cesariano.

Nowhere was that new commercialism more evident than amongst Lazio's Irriducibili. To begin with Diabolik and his crew were just selling their Lazio gear out of cardboard boxes and temporary gazebos. Business was booming. They had no overheads and yet they had queues of people wanting to pay for their clobber. The price differential between their counterfeit shirts and the real thing was huge, and it was, anyway, far cooler to have a Lazio shirt with the Irriducibili's Mr Enrich logo than the Puma one. The idea that local lads from Rome were taking on a global clothing company only added to the allure. In addition, those from the streets knew what the very latest pose was. Yuri was put in charge of the marketing operation and, he said, 'It's a very smart management. We're very attentive to the trend of the moment.' Nor did they have rivals. If anyone else set up a stall without their permission, they were dealt with. One man, who knew Diabolik, says that he was all smiles until, out of the blue, he would pull out a pistol.

The distance between what the Irriducibili said they were doing and what they actually were doing grew ever larger. When Lazio's owner tried to cash in on his star player, Beppe Signori, by accepting a 25-billion-lire offer from Parma, the Irriducibili rioted. Windows were smashed and skips set alight. They threatened a fans' strike for the whole of the following season. It was true, obviously, that fans were desperate not to lose the diminutive striker to a Serie A rival, but Diabolik and his crew fuelled the riot for other reasons. It was a show of muscle to the owner. They wanted more free tickets to matches and a slice of the stewarding contracts. Diabolik realized that hundreds of hot-headed ultras could easily be bounced into outraged riots and indignant strikes, so he encouraged the mayhem. The sale of Signori was called off.

Over the next few years the Lazio owner, Cragnotti, was repeatedly forced to give in to the Irriducibili. In 1999 he announced that the ultras would have to pay to watch the team train at Formello and that away-day packages could only be organized through the Francorosso tour company (not the ultras). One of the Irriducibili beat up the man Cragnotti had sent to negotiate with them and both proposals were dropped. The Irriducibili could continue working as tour operators, making money out of their own fans.

In 2000 the Irriducibili were even given occasional gigs organizing the stewards in the Stadio Olimpico. The awarding of stewarding contracts became, over the years, one of the key areas of collusion between clubs and ultras. It was obvious that if the ultras were given the stewarding contract, there would be no trouble, and if they weren't given it, there would be. It was just another way to keep them sweet. It wasn't only club owners who could feel the heat. In their pomp, the Irriducibili had 6,500 paid-up members. On one occasion (unhappy with its reporting) they all boycotted the *Gazzetta dello Sport*, reducing its sales, so they said, by five thousand. They became an important political lobby, too, visited by aspiring politicians like the former Lazio player Luigi Martini, who was standing as a candidate with the right-wing National Alliance.

By then they also had a fanzine, *The Voice of the North*, selling thousands of copies every week. Soon there was a radio station of the same name. The singular 'voice' was telling: there was only one line. If anyone cheered or applauded during a 'fan strike' they were hospitalized. Not even a *Daspo* (stadium ban) could keep Diabolik away from the ground. One eye-witness from the time remembers a policeman seeing Diabolik, then banned, strutting along the athletics track around the pitch as if he owned it.

'At least don't make it so obvious,' a policeman said, suggesting Diabolik should keep a lower profile.

'Fuck off, don't fucking break my balls,' the *capo-ultra* snapped.

He seemed to enjoy an astonishing level of protection from the police. One police union representative complained that Diabolik had the phone numbers of police functionaries and went in and out of police stations 'in a way that not even I can do'. 'There was,' one Lazio ultra remembers, 'a total coexistence at every level.'

Nobody knows how many free tickets the Irriducibili were receiving but given the stadium capacity was over 70,000, it seems safe to assume they were getting hundreds of complimentary tickets from the club. When Diabolik stood at the turnstiles, he could get anyone into the ground, whether they had a ticket or not.

These were years in which the Irriducibili became famous for antisemitism. In a derby match against Roma in 1999 they displayed a banner with the taunt: 'Auschwitz is your homeland, the gas-chambers your houses.' In 2000 they wrote a dedication to a Serbian war-criminal, Zeljko Raznatovic: 'Honour to the Tiger Arkan.' It was, wrote Valerio Marchi, 'the umpteenth signal of a taking of power, in the terraces all over Italy, of a generation of hooligans evermore attracted by political extremism, by now prevalently orientated to the most racist and radical right.'

When those and many similar banners became national scandals, the Irriducibili felt misunderstood. They had always tried to avoid using swastikas (they did so only on one occasion, against the far-left ultras of Livorno). The Irriducibili leaders, in fact, willingly denounced Nazism but there was always, very quickly, a 'but'. 'I personally thoroughly condemn the Nazi crimes,' said Paolo Arcivieri, 'but at the same time I'm against the people of Israel who I consider intolerant and incongruent...' Toffolo is equally fast with his 'but': 'The swastika is, for me, a horrendous symbol because in its name brutal crimes have been perpetrated, but the hammer-and-sickle is its equal, a symbol which should be condemned...'

Part of the problem was that these men – who by their own, proud admission, had never finished their schooling – were conducting a historical debate through one-liners painted on banners that could be seen by millions of TV viewers. Never did British hooligans hold such a grip on national historical debate as the Irriducibili, with their bizarre notion that because dictators had convictions they shouldn't be repudiated. Yuri, another Irriducibili leader and – according to him – a communist, said: 'I believe that Hitler and Stalin were great historical figures, as was Mussolini, who it's right should be remembered as a great statesman. Maybe they made mistakes in committing the crimes they did, but I don't feel able to condemn them because they believed in something.'

It was a period in which the Irriducibili were gaining in strength because the team seemed to be winning everything. In the final of the European Cup-Winners' Cup in 1999 Lazio beat Real Mallorca. Wearing an odd yellow-and-black strip, Christian Vieri scored the first goal, meeting a cross from deep with his head, pushing out his chest to loop the ball over the keeper. Real Mallorca equalized with a tap-in from Dani but then Pavel Nedved – on the edge of the penalty area and with his back to goal – spun and hooked the ball into the net.

That year they beat Manchester United in the European Super Cup, and then went on to win Serie A in the 1999–2000 season. Managed by Sven Goran Eriksson, it was a team that had everything: muscle, fantasy, goals and good luck. It was an international mix, combining Argentinians, Serbs, Portuguese and many Italian greats like Alessandro Nesta, Roberto Mancini and Simone Inzaghi, as well as the Chilean Marcelo Salas and the Czech Pavel Nedved. Towards the end of that season a series of bizarre refereeing decisions helped Juventus repeatedly win matches (years later, it was revealed that the club had a huge influence over referees). Before the last game of the season the Lazio ultras organized a funeral procession under the slogan, 'Football is dead'. There were fights with police in Via Allegri in Rome, outside the headquarters of FIGC (the Italian FA). As it was, the gods intervened. Torrential rain in Perugia meant that Juventus lost while Lazio comfortably won 3–0 against Reggiana. Lazio had won their second *scudetto*.

What for fans represented sporting ecstasy was, for Diabolik, a business opportunity. They already had a 600-square-metre warehouse full of berets, Babygros, slippers, beach towels, watches, lighters, military paraphernalia, fridge magnets and car stickers – anything a Lazio fan might need to show their allegiance. Now they wanted their own shops. They put up posters all over the city, advertising a new brand, 'Original Fans', and the opening of a store. The logo was the bowler-hatted midget, Mr Enrich, swinging his boot.

When Grit, the ousted founder of the Irriducibili, saw the poster, he stopped in his tracks. It was his logo and it had been snatched from him by force. 'I was disconcerted and shocked,' he wrote in his memoir. 'I looked at the poster and, on reflection, came to the conclusion that it was the beginning of a slow demise of the famous ultra mentality: whilst in the 80s and 90s certain behaviour was codified, in the 2000s the most absolute hypocrisy was released.'

The Irriducibili began opening shops all over the capital. Some were little more than single-room stores in the suburbs but others were glitzy boutiques in the city centre. By 2003 they had fourteen outlets. It was largely a cash-in-hand business, so the real income was probably far higher than the 210,000 euros the 'Original Fans' brand declared that year. No one doubted Diabolik's business nous, only his morals. 'If he weren't a gangster,' one Lazio fan said to me, 'Diabolik could have been a CEO.'

The benefits weren't only financial. In part, the stores spread the chromatic conformism vital to any gang. They created a network of contacts, making ever more porous that membrane between ordinary fans and the tight-knit crew that controlled the terraces. The 'Original Fans' empire meant that the emperor could now reward those who were most loyal to him by offering paid employment. With the cashflow, the contacts and the loyalty, Diabolik now had much greater ambitions. He started toying with the idea of actually buying Lazio itself.

2001, Piazza Alimondi, Genova

By the turn of the millennium Puffer was the undisputed leader of the Genoa ultras. Shortish, shaven-headed, smart-casual and with a slightly high-pitched voice, he was usually charming and generous. But he had a temper so violent that when he lost it the only thing to do was agree with him as fast as possible. If he sensed a threat he would attack first. 'He's a refined, loveable man', says one Genoa ultra, 'but I wouldn't ever want him as an enemy.'

Puffer had always loved pistols. When he was doing his military service in the mid-1980s he had proved an excellent shot at the firing range. The cadets were blindfolded and told to dismantle, and reassemble, their weapons. Puffer was so fast that his superiors tried to persuade him to stay on in the military. 'You're born to do this,' one of them told him. He wasn't interested but the love of handguns never left him. He had a collection of guns in his home.

In 2001 one of the Genoa ultras was in prison for drugs offences. Cyclops was a simple man but a proper bruiser. He was burly and had only one eye, having lost the other to the end of a flagpole. He had been arrested in possession of three hundred grammes of cocaine and twenty-one false 50,000-lire notes. His wife had financial worries and Puffer had told another ultra to take care of her. '"Do her shopping," I told him, that sort of thing. I told him two or three times. I said, "You're not doing right by her."' The two men arranged to meet up to sort it out.

'I'm going to go and do Puffer,' said the ultra as he left '5r', the historic HQ of the Genoa ultras. Someone overheard the threat and phoned Puffer to tell him to be careful at the meet-up.

A few minutes later the two men were walking towards each other with the sort of speed and intent that spelt trouble. The ultra had the heavy metal of a steering lock in his hand, so Puffer pulled out his pistol. 'Pam, pam, pam, three shots in his ankle,' he tells me. 'He fell onto his knees and wet himself. He's disappeared from circulation now. Last I heard, he was living in Santo Domingo.' He likes telling the story.

Puffer was arrested two weeks later, the day after the Genoa–Sampdoria derby. Because he had shot low, he wasn't tried for attempted murder and he was only sentenced to a year in prison. By the time he came out, people knew not to mess with him. 'The message to everyone,' a magistrate told me, 'was: if you behave badly, I'll shoot you.'

It wasn't the only shooting in Genova that year. In July the G8 summit took place in the city. Hundreds of ultras from across Italy, and thousands of protesters from across Europe, travelled to the Ligurian capital to march against what they perceived as the capitalist superpowers. 'Another world is possible' was the slogan. What happened that grim weekend was later described by Amnesty International as 'the most serious suspension of democratic rights in a Western country since the Second World War'. Police shot dead one man, Carlo Giuliani, in Genova's Piazza Alimondi and, during a night-time raid on a school being used as a dormitory, 346 police brutally assaulted ninety-three people: one sixty-two-year-old man had ten ribs, an arm and a leg broken. A British journalist lost sixteen teeth, suffered eight broken ribs, a collapsed lung and fell into a coma. In all, sixty-eight people suffered comparable injuries. The floor, walls and radiators of the school were covered in bloodstains. Police later planted evidence to justify the attack. Fifty-nine people were later beaten up and tortured in police barracks in Bolzaneto.

The Italian police suffered a global PR disaster at the G8. Many of those beaten and tortured were foreign journalists and peaceful protestors. The only way to redress their reputation was to unearth political terrorists who might, in some way, retrospectively justify their heavy-handedness and, perhaps equally importantly, foot the bill for the damage done to the city.

November 2002: Claudio arrested

It was shortly after midnight on 15 November 2002 when Claudio's doorbell in Cosenza rang. Policemen with balaclavas and guns came into the flat and told him that he was being arrested for 'subversive association and conspiracy against the economic order of the state'. He and various other 'no global' agitators were being fitted up as the fall-guys for the G8 disturbances.

'You're going to the maximum-security prison in Trani,' they said. By then Claudio had become, like his parents, a school-teacher. One of his first thoughts was who would cover his lesson tomorrow. He picked up a copy of Leopardi's *Canti*, said goodbye to his wife, whose birthday it was the next day, and was escorted by the police to the prison in Puglia. Outside it were various protestors, holding up banners in support of their arrested comrade.

The smell of the prison struck Claudio more than the noise of metallic locks: not just the odour of shit from the cells but the constant smell of people getting high on cooking gas. The only other substance for a buzz was coffee, rolled in plastic bottles from one cell to another.

Over the next few days he started receiving messages. The prison chaplain came to see him. 'Padre Fedele called me,' the chaplain said. 'I tried to calm him down, because on the tele-phone he was shouting continuously. He's very irate. He says that you guys are exceptional rebels. He said that he considers you his children and that he won't let any harm come to you.'

Then he received a telegram from his schoolchildren which made him well up: 'We're with you and await your return and

your smile. We love you. Come on Cosenza!' Later, he was trans-
ferred to a prison in Viterbo and ended up in a cell with his old
friend Gianfranco. Together they chatted, trying to understand
how they had ended up here. In the late 1990s the Italian police
had been desperately attempting to impose law and order in
Italian stadiums. Since the terraces had always been autonomous
zones – 'prisons where there was liberty' – the ultras always
defended their turf against what they saw as any invasion. In
1998, before a Coppa Italia game between Cosenza and Lazio,
the Guardia di Finanza aligned sniffer dogs at the entrance to
the *curva*. 'Since the average of [dope] smokers in our terraces is
every other fan,' Claudio remembers, 'they were arresting dozens
of us. Not criminals, just young lads from the countryside.' The
injustice angered the anti-prohibitionist Cosentini. Within ten
minutes the stadium bathroom had been stripped of everything
useful as a missile, and the Guardia di Finanza was attacked and
forced to retreat.

Shortly afterwards the San Vito stadium upgraded its security measures, trying to ensure that only those with tickets could
get inside. In a game against Pistoiese one young man decided to
climb the high iron grid. When he dropped down the other side,
he was – in front of all those queueing at the turnstiles – beaten
by police. Once again the sense of injustice riled the masses who
watched as an unarmed boy was beaten by three policemen,
smacking his head with their truncheons. Once again, the
ultras organized and attacked hard, going up against dogs and
truncheons armed with stones and flagpoles.

Every week there seemed to be an escalation. Soon, nautical
flares were replying to the police's tear-gas cannisters, which were
fired – the ultras maintained – at head height. Police vehicles were
ambushed. Fans were arrested and beaten up. It was happening

in every stadium in Italy but the circumstances in Cosenza were unique. Here the ultras seemed dangerous not because of the violence but because of the consensus they enjoyed. Their fanzine had become a source of counter-information that revealed all manner of skulduggery in city hall. The buildings they occupied weren't crusty dens of criminality but open centres of creativity that enriched the city.

The habitual rebelliousness of the city must have seemed dangerous to the Establishment and they began to investigate the ultras in a more methodical way. Because a series of paper bombs had exploded outside the offices of regional quangos at night, the police – always alert for political terrorism after the bloodshed of the 1970s – wondered whether an armed insurgency was imminent. Even if it wasn't, they could use the bombings to decapitate a movement that was becoming ideologically subversive. Their trouble was that, as Piero had always said, Cosenza didn't have bosses. There was no clear leader of the ultra movement: it was chaotic, instinctive, unplanned.

But the authorities decided that Claudio – the boy who had grown up on the balcony opposite Piero, and now a teacher in his late twenties – was the mastermind. It was a foolish choice of target. Like so many ultras, he had lost his father young and was, in some ways, the adopted son of the *curva*. He was well-read and well-connected, eloquent and funny, but also combative and committed. When he discovered a police bug in his car, he called a press conference and wore furry handcuffs.

Very soon the battle became serious. In the dying minutes of the last day of the 1999–2000 season police stormed the Cosenza *curva*. There had been no disturbances all afternoon – it was a game without anything at stake and many of the ultras were wearing flip-flops – but police ran in, shouting Claudio's name.

As he sprinted away from the helmeted men, he fell, breaking his tibia and fibula. The police set on him, beating him with truncheons and fists. One young policeman tried to stop the violence. 'Stop it, stop it,' he shouted.

One of the first people to visit him in the hospital was Padre Fedele, dressed in a doctor's white coat. Twenty or so ultras were protesting outside the hospital. The atmosphere was so inflammable that the surgeon wheeled Claudio onto a balcony to calm things down. But the confrontation with the police continued. Weeks later, his leg in traction at home, Claudio's home was raided at 4 a.m. Police removed fifteen years of ultra archives. Within minutes Padre Fedele arrived and, ever protective of his adoptive son, lost his temper with the police. 'You shouldn't be here,' he screamed.

It seemed, to many in the city, absurd. With all the criminals in Calabria, and even within the ultra movement, to choose from, the police were picking on a schoolteacher whose only crime was *lèse-majesté*: criticism of the Establishment in general and of the police in particular. His was an antagonistic voice, certainly, constantly accusing the police of violence. 'Indiscriminate beatings, arrests without guarantees,' Claudio later wrote, '[the atrocity in] Genova isn't an exception but the rule.' He was adamant that it was the militarization of the police that had made the ultras violent and not vice versa. He never denied being a participant in fights. But to most people Claudio seemed the noblest expression of the movement: mentored, as a teenager, by a Franciscan friar, he saw in the terraces the possibility of an alternative world, a place where the dispossessed and the weakest could gather and find protection.

But by now the police were investigating a political network called Rebel South, in which Claudio and other radicals were involved. Police tried to tie the night-time explosions of the 1990s to the group. It was tenuous to say the least but that was the reason for his imprisonment. Claudio was released, pending trial, a week later. He didn't reach Cosenza until dawn, just as the rising sun was kissing the Silan mountains to the west. But there, waiting by the motorway exit, were a hundred or so ultras, singing and clapping as his car came into view.

The ultra world is often defined by hatred. But Claudio, writing about that dawn, showed that an ultra is also inspired by the opposite: 'I decided to love you [Cosenza] years ago, when I started proudly to wear the colours of the city. For an ultra, the feeling of appreciation towards one's own land is written in our DNA. I love your history, Cosenza. I love your legends. I love your rivers and I love the old city. I love your sky and the two mountain ranges which hug you. I love the villages which surround you. I love the gypsies and migrants. I love the Ciroma radio and all the liberated spaces. I love this terrace and its colours. I thank mother nature that I was brought into the world here, at the confluence of the Crati and Busento rivers.'

A laborious trial later cleared him and his alleged accomplices of all charges. But what that arrest, and many others, showed was how much the police and ultra groups were now targeting each other. During 2002–03 there were 51 per cent more stadium-related arrests than the previous season. The figures published by *Gnosis*, the online magazine of SISDE, an arm of the intelligence services, suggest that whilst there were many fewer actual incidents (a reduction of 40 per cent every year), the violence of those incidents was increasing, with the number of those wounded actually on the rise: from 400 in the 95–96 season to almost 1,200 four years later. Another clear change was the fact that ultra groups, as much as targeting each other, were now fighting pitched battles against public officials. Of the 850 injured in the 2002–03 season, 612 were from the 'forces of order', an increase of 72 per cent on the previous year. Even allowing for the cynic's response that the police had an economic incentive to claim injury, it was clear that the ultras had a new target.

Threatened by what they saw as a resurgent fascism within the movement and targeted by an authoritarian police force outside it, left-leaning ultras decided it was time to fight back. Ever since 1997 an organization called Progetto Ultrà had run a tournament called the 'Anti-Racist World Cup' outside Modena (the slogan echoed that of Genova's G8: 'Another football is possible'). In 2002 a movement called the Ultras Resistance Front was born. It was founded by Livorno's (notoriously far-left) ultras and immediately supported by Ancona's Ultras and Ternana's Freak Brothers. Soon other groups that were traditionally from the anarchist or antagonist traditions – Caserta's 'Against Racism', Cosenza's Rebel Fans, Sambenedettese's 'Nucleo', Modena's 'Brigate' and Venezia's 'Rude Fans' – joined the resistance. That summer, in Narni (the geographical centre of Italy), they organized an international anti-racist rally.

Whilst many far-right ultras had assumed that the vaunted 'ultra mentality' was a perfect fit with fascism, those in the Ultras Resistance Front made a case for the opposite: sport, they said, knew no skin colour, only the colour of the shirt. Fandom was about association, which was, after all, where the word 'soccer' came from. The ultras were partisans and freedom-fighters, they said, able to liberate spaces from the control of a corrupted system. They were, they said, creating alternative communities based on the values of ultra fandom. As Marco De Rose (one of the Rebel Fans) wrote in his book, *Controcultura Ultras*, 'The ultras are the most true and rebellious part of society, a social force for aggregation and participation... but the real struggle of the ultras is in the streets and the squares.'

If the left-leaning ultras were taking the fight elsewhere, it was partly because football was increasingly unreliable as a sport. For a decade Cosenza had seemed a pretty crooked club: the cars of critical journalists or investors were shot at or burnt. When one mafia *pentito*, Franco Pino, alleged that results had been altered in return for cash, nobody was even surprised. The club president spread his bets and bought a second club, Spal, in Ferrara. The team was docked nine points for financial irregularities. It returned to Serie B in 1998 but then, in 2003, there was another 'Caso Catania', in which various teams lodged appeals to be promoted because one or other rival team had fielded disqualified players. Cosenza, which had gone bankrupt with debts of over €12 million, was relegated by the lawyers. The following season there were two teams calling themselves Cosenza: Cosenza FC and Cosenza Calcio 1914. Fans were so incensed by this situation that during the derby between the two teams, they occupied the pitch and stopped the game going ahead. Cosenza Calcio 1914 went bust in 2005, and then Cosenza FC, having changed its name to the Associazione Sportiva Cosenza Calcio, collapsed in 2007. A suburb of the city, Rende, then changed the name of its team from Rende FC to Fortitudo Cosenza and became the 'official' team. It was sometimes hard to understand who you were supporting any more.

But often the retreat from the terraces was an admission that the fun was finished and that the stadiums only offered bulletins of deaths. In 20 September 2003, in Avellino, Sergio Ercolano tried to slide down a perspex roof over the stadium's gym to escape fighting and fell a dozen metres onto a concrete no-man's land. Fans called the emergency services and screamed at the police. When the ambulance arrived, nobody could find the key to unlock the door to the passageway where Ercolano was lying motionless. For the next half an hour, the ultras took almost complete control of the ground. They ran onto the pitch with sticks and chains, beating the police. The ground was united in singing '*assassini*' to the men and women in blue helmets. One policeman was stabbed, another had a heart attack. Ercolano died in hospital the following Monday afternoon.

Even those ultras who believed that incompetent ticketing and police brutality were equally responsible for what had happened felt that the game was up. The battle in the stadiums could only have one victor and the minority of left-leaning ultras decided to pick a fight on other terms. 'It takes courage,' said the Associazione Noi Ultras after Sergio Ercolano's death, 'to desert a war which is, however, lost.' But, the Association said, there was 'a war to fight on another plain, with other arms: solidarity, sporting passion, the desire to be a part of something. To be squashed by a violence-repression-violence logic will serve only to generate more tears, more pain, more anger.' Ercolano's father joined the Battito Azzurro ('Blue Heartbeat') fans' organization, run by the former *capo-ultra* of Napoli's glory years, Pallummella, which was campaigning for a return to simpler, safer Sundays.

There's a proverb in Italy which says that 'to know the truth you need to listen to two liars'. It expresses the notion that everything is *fazioso* (sectarian) and that if you confront two fables, you'll begin to see what is false and be able to feel the contours of the truth. But it also hints at a willingness to lend an indulgent ear to all and sundry and do away with any acoustic quality control.

It's almost as if there's a conversational quicksand into which everything will sink. Relentless rhetoric insists and persuades and disorientates, until there's nothing solid onto which you can grab hold.

That's certainly the case when you try to define fascism. Mussolini himself liked to boast that his ideology was 'the church of all the heresies', implying that there were no orthodoxies to it at all. 'We don't believe in dogmatic programmes,' he said on another occasion, 'we allow ourselves the luxury of being aristocratic and democratic, conservatives and progressives, reactionaries and revolutionaries, legals and illegals...' It was totalitarianism mounted on slipperiness. 'Mussolini did not have a philosophy,' Umberto Eco once wrote. 'He had only rhetoric. Fascism was a fuzzy totalitarianism, a collage of different philosophical and political ideas, a beehive of contradictions.'

In some ways, that unifying personality cult is continued by some of the biggest ultra groups. Juventus's Drughi have a portrait of Mussolini in their headquarters; Roma's Boys have his bust. You lose count of the number of times you see him – or Julius Evola or Gabriele D'Annunzio – in their HQs. There is lots of playing with symbols. Any Roma Boy who was given a stadium ban used to be given a miniature double-headed axe. In terms of recruitment, there was a 'pull' from the HQ of those firms, which made you feel pretty invincible once you were inside; but there was also a 'push' from political parties, sending their young men into the terraces.

Roberto Fiore, one of the founders of the extreme-right Terza Posizione who had made his fortune in London, returned to Italy in 1999 having founded another fascist movement called Forza Nuova. Fiore was a clerico-fascist, close to the extreme dissident Catholics of the Society of Saint Pius X, and he saw the terraces as a major site of missionary outreach. Soon the banners seen in the stadium were reflecting his influence. On 27 October 2002 one exhorted fans to attend the celebration for the eightieth anniversary of Mussolini's march on Rome. 'March, don't go rotten,' it said. In 2006 another banner used the old slogan of the Teutonic knights and Nazi Germany: *Gott Mit Uns* ('God is with us'). It has now become a common inscription on ultra scarves. Inter ultras began singing, 'We're the ones who took Anne Frank.' Another frequent banner on the terraces was 'Santa Teppa', the phrase Mussolini once used to describe his black shirts: 'holy thugs'.

This infiltration of the terraces was partly because the far right had borrowed a strategy from the Marxist philosopher Antonio Gramsci. He urged 'cultural hegemony', meaning the creation of political consensus through cultural conversion. The far right gave this strategy a new name – 'metapolitics' – and another neo-fascist party, called CasaPound in honour of the late fascist evangelist, the American poet Ezra Pound – was particularly adept at this cultural infusion. Here, too, there was plenty of ideological contortionism. CasaPound started describing itself not as fascist, but as *estremo centro alto* ('extreme, high centre', the name of a song by its founder Gianluca Iannone's rock band, ZetaZeroAlpha). It opened gyms, pubs, parachute clubs, subacqua clubs, motorbike clubs, football teams, restaurants, nightclubs, tattoo parlours and barbers. Then CasaPound militants set up a Roma ultra group called Padroni di Casa ('Landlords of the House').

Fascism, it was clear, was suddenly fashionable. Its symbols (the lictor's bundle, the Celtic cross, the double-headed axe), its look (shaved heads and sartorial sameness) and buzzwords ('honour', 'loyalty', 'youth', 'action') became ubiquitous on the terraces. Groups announced their politics by the use of the font of Ultras Liberi, often written in white lettering on a black background and overlaid with tricolour ribbons. Style had always been integral to fascism's appeal: himself a silver-tongued poseur, Mussolini once bragged that 'fascism has brought style back into the life of the people: a way of behaving, meaning colour, force, the picturesque, the unexpected, the mystical...' For a subculture so conscious of style as that of the ultras, the vogueishness of the far right was particularly appealing.

In those first years of the twenty-first century it felt as if the political wind was only blowing in one direction: Gianni Alemanno – a man then married to the daughter of the political terrorist, Pino Rauti – was a minister in Berlusconi's government (he would later become Mayor of Rome). The birthplace of Mussolini, Villa Carpera, was bought and turned into a museum of fascist paraphernalia in 2001. Heresies were becoming the orthodoxies once again.

2003, Genoa

In 2003 one of the hardest nuts of the Genoa ultras died. Claudio Natale was known by everyone as Speloncia. He was renowned as a proper street fighter, as befitted a man who had Benito Mussolini's face tattooed on his forearm. In his memory a new firm was created: the Brigata Speloncia. Many people assumed it was fascist, and it's true that its adherents were 'nostalgics', but they claimed they checked in their politics at the turnstiles, refusing – in old ultra tradition – to allow politics to enter the terraces. Puffer, who became the leader, claimed that they wore black shirts as a sign not of political ideology but of mourning for Speloncia.

That same year a businessman called Enrico Preziosi bought Genoa. He had moved north from Avellino, ending up in Milan where he produced games and toys, including one called 'Hit the Referee'. His role-model and mentor was Silvio Berlusconi: at one point Preziosi was spending almost 40 per cent of his company's income on buying advertising space on Berlusconi's TV channels. By 1994 Preziosi had a turnover of 100 billion lire and 200 employees. He bought a small club, Saronno, taking it from the Interregionale championship to C1. Then, in 1997, he bought Como, promising to take it into Serie A in five years. In 2002 he had done it through a combination of ruthlessness and instinct for promising players. Then, in 2003, he sold Como and bought the oldest club in Italian football, Genoa.

21 March 2004, Rome: 'The Derby of the Dead Baby'

It was the derby: Lazio–Roma. Both teams had, in recent history, won the *scudetto* and there was a real bite to the encounter. Francesco Totti was at the height of his powers and scoring incredible goals: that strike against Juventus from thirty-five yards out, hit so true it had no bend at all... the third goal against Sampdoria when he dribbled from inside his own half, only it wasn't a zigzag dribble but a sprint in which Totti just saw who was coming and angled his run so that he was untouchable. And then he had the coolness, having beaten the whole defence, to dummy a shot, watch the keeper drop, and dink it in.

He often lobbed the ball, as if time slowed and only he, in the whole stadium, had the composure and vision to chip rather than drill. It was like that fifth goal against Lazio in the derby a couple of years before. It was so impudent that the commentator laughed. Against Inter, when Roma won 3–2 away from home, he jumped through one lunge, found himself surrounded by three Inter players, freed himself, ran and then looked up and, instead of going for power, lobbed it over the keeper. Even the Inter fans were on their feet applauding him.

That week, as usual, the radios of the city's taxis were all tuned to the gurgling chat of the capital's football phone-ins. But that Sunday evening outside the Olimpico something was different. As fans got closer to the stadium, arriving from the footpath along the Tiber, they heard screams and sirens, saw flashing lights and the fizz of tear gas. The serenity of the spring dusk gave way to scenes from a battle.

It seemed to many ordinary fans as if the police were drunk on power that night. At one point a tear-gas cannister was even fired into the main stand. 'The cannister,' said one fan, 'fell fifty centimetres to my left. I had the feeling that my time had come and that I wouldn't be going home.' The most common metaphor used by fans – both ultras and ordinary aficionados – was that it was like a war-zone: the noise, the smoke, the shouts, the fear. Even the Lazio captain, the Serbian Sinisa Mihajlovic, used the same metaphor: 'I was reliving the scenes that had bloodied my own country.'

But it was one-sided warfare. The *celerini*, the 'riot police', were disguised, shielded and tooled up with tasers and truncheons. The ultras were mostly unarmed, their weapons were just their feet, fists, belts and voices. Their only other advantage was their ancient weapon of force of numbers. There were soon

80,000 fans in the stadium, outnumbering the riot police by over a hundred to one. That crowd was, by kick-off, seething and hysterical. No one understood the cause of the police brutality. Many were shouting or crying. People heard things and misheard them. Others phoned home to see what the news was saying.

Crowds have often been compared to beasts or to fires. There's something beyond control, beyond agency and intention, to a mass of humans. They're untamed and noisy, which means whispers are misheard. One fan had gone to the ambulance crew to get medical attention. He thought he heard the nurses talking about a death. Another saw a fan laid out on a stretcher, with his face covered by a sheet because all the tear gas had caused an asthma attack. The fan assumed it was a dead body. Marco, one fan, said that 'the news travelled fast... a boy next to me said "I've phoned home and there are two kids dead." I saw absurd scenes: people crying and shouting and we didn't know what to do.'

People were hearing things, and repeating them, and asking questions that morphed into statements. The more people asked, 'Has someone died?', the more believable it became, whatever the reply. Soon – in the chaos of that evening – a rumour began that a baby had been killed by a police vehicle. Like all oral storytelling, it seemed to give sudden meaning to the group's anxieties. It was a grippingly believable rumour.

At half-time, the Roma ultras removed all their banners, a gesture akin to lowering a flag, a sign of respect in the event of death. Even people watching at home on TV realized something strange was going on. Fabrizio Toffolo, one of the leaders of Lazio's Irriducibili ultras, was under house arrest. 'When at the end of the first half,' he said, 'the banners in the south terrace were removed, it was a signal that something serious had happened...' Even those who were uncertain what to believe were so incensed by the treatment they had received at the hands of the riot police that they, along with the rest of the stadium, began screaming *'assassini, assassini'*.

There was a denial, over the stadium's PA system, that anyone had died: 'the *Questura* communicates that the news is absolutely without foundation.' Very few believed the announcement however. Given the disturbances outside the stadium, the rumours of a baby's death seemed every bit as credible as the denial. Within minutes all sides of the stadium were shouting for the match to be called off. *'Sospendete la partita,'* they shouted. 'Stop the game.' The chant, in unison around the stadium, convinced the last doubters that something terrible really must have occurred.

There was righteous indignation in the chant. Just ten days before, Roma had played Villarreal in the Uefa Cup. It was on 11 March, the same day in which 192 people lost their lives in Madrid in the Al Qaeda bombings. The fans had been adamant that the match should be postponed as a mark of respect but nothing – not even that horror – could stop the show business. This time, on their own turf, they were determined that the show shouldn't go on.

The second half kicked off. The game was nil–nil but the atmosphere was so strange that even the players seemed reluctant to go on, deliberately kicking the ball into the stands. At 21.34, in the fourth minute of the second half, the referee blew his whistle and suspended the game. Three Roma ultras were on the pitch and Francesco Totti, the iconic Roman captain, went to talk to them.

'Francé,' said one of the ultras, 'you have to stop the game. Give me your word of honour. Now go and tell the others.'

'But the speaker,' Totti tried to push back, 'said that no child has died.'

'I'm telling you that's the way it is. Even his parents have called from home. The game can't be played.'

As he was walking away, Totti looked over at his teammates and club officials and said: 'If we play on, they're going to kill us.' Interviewed by police, Totti denied having been threatened but said that 'a heavy atmosphere had been created which left one to guess that something serious could have happened if the game had continued...' At 9.59 p.m., after a phone consultation with the head of the Italian Lega Calcio, Adriano Galliano, the referee decided to postpone the game.

The iconic non-match was given the ironic title, 'the Derby of the Dead Baby'. There had been no death, but tellingly more people were convinced by a rumour than by a reality narrated by the authorities. It was an indictment of the lack of trust in the police and *Carabinieri* that the vast majority disbelieved the truth and gave credence to an invention instead. Perhaps it was just an indication – as the ultra-watcher Diego Mariottini put it – that in Italy 'the truth is less true than elsewhere'.

Many didn't believe that it was merely a rumour that got out of hand, however. They thought that there had been a deliberate design behind the evening. It seemed an eerie warning from the ultras as to what could happen if either Lazio or Roma were to go bankrupt (less than a week before that non-game trade in Lazio shares had been suspended). As always in the ultra world, it was hard to disentangle self-righteousness from arrogance. The menace the ultras could conjure up seemed deliberately over-powering, as if they were sending a message to the super-rich sport: 'We're still here, and we can veto your money-making enterprise. We can put a stop to all this unless you cooperate with us.'

Many groups were, by then, enjoying a parasitic relationship with their club. The ultras could call a 'fans' strike', refusing to go to the ground for a period. But the main tool they had in order to force club owners to compromise was related to what was called 'objective responsibility'. According to Italian law, if explosives or racist chanting were present within a stadium the club itself was held responsible, invariably being subjected to large fines, docked points or stadium closures. It was, for ultras, an open goal. If the club presidents didn't provide the ultras with what they wanted, a few racist chants or objects thrown on to the pitch could bring them to the table. The figures demonstrate just how powerful the ultras' bargaining position is: between 2014 and 2019 fines due to ultras' actions cost Roma €1.2 million, Napoli €524,000 and Juventus €364,000.

What the ultras wanted was usually very simple. Merchandising concessions and donations towards the cost of material for operatic choreographies were the bare minimum. What they really wanted were tickets. Few clubs didn't come to an arrangement. Some gave the ultras free tickets, others sold them. But even when they had to pay for tickets, the groups could double their money by fleecing their fellow fans, increasing the price as high as demand would allow. They actually helped keep ticket prices expensive. And the bigger the club, of course, the higher the demand and the greater the profits. One police investigation in Napoli overheard one man saying to another: 'We live on tickets, we live on Napoli football club.'

Over time, the grey area between football clubs and their ultras became normalized. Whilst both sides – owners and ultras – were often scathing about the other in public, in private they formed a symbiotic relationship. The ultras could threaten public disorder on behalf of club presidents when legal, sporting and judicial decisions were pending. In 2003 various Serie A clubs, including

Lazio, were so seriously in debt that it seemed likely many would go bust. It suited the clubs to have thousands of ultras on standby, as it were, ready to riot if their beloved clubs were made extinct by the application of the law. Fear of rioting (and the political cost of losing voters) encouraged the government to pass what was called a 'debt spread' law, allowing repayment of evaded tax over many years. 'In this way,' wrote the criminologist Vincenzo Scalia, 'a financial problem is turned into a public order one, thus urging a political intervention.'

Writing in 2007, Alessandro Dal Lago noticed this shift whereby they became the foot soldiers of the club's interests: '… the ultras (certainly, not all of them, not always, not in all the stadiums) ended up being used for internal struggles within clubs, to support this or that president, to impose an increase in the price of tickets or simply to sustain the politics of the new signings…'

But it was at Juventus that the relationship between ultras and club was most entangled. The deal was that the club would supply the various ultra groups – Bravi Ragazzi, the Drughi, Tradizione, Vikings – with hundreds of tickets as long as the behaviour inside the ground caused no difficulties for the club hierarchy. 'The compromise was this,' the former commercial director, Francesco Calvo, later told investigators: 'to guarantee a safe game, I gave in regarding the tickets, knowing that they were making money. I maintained that a mediation with the organized fans was, however, a good solution for everyone.'

Before the start of each season, the various *capo-ultras* would request hundreds of season tickets from the complicit club. Since tickets, by then, were sold to named individuals with ID cards, the touting could only work with the connivance of stewards on the turnstiles, who turned a blind eye to the discrepancies between the name on the ticket and the name of the person holding it. It was common to see the tough ultra crews crowding around stewards for the hour or two before every game, making sure that they were behaving themselves.

As well as season tickets, additional tickets were also given to the ultras for every game. One Drugo, for example, later revealed that his gang would request 300 tickets per game. Sometimes they were given for free but, more often, they were just given on credit and in bulk. The ultras paid the club back after the match, once they had sold the tickets at profit. The various ultra outfits had effectively become, with the blessing of the club itself, sub-contracted ticket offices.

It was an arrangement that made them vast sums of money. The Turin *Carabinieri* estimated that ticket-touting by Juventus ultras yielded between €13,500 and €15,000 per game. 'Tickets which were bought at face value, or even received for free,' their report said, 'were being sold on with a mark-up of €100–€200.'

Present Day: Another Game

Brescia's ground is hemmed in between the foothills of the Alps, with fog drowsing between the peaks. But it's mostly empty. There are only 5,000 spectators for a big Serie B game.

Now Cosenza are back in Serie B, the team is playing many games in the North and it's a chance to show how they deal with hatred. Donata Bergamini is here, and Elastic leads the singing in memory of her late brother.

'Fuck off Cosenza,' chant the Bresciani. In their knee-jerk outrage at this unoriginal insult, many Cosentini offer the same chant back. Elastic scowls furiously, enraged that any shout from our midst has arisen without his say-so. 'We don't give a shit what they do,' he screams. He pulls himself tall on the railings and there's a hint of a smile to his snarl.

'You' – he's got the megaphone to his mouth and is bouncing his forehead backwards to the Brescia ultras 200 metres away – 'are Catanzaresi.' It's a chant of hatred and humour at the same time. We're accusing these proud Northerners of being Calabresi from Catanzaro, somewhere they probably couldn't even find on a map. But we know what it means and keep it going, even though the stadium announcer reminds us that 'territorial discrimination' (basically internal racism) will be penalized with the appropriate sanctions. 'You are Catanzaresi,' we keep chanting, defining ourselves by what we're not.

Then, to show it's just fun, we rattle off the line that 'the Lombard League said we [southerners] were a bastard race'. The chorus is a way of shrugging it off: SkinnyMon, Chill, Vindov and I link arms, bouncing left as the row in front of us is bouncing right, 'la-la-la-ing' to the Speedy Gonzalez melody as if we had our fingers in our ears.

2005, Genoa

In the spring of 2005 Alberto Lari, a Genovese magistrate, suspected that the Genoa ultras were receiving information on match outcomes from within the club itself. Lari sought permission for his men in the *Carabiniere* flying squad to wiretap some of the staff of Genoa football club, including the phone of the president, Enrico Preziosi.

It was a very sensitive stage of the season. Genoa needed three points for mathematical promotion to Serie A and there were two games left. The club had a scowling manager with a voice like a Vespa – Serse Cosmi – and a reliable goalscorer, Diego Milito.

Piacenza was the penultimate game. It was 5 June 2005. Fifteen thousand Genoa fans made the trip across the Apennines. Some middle-aged men even ran there in a relay. It was an exodus of cars, bikes and vans, all decked out in red and blue and with the yellow griffon. But the game didn't go as planned. As time was running out, Giorgio Di Vicino, a Neapolitan journeyman on loan to Piacenza, scored a stunning free kick from 30 metres out, curling it left-footed into the top corner of the goal. It was his first and only goal for the club. The thousands of Genoa fans were silent. They barely heard the raucous insults from the other end of the stadium. After a season of brilliance, the squad seemed to have run out of steam, or luck, at the business end of the season. Everyone was suddenly sober. The team had blown its match-point.

The final game of the season was at home, against a Venezia team that was bottom of the league and going bankrupt. Lines of red and blue balloons hung on parallel wires between palazzi. Plastic flags were taped to the plane trees of the long boulevards and onto lampposts. That iconic date of 1893 was spray-painted onto walls. It was Genoa's biggest game for a generation. 'Old griffon,' said one banner above the traffic lights, 'open your wings. It's time to fly.'

The innocent hope of fans contrasted with the cynical certainty of people who already knew the future. Police had placed a bug in the Novotel hotel in Genoa where the Venezia players were staying before the game. One of them had played in Ternana when a current Genoa Sporting Director had been there.

'Will you send flowers to my wife?' the Venezia player asked the Genoa official.

'Don't worry, there will be flowers and fine wine for everyone,' the club official replied. It seemed an obvious code for the financial rewards of letting Genoa win the game.

Just before kick-off, at 12.58, two *Carabinieri* monitoring the phone-tap listened in on a phone call from Enrico Preziosi, the Genoa owner. He was speaking to one of the team managers of Venezia, Franco Dal Cin.

'It's all OK,' said Dal Cin, 'we couldn't have done better than this.' When the team line-ups were announced, it seemed strange that many of Venezia's star players – Esposito, Savino Guidoni, Andersson and Collauto – were absent.

In the stadium the choreography was stunning. One side of each stand waved red flags, the other half blue. Each stand was perfectly divided into those two colours. The game kicked off and Genoa played decent football. But early in the game, a long, diagonal ball came to Gonzalo Vicente, the Venezia attacker, unmarked at the far-post. It was a simple tap in.

The *Carabinieri* listened to Preziosi's phone conversation with Pino Pagliara, a Venezia staffer, in the midst of that turbulent half. 'What the fuck is happening?' screamed Preziosi. 'What are those guys doing? They scored by mistake. We had an agreement.'

Genoa kept coming forwards, shooting from all angles, but the ball just wouldn't go in. They hit the crossbar. Milito went close. Then Marco Rossi crossed from the right and Milito jumped slightly, bending his right leg so that he almost stamped the ball in with the outside of his right ankle. The energy then, the euphoria and relief, were almost libidinous. People were screaming, jumping, hugging. 'Milito!' screamed one commentator for the local radio, again and again: 'Milito! Milito! Milito!' It was one-all.

At half-time, the two *Carabinieri* monitoring the phone-taps listened in. Preziosi was still furious, screaming at one of the Venezia staff: 'What the devil are they doing? It wasn't supposed to go like this. We had an agreement.'

'Stay calm,' the Venezia man replied, 'we'll sort everything out.' Venezia's Czech goal-keeper, Martin Lejsal, was replaced by a nineteen-year-old rookie, Riccardo Pezzato. Within a few minutes of the restart, Rossi tapped in after the Venezia keeper had blocked a shot with his legs. It was even more raucous now. No neutral could remain unmoved. Luis Oliveira equalized with a header for Venezia but then a cushioned header put Milito into the penalty area and, drifting between two defenders, he smacked the ball into the roof of the net. Even in slow-motion the ball moved fast. The score ended 3–2 to Genoa.

There were riotous celebrations that night. As Enrico Preziosi walked the streets, he was hugged by fans. '*Grazie, Presidente*,' said one, '*grazie, grazie*.' He was given a crown made out of gold card and a flag that said 'The King of Genova'. Car horns sounded throughout the night. It was a contagious cacophony. Even the next morning, as people went to work, there were still dazed fans wandering the streets and sober-seeming commuters honking their horns and reigniting the noise.

The day after the match Pino Pagliara phoned a colleague from Genoa: 'Oh, what's happening?' Pagliara asked. 'Deals should be respected.' He was told to go to Cogliate, the head-quarters of Enrico Preziosi's Giochi Preziosi empire on Tuesday at 10 a.m. When he emerged from the building that Tuesday morning, police moved in and found that the bag he was carry-ing contained €250,000. Pagliara stuttered that it was for the sale of a player but the evidence against both clubs was overwhelming.

As the story emerged, Preziosi – like many presidents – tried to turn the threat of ultra unrest to his advantage. 'If Genoa is demoted to Serie B,' he said, 'there will be another G8.' The club was actually demoted to Serie C. Fans were, understandably, furious but they were uncertain whether their anger should be aimed at their scheming president or the Italian FA. Riots ensued throughout the city. Wheelie bins were burnt and windows and cars smashed.

Some wondered, however, whether the ultras were, like ordinary fans, the victims of the stitch-up or, like Preziosi, the beneficiaries of it. Genoa's ultras were indignant that they were associated with the match-fixing. From their perspective it was all hearsay. Many fans, they said, come up with phrases that might sound like certainties: 'We're definitely going to win this', or 'It'll be 2–0, don't worry.' It was just, Puffer told me, 'bar chatter'.

But the investigating magistrate had recordings of conversations between ultras which seemed to suggest that they actually had inside information on matches. He was repeatedly threatened, receiving a trigger in the post. Graffiti against him was left outside his daughter's school. When one journalist reported on the story, he was given a police escort. For the entirety of the following season, there was a banner in the *gradinata nord* saying: 'We don't buy the *Secolo* [the city's newspaper]'. The paper's windows were smashed and other graffiti urged execution of the editor. Years later the editor offered me a succinct analysis of the ultra world: 'For the most part it floats in the borderland between legality and illegality. It often slides onto the wrong side.'

A few months after that tumultuous summer, the head of the Association of Genoa Clubs organized a meeting near Rapallo between Preziosi and the club's leading ultras. It was supposed to be an occasion to clear the air but it turned into a verbal mugging of the President.

'When you came to us,' one of the ultras said to Preziosi, 'and told us, "I've bought all the games, I've bought the lot", no one said anything. OK? Nothing. Fine, maybe it suited us, but we have a vow of silence, a blood pact, President. You should know that it'll remain a blood pact.'

Preziosi kept denying everything. He was interrupted and shouted at and rough-housed. 'Just let me talk a bit,' he pleaded. 'Just give me the chance to talk a second.' The successful businessman seemed so intimidated that he started insulting himself: 'Shit that I am... I'm a dick...' It was almost as if the hierarchy had been inverted, with the ultras assuming control and Preziosi pressured and belittled.

One ultra was recording the conversation and was bullying Preziosi for, investigators assumed, a confession that could serve for blackmail. Preziosi was repeatedly asked what, exactly, had happened in the previous season. The more he came up with bizarre and unbelievable explanations for his behaviour, the more irascible the ultras became.

The recording came to light a few months later, in November 2005, when Puffer was again arrested. His wife had phoned police saying that he had threatened to kill her. He was arrested as he was driving towards her house with two guns. His residence was searched and investigators discovered the recording of the Rapallo meeting.

The events of 2005 cast Genoa in a dark light. The ultras weren't involved in organizing match-fixing but through their connections at the club they might have had foreknowledge of it and – through betting – have profited from that knowledge.

They had also, it seems certain, tried to entrap the hapless Genoa president into a confession so that they could profit further. One Genoa ultra, with decades of '*militanza*' behind him, describes Puffer as 'very intelligent, a born leader, but clearly attracted to the dark side'. In those years the ultra scene in Genoa was beginning to appear like the wild west. In 2006 a man nicknamed 'the shark' – who had previously been in prison for throwing his girlfriend off a balcony – shot two fellow ultras in the legs with a Smith & Wesson pistol at the famous '5r' HQ.

But the difficulty of writing about criminals amongst the ultras is that, in many ways, they're only partly representative of the movement. It's like the old truism that a falling tree in a forest is louder than thousands growing in silence. Every time you go to the *gradinata nord* in Genoa you'll see ultras handing out free flags to newborn babies being carried by young mothers in marsupials ('Born a Griffon' say the flags). There are ultras who love this club so much that they go on pilgrimage to the grave of the club's founder, Dr Spensley, in Germany where he died in the First World War (the grave was discovered by two Genovese scout leaders in 1993). Roberto Scotto is still working in the Genova Insieme cooperative, helping out anyone in the city who has fallen on hard times. Each time there's a natural disaster – and Genova often suffers fatal floods – the ultras are always on the frontline.

That diversity is evident amongst the ultras of every team. In Catania the career paths of various ultra leaders show how impossible it is to box them into labelled compartments. Ciccio 'Fascista' has now died. Stickers of his unshaven face are all over the Curva Sud. The leader of Catania's Irriducibili has been imprisoned for extortion, including demanding five grand from a player and a few hundred thousand from a film producer. And yet another former ultra, a member of the Indians back in the 1990s, was previously an MEP and is now the city's mayor.

Shortly after Genoa's match-fixing scandal in 2005, the club's former coach, Franco Scoglio, died. He had once joked he would die talking about the club he loved, and that's how it happened. He was live on television, arguing on the phone with the club's president, Preziosi, in his passionate, eloquent way. Suddenly, he slipped in his chair and fell to his right. He never regained consciousness. It was an occasion for the Sampdoria ultras to show their wit. Since Scoglio had died on the phone to Preziosi, the Sampdoria ultras – pretending that they thought he had telephonic powers of extermination – hung out a banner: 'Preziosi, call my mother-in-law.'

The ultras had always had a great sense of humour. An Ancona group once had a counterfeiter who turned out forged tickets. At the bottom, in tiny letters, he wrote: 'This is a false ticket, but no one will realize anyhow.' Often the banners were punchy one-liners, usually the result of late-night drinking sessions in the group's favourite bar as everyone came up with suggestions. They could be surreal ('Genoa Cod') or silly ('Honour to Sylvester the Cat'). Even the names of the groups were often inspired. In 1997 various female ultras in Cosenza founded a new group called Curvaiole, a play on words that meant both 'terracers' and 'curvies'.

23 January 2006, Cosenza

'They've arrested the Monk.' Word went round very fast. People phoned friends and turned on the TV. 'Padre Fedele is in prison.'

The accusation was that he had repeatedly raped a nun within the 'Franciscan Oasis'. In the legalese of the arrest warrant, he had forced a Sicilian nun to 'conjoin' with him. Behind that flat term, the details of the five attacks – between February and June 2005 – were gothic. The attacks are alleged to have taken place five times. After he gave the nun in question, who lived at the Oasis as part of the Poor Sisters of San Francis, a pill to make her compliant, he allowed others to rape her and filmed the violence. Before the first rape, on 28 February, Padre Fedele was supposed to have insinuated that he knew a Messina mafioso as a way to intimidate her. It was claimed that the next two rapes were watched by perverts who had paid six-figure sums. Later, the nun allegedly received threats: 'Be careful what you do, we're very close.' The most non-violent of all ultras, the one who had spearheaded the campaign for peace within the sport and had been a vocal supporter of a centre for victims of domestic violence, was himself now accused of the worst violence.

Salacious wiretaps of Padre Fedele talking dirty on the phone were released by the investigative team. Soon, newspapers were reprinting intimate telephone conversations in which the charismatic monk asked women about their breasts and underwear and where he could put his hands. Padre Fedele vehemently denied the accusations. On the day of his arrest he said: 'Today is the most beautiful day of my life because I feel closer to Jesus Christ, persecuted and crucified.' There were various journalists outside the prison, and standing alongside them were Drainpipe, Claudio and his wife. 'We'll never believe it,' they shouted.

Later that night other Cosenza ultras gathered outside the prison. They kept singing the song that Padre Fedele had popularized in the stadium: 'Maracanà, maracanà, we've come this far, and we'll sing and we'll shout, come on Cosenza, olé olé.'

They brought along the *striscione* that bore what had become Padre Fedele's motto: 'Fanhood yes, violence no, peace.' Over the decades, thousands of ultras had been imprisoned. Invariably, their names were chanted and their freedom pleaded. But this arrest put all those other ones into the shade. At the game the following Sunday, at home to Ragusa, a simple banner appeared: 'Free the Monk.'

The arrest of Padre Fedele, the portly, red-blooded man who had served as a spiritual guide to the ultras of not just Cosenza but of Italy, became a national sensation. Everyone tried to understand quite who he really was. His friend, the pornstar Luana Borgia, said: 'Let's say he's a monk who definitely isn't indifferent to female charm.' She spoke of how he had 'a long eye' for women. A journalist who knew him well, Emanuele Giacoia, described him as 'exuberant, open and generous' but with a character that was 'fiery, sometimes uncontainable'. Many women were angered at the sight of an alleged rapist being immediately defended by a male-dominated gang. Although there were many women who stood by him, none were as notorious as Cosenza's (mainly male) ultras.

Padre Fedele had always longed for the limelight. His desire to be the protagonist was almost pathological. But now the national spotlight was on him and instead of adulation, there was vilification. TV shows and newspapers satirized his weaknesses. People he had worked with in Africa accused him of womanizing. Journalists who used to love the fireworks he could produce now wrote wistful profiles of their fallen hero.

Most people outside Cosenza simply assumed he was guilty. In an era in which the libidinous criminals of the Catholic Church were being revealed across the globe, Padre Fedele seemed another example of brutal power being disguised by piety. It was alleged that he had persuaded other women to have sex with him in return for helping their asylum applications. In the past he had sometimes appeared mildly ridiculous, but never so sinister.

The Cosenza ultras stood by him, however. They simply didn't believe the accusations. Drainpipe wrote a long, open letter to Padre Fedele in prison. 'You took me to Africa,' it said, 'where you showed me what it meant to run a leprosy clinic, what it meant to construct a nursery in the desert, to feed starving children who before meeting you had only known cassava and locusts. We've argued a thousand times. Never, never, never in these three decades would I have ever thought, even for a moment, that what they are accusing you of was a possibility.'

Drainpipe had often slept in the Oasis as a night warden and was sure that he would have known if something were amiss. He affirmed that Padre Fedele had shown the ultras 'a way of solidarity and true love towards those who are suffering and are among the forgotten of this planet'. He said Padre Fedele had only ever shown 'clear love towards the marginalized'. Claudio remembers that Padre Fedele was accused of the one crime that the ultras would have found unforgiveable: 'We would have forgiven him anything, even murder, but never rape.'

Many of Padre Fedele's friends felt that he had been framed. It was as if someone had deliberately looked for his weak spot – and few denied that women were his weak spot – and thus arranged the accusations. They were, for many, simply too gothic to be believable: the mystery pill, the six-figure sums – first €160,000 then €100,000 – to watch the rape, the Mafia threats. They read like a crime novel.

To those ultras in Cosenza who had been repeatedly arrested or even sectioned, it looked like another stitch-up. They knew Padre Fedele could be a *buffone* (a clown) and a bruiser. He was a *casinista*, a troublemaker, like his ultras. He had showily slept under bridges to highlight homelessness or gone on hunger strike because Cosenza might be relegated. But Padre Fedele had often denounced sexual violence. His battle on behalf of a young woman had led to the arrest of seven people. He had courageously denounced drug-dealers. He had built a multi-million pound 'Oasis' over which Church authorities were casting an envious eye. He had also denounced corruption in – and naturally proposed himself as the new head of – a hospital that later became the biggest bankruptcy in Calabrian healthcare. Far from being a rapist, his supporters said, Padre Fedele was actually a stone in the shoe of the corrupt.

Drainpipe dared write as much publicly. In the Cosenza fanzine, he wrote that 'the hierarchy of the Cosentine church is completing a project which they had in mind for a long time and which has one great obstacle: Padre Fedele'. He accused the Church of wanting to take over the Franciscan Oasis, to turf out the needy and to turn it, effectively, into something more like a hotel because 'they know only one God: money'. Claudio, as editor of the magazine, was sued for defamation by the Bishop, and declared himself 'ready to burn on the bonfire' rather than renounce what had been written. He repeated the conviction that there was a 'conspiracy' against Padre Fedele.

February 2006: a Lazio take-over bid

In July 2004, Lazio had been bought by a man called Claudio Lotito. Lotito had made his money (like many football owners) from cleaning and refuse contracts with local governments. Lazio supporters were suspicious. Lotito had married into one of the richest (and Roma-supporting) families in the capital, called Mezzaroma. As well as their involvement in Roma, members of the family were also involved with Siena and Salernitana football clubs. The manner in which he had bought the shares was also obscure – many felt he had used third parties to disguise the extent of his ownership.

Although Lotito had rescued Lazio from bankruptcy and possible extinction, there was soon a nasty surprise. The club was invoiced for €107 million for unpaid taxes by the Agenzia delle Entrate (the equivalent of HMRC). Repeatedly in the past, the debts of football clubs had been eased by government legislation, and Toffolo and Diabolik, two of the Irriducibili leaders, felt that a whiff of cordite might nudge the tax authorities towards indulgence. They organized a protest involving thousands of fans which, unsurprisingly, turned violent. Many supporters and police were hospitalized. The ultras were publicly demonstrating the chaos they could cause if the government didn't offer debt relief, which is exactly what happened. The government of Silvio Berlusconi spread the debt over twenty-three years.

In many ways, the ultras were just defending their club. But they had also performed a huge favour for their new president and there was an expectation of something in return. Lotito, however, made no concessions. The stewards on the turnstiles became officious. There were no more free tickets. Banners were confiscated. The terraces, and especially the spaces beneath the stairs, were no longer souks. 'He's taking our bread,' Diabolik said on the phone to Toffolo. 'This guy isn't letting us work.' It was very clear that there was going to be no quid pro quo.

The Irriducibili decided to protest. They smuggled in banners – 'Lotito Enemy of the [Curva] North' and 'The Battle-cry is

Lotito to the Executioner' – and began an assiduous campaign of intimidation. Manure was dumped outside the club's headquarters. Messages were faxed, posted and left on his windscreen. 'Be careful of your beautiful little wife,' said one. 'If you don't want to find him dead with his throat cut,' said another message left at the club, 'that bastard, disgusting pig has got to go. We'll cut him to pieces if that bastard doesn't go.'

The threats continued throughout the autumn of 2005. It was a period of many extremist gestures: a swastika was displayed during the game at Empoli in November, and another, plus a Celtic cross, at Livorno in December. The chants were politically similar: 'Duce, Duce' and 'Livornese Jew'. At Lazio–Ascoli in January, a banner read: 'No one will touch our [Roman] salute.' Very often such sentiments are the first exhibits in the case against the Irriducibili's political extremism, but they invariably appear when the ultra group is putting pressure on the club owner (who has to pay the fines and suffer the consequences of stadium closures).

Police had, by then, been alerted to the death threats made against Lotito, and the phones of the Irriducibili leaders were tapped. In one intercept, Toffolo gives an eloquent description of how he sees the role of the ultras: 'These people have to understand that we are the trade union.' To one listener he boasts: 'You're about to talk to someone who represents 15,000 people.'

The Irriducibili duly called a fans' strike. But it began to hurt them as much as it did Lotito. The thousands who didn't go to games didn't spend their money in the Irriducibili's shops to get kitted out for match days. In a text message, Diabolik wrote: 'If this bastard doesn't go, we're ruined because from this year we've started to dip into the other account that until now has never been touched. With costs higher than income we can't do anything other than end up bankrupt.'

It looked as if the good times were over for the Irriducibili but a solution was on the horizon. A Neapolitan businessman was planning to buy Lazio and had identified the old Lazio hero, Giorgio Chinaglia, as the ideal man to front the takeover bid. He wanted the Irriducibili as the foot soldiers who could force Lotito to, as they said, 'sit at the table'. During that 2005–06 season, the Irriducibili were in almost daily contact with members of the consortium. They were given funds for anti-Lotito banners and their radio station was granted the exclusive rights to any interview with the legendary Chinaglia. People who appeared to side with Lotito – a Sky sports analyst, the team coach, one of the players – were threatened and insulted. Others were invited to dish dirt on Lotito and were denounced when they didn't. Even some members of the Irriducibili complained about the ferocity of the campaign. Yuri fretted on the phone to Diabolik that Toffolo had his 'twenty veins' out, shouting at a woman who had defended the coach. 'We need to make friends, not enemies,' Yuri said.

Toffolo was equally incandescent during phone-ins on the group's radio station, The Voice of the North. When one listener disagreed with him and defended the coach (who had insulted the ultras by dedicating a victory to the president and not the fans), Toffolo rounded on a fellow Lazio fan: 'What's your problem, you jerk? I'll come and grab you in your home. What's your problem, villain?'

From reading the transcripts of months of phone calls as the Irriducibili tried to enable a takeover of their team, a sad, sordid world emerges. The Irriducibili come across as both menacing but amazingly unrealistic. At one point, Toffolo, half-dreaming, says, 'I've got Lazio in my hands.' 'I'm a power,' he boasts. He starts calling Chinaglia 'the President'. (Years later a medical report described Diabolik as suffering from 'symptoms of psychosis and mental instability', but since that document was provided by his defence team to arrange his release from a custodial sentence, it should be taken with a pinch of salt.) Theirs was a nihilistic world in which the only languages spoken were brute force and cash-in-hand. One of the Irriducibili's leaders said to a person who wasn't cooperating: 'I don't care anything for ethics. We're on the streets and on the streets anything can happen, understood?'

Chinaglia himself seems rather dim, never quite understanding all the machinations going on around him. He had already been used as an unwitting figurehead when money-launderers tried to take over Foggia football club the year before, but despite that takeover bid landing him in trouble, he couldn't resist the temptation to be in charge of his beloved Lazio for a second stint. This strong, stubborn man seemed to reflect perfectly the self-perception that many Laziali had of themselves, and he understood the Irriducibili's needs. 'If things work out,' Chinaglia told the ultra group, 'I would like to put a few things together, understand? We'll see.' He was offering to throw them the scraps again.

The problem was that the money for the takeover was coming from Neapolitan sources which were very suspect. In the subsequent arrest warrant, the investigating magistrates wrote that the man putting up the cash was 'tied up with a Camorra [the Neapolitan Mafia] association called the Casalesi clan. He had available a very considerable sum of money – equivalent to $21 million – locked-up in investments in Hungary. It's a sum absolutely disproportionate to his legitimate activity.' Put simply, the

Lazio takeover bid appeared to be funded by organized crime and Chinaglia was, as the arrest warrant said, 'a screen'.

Chinaglia's reaction to the news that organized crime was recycling money to buy his beloved club, exploiting him as the figurehead, was either naïve or wilfully myopic. Asked if he had complete trust in his backers, he replied that he trusted them 'because they had loads of money'.

2006: Eboli v. Cosenza

Since the advent of smartphones most groups have avidly filmed their fights. The footage isn't, for obvious legal reasons, uploaded to public sites, but most are only too happy to pull out their phone and show you some of the best. It's their equivalent of the slow-motion replay.

'This is the throwing of the stones,' Left-Behind once said to me, as we crowded round his phone. It sounded like a regular liturgical event: *il lancio delle pietre*. 'And this is the charge.' When you've watched hundreds of those films, a pattern emerges. The events are usually captured from inside cars or coaches, with a sardonic running commentary: 'Here come the cops' or 'I wouldn't go down that street, matey-boy.' You can only see a few heads, and sticks, bobbing in the distance. There's invariably the sound of sirens. Anyone who wants to join in can get out, anyone who wants to watch can get inside and, like everyone else, film the fun from fifty metres away.

It's usually a game. Years ago the Barletta ultras lined up barrels of firecrackers by an embankment, lighting them all just before the convoy of half a dozen Cosenza coaches came by.

Marco had his head out of the sunroof of the coach, trying to see what all the explosions were, and saw the rival ultras at a distance, insulting and laughing. So, the convoy stopped and a few men got out, grabbed the metal traffic hurdles and used them as blunt batons to charge the Barletta fans. It was exciting but no one really got hurt. You can often see in these filmed fights the plain-clothes policemen just a few metres from the action, one hand in a trouser pocket, wearing a white shirt and speaking calmly into a walkie-talkie. It's striking how contained the action is.

When you compare reports – from police and journalists – with what you actually see, you realize that everyone is exaggerating. The police over-egg the depravity because it's their job to spot danger (and, maybe, because that way they receive larger budgets, man-power and overtime). Journalists, of course, relish the news of blood and do nothing to diminish the stories. And ultras themselves want to appear as hard as lump-hammers, with each retelling adding new details.

Sometimes, though, the game goes wrong. Everyone in Cosenza remembers Eboli in 2006. It was supposed to be a friendly occasion but it's very often friendly games that have the most vicious fights. Two or three Cosentini went into a bar in the town. Versions of what they did vary. They either didn't pay for their drinks or were making lewd comments to the barwoman, who was the wife of the local crime boss. The husband got in his car and, as the lads were going to the stadium, mowed them down.

The fights then got serious. Although the Cosentini ultras are fun-loving jesters, when they decide to fight, they really go for it. There's a speed to them which is unpredictable and a strategic nous which comes from experience. Incensed that an ultra brother had been knocked down by a car and that the game was still going ahead, one Cosentino ran onto the pitch and punched the Eboli goalkeeper. The fights went on all afternoon.

Many people took a hiding – slaps and punches and kicks, but nothing too dangerous. But pride was hurt, and as the crowing Cosentini walked back to their coaches, they saw that the unarmed play-fight had turned into something else. People with axes and machetes chased them, and one lad with learning difficulties got left behind. Drainpipe and Barbara went back for him but were taken hostage. From the coaches you could see a hundred men surrounding them. You can hear, during the usual filming from inside the coach, people suddenly screaming in terror.

The proper criminals had turned up, and one of them spat at Drainpipe: 'You fuckers have broken our balls. Now you pay for everyone.' They were stripped of their wallets and given a beating. 'I thought that I was going to lose my skin there,' remembers Drainpipe.

Eboli was one of those rare occasions in which the ludic fight became very real. When you're an imitative teenager chanting 'You have to die' every week, it's hard to know that it's only a taunt. But Eboli was also an occasion in which ultra violence was taken on by (at least as the Cosentini tell it) the Mob proper. This wasn't ultras against ultras, but ultras against professional criminals.

When the violence was truly grim, though, there were always consequences for the leading group. After Eboli, the Cosenza Supporters decided to dissolve, leaving other groups in the field: Cosenza Vecchia, Alkool Group, Rebel Fans, Mad Boys, Amantea and the Allupati. As one group folded, the personnel bled into others. Everyone knew each other anyway. The boundaries between each group were porous. The same happened on all the terraces: there were feuds and friendships and reconciliations through the decades. But there was always strength in numbers, and so inevitably the entry requirements were low. The more youngsters you could pull in, and the more mental they were, the stronger your group. The terraces filled with hot-tempered types who knew no boundaries, especially that very thin one between facsimile and real violence.

Present Day: Venezia v. Cosenza

As soon as you're beyond San Marco and the Bridge of Sighs, the tourists thin out. It's two days before Christmas and small groups of Cosentini with red-and-blue scarves are walking along the waterfront boulevard that leads to the second-oldest stadium in Italy: the Stadio Penzo. If Venice is a fish, it's on the very southern tip of the tail fin, past the Arsenale and the Biennale Gardens.

The stadium is squeezed between a marina with its slim, white yachts and the leafless lime trees. The north stand for away fans is made of scaffolding poles that seem, from a distance, little more than matchsticks. There's a friendly atmosphere, partly because it's Christmas, but also because Venezia and Cosenza used to be twinned. 'How's Padre Fedele?' asks one of the Venice fans. Wherever you go, everyone asks after the Monk.

As you go to the stadium, there's a toilet block with a message spray-painted in huge letters, in English: 'Fight Fascists, Eat Nazis.' It's bitterly cold up in the scaffolding-stand, with its green, orange and black seats. All the groups are there: the Irrequieti ('the restless'), Amantea (the seaside town), the Allupati (a play on words between 'horny' and 'wolf'), Anni Ottanta (the 80s gang) and all the others. There are a few families too, the exiled Cosentini living in the North, who want their frozen children to experience a little bit of their home town. The ultras do a bit of outreach, offering the kids scarves and sandwiches.

Elastic is leading the singing as usual. One of the numbers is a bit of a mouthful – 'Orange-green-black-red-and-blue' – since an old twinning with Venezia has been recreated and is now being cemented in song by uniting the colours of the two teams. It feels a bit like 'I can sing a rainbow', which is, perhaps, part of the point: the closeness between the two groups of fans is the inclusivity encapsulated in the rainbow flag. It was here, in Venezia, that the 'Associazione Noi Ultras' was born, aiming 'to defend and enhance the sociable, unifying and cultural aspects of ultra fandom against xenophobic and racist degenerations'.

The ultras here have raised thousands of euros for charities like Emergency, for earthquake relief in Aquila, for the Green Cross and for the relatives of sick children. Throughout the 1990s one of Venezia's most charismatic ultras was El Bae ('Balls'). He was a left-wing activist, drawn towards the city's social centre, called Rivolta, and working as a cook in its 'hostelry of the dead cop'. He dreamt of going to help the Zapatistas in Chiapas, Mexico, but died in 2001, aged only forty, before he could make the trip. Shortly after his death, his friends from forty different fan groups raised money to rebuild a village in the Lacandon jungle in Chiapas, in his name. Calling the project 'the stadium of Bae', they built an aqueduct, a football and basketball pitch and a doctor's surgery.

'The mistrusted are always present,' we chant, clapping our hands fast. 'The mistrusted are always present.' Every time you despair of this numbskull world, you glimpse the beautiful flowers that emerge from the memory of dead ultras. Maurizio Alberti was an ultra from Pisa who died of a heart attack on the terraces when medics, assuming he was simply drunk or high, failed to take his condition sufficiently seriously despite being informed that he had a pacemaker. Since his death in 1999, the Curva Nord of Pisa has created a movement called Mau Ovunque ('Mau everywhere'), opening a play park in his name for disabled children.

It's a good game. Cosenza attack constantly but hit the cross-bar and the post in quick succession. At half-time, we go to the top of the stand to look for Chill, who has made this 2,000-kilometre round trip despite being banned from the stadium. We can't see him. 'He'll be in a bar somewhere,' reckons SkinnyMon.

'Long way to come for a drink,' says Left-Behind.

In the second half, Venezia are pressing for a goal but the game seems to be drifting towards a nil–nil. Between songs Vindov tells me about a feud that happened here back in 2012. There was a serious brawl between Venezia's own ultras, between the far-left Gate 22 and the far-right Vecchi Ultrà. One of the Gate 22 boys was scared for life after being beaten by a man with a knuckle-duster, so a few months later the boy's brother sought out the man from the Vecchi Ultrà and attacked him with a hammer, putting him in a coma. 'Since then they've tried to keep politics out of the terraces,' he says.

'Bet they have,' says Left-Behind.

Whilst we're talking, the ball breaks to Domenico Mungo, who launches it to the right, towards Jaime Báez. It's a sudden counter-attack and Venezia are exposed. Báez takes a touch and then plays a perfect diagonal ball to the far side, where Tommaso D'Orazio doesn't break stride, hitting the ball with his left and burying it in the far corner. Suddenly there's that blissful erasure of anything that separates us from each other. You hug, kiss, high-five. You bound down towards the turf, almost falling over the seats as the mass of humanity pushes you from behind. It's as if we've become a living organism, unable, briefly, to move with any autonomy. (Later I find that section from Elias Canetti's great book, *Crowds and Power*, in which he expresses this sense of almost ecstatic union. 'Only together,' he wrote, 'can men free themselves from their burdens of distance; and this, precisely, is what happens in a crowd. During the discharge distinctions are thrown off and all feel equal. In that density, where there is scarcely any space between, and body presses against body, each man is as near the other as he is to himself; and an immense feeling of relief ensues. It is for the sake of this blessed moment, when no one is greater or better than another, that people become a crowd.')

That density and equality linger for an hour or more after the game. And because it's Venice, and Christmas, and a victory, a hundred of us are singing loudly through the narrow streets, the raucous unison bouncing off the water and the walls. 'How beautiful it is,' we sing yet again, 'to get out of the house, to go to the stadium, to support Cosenza.' We pass our Venetian friends and briefly sing the rainbow song, before going back to the old favourites. We pile onto a boat-bus without tickets, overwhelming the inspector with a mixture of menace and humour. As it speeds along the Grand Canal, everyone is singing, banging hard on anything to hand. Red-and-blue flags – with Cosenza written on the horizontal – are hanging out of the windows, and the more tourists gawp at us, the more noise we want to make. Not just to show them that Cosenza has conquered this ancient city but to keep ourselves dense and united. Because any minute we'll all go our separate ways and the world will seem colder and lonelier again.

2007, Cosenza

In January 2007, just short of his forty-sixth birthday, Piero Romeo suffered a cerebral aneurysm. He was paralyzed down his left side. Though he was lucid, the quickest wit of the *curva* was suddenly slow and slurring.

It's noticeable how often terraces throw up characters who reflect, in some ineffable way, the contours and crevices of a city. The grief about Piero's illness was profound not just because of his personal situation, but because he seemed to encapsulate all that was best about the Cosenza *curva*. He, more than anyone, had lived by the motto the Cosenza ultras had once put on a banner: 'Our happiness will bury you.' To him, being an ultra was about being a prankster, putting one over people in power, especially the police. It was about getting around the rules to have a laugh with your mates during the party on the terraces.

Now he was ill, everyone started telling the old stories about him. How, during an away game at Catanzaro, he had smuggled 5,000 balloons in the shape of rabbits into the stadium (the symbol, like a chicken in English, of a coward). Half were red, half yellow. Once in the stadium, everyone inflated them and waved them at the hated local rivals. Another time, he had made the Cosenza goalkeeper, Sorviero, promise to jump the deep, concrete ditch behind the goal into the *curva* if the team was promoted: there's a famous photo of the goalkeeper, mid-air, jumping into Piero's arms. Even the players loved him, they said, and took absurd risks for him. He was constantly doing things to make people laugh, like sending a telegram to a friend who wasn't replying to his calls: '*Vu rispunna a su cazzu' i telefono?*' – 'Do you want to reply to the fucking phone?' He lived simply as an irreverent sprite, expressing an instinctive solidarity with any underdog. He would get furious if anyone referred to the homeless men and women he served in the foodbank as 'hobos' or 'bums'. And now he was the underdog, trapped in a deteriorating body, and it felt as if the whole of the *curva* was mourning the man who never wanted to be its leader.

Before his illness, Piero's 'Monk's Group' had become 'Vino e Gazzosa' – 'Wine and soda-water'. The Nuova Guardia had started to call themselves, ironically, the BDD. When one boy was handed back to his mother, the police told her that he had been found amidst a 'band of druggies and delinquents', and inevitably the insult stuck. By 2007 two of the most active ultra groups in the city were Rebel Fans and Cosenza Vecchia. Their headquarters were inside a squatted building near the railway station called Rialzo. It was one of those Cosenza spaces that became a home for ex-offenders, the homeless, for immigrants and ultras. It was home to the city's mosque and became a celebrated concert space, even hosting the Skatalites and Subsonica. 'Let's take back the city' was one of the occupiers' slogans.

Those ideals, of course, often came up hard against reality. One of the occupiers' other slogans was 'Against heroin, indifference and job insecurity' but many of the Rebel Fans were struggling with addictions. The squatters were protesting illegality and the incessant 'cementification' of the city, and yet found themselves living in the cold, bare concrete as illegals. But just as the ultras inverted everything you thought you knew about football, so the Cosenza squatters inverted the notion of illegality. The football team that emerged from Rialzo was called Clandestino United. Just as he was being vilified for alleged criminal offences, the squatters spray-painted 'Long live Padre Fedele' on the walls. It was like that chant from the terraces repeated at every game: '*diffidati sempre presenti*' (those who society mistrusts are always, in these spaces, present). The sadness at Piero's paralysis was tempered by an awareness that, at least, his revolution lived on.

2 February 2007: Death of Filippo Raciti

It was the weekend of the Sant'Agata celebrations in Catania, one of the biggest Christian festivals in Europe. The *centro storico* was candlelit and there was so much wax that young boys were scraping it off the cobbles to make, and sell, new candles. The elegant citizens were eating late-night pastries as the suburbs boomed with fireworks and songs.

It wasn't the ideal time for the biggest Sicilian derby for decades: Catania–Palermo in Serie A. The Sant'Agata spectacle was due to go on all weekend, so the *Questura* had scheduled the match for 6 p.m. on the Friday before the Sant'Agata processions began in earnest.

Looking back, the mixture of ingredients was so explosive that a tragedy was almost bound to happen. Just the week before, on 27 January 2007, a forty-one-year-old club official from Sammartinese, Ermanno Licursi, was beaten up during a mass brawl at the end of a game against Cancellese. He collapsed and died in the changing room shortly afterwards.

The Catania ultras were enjoying what Spampinato calls 'a time of maximum splendour: over the years we had make it clear that Catania wasn't a land to be conquered, that here it wouldn't be a walk in the park. If you arrive en bloc, and I want to come and find you, I will.' There was plenty of previous history between Palermo and Catania. Both sets of fans wanted 'contact'. It was what Spampinato 'wanted, studied, looked for and consumed. Game after game, we go and look for it.' Fighting with Palermo ultras was, for Spampinato, 'the rule for the red-and-blue ultras'.

Organizationally, the match was a mess. For years, quite a few Catanesi had wandered into the stadium waving just their supermarket loyalty cards. Things had tightened up a bit since the club had gone into Serie A but many toughs could still blag their way into the stadium. Some knew the security men. That was one of the police complaints – that clubs were complicit with ultras because the juicy contract of stadium security was always a compromise between the interests of the president and the ultras.

That season everyone wanted to be at the stadium. Not only because it was the derby, and in Serie A, but because Catania had been playing fine football. At the beginning of February Catania was fourth in Serie A. Part of the reason was a local attacker called Giuseppe Mascara, a man whose every other goal was a collector's item.

Not since Scoglio discovered Schillaci had Sicily produced such an original, lovable top-scorer. But whereas Schillaci was all fire-and-eyes with a furious shot, Mascara was impish. From inside the crowded box away at Catanzaro the previous season, he had scored a goal that was more like a golf-chip. Against Inter, at the San Siro, he had nonchalantly flicked the bouncing ball up with his right boot and speed-lobbed it into the net, leaving the keeper flapping like a fly in a spider's web. As if any additional spice were needed for the fixture, Mascara had previously played for Palermo, scoring eight goals in thirty-four games.

Palermo and Catania are separated by 190 kilometres. The Palermo ultras were given a police escort to the city on the other side of the island. But that escort had been ordered to go slow, at a maximum speed of 60 kph. The police plan was that the Palermo ultras would arrive when the match had long-since started, and that they would be so eager to consume the football spectacle that they wouldn't then go looking for a scrap. The police intelligence was deficient. Any ultra forced to miss half a match would arrive at the stadium alight with righteous anger. All that money they had spent, all the nights planning what to do, what insult to shout, where to seek out the Catanesi and teach them a lesson in their own city... only for the police to get them there with half the game gone. By the time the Palermitani got to the Cibali stadium, they were raring to smash the place up.

The game was already well underway when, eye-witnesses say, the police fired a tear gas cannister into Spampinato's Curva Nord at the start of the second half, just as the Palermitani were arriving. The *curva* dispersed, spreading out like a threatened shoal. The hardest ultras, as always, headed outside. Soon there was so much tear gas in the air that the game had to be suspended.

The underside of the Curva Nord of the Cibali is like all stadiums: the backside of concrete stairs, large areas of hard-standing, the odd glass booth. There are bushes sprouting from concrete tubs, lots of graffiti against the state. This was where it kicked-off. Now hundreds of Catania ultras were outside and tooled up. Palermitani ablaze at injustice were the enemy. In the middle, the police whom both sides hated for keeping them apart.

Catania ultras were running backwards and forwards, throwing stones over the transparent shields of the police at the Palermitani. Flares were thrown by the ultras, their orange glows mixing with the scalding tear gas. People grabbed anything they could: loose stones, hub caps, ripped-up asphalt. One kid, a six-foot, sixteen-stone teenager called Antonino Speziale, had gone into the toilets and smashed off a leg supporting a washbasin. Vehicles came steaming into the area, with sirens and sweeping blue lights. It was now a three-way fight.

Inspector Filippo Raciti arrived at 7.07 p.m. Soon afterwards, the police driver, Salvatore Lazzaro, saw a flare roll under a police Landrover Discovery. He quickly put the vehicle into reverse. On his first witness statement, that driver said: 'I moved the Discovery a few metres and in that moment I heard a blow on the vehicle and I saw Raciti who was on my left... bring his hands to his head.' At roughly the same time, Speziale was coming out of the bathroom with the leg of the wash-stand.

An ambulance was called for Raciti at 8.30 p.m. He had been complaining of dizziness and chest pains for over an hour. It wasn't certain what had hit him – the reversing vehicle or Speziale's ceramic bracket. It could have been anything. Visibility was worse than on the Po in winter and the sky was full of flying objects.

Inspector Raciti died that evening, having said to one of his colleagues: 'Make sure that bastard pays, the one with that hair, robust, the *Questura* knows who he is.' Raciti implied he had seen who had hurt him, but he couldn't name him.

His funeral was held on the Monday, 5 February. The Catania ultras hung out a large banner: 'The real Catania is that which weeps for its son, not for who kills him. We are Catania.' In private, though, many ultras were saying the opposite. Many would echo what one said, bluntly, in Giuseppe Scandurra's *Tifo Estremo*: 'What I've got to say about what happened in Catania is short but very clear: one–nil to the ultras. We, and there are many of us, have never forgotten Carlo [Giuliani, killed at

Genova's G8] and all the other dirty deeds they have done to us. I just hope this is only the beginning... death to cops.'

The crackdown was swift. Fifteen fans were arrested, four of them minors. Amongst them was an activist in the neo-fascist organization, Forza Nuova. One ultra group, the ANR (the 'Non-Recognized Association'), was found to be holding guns. The house of the stadium's custodian was raided, revealing baseball bats, ball-bearings and a sweatshirt emblazoned with 'ACAB' (an acronym for 'All Cops are Bastards'). The custodian was so incensed by the raid that he screamed at the police, 'Go away, you're just a fistful of bastards and villains. They did a good job throwing bombs at you. They should have killed all of you.'

That defiance was echoed by other ultras interviewed in the aftermath of Raciti's death. 'What we really want to say to all those who behave as if we don't exist is "here we are",' said one. 'Not only do we exist, but we're able to break your arse whenever and however we want.' Another fan underlined how much the police were now, more than rival fans, the intended enemy: 'At the stadium we always win because we don't go to watch the game but to fight the police.'

In this respect Catania ultras were no different to most others. There was, by now, a visceral distrust of the state and the police amongst Italian football's toughest fans. That ACAB acronym was now common all over Italy, especially around the stadiums. *Sbirri* – cops – were the butt of much urban graffiti. Policemen escorting ultras were used to listening to one almost-military song, sung aggressively in their faces: 'As soon as I arrive in the police station, the cop should tremble. The law doesn't scare us, the state won't stop us, we will not stop, because everyone knows the life of the ultra knows only two laws, violence and attitude.' That hatred for the police was particularly problematic on an island where the Mafia's law of antagonistic silence was always hard to break. It seemed to many as if the ultras were driving a wedge into the fragile cooperation between police and the people. Although they claimed to be different from the professional criminals, the ultras were serving their purpose, creating a hatred and suspicion of the police that could only hinder the fight against the Mafia. It showed an overlap of attitudes between the organized fans and organized crime.

The authorities were desperate to find a guilty party. They had watched all the CCTV from the 2 February riots and had seen Antonino Speziale – in his 'Champion' sweatshirt – emerging from the loos with the basin stand. When they looked into his background, he seemed to fit the bill. He was a regular around the stadium, attending a technical college fifty metres from the ground. He was part of a group called the Skizzati, 'the squirted' or 'splattered'. He had the symbol of Catania Calcio, an elephant, tattooed on his right arm. Speziale, by then seventeen, was arrested and charged with involuntary manslaughter.

It wasn't only the ultras, however, who were convinced that the police had the wrong boy. He wasn't a football nut but a rugby player, 'all fat and no brain' according to a friend. He had a huge, pock-marked face and he was always the one in the group people took the piss out of. If anything, he seemed a bit of a softie, helping out his grandmother at her florist's booth. He was the sort of dim underdog led astray because he longed to be included in the gang. He admitted taking part in the riot but he was adamant that he hadn't killed Inspector Raciti.

The forensics reports were inconclusive. The RIS (a forensic investigation unit) in Parma doubted, in its tortuous prose, that the basin stand could have caused the fatal injury: 'Whilst not being able to express a definitive diagnosis, the hypothesis of its unfitness seems to reunite the major probabilities.' Even more damaging for the prosecution was the fact that RIS revealed that they had found, on Raciti's protective vest, 'fragments of a blue colour which are made of a modified acrylic resin with nitrocellulose and with a large presence of titanium bioxide...' The implication was clear – Raciti may well have been hit, and killed, by the reversing blue Discovery.

For years ultras all over Italy had held onto that description of 'fragments of blue resin' as evidence of their generic innocence and of the stupidity of the police. Although Speziale was found guilty at all three levels of Italian justice, and sentenced to eight years, the 'Speziale Libero' slogan ('Free Speziale') quickly caught on, becoming shorthand for support of ultras and hatred of the 'forces of order'.

The ultras had always relished having bad taste. Being offensive was part of their famous 'mentality'. Now a new chant, reinventing that famous line about astonishing feats at Catania's stadium, celebrated the suspicion that Raciti had actually been killed by his own colleague reversing the Landrover. 'Sensational news from Cibali [Catania's ground],' they sang. 'They've run him over with a Discovery'.

11 November 2007, Arezzo

The hatred between the ultras and the 'forces of order' might have dissipated over time if another death that year hadn't made it far greater. Gabriele Sandri, or 'Gabbo', was a twenty-six-year-old DJ from a smart suburb of Rome called Balduina. He was a tall, gingery-blond with a big smile. He was always well dressed. His father had a fashion store and he liked showing off his latest tattoos. His mother was a casting director in Cinecittà, and Gabbo had seen all the old Italian comedies set around his own city. Now, as a DJ, he was beginning to get gigs all over the country, especially in Sardinia during the long summer.

Gabbo was a Lazio nut. He had come of age watching the golden years of the early noughties: Sven Goran Eriksson's tough but exciting team of winners. He had a Vikings scarf but had been on Irriducibili marches too, like the one protesting against the sale of Beppe Signori to Parma in 1994. He was friends with one or two of the Under-21 players who had been to his sets. Many of his friends were part of In Basso a Destra ('Bottom Right', a name which hinted not just at where they stood on the *curva* but also at their grass-roots far-rightism).

The night before the game he was at the decks in the Piper nightclub until almost sunrise. He went home, had a quick shower and went out again, meeting his mates in Piazza Vescovio outside the Excalibur pub. Nine of them, in two cars, were heading to Milano to see the Lazio game against Inter. Gabbo got into the grey Renault Scénic, driven by his friend Marco, known as 'Ovo'. Ovo was a member of the neo-fascist organization Forza Nuova and had been arrested by police for carrying a knife at a Lazio game in April 2006.

After a couple of hours, they stopped in a service station, Badia al Pino Est, southwest of the Tuscan city of Arezzo. In the same service station were five Juventus fans from the Juventus Club di Roma. They were on their way to support Juventus at Parma. Insults between the two were inevitable and the ultra code called for the insult to be avenged physically. There was a *zuffa*, a 'struggle' or 'scrap': shouts, fists, kicks.

On the far side of the motorway, a traffic cop had heard the fight. He put on his siren and ran up the bank to see more. The ultras quickly dispersed, the Juventini getting back into their car and, as they sped off, opening a door to knock one of Gabbo's mates over. The Laziali chased the car on foot, hoping to smash a window, but it was gone. The fight was over almost as quickly as it had started.

Gabbo was in the back of the Scénic, sitting in the middle between his two mates. Just as the car was pulling away, the traffic cop, Luigi Spaccarotella, screamed at them to stop. It was 9.18 a.m. Spaccarotella was over-excited and pulled out his Beretta 92SB, a semi-automatic pistol. The car was 66 metres away. The bullet, travelling at 385 metres a second, left a tiny hole in the side of the Scénic and entered Gabbo's neck. The other passengers barely realized what had happened. There was a faint noise and nothing more.

By the time the other lads understood, they were already racing north on the motorway. Gabbo was slumped, wheezing, and blood was coming out of his mouth and neck. They called an ambulance and pulled off at the next exit. Marco was so anxious that he smashed through the barriers of the motorway pay-booth. The doors of the car were thrown open and the paramedics moved in but there was nothing to do. Gabbo had died.

Before lunch that Sunday, the news of his death was made public. A press release from the police suggested that their officer had merely fired in the air but that official line was quickly ridiculed. There were plenty of eye-witnesses who had seen Spaccarotella plant his feet, straighten his arms and take aim. Word got around very quickly and as ultras were journeying to their games, they stoked each other's anger with stories about earlier police slayings.

The ultras never denied being violent. But they were adamant that there was violence on both sides and the lack of consistency in reporting and punishing that violence infuriated them. Back in February 2007 the entire league had been suspended to mourn Inspector Raciti. The idea that the same thing wouldn't happen now that the roles were reversed – a policeman killing an ultra – seemed illogical. Inter ultras, twinned with Laziali, unfurled a banner within hours of Gabbo's death: 'For Raciti you stop the league, the death of a fan has no meaning.' Parma fans raised an egalitarian banner, echoing the one written in 1993 for another alleged victim of police violence: '*La morte è uguale per tutti*' ('Death is the same for everyone').

The most violent protests were in Bergamo and Rome. Il Bocia and his Atalanta ultras in Bergamo decided to stop the game at any cost. A few minutes into the home game against Milan, two dozen hooded ultras, with scarves covering their faces, started kicking the inch-thick plexiglass between themselves and the grass. It billowed like clingfilm, eventually shattering in two places. Soon there were two big holes. After a quick consultation with the players and police, the game was called off.

In screaming for the games to be postponed out of respect for a dead fan, the ultras were assuming an original position. Until the early noughties, they had proudly been the most demented devotees at the football temple. But now, as with the 'derby of the dead baby', they were actually sometimes agitating for games not to go ahead. It was like an alcoholic not just passing a pub, but protesting against it. They, of all people, were asking that the football juggernaut occasionally pause and mourn. It was both logical and paradoxical: they didn't see themselves as apostates but as the faithful resacralizing games by violently stopping them.

That evening there were serious riots in both Rome and

Milano. Even those who had never known Gabbo felt he was one of them. The Roma–Cagliari match was supposed to be an evening kick-off and by late afternoon 400 fans – both Romanisti and Laziali – were marauding. Between the Stadio Olimpico and Ponte Milvio, the pedestrian bridge over the Tiber, skips and motorbikes were overturned, a bus was set alight, the offices of CONI (the Italian International Olympic Committee) were invaded, and its windows, computers and clocks smashed. Three police stations were besieged. Although chaotic, it seemed well-organized. 'It's not easy to attack three police stations and the offices of CONI,' said one Home Office minister, 'unless you've got a military strategy.'

The police had always been seen by ultras as the armed wing of the Establishment, and since ultras saw themselves as the armed wing of the resistance, it was inevitable that the two would come to blows. As Valerio Marchi wrote in his essay, 'I am an ultra and I'm against': 'For the police the ultra is a figure to control and repress because he's subversive, and not because of what [crimes] he could commit. For the ultra, the police are part of a third tribe which wears the coat of the system and which beats up, arrests and issues restriction orders not to restabilize order but to defend their interests.' It's a point of view repeated by almost everyone within the movement. As one of the characters says in Nanni Balestrini's novella, *I Furiosi*: 'The police, too, are ultra gangs, so are the *Carabinieri*, and as with us they too have groups which are more tight-knit and which always want to fight.'

If an increased politicization of the terraces created divisions (both internally, within the same terrace, and within the movement as a whole), hatred of the police united all political sides of the terraces, from far right to far left. They would sing 'Landslide, a terrace landslide on the Italian police, a terrace landslide on those sons-of-bitches', a song written by Erode, a left-wing post-punk band from Como. From the outside, that visceral disdain for the police appeared Mafia-like, delegitimizing law-enforcement and refusing all cooperation with it. But from within the ultra world, the disdain was born of a profound sense of injustice. They would point to a long list of victims of police brutality: Giuseppe Plaitano killed by another police bullet in April 1963, the Trieste fan Stefano Furlan who died of brain injuries inflicted by a police truncheon in 1984, the Atalanta fan Celestino Colombi slain by a heart attack after a police charge in 1993. Exactly the same thing had happened to Fabio Di Maio, a Treviso fan in 1998. Alessandro Spoletini, a Roma fan, had spent a month in a coma after a brutal truncheoning in 2001. For months newspapers reported the case as one of ultra, rather than police, brutality. Brescia ultra Paolo Scaroni, a farmer and rock-climber, was savaged by police in Verona in 2005 when no disturbances were taking place. He too spent a month in a coma and, when an investigation was eventually begun, it became apparent that witness statements had been doctored and CCTV footage was missing. Years later a court found that his had been a 'gratuitous and unmotivated beating' but since police wore no identification, it was impossible to determine the guilty party. 'The thing which hurts most,' he said in an interview years later with *Espresso*, 'is that they've deleted my childhood and adolescence. I've lost all the memories of the first twenty years of my existence.'

In those and many other cases, the police version was repeated *ad nauseam* by work-shy journalists who didn't want to sour their contacts in the *Questura*. Clichés about rioting thugs were churned out, meaning that even when they were the victims, the ultras were still the scapegoats. What incensed the ultras wasn't just the brutality – that was part of the deal. It was the fact that only one side of the story was ever told (their violence, not that of the police), and that there were stiff sentences for ultras but guaranteed impunity for police. It seemed as if journalism, and justice, were stacked against them. Here, too, was another feedback loop: the more ultras felt that journalists were reporting only the police side of the story, the more they chanted 'Journalists are terrorists' and the like, which only persuaded most investigators that it was safer to source their information from the *Questura*, not the terraces.

Often the victims of police brutality weren't ultras but ordinary citizens like Federico Aldrovandi (killed by police in Ferrara on the same day that Scaroni was beaten) or Giuseppe Uva (beaten to death for having moved some traffic cones for a lark when drunk in Varese) or Stefano Cucchi (who died at the hands of *Carabinieri* in Rome). Their names were added to all the others memorialized by ultras in matches. 'La legge non è uguale per Cucchi', said one Torino banner, a parody on the ideal of equality before the law ('The law isn't equal for Cucchi'). The ultras felt it was a repression of freedom of expression that, from March 2007, banners now had to be approved by the authorities. When, in November 2012, a Cosenza player revealed a T-shirt saying 'Speziale is innocent' (the man convicted for killing Inspector Raciti), he was banned from football for three years.

To the police, however, the ultra world appeared a '*collante*', an 'adhesive' that held together an underworld of criminals. It was a world in which the colours of a team were now secondary to the colour of money. In May 2007 seven members of Milan's Guerrieri were arrested, accused of extortion, violence and threats towards the club they were alleged to be supporting. The CEO of Milan, Adriano Galliani, was even given a police escort. Almost identical charges had previously been brought against Roma ultras when two former leaders of the far-right organization FUAN (the 'University Front of National Action') attempted to extort tickets and away-game packages from the club.

The traditional rivalry between many ultra groups had been superseded by political similarities. All the major firms of both Lazio and Roma were now avowedly fascist. On the Roma side were Tradizione Distinzione, the Boys and Bisl ('*basta infami, solo lame*' – 'enough villains, only blades'). Apart from the Irriducibili, the Laziali had Only White and In Basso a Destra. It was a similar story in Milan. 'Kassa' and 'Peso' of Milan's Guerrieri had opened a fascist night spot called Lux. Another Guerriero was tried for attempted murder. 'Todo', the head of Inter's Irriducibili, was a founder of an extremist club called Black Heart, and was a former adherent of Skinhead Action. A year later, after a fire had destroyed the premises of 'Black Heart', it rented new premises in Via Pareto from a former NAR terrorist. It was here that 'Todo' opened a shop – 'Il Sogno di Rohan' ('The Dream of Rohan' – more Tolkien) – selling neo-Nazi paraphernalia. In 2011 another neo-Nazi organization, Lealtà Azione ('Loyalty Action'), was founded and based in the same complex.

It was often at funerals that you could glimpse how the ultras' original separatism – keeping rivals, business and politics at bay – had now been replaced by cooperation. When the leader of Roma's Boys, Paolo Zappavigna, died in a motorcycle accident in 2006, his burial was a reunion not of Roma ultras but of the city's fascist fraternity. The same happened at the burial, in Milan in 2007, of Nico Azzi, a former terrorist in the Fenice organization. His funeral was attended by the leading Alleanza Nazionale politician Ignazio La Russa, as well as representatives of almost all Milan and Inter ultra groups. It seemed that, far from being 'beyond', many ultras were now in the midst of the political and entrepreneurial worlds.

That fatal year of confrontation between the ultras and police that changed everything. The Italian state designed a series of measures that slowly split and splintered the movement. Legislative attempts to exert control had, in truth, begun two years earlier. Under the so-called Pisano Decree, any stadium with more than 10,000 seats was supposed to have electric turnstiles, CCTV and frisking of all fans. Then, in the aftermath of the killing of Filippo Raciti, in April 2007 a new law banned the sale of more than four tickets to the same person. *Daspos* (stadium bans) were increased, so you could now receive a ban from one to five years for lighting a flare. Anti-Mafia measures were to be deployed against fans, enabling surveillance and the confiscation of property from those who might be violent. There would be custodial sentences of one to three years for those who broke the terms of their Daspo, and one to four years for the throwing or use of dangerous materials. Climbing a barrier brought a year's jail term and a fine of between a thousand and five thousand euros. Arrests could also now be made in a different way: rather than *in flagranza*, the terminology was *quasi flagranza* ('almost flagrant'), meaning that people could be arrested up to forty-eight hours after an event, when the individual ultra was well away from his mates. There were now sentences of four to sixteen years for attacks on public officials. Worst, for the ultras, was Article 9, in which anyone suspected of 'episodes of turbulence' at past games could be excluded from the purchase of tickets. 'Suspicion' and 'presumption' – not even a definitive sentence – were the bases on which ultras were now barred from their temple, and it only served to increase the rancour between both sides.

But the shrewdest measure imposed by the state was the introduction in August 2009 of the *Tessera del Tifoso* ('the fan's card'). It was a sort of loyalty card issued by clubs, without which fans were unable to purchase tickets to games for which it was decided that the *tessera* was necessary (usually high-risk matches and away games). Many clubs saw a financial, as well as a law enforcement, opportunity and turned their particular *tessera* into a debit card, enabling fans to purchase merchandise in the club shop.

The *tessera* was the antithesis of ultra ideology. Many felt it was both an example of *schedatura* (state surveillance) and a capitalist perversion of their temple. But opinion about what to do was divided. Some groups, like the Veronesi, decided to adopt the *tessera* en masse. In other terraces, many older ultras didn't think it was worth the fight and urged the younger hot-heads to acquire the card and get on with it.

But the purists took a stand. At every match new chants began against the hated loyalty card, among them 'And I will not be carded' and 'Carded ultras, servants of the state'. Many terraces, previously united, were suddenly split along ideological lines, with both sides bitterly accusing the other of betrayal. One group stood accused of selling out to the state and playing by their rules, whilst the other was accused of forsaking the cardinal rule of the ultra world – presence – and of no longer supporting the team. In any ultra context, mention of the *tessera* became the conversational equivalent of popping the pin out of a hand grenade.

Over the years there had been many attempts to unite the ultra movement. There had been conferences and peace summits.

The nationalist wing of the movement tried to create an ultra group in support of the national team under the (usually far-right) Viking banner. None of those initiatives were particularly successful because of the infinitely fractious nature of Italian fandom. But whilst the hated *tessera* divided the ultras in practice, it also, paradoxically, united them in theoretical opposition. In a strange way, the *tessera* provided that sense of repression which, according to Elias Canetti, is vital to the defiance of a group. 'One of the most striking traits of the inner life of a crowd,' he wrote, 'is the feeling of being persecuted, a peculiar angry sensitiveness and irritability directed against those it has once and forever nominated as enemies… whatever they [the enemies] do will be interpreted as springing from an unshakable malevolence, a premeditated intention to destroy the crowd, openly or by stealth.'

It was as if the ultras had found a new calling: the fight not only against each other but against repression. It was common for them to travel hundreds of kilometres to games and, having neither the *tessera* nor, consequently, a ticket, they would stand outside the ground chanting that they were the '*non-tesserati*'. Often opposing ultras, from inside the stadium, would applaud them. And, equally frequently, the police or stewards would fudge the rules and allow them into the stadium anyway as they could cause less damage inside than out.

Pino Coldheart, the leader of Juventus's Drughi, was released from prison in February 2005 after serving his sentence for the armed robbery in which a *Carabiniere* was murdered. Such was his notoriety that even opposing ultras from Roma held up a banner the following Sunday at Juventus's ground: '*Ciao Pino. Bentornato*' ('Hi Pino. Welcome Back').

But he didn't like the limelight. A man of very few words, he was so silent it could be unnerving. Normally he just listened and watched. When he did speak, everyone obeyed because they trusted his shrewdness and because it wasn't worth your while to disagree. He had been inside so long that the outside world itself seemed odd to him – faster but more superficial, both richer and yet somehow impoverished. The ultra world, too, was almost unrecognizable. There was so much money in football, he realized, that even a tiny slice of the action could make a *capo-ultra* rich.

In Pino's absence the Drughi had lost supremacy on the terraces. Now he was out of prison, the plate tectonics of the terraces were shifting. In the summer of 2005 an ultra from a rival Juventus group was stabbed. The feud lasted more than a year. In the summer of 2006 two Drughi (including Pino) were stabbed and fifty fans arrested in clashes between different Juventus ultras in Alessandria. Some of the major ultra groups moved to the Curva Nord of the old Delle Alpi stadium, leaving the Drughi to battle it out with the Bravi Ragazzi ('Goodfellas') for control of the south terrace. In March 2009 Pino was again wounded by three thugs who police believed to be from the Bravi Ragazzi group. The leader of the Bravi Ragazzi, Andrea Puntorno, had an arm broken in a fight. Umberto Toia, the leader of another group, Tradizione, was beaten up outside his bar (Black & White) and shots were fired against its metal shutters.

It wasn't just established ultra groups who were vying for access to the tens of thousands of euros available from ticket touting. Organized crime began casting an envious eye at the easy money to be made. The attraction wasn't just the profits but the impunity that accompanied them. Ticket-touting wasn't a criminal offence (in the jargon, it was called an 'administrative offence') and it carried an almost negligible risk compared to drug-dealing. It was also a chance to invest and launder capital amassed from the drug trade. Some policemen speculated that the violence against *capo-ultras* wasn't only inflicted by rival ultras but also by mafiosi who hadn't received the return they expected from tickets in which they had invested.

For their part, various ultra gangs were receptive to mobsters on the terraces because they could enforce order. They carried a threat of such lethal violence that the *capo-ultras* now felt protected, even untouchable. There wouldn't be any more broken arms and stabbings, they hoped, if they stood alongside notorious underworld figures. For those ultras, like Andrea Puntorno, who doubled as drug-dealers, the Mafia also offered new supply chains, contacts and distribution channels. Two worlds that already seemed to overlap now became, on certain terraces, even closer.

The result was that each Juventus ultra group forged an alliance with one or two Mafia clans. Puntorno was known to be close to the Sicilian Li Vecchi family and the Macrì clan in Calabria. It wasn't as if the ultra bosses hid those connections. It actually suited them to boast about their underworld connections in order to increase, exponentially, the fear they instilled: Loris Grancini, leader of Juventus's Vikings, once boasted: 'It's true, I'm very close to the [Calabrian] Rappocciolo clan.' Pino Coldheart himself, calling on contacts he had made in prison, approached Placido Barresi, the head of the Piedmont arm of the Calabrian Mafia, the 'Ndrangheta. Years later, an aged Barresi would admit that 'united Calabria' had infiltrated the Juventus terraces.

By 2010 the Italian secret services – the Agenzia Informazioni e Sicurezza Esterna, known as Aise – were aware that the

Juventus terraces were becoming a home not just for political extremists from the far right but also for Mafia outfits. The agent commissioned to investigate that murky world needed an informant on the inside. The man he found was embedded deep within the Drughi but was also a gregarious, friendly man: Ciccio Bucci.

By then, after years of frenetic dealing and late-night dashes back to Turin, Bucci and his wife had drifted apart. Football, and his phone, seemed to interrupt everything. He was rarely at home and when he was, his wife felt he was too indulgent towards his son, Fabio. He would spoil him in the way absent parents often do. Gabriella didn't like it when Bucci took their young son into the city for sleepovers. Eventually, the pair separated but remained on good terms. Bucci bought a small flat in the next-door village, in Margarita, with its petite castle and rust-brick church. By then he was so close to Juventus staff that he sometimes slept over at the flat of Stefano Merulla, the head of the club's ticket sales division.

In many ways, he was actually closer to the club hierarchy than he was to the Drughi. Since Pino Coldheart had come back on the scene, Bucci felt he was being slowly sidelined within his own group. Bucci's quick patter and matiness contrasted sharply with Pino's brooding, reticent presence, and Bucci felt constantly judged. It was as if his place in the crew, his whole income even, were under threat. There were new faces that he had never seen before, Calabrians who seemed to be suddenly at the centre of the action. Sometimes, speaking on the phone to his handler in the secret services, Bucci felt relief at being able to let off steam. Since his marriage had broken down, it was the only time anyone seemed to listen to him.

––––––

2011–12, Genoa

When Puffer emerged from prison, having served his sentence for threatening his (now ex-) wife, he seemed different. On the day of his arrest in 2005 he had decided – after twenty years of heavy use – to give up cocaine. In prison he had read all the works of an Italian sociologist called Francesco Alberoni and had sat through two-hour sessions with a prison psychologist every Tuesday afternoon. 'It helped me become more patient and self-critical,' he remembers.

Like a lot of people in recovery, he had put on a bit of weight. His head was still shaved, his face taut, but he looked rounder. 'I'm now a breathless old nag,' he joked with a wheezy laugh. He was approaching his fiftieth birthday and had started to dress smartly. Under his Burberry jacket, his initials were stitched into the paunch of his immaculate blue shirt with its cut-away collars. He had designer glasses, a black-and-silver Rolex and brown suede shoes with raffish green laces.

He had started to build a bit of a business empire. He opened one restaurant in 2002, in Piampaludo just west of Genova, and then in 2010 opened another in Urbe, near the Piedmont border. Soon he would add a focaccia bar to the business. When he was released from house arrest, his friends organized a party to celebrate his new-found freedom. Many ultras were there, as were a few players from Genoa, including Omar Milanetto and Beppe Sculli.

Piazza Alimondi was now his kingdom. He lived in a flat above it, while '5r' – the historic headquarters of the Genoa ultras of which he was the leader – was just off it. When he sat in the bar underneath his house, drinking red wine in the early afternoon and smoking his Camels, passers-by would constantly shout hello. If he ate a quick bowl of pasta – he was given the 'high table' in the corner – so many people shook his hand that it was hard to eat. He would hold out his left hand whilst he ate with his right.

The fear he had inspired in the past was now mixed with affection. He was generous, buying people drinks or giving coins to passing beggars. Now he was single, he put up young lads who were in trouble, even Sampdoria fans. He was hard with them to help get them off drugs: 'I'll break your other leg if you go back on that shit,' he would say. Now, he complained, anyone could get hold of drugs. 'They're the only thing in the last thirty years that have gone down in price.'

He still exuded authority. At every meeting in 5r, with people packed on the red-and-blue benches along the walls, or drinking Ceres and playing table-football, people listened the minute he spoke. He passed on the intelligence he had heard about CCTV, about police operations or opposing fans.

In May 2011 there was a strange meeting in a restaurant, Coccio, in Sturla, an eastern suburb of Genova. It was mid-afternoon and the restaurant was closed to the public. At the meeting were two footballers, Domenico Criscito (Genoa) and Beppe Sculli (Lazio), two ultras (Puffer and Cyclops) and a Bosnian criminal called Safet Altic. It was a rum crowd. Safet was a Bosnian debt-collector for the Sicilian Fiandaca clan who had also, in the past, been involved in jewellery heists and drug-dealing. He was so well-known to the Lazio player, Sculli, that the latter called him '*fratè*' ('brother'). Sculli himself was one of the most opaque of Italian footballers from recent decades. The grandson of a convicted Calabrian mafioso known as U Tiradrittu ('Mr Straight-Ahead'), he had already been banned from football for eight months in 2001 for match-fixing in a game between Crotone and Messina. He had played for Genoa for years but had recently moved to Lazio.

The reason for the meeting was obscure. Coming four days before Lazio played Genoa, it appeared an opportunity to agree what should happen in that game and, presumably, to distribute the cash required to make it happen. The meeting was photographed because magistrates in Cremona were investigating a match-fixing syndicate. There were investors from Singapore and Hungarian, Albanian, Macedonian and Italian criminals who had established contact with footballers in Serie B and A. An investigating magistrate later wrote that there were 'significant elements to affirm that Sculli, just before Lazio–Genoa of May 2011, took on the role of "collector" of a notable sum of money to fix the match.' Sculli, the magistrates noted in their roundabout way, 'isn't extraneous to the world of organized crime'. Before the game, there were an astonishing number of phone calls between players and criminals, referring cryptically to the delivery of 'watches' or 'documents'. Two days after the main meeting in the Coccio restaurant, Safet Altic met the Genoa midfielder Omar Milanetto in Bar Groove in the city centre.

Subsequent confessions revealed that the game would be 1–1 at half-time, and that there would be more than four goals scored overall (it finished 4–2). The bookmaker, SKS365, received (and duly denounced) an anomalous volume of wagers on precisely that result. Even without the hindsight of confessions and investigative wiretaps, it was obvious to anyone who watched the game that it was a strangely meek encounter. Many of the opposing players that day knew each other from having played together in Modena years before. Once the 1–1 score had been reached by the twelfth minute, the players stopped attacking. 'There's little freneticism,' bemused commentators said, 'so many errors in passing, even from good players… it's an incredible thing… they're passing the ball around ad infinitum…'

Two days after the game, on 16 May 2011, there was a meeting in Milano involving Sculli, two Genoa players and many of the criminal fixers. It was, one assumes, a chance to settle accounts and maybe even agree future fixes.

Within weeks of that infamous Lazio–Genoa game, the *calcio-scommesse* ('football betting') scandal broke and various players were arrested. At first eighteen clubs and twenty-six players were under investigation. But the scandal kept getting bigger and a second investigation, called 'Cremona-bis', involved twenty-two clubs and sixty-one players. A third one ('Cremona-ter') looked into thirteen clubs and thirty-five players. Other trials with multiple accused began in Bari, Naples and in Bari again. There were a fourth and fifth investigation in Cremona, and another one in Genoa. Every thread that was pulled seemed to unravel the seams of the footballing world and reveal a sordid world of cash and duplicity. Sporting heroes like Beppe Signori and Cristiano Doni suddenly seemed very different. In the words of one of the cynical fixers, Hristiyan Ilievski, it appeared that Italian football 'wasn't a game but a compromise'.

The country had always had a problem with match-fixing (there were similar scandals in 1980 and 1986), partly because it was a particularly attractive scam for organized crime: although the financial rewards were great, the punishments were, as with ticket-touting, minimal. 'It's the cleanest dirty business in the world,' joked Ilievski. Both a prosecutor in Bari and the head of Fifa's security commission estimated that €12 billion was bet through unofficial channels on Italian football every year.

The vast majority of ultra groups were aghast at the revelations of match-fixing. For them, buying or selling games was just another example of how they had been betrayed by greedy players. The scandal merely underlined the ultras' conviction that, with so much wrong in the sport, it was absurd to scapegoat them alone. But because they invariably occupied that grey area between legality and illegality, and often had contacts with both players and the underworld, it was perhaps inevitable that some groups would be drawn into the money-making wheeze. One of the match-fixers called Genoa 'our Gomorrah', and the strange meetings there spoke for themselves. But in Bari, too, the ultras saw a chance to turn a profit. Since the club in that 2010–11 season was as good as relegated (and match-fixing invariably took place towards the end of a season when mid-table clubs had little to play for and others were desperate for points), three *capo-ultras* approached the players. 'You're bottom,' they said (remembered the club captain when interviewed by police). 'You've had a shit season. Tomorrow you've got to lose. Basta.' One of the players was slapped. Another eye-witness remembered the threats. 'Until now we've let you live peacefully even if the team has been shit and you're practically relegated. We haven't broken your balls, we let you go out in the evenings with your families. But now you've got to give us a hand, the music is changing...'

The players allege that they told Bari's sporting director of the threats and that his advice was to 'close your eyes and shut your mouth'. The team lost the next two matches 1–0, away to Cesena and at home to Sampdoria. Three weeks later, one of the players at the centre of the match-fixing scandal, Andrea Masiello, deliberately scored an own-goal in the derby between Bari and Lecce to give Bari's closest rivals a 2–0 victory.

———

13 December 2011, Florence

Until the 1990s, Italy had been an almost exclusively monocultural and monoracial society. In the 1981 census there were only 321,000 foreigners in the country. By 1991 that number had almost doubled and in the 2001 census there were 1,334,889 non-Italians officially resident in Italy, with far more living as 'clandestines'. By 2015 the official figure went above five million for the first time. The consequence for ultra groups – many of which were becoming stridently right-wing and nationalist – was an almost complete inversion of the movement's founding ideals. Where before the terraces gathered many of society's excluded, now they seemed to unite against the racially different. Rather than offering belonging, certain terraces became bulwarks against those who, they said, didn't belong.

Incidents of what's known as *'squadrismo'* were increasingly common. One anti-fascist watchdog counted, between 2005 and 2008, 330 acts of fascist aggression. In 2009 *Blocco Studentesco* – CasaPound's youth movement – came to Rome's central square, Piazza Navona, armed with truncheons painted with the Italian tricolour, which they used to beat up left-wing students. When one TV programme criticized *Blocco Studentesco* its offices were 'occupied' by CasaPound militants. Two years later that atmosphere of hatred led, inevitably, to the loss of innocent lives. On 13 December 2011 Gianluca Casseri, a militant in the CasaPound base in Pistoia, left home with a Magnum 357 in his bag. He was a taciturn loner, fifty-years-old, rotund with short, grey hair. He was a self-published author, writing a biography of the Italian neo-Nazi intellectual Adriano Romualdi (son of a former MSI president and protégé of Julius Evola) and a fantasy novel, *The Keys of Chaos*. On that December morning Casseri had a clear plan: to shoot as many immigrants as possible. He went to Piazza Dalmazia and, at 12.30 p.m., killed two Senegalese men, Samb Modou and Diop Mor. He shot another man, Moustapha Dieng, in the back and throat and then drove off in his blue VW Polo. Just over two hours later Casseri was at the city's central market, where he shot Sougou Mor and Mbenghe Cheike, who survived the attack. He then turned his gun on himself in the market's underground car park.

Sometimes the attacks on immigrants were a calculated warning by organized crime. When six innocent bystanders – from Ghana, Togo and Liberia – were killed in the 'Castel Volturno slaughter' in 2008, it was interpreted as a warning by the Neapolitan Mafia, the Camorra, against the activism and entrepreneurialism of the immigrant community. Racism certainly played a part but it was as much old-fashioned criminal marking of territorial control for commercial exploitation. But often the violence was sheer and senseless hatred. Between 2011 and 2014, fifty-nine Bengali men and women were admitted to hospitals in Rome with severe cuts and fractures since one of the games played by Forza Nuova militants was to find a solitary Asian person and, as a group, attack them. As one militant proudly boasted, it was like having a coffee after a meal: 'At the end of the evening we do a Bengali.'

22 April 2012, Genoa

Sometimes they managed to storm the bastille: not just take control of the streets, but of the stadium as well.

The Genoa–Siena match was, from a Genoa point of view, going terribly. The club was close to relegation and, despite playing at home, found itself 3–0 down to Siena by half-time. The ultras in the *gradinata nord* were shouting and gesturing. It wasn't the usual co-ordinated singing but individual shouts as if there were rebellion in the air.

In the fourth minute of the second half Siena scored a fourth goal and the ultras started moving. The head of the stewarding operation realized it was becoming dangerous and decided to pull his stewards out of the *gradinata*. But when the door was opened, about two hundred ultras, led by Cobra and Cyclops, burst through. They forced the next gate into the main stand. Soon they were centre stage, standing on the plexiglass above the pitch. Theirs was a montage of rage and intensity: the unison chants, the identical gestures of arms going backwards and forwards in the air. Flares and paper bombs were being thrown onto the grass. In the eighth minute the referee suspended the game.

The Siena players walked to the changing rooms but the Genoa players couldn't. Cobra and his mates were standing on the white players' tunnel, its ribs bending like an accordion. The Genoa players were in the centre-circle with police, journalists and club officials. Suddenly, the ultras seemed to be in charge. They were jabbing their fingers at the grass in front of them as a summons. 'Come here, pieces of shit,' they shouted. Some made throat-slitting gestures. 'We are Genoa,' they said. 'We'll come and get you tonight by the seaside,' Cyclops bellowed. 'We'll see you this evening.'

The tableau was hypnotic. The commoners – a dark mass of men dressed in shades, hoodies and jeans – had complete control of the aristocrats of a Serie A game. The Sky commentator called it 'surreal and grotesque'. Marco Rossi, the club captain, walked over to the group that was now chanting rhythmically: 'We are Genoa!' The ultras demanded that the players remove their shirts because they weren't worthy to wear the colours. The commentator from RAI (the state broadcaster) tried his best to sympathize with the ultras. 'Fans' anger should always be listened to,' he said. 'It's always the fruit of great love... even hatred is the child of too much love.'

Enrico Preziosi, the club president, was on the pitch, concerned that the club would be docked points if the game couldn't continue. He agreed that the players should remove their shirts, a symbolic surrender to the ultras. Rossi took off his shirt. Other players did the same and Rossi gathered them up. One player was crying. 'There's great sadness in these images,' the RAI commentator said. 'This is a command, it's blackmail, it's intimidation.'

The symbolism of that afternoon was eloquent. Young players were crying and denuded, standing far below older men who were threatening them with violence. But Beppe Sculli – the Calabrian with underworld connections and a match-fixing history, who had now returned to Genoa from Lazio – refused to remove his shirt. What might have appeared brave defiance was actually a meeting of minds. He climbed up towards the top of the players' tunnel and he and Cobra put their heads together, arms around the back of each other's heads, whispering. 'Sculli is one of us,' the ultras started shouting. Sculli, having spoken to Puffer on a club official's phone, persuaded the ultras to end their protest. He shouted at his captain to take the shirts back to the players. The game was back on.

As with so many iconic events involving the ultras, it could be read in diametrically opposing ways. On the one hand, the

Genoans had merely done what every ultra group in Italy dreamt of doing: they had publicly reasserted that the shirt was more sacred than the overpaid players, even more sacred than the sport itself. They had defended the colours of the city against humiliation and, apart from barging a few stewards out of the way, hadn't committed any crime. 'It was the most civil protest,' Puffer told me, 'there's ever been in the world of football.' Many remembered the words of Fabrizio De André, the Genovese singer-songwriter, who in his brief scribblings about fandom once wrote that 'an easily influenced individual, who is continuously taught by society that life is only a knife-fight for survival, will easily become a fanatic… and will consider defeat as a personal tragedy caused by others and against which he will carry out acts of violence either before the defeat to avert it, or afterwards to avenge it.'

Others, though, felt that the afternoon finally exposed the intimidation that had always bubbled in the background of ultra life. Just a few months before, the ultras had surrounded the players at training and, according to some, had so taken against a player that he was sold. Preziosi, in a press conference after that Siena game, gave his version: 'We've always been scared of these people: "I'll grab you", "I'll split you", "I'll break you". They come to your home, they come to the stadium, they slap the players. They know everything about everything. We accompany them with a sense of unease but also with fear.' They were the 'evil of Genoa', he said, and should be in prison.

Events over the following months persuaded many that Preziosi's analysis was close to the mark. The fear instilled by the ultras was such that only one of the stewards present that day dared identify the protagonists to the police. A few months later, one of the leaders of the Genoa–Siena insurrection – a Sicilian with convictions for drug-dealing who was later caught up in a drugs murder – was arrested for beating up a car mechanic for having not done some repairs fast enough. He and his brother had so much blood on their shoes and clothing that they pretended they had fallen off their moped.

Since that ultra was the son of a Sicilian mafioso, it began to appear, not for the first time, that the ultras were surrounded not just by petty criminals but by the professionals. The Italian parliament's anti-Mafia commission published a report in December 2017 entitled 'Football and Mafia', in which it pointed to Genoa as an example of 'the acquisition by a section of ultra groups of the methods of organized crime'. The Commission interviewed the Genova District Attorney, Francesco Cozzi, who said that the ultras 'impose themselves through implicit threats… by their characteristics and because of their pedigree. Applying the mechanisms of organized crime, they exercise an intimidatory power to influence the decisions of the club.'

The ultras' ability to suspend games, though still rare, was becoming more common and more creative. On 10 November 2013 the Salernitana–Nocerina derby produced a parody that no one had ever seen before. Within fifty seconds of the kick-off, the manager of Nocerina had made three substitutions. Then, in the next twenty-one minutes of play, one Nocerina player after another fell to the turf, clinging calves and ribs. Because the total number of allowed substitutions had been made, there were no replacements so the away team was reduced to ten men, then nine. When the number got to six, the referee was obliged by the rules to abandon the game. At that moment, a plane flew overhead with a banner trailing behind. In red capital letters it said 'Respect Nocerina and her Ultras'.

The back-story was that the Nocerina ultras had been banned

from the match, even though thousands had acquired the *tessera*, or 'supporters' card'. They were so incensed that they somehow persuaded the players to feign injuries. The method of persuasion was the mystery. It was easy for national media to portray Nocerina as a site of Mafia-like intimidation, not least because of completely unrelated deaths there. The father of the club owner had been killed in gang warfare years before, and one of the club's leading ultras was shot dead just a month before that iconic non-game.

But the ultras told a very different story. They were on good terms with the players, who wanted to show solidarity with their supporters. There had been no threats, only pleas. Aniello Califano's memoir of being a Nocerina ultra put his finger on why going to a game mattered so much: 'Those colours for us are our freedom; they are our victory against the time...' The terraces were where they could redeem all the wrongs they had endured: 'We are our land, long-suffering, exploited, scorned but unique, loved and full of real life. And that's why, so long ago, we made our flag from our own anger.' If the ultras couldn't go to a game, they would make sure no one else could either.

Present Day: Verona v. Cosenza

Blue lights illuminate the way to the stadium like a runway. There are metal-plated vans and unmarked cars with rotating blue lights parked up at the motorway exit and at the roundabouts. Police officers stand in groups of a dozen, with helmets, visors, leg-guards and truncheons. The car park for away fans is a cage. A metal gate is slid open and closed behind each car and coach.

These sorts of cemented spaces with little history or meaning – motorway service stations, car parks, ferry-port forecourts – are the natural habitats of the ultras. The soulless backdrops make what Durkheim called the 'collective effervescence' all the more evident. The ultras bring their colours to the grey spaces, their energy to the passive, they bring their sense of rootedness and belonging to places that are, by their very nature, temporary shelters for itinerants. Maybe that's why, on all our away-trips, we never stop at the sea or a lake or a mountain. It would take the attention away from ourselves, from the effect we have on these dull canvasses. And there's a relish in the self-perception of being the urban underclass, the cockroaches who inhabit the darkest corners and only come out to spook the salubrious salons of straight society. In this grey suburbia it sometimes seems as if the football pitch is the only patch of lush, verdant turf left.

The boundaries are so firmly enforced now that there's no transgression or trespassing. Pitch invasions are impossible. The ultras are still nomadic but always on someone else's terms. We're kept caged, kettled, scorned, evicted. The floodlit grass is nothing to do with us any more. It might just as well be the end of the rainbow. We're not even interested in our champions. As one recent Udinese banner said: 'Only for the shirt, not for whoever wears it.'

The strange thing is that the people gathered here are not remotely an underclass. The cars, clothing and careers of this group speak of success and social integration. It's almost as if we're role-playing at being the dregs, relishing our collective descent into an underworld. And the relief of the collectivity is that our atomized lives suddenly come together in a world that is, finally, binary: it is simply and blissfully just us against them. *Mors tua vita mea*: your death, my life. No nuance, no complexity. There's a decent party going on now, with all that entails: drinking, smoking, singing, dancing, flirting. Two blokes are even fighting but they looked so smashed that they probably don't even know what it's about.

This game is even more binary than most. It's a grudge match – the most left-wing, Southern ultras coming up against the most right-wing, pseudo-Aryan ones – and so the authorities have rescheduled it for a Monday night at 9 p.m. It's a 2,000-kilometre round trip from Cosenza but a few hundred supporters are here, probably about half of whom live in the North. Exiles are greeting old friends. The temperature is well below zero and everyone is singing: 'Veronesi should be strung up', 'Veronese, piece of shit' and, since Romeo's squeeze came from Verona, 'Juliet is a whore'.

The floodlights, rectangles of white, tower above the mighty Bentegodi stadium. Eventually we shuffle through the turnstiles. We keep singing as we're split up, stewards frisking, *Carabinieri* filming. 'How beautiful it is, when I get out of the house,' – the noise is raucous – 'to go to the stadium, to support Cosenza. Oh, oh, oh, oh...' Through more turnstiles – with their two-inch thick horizontal bars – and then up and up into the very top of the stadium. It's vertiginous and from up here – the far side of the damp, blue running track – the players are tiny. It's like trying to watch TV from the other end of the house. The stadium is less than a quarter full, the result of scheduling with public order, rather than public engagement, in mind.

The Verona banners give an idea of their anglophilia. There's a huge Union Jack and many groups with English names, including 'Hell' (Verona's full name is Hellas Verona) and 'The Geekers'. There are hints of jokey eroticism – 'Calcio Club Osé' – plus the usual memorializing of dead ultras. There are religious borrowings – 'I believe', says one banner, 'I will rise again' – and hints of unorthodox extremism, like 'Bassa Estrema' ('Extreme Base'). Another banner says, 'Against all drugs'.

Elastic is on the megaphone. He's hissing into it to make everyone silent. His lieutenants in the front rows turn around and shout 'Oh!' to the back rows where there's still chatter. Discipline descends and it's all quiet. Everyone is looking at Elastic, who can read the mood like it's a book. Everyone here wants to stick it to the blue-and-yellow fascists on the far side of the stadium and so the opening song is 'Come on Cosenza' to the tune of that old partisan favourite, 'Bella Ciao'. As if to underline the political differences, one Cosentino is holding up a banner – in Verona colours – saying 'Refugees Welcome'. Another flag just says 'We are who we are'.

There's a reluctant respect for the Veronesi, though, despite all the political differences. Although they have a reputation for being fascists, that extremism is partly about riling the righteous. Certainly, many are true-believers but, like the Laziali with whom they are twinned, others play up to it because that's just what they've always done. It's part of the tradition by now. And if from the outside the Veronesi ultras all appear to be fascists, in reality it's far more heterogenous. Under the Hellas banner, there are plenty who are keen to keep the terraces apolitical. Some – a small minority – are even anti-fascists. The ultra world is not just a place where political extremism thrives, it's also the place – perhaps the only one – where political extremisms occasionally make peace and rub shoulders.

'Ultrà', we chant, clapping hands quickly, before shouting again, 'ultrà'. Elastic starts the Marseillaise but the troops go off too quickly and he rolls his eyes. He wanted it slower. He hisses everyone quiet, smiling at the enthusiasm. Most cheerleaders on a megaphone have to encourage more singing, but here it's as if he had to slow them down.

Verona are playing incisive football, sliding in clever balls behind Cosenza's back four. They take the lead and suddenly the sulking ultras on the far side of the stadium are booming. Verona score again shortly after half-time. It's strange but that second goal doesn't interrupt our singing. 'I'm mistrusted,' goes the melancholy lament, 'photographed, because any excuse is an accusation of crime, but I've got by, I haven't given up, and in life I'll always be an ultra...' It keeps going on repeat for five minutes. 'I'm mistrusted, photographed...'

The game goes on far away, like watching ants on a snooker table. Because we're right under the roof, our singing rebounds loudly and it's more fun watching ourselves than the match. Almost all the photographs and videos people are taking on their phones are of the singing and bouncing and debauchery. But just as we're singing a strange version of 'You'll Never Walk Alone', with scarves pulled tight, Cosenza score. Almost no one realizes. It's only when you see, through the taut scarves, the players hugging and walking back towards the centre-circle that you realize it's a goal. We just keep singing like nothing has happened.

But as the match progresses, people are straining to see what's going on. Usually, only Elastic with his lieutenants decide what is sung but there's an unstoppable mutiny in the ranks as the two hundred spontaneously start chanting incessantly, 'Lupi, Lupi, Lupi, Lupi'. Elastic smiles wearily and turns around to see what's going on. There are only five minutes to go and Cosenza are pressing for an equalizer.

Suddenly, Cosenza score again – another obscure goal that no one saw – but the place explodes now. Strangers hug. Even the growlers are grinning, pumping their fists and their fingers towards the yellow terrace at the far end. Now you can behave however you like because the regimentation has broken down and people are walking up and down the seats, waving their arms in the 'suck this' gesture.

Both teams are now playing for the winner and it's an open game. The fact that Cosenza have come back from 2–0 against the hated, fascist Veronesi is poetic and the songs take on a more playful tone. We sing about being 'Southern peasants' – *'terrun terrun'* – and, to a melody that is almost The Crystals' 'Da Doo Ron Ron' about how 'we'll never leave you, we'll always be by your side'.

The final whistle goes. A 2–2 draw. We're locked up for another hour to make sure that there are no fights with the Veronesi, so we rile the departing locals with 'You're staying in B' and 'You can only win at the table' (since the game back in the summer, unplayable because of the pitch, was awarded to them by authorities 'at the table'). Then, after midnight, we're ushered back into the caged car park. There's more singing and drinking, and slowly the cars and coaches disperse, heading to the motorway between the blue lights. We'll be back in Cosenza just in time to start work in the morning.

February 2011

Piero Romeo, the ultra felled by an aneurysm and whose health had been declining for years, died in February 2011. His coffin was taken to the Curva Bergamini after the funeral, where it was draped with red-and-blue scarves. Flares were lit.

A few weeks later, Cosenza were playing against Nocerina, with whom there had been, for years, a twinning. The Nocerini had brought a banner saying 'Fly, Piero, and amaze paradise'. The whole afternoon was supposed to be a memorial to the late leader. There are differing versions of what actually happened. Some say the Nocerina fans had a tricolour, which to the anti-nationalist Cosentini was paramount to a declaration of fascism. Others say the incidents were provoked by Cosentini, who insulted the visiting fans for having adhered to the hated *tessera*. Whatever the reason, the Nocerini ripped up their banner, a tribute to Piero, and a grieving Drainpipe – watching aghast as the tribute to his best friend was ruined – left the stadium, vowing never to step foot again in the Curva Sud.

It was an example of how twinnings can suddenly end and decade-long friendships evaporate in an afternoon. There are many reasons for twinnings between ultra groups. Sometimes it's political affinity, like that between Lazio and Inter ('A Roman salute to the real Milan' said one rhyming banner by the Laziali) or between Cosenza and Ternana. The Genoa–Napoli twinning was cemented in 1982 when a 2–2 draw relegated Milan, whom both sets of fans hated. Fiorentina ultras are so anti-Juventus that they are naturally twinned with Torino (Torino is also ever-grateful that Fiorentina lent the club players after the Superga tragedy).

These twinnings mean that when the two teams meet, you're guaranteed not urban warfare but a liquid lunch. Twinned ultras will be invited to each others' end-of-season football tournaments. Quite often marriages and children result from that interaction, a classic example of how hostility and hatred between ultras can be reduced by contact. When visiting twinned groups, the delicacy and etiquette are very pronounced: pennants and scarves are swapped, threnodies to late ultras read out, cheap commemorative shields handed over. The encounter is fed back to the next meeting with words of almost medieval admiration: 'exquisite', 'knightly', 'genteel'.

Plenty of famous twinnings have been broken, the affection replaced – like divorcing couples – with scorn and hatred. Those between Atalanta and Roma, and Verona and Inter, both broke down. They say the Genoa–Cosenza twinning was strained, if not ruptured, by the Genoani inviting Cosenza's Calabrian rivals (and often far-right) Lamezia fans to the San Vito stadium at the turn of the millennium. The thirty-seven-year twinning between Napoli and Genoa was terminated by Napoli ultras in the spring of 2019 when Genoa remembered, with a banner, the dead Varese ultra, Dede, who had ambushed them. When there are break-ups, personal friendships usually survive but understanding the reason for the break-up is always hard. As Alessio, one of the founders of Spal's Gruppo d'Azione, once said: 'To make an alliance is an important thing because it means your group is recognized as such by another group from another *curva*, maybe even outside your country. Then who manages to have more twinnings is also the most strong, in the same way that who manages to break historic alliances demonstrates they have the power to do so.'

Present Day, Milano

Back in February 2009 there was a Milan–Inter derby at the San Siro. For years, a peace deal had held between the two Milanese clubs, and violence was rare between the various ultra groups. On that occasion, however, a Milan banner was hung on the railings from an upper tier and came lower than intended, blocking the view of the Inter fans just below. That, at least, was the excuse. They tugged at it hard, ripping it. The damaging of a banner was an affront to the group, and Milan's ultras quickly came down, some slipping their chunky watches round their fingers to use as brass-knuckles.

Luca Lucci – known as il Toro, 'the Bull' – was at the forefront. He didn't look bullish. Then aged twenty-two, he had a thin face with a pointy nose and a shaved, scarred head. But he charged the same way, piling in with his head down. He aimed for the leader of the Banda Bagaj group, meaning the 'lads' gang' in Lombard dialect. One of its leaders was Vittorio Motta, who was now protecting his own group's herald. Punches arrived from behind. Motta later described one particular punch: 'It was anomalous, a very strong pain, a tremendous pain. I removed my hand and looked: I found blood, many tears and a gelatinous substance.' Motta had lost his eye in the fight. The Bull was prosecuted and obliged to pay compensation but three years later, Motta took his own life.

By 2018 Lucci had become one of the undisputed leaders of Milan's Curva Sud. He and his mates met in a club called Al Clan, in the Sesto San Giovanni suburb in the northeast of the city. Police had planted a listening device in the building, as they suspected Lucci of drug-dealing. They filmed him taking delivery of marijuana and cocaine at the crack of dawn at Al Clan, receiving them from an Albanian gang who were importing from Spain. He was arrested in June 2018 and pleaded guilty to drugs offences, receiving an eighteen-month suspended sentence.

There was nothing particularly unusual about ultras being

involved in drug distribution. In many ways, it was hardly surprising. They were regularly travelling all over the country in convoy, tooled up and almost untouchable. Drugs busts in the ultra world were common. In 2016 the *Carabinieri* arrested an ultra from Genoa, Davidino, who had two garages full of narcotics – twenty-six kilogrammes of hashish, eight kilogrammes of marijuana, 1.1 kilogrammes of cocaine and seven of ecstasy. There was also €18,000 in false notes, along with bullets, two pistols with the serial numbers filed down and silencers. There was a theory that ultras were being used merely as the foot soldiers for the Mafia: people with whom one could park the product or weaponry.

But there was something different about the Luca Lucci case because it revealed that politicians, from the unknown to the most notorious, enjoyed intimacy with his world. One of the men arrested with Lucci was called Massimo Mandelli, head of Inter Milan's volunteer stewards and a candidate in local elections with CasaPound. And only a few months after Lucci's arrest, during celebrations for the fiftieth anniversary of Milan's ultras, the Minister of the Interior and the most powerful politician in the country, the Milanista Matteo Salvini, warmly shook hands with him. Salvini – who was also deputy Prime Minister – said: 'I'm a suspect amongst suspects.'

It seemed more than a repetition of that old Italian plea for impunity, percolated through Catholicism's notion of us all being fallen sinners ('Nobody is innocent, so we're all equally guilty'). It was a choreographed show of support from one of the highest officers of state to an underworld that, in many ways, embodied his electoral base and his political philosophy: the defence of your own and an aggressive rejection of those with different colours. In March 2019 a comparable incident occurred prior to the Inter-Milan derby: the security detail of the San Siro stadium refused to allow a choreography paying tribute to the Blood&Honour group and commemorating 'Dede', the ultra killed in the ambush of Napoli ultras on Boxing Day 2018. At Salvini's behest, the Interior Ministry over-ruled the decision, meaning that a game broadcast by Sky contained a huge homage to a neo-Nazi group. Two months later a publisher with very close links to CasaPound, Altaforte, published a hagiography of Salvini in the form of his replies to one hundred questions.

In 2008 the Juventus board of directors approved the designs of a new stadium. The board had previously agreed to buy a ninety-nine-year lease from Turin city council to the ground beneath the old stadium that they had shared with Torino, the Delle Alpi. Construction work began in 2009.

Juventus was then, by the club's high standards, at a low ebb. It hadn't won the Serie A title since 2004 and hadn't claimed the Champions League since 1996. The club was desperate not only for sporting success but also for a tranquil relationship with its fans. The club decided that all the ultras should be seated together, in the Curva Scirea of the new stadium. That was the area for which Juventus would provide hundreds of tickets to its ultras on the condition that they were well-behaved. Given the money those ultras were making, they were unlikely to do anything to rock the boat. One *capo-ultra* – Andrea Puntorno, from the Bravi Ragazzi – later boasted that he bought two houses, an Audi and a bakery from the proceeds of ticket-touting.

The new stadium was, for a club with such a large following, curiously modest. There was space for only 41,500 spectators, meaning that demand was always far higher than supply.

Puntorno's wife recalled that he would bring home up to €30,000 after an important match – three hundred tickets sold at a hundred euros each meant that in a day, one ultra group could make more than most people's annual salary.

It was a strange quid pro quo. Even after the inauguration of the new stadium in 2011, the commercial development of its curtilage, in an area called Continassa, was held up by a travellers' encampment. The club wanted to build something called the 'J-village', complete with a museum, medical and training facilities and so on. The presence of travellers living in vans and tents was clearly an obstacle. The ultras dealt with the problem. On the age-old and invented pretext that an Italian teenager had been raped by travellers, the Bravi Ragazzi rallied a mob of a few dozen men and set fire to the whole settlement. 'Let's burn them all,' said one of the leaders. There was never any suggestion that the ultras were commissioned or encouraged by the club hierarchy but it was blatantly clear that their actions – literally clearing the ground – were advantageous to the sporting superpower.

There also seemed to be a new-found *pax ultra* amongst the club's various gangs. Italian Mafias had always known that business, and invisibility, were put at risk by open warfare, and the various criminal clans who were now intertwined with Juventus's ultras encouraged them to put aside their feuds for the sake of business. Some of those clans were now investors, putting up cash for the ultras to bulk-buy tickets. They also taught them how to find a convincing explanation for their new-found cash: complicit betting shops would provide winning lottery tickets but not the pay-out. It was enough to explain away tens of thousands of euros in cash. In one betting shop in Cuneo, near where he lived, Ciccio Bucci had won the lottery so many times that he appeared to have amassed winnings of €200,000 over four years.

In 2013 two Calabrians were holding a series of meetings to seek permission to set up their own ultra gang. Saverio Dominello and his son, Rocco, were suspected of being part of the Rosarno clan involved in extortion in small towns between Turin and Milano. They had got mixed up in nightclubs, narcotics and even attempted murder. Saverio was a man of few words but Rocco was often described as *garbato*, 'smooth' or 'graceful'.

From recorded conversations in the spring of that year, investigators realized that the Dominello family were planning to move in on the ticket-touting business in Turin and form their own ultra group called the Gobbi ('hunchbacks' being the pejorative name for supporters of the 'old lady'). Since the ultra world was as territorial as drug-dealing, Saverio and Rocco Dominello knew that they had to tread carefully. 'If the plate is round,' Saverio Dominello was recorded as saying, 'it'll be cut five ways.' This was old-fashioned *spartizione*: slicing up the profits between different cartels.

Slowly, other interested parties were sounded out. Loris Grancini, the head of the Viking Ultras, gave his assent. 'Ndrangheta strongholds in the South gave their agreement. The man fronting the new ultra group, who was under police surveillance, boasted over the phone about having the support of Mafia clans: 'We've got our backs covered, we've got the Christians who count. What the fuck more do you want?' There was just one more man who needed to give his blessing, the man the police called the 'Scarlet Pimpernel' of the ultra world, Pino Coldheart of the Drughi.

On 20 April 2013 the Dominellos and their sidekicks held a meeting with Coldheart. The Dominellos arrived with ostentatious humility in a Fiat 500; Coldheart rolled up in a Series 1

BMW. They met in the Caffetteria del Portico in Montanaro for almost two hours. A police listening device was hidden in one of the sidekick's cars and they heard boasts about the power of the nascent Gobbi: 'You've had the honour to sit at table with Coldheart... no one can touch you. You're the number one... you can dictate the law if anyone behaves badly.'

The next day, in a crunch match against Milano on 21 April 2013, the new Juventus group announced itself with a huge banner in the stadium. The B's of 'Gobbi' were back-to-front, looking like '88', which many neo-fascists use as code to refer to HH, or 'Heil Hitler' – H being the eighth letter of the alphabet. The Calabrian Mafia, the 'Ndrangheta, now had its own ultra firm inside the stadium of Italy's biggest football team.

The smooth Rocco Dominello quickly became extraordinarily influential amongst both Juventus officials and different ultra groups. He was introduced to Stefano Merulla, the man responsible for Juventus's ticket office. He became an apparently intimate friend of the Juventus security manager, Alessandro D'Angelo, addressing him as 'Ale'. By June 2013 Dominello was giving him orders. When D'Angelo told Dominello that the rival Viking's allocation of tickets had been reduced, Dominello said arrogantly, 'Like I told you to.' Dominello boasted to the club's security manager that people 'are scared of me'. He once even received tickets directly from the director-general and arranged a face-to-face meeting with him.

Juventus did nothing to halt Dominello's rise. In January 2014 a Swiss citizen complained to the club that he had paid €620 for a ticket worth officially €140. Internal checks by the club proved that the ticket had been supplied to Dominello by D'Angelo. A week after the Swiss fan's complaint, D'Angelo squared the situation, telling Dominello that they would find a way to get him tickets using 'a different code'. Bucci's friend, Merulla, was beginning to have suspicions about Dominello: 'I don't know what job he has, I don't know what influence he has...' He seemed, said Merulla, 'mysteriously powerful' – often code, in Italy, for mafioso.

Part of the problem was that Juventus' security manager didn't seem very good at security. He had been appointed, in part, due to a childhood friendship with the Juventus president, Andrea Agnelli (they had grown up together since D'Angelo's father had been the chauffeur to Agnelli's father, Umberto). Investigators were wiretapping his phone, and as you read the transcripts of D'Angelo's sweary, sloppy conversations, it becomes clear that he was doing little to distance himself from the tough-nut ultras and was turning a blind eye to their darker dealings. One judge later wrote that D'Angelo and Juventus appeared to behave with 'subjection and submission' with regard to Rocco Dominello.

Through 2014 the ultras were becoming more menacing. For the Juventus–Torino derby that spring, Pino Coldheart called a fans' strike in a show of power to the Juventus hierarchy. The pretext for the strike was the stadium bans that various ultras had received after fights with Atalanta fans, but the reality was that the Drughi wanted to receive more tickets and at cheaper prices. For years, D'Angelo had looked to Ciccio Bucci as the go-between to shore up the Juventus-ultras compromise but now he phoned the Calabrian, Rocco Dominello, instead: 'I want you [ultras] to be calm, and us [Juventus] to be calm, and we'll travel together.'

Bucci must have sensed that his influence was on the wane. Dominello had become the main interface between the club and the ultras. At the end of that season Bucci was beaten up by Pino Coldheart. Nobody knows the reason, though it seems a logical speculation that either Pino had discovered Bucci was working as an informant or that he simply wanted him out of the way. Bucci was so spooked by the beating that he decided to leave Turin, going back to Puglia for a year. He lost eight kilos and told his ex-wife that people were trying to 'take him out'. His phone was no longer ringing and, back in San Severo, he spent much of his time caring for, and arguing with, his ageing parents. It seemed as if he was losing everything he loved.

3 May 2014: Coppa Italia Final

On 3 May 2014 Napoli was playing in the Italian cup final against Fiorentina. Managed by Rafa Benítez, it was a strong team with the free-scoring Argentinian Gonzalo Higuaín up-front and Paolo Cannavaro bossing the defence.

On the Saturday afternoon before the game, a convoy of coaches was stop-starting along Viale di Tor di Quinto in Rome. You could see, in the windows, the light-blue flags and scarves of Napoli fans. In the 1980s there had been a twinning between Roma and Napoli. Roma's Fedayn had even been guests in the Neapolitan stadium's Curva B. But then Roma's Boys had attacked Napoli fans and deliberately broken the friendship, and ever since there had been hatred between the two.

The Napoli fans saw someone run towards one of the coaches and throw something underneath. The explosion was so loud that it seemed to rock the whole vehicle. Suddenly, there was smoke pouring out from underneath the chassis. Napoli fans were piling out of nearby coaches. It was just a paper bomb and there was no damage done but now the fans were on the streets, exposed. They saw a group of men in helmets and balaclavas jeering at them from a sidestreet. Ciro, a thirty-one-year-old man who had a carwash outlet in Napoli, led the chase.

Ten seconds later there were four syncopated shots. The noise – cold and metallic – ripped through the streets. Ciro fell sideways. The bullets from the Beretta had torn through his arm, his lungs and lodged in his spinal cord. Two other men were injured.

'*Il chiattone, il chiattone,*' Napoli fans shouted. 'The fat man.' They rushed him and he lifted his gun again but it jammed. The fans moved in on him, hammering him with their fists but he was so insulated in flesh – and some thought he must be high – that nothing seemed to hurt him.

'Give it to me harder,' he shouted. 'I don't feel it.'

Ciro was carried back to the main road. He was sagging badly and his friends tried to get his rucksack off his back. Police arrived. A helicopter was stuttering overhead. An ambulance took Ciro to hospital. The shocked fans in the coaches saw police leading away the suspect.

After that, it was surreal to go to a game of football. Napoli won 3–1 but the memorable image from the match was a Napoli ultra – nicknamed 'The Swine' – sitting on the railings at the centre of the terrace, screaming at the players to stop the game. He had inked arms outstretched and a black T-shirt saying 'Speziale Libero'.

Ciro slipped in and out of consciousness over the next seven weeks. Lazio ultras paid for his mother to stay in a hotel so that she could be with her son. Slurring his words, he identified from photographs the man who had shot him. It was a forty-six-year-old called Daniele De Santis. Ciro Esposito died of multiple organ failure at the end of June.

De Santis was well-known to police. Nicknamed Gastone, and with 'Roma' and 'SPQR' tattooed on his knuckles, he was a Roma ultra who liked to think of himself as a modern-day Roman legionary. He had been present at the riots in Brescia in 1994 and had previously been accused of threats to the Roma club hierarchy. He lived in the same street where Ciro had been shot, surrounded by runes, Celtic crosses and posters of fascist martyrs,. He had spent the previous night snorting cocaine with two prostitutes. He was convicted and sentenced to twenty-six years in prison, reduced on appeal to sixteen.

In Napoli, as the city mourned Ciro Esposito, his relatives were adamant that they wanted no revenge or violence in his name. Graffiti in blue lettering around the city reiterated the point. 'Scampia [his suburb] doesn't want revenge, only justice' said one, 'You can't die of love' another. His mother, Antonella Leardi, was softly spoken but resolute: 'I've always said it and always will: the ambush in Tor di Quinto was a fascist and racist ambush.'

In a communiqué, Roma's Curva Sud attempted to distance itself from the act: 'For us the death of Ciro Esposito is an abnormal tragedy which, for the way it came about, is beyond the bounds of the ultra world.' But loyalty didn't allow Roma's Curva Sud to distance itself from the murderer: 'The Curva Sud remains and always will remain at the side of its son, we will never renege on our brother, whether right or wrong. This is what life, and the street, has taught us.' There were long banners pouring scorn on Ciro's grieving mother ('How sad to turn a profit from a funeral using books and interviews'). Years later, when Roma ultras went to Liverpool – on the occasion in 2018 when the Irish Liverpool fan, Sean Cox, was punched and reduced to a coma – a banner saying 'DDS [Daniele De Santis] With Us' was held up as if the murderer were an icon for the terraces.

———

2014: Lucca–Luhansk

Andrea Palmeri liked to call himself the 'Generalissimo'. He was the leader of an ultra group from Lucca, in Tuscany, called Bulldog. The group drew in elements from all the far-right parties, from CasaPound, Forza Nuova and the Skins, and they spray-painted slogans like 'Hitler for 100 years' and 'Priebke is a Hero' on churches working with refugees. Most collected knives, tattoos and convictions for assault, fighting less against other fans than their political enemies. In 2014 Palmeri was on trial for conspiracy, grievous bodily harm, aggravated assault and possession of a knife.

Palmeri was facing the probability of a custodial sentence and decided to drive his BMW 3,000 kilometres away, to the breakaway Luhansk People's Republic, in Eastern Ukraine. There he had Russian contacts. A fugitive from Italian justice, Palmeri became both a mercenary, fighting for the Russian nationalists, and a propaganda tool, publishing photographs of himself online to his thousand followers on Facebook: the 'Generalissimo' doing humanitarian work in an orphanage, and – more often – snaps of himself, topless, hugging a gun or a blonde woman. He was soon joined by other neo-fascist mercenaries (or 'contractors') from Italy: 'Archangel' (the son of a politician from the Lega Nord) and Spartacus (who in an interview said that every time he shot a Ukrainian, he imagined he was firing at a politician from Brussels).

Over the next few years, the former *capo-ultra* became an important bridge between Italian neo-fascists and Russian nationalists. Moscow was deliberately using far-right groups in Europe to undermine the continent's political consensus and stability. In March 2015 fascist groups from across Europe were invited to Saint Petersburg to the 'International Russian Conservative Forum'. As well as the British National Party's former leader, Nick Griffin, and members of Greece's Golden Dawn, various Italian fascists were present including Roberto Fiore, Forza Nuova's founder and a close friend of Griffin. 'We are the avant-garde of a new Europe that will very soon emerge,' he said. 'It will be a Christian Europe, a patriotic Europe, and Russia will not just be a part but a leading force.'

The link between Italian neo-fascists and Russian nationalists was based upon disdain for the alleged 'effeminacy' or 'decadence' of Western politics. They both disliked its advocacy of gay or women's rights and its embrace of multiculturalism. Wooed by Moscow's white machismo, many Italian fascists now looked to Russia as a bulwark against what they saw as the disintegration of Western values. They avidly read works by the prolific fascist writer (and former adviser to various figures in Putin's regime) Aleksandr Dugin. He promoted 'Eurasianism' – a new continent centred on Moscow – and enticed Europeans from the far-right into a fringe organization called the European Communitarianist Party. Eastern-looking Italian fascists also had ties to a neo-Nazi organization called Rusich, inspired by Pan-Slavism and by a longing to recreate a twenty-first-century nationalistic version of the USSR.

That a *capo-ultra* could become a militant in these geopolitical games shows how far the ultras had changed in half a century. Few, it's true, became mercenaries like the self-styled 'Generalissimo', but his propaganda from the front-line was inspirational to fascistic ultras back in Italy. Here was a leader of the terraces who, hounded by 'Communist justice', had fled abroad to fight against the decadence of Europe. He had turned his guns, quite literally, on the West.

In reality, he seemed to be fighting imaginary demons. Like his colleague 'Spartacus' pretending he was firing at EU politicians, Andrea Palmeri conflated Ukrainian soldiers with anti-Nazi freedom-fighters from the Second World War. 'I swear, it's tiring catching them. Fuck, they really move like partisans,' he said to a friend on the phone. In August 2018 a European arrest warrant was issued for Palmeri. Because he remained in Russian-partitioned Eastern Ukraine, it had no effect other than cementing his reputation amongst his ultra admirers as a courageous combatant against liberal democracy.

By then, combativeness was what a lot of Italians were longing for. The country was facing an unprecedented crisis of confidence. In 2015 youth unemployment was over 40 per cent. There was an exodus of young Italians abroad, seeking a more meritocratic society outside the country's borders. In the same year Italy's national statistics office suggested that almost five million Italians were living in 'absolute poverty'. The degradation in certain suburbs suggested that the Italian state was, in places, almost entirely absent.

Peoples' insecurities were fuelled by a media that gave almost unlimited airtime to ambitious politicians who spoke about a crime epidemic caused by illegal immigration. National security, the narrative went, was threatened not by corruption or organized crime but by refugees. The argument went that a coalition of peaceniks and 'immigrationists' had deliberately concocted multiculturalism and had sacrificed sovereignty and indigenous (white) populations in the process.

The man who, slightly surreally, was held responsible for this conspiracy was the Austro-Japanese philosopher Richard

Nikolaus di Coudenhove-Kalergi. After the horrors of the First World War, he had been inspired by the notion of post-nationalism, publishing *Pan-Europa* in 1923. Long-admired as an eloquent voice for international cooperation, Kalergi became the *bête-noir* of fascists when the Austrian neo-Nazi and Holocaust-denier, Gerd Honsik, ascribed to him 'the Kalergi conspiracy' to eradicate native Europeans from their homeland. In an era of mass migration, economic stagnation and profound discontent about the distance between the people and the per-ceived 'elites' of international politics, Honsik's theory was like water to parched ground. It was absorbed and diffused, and those who felt quenched by it wanted more. The idea that migrants were deliberately being foisted on impoverished and ignored Italians by a European elite was captivatingly simple, and chimed perfectly with many peoples' sense of vulnerability.

At the same time the fringe French writer Alain de Benoist and his Nouvelle Droite philosophy (broadly rejecting multi-culturalism and globalization) were becoming voguish in far-right circles. De Benoist was even interviewed by *American Renaissance* magazine and invited to speak at the National Policy Institute. Another French writer, Renaud Camus, published a book called *The Great Replacement*, in which he spoke of the idea that native Europeans would soon be completely sidelined and displaced by waves of immigrants. This was the beginning of an 'Identitarian' movement, in which everything you thought you knew was inverted. Universalism was just Western imperialism, which in turn caused globalization and homogenization. True pluralism – 'ethnopluralism' – meant racial separation.

These ideas influenced both Steve Bannon at Breitbart and the American Alt-right leader Richard Spencer and chimed well with Italian politicians and extra-parliamentarians on the right.

CasaPound's 'cultural attaché', Adriano Scianca, published a book called *The Sacred Identity*. 'The cancellation of a people from the face of the earth,' he wrote, '… is factually the number one [aim] in the diary of all the global oligarchs.' It sounded absurd but the paranoid notion got traction and very quickly racial distinctivism became CasaPound policy. Throughout 2014 and 2015 CasaPound rallied protests against 'asylum centres'. Every time a vacant building was converted into an asylum centre for refugees, in Infernetto and Casale San Nicola and Tor Sapienza, CasaPounders would make friends amongst the locals, distributing food parcels, fixing their plumbing, removing rubbish, and offering strategies and strong arms. Immigration was, according to CasaPound, a question not of racism but of legality and economy.

Normally the significance of these instances of extremism was minimized as the acts of fringe fanatics. But the fringe fanatics were becoming the political mainstream. In February 2017 (a year before his party won over 17 per cent of the vote) Matteo Salvini spoke at a rally of the Lega, the party of which he is leader. 'Italy needs a mass cleansing,' he shouted into the microphone. 'Street by street, suburb by suburb, with strong methods if needed, because there are entire parts of Italy out of control.' A year later, during his successful election campaign to become the governor of Lombardy, the Lega politician Attilio Fontana pressed the same button: 'We need to decide if our ethnicity, if our white race and our society should continue to exist or should be cancelled.'

The politicians of the Lega were, by now, deploying exactly the same 'Identitarian' discourse that had proved so successful for the fascist parties of Forza Nuova and CasaPound. Ever since 2014 Salvini had been reinventing both himself and his party. The Lega Nord had always been a separatist, or federalist, movement, and its founder, Umberto Bossi – though virulently xenophobic – was also a lifelong anti-fascist. Salvini, though, knew which way the political wind was blowing and throughout 2014 and 2015 he assiduously courted the far right. He shared a platform with CasaPound in 2014 at an anti-immigration rally called 'No Invasion' and in February 2015, in Rome's Piazza del Popolo, he launched – alongside CasaPound and a delegation of Greece's Golden Dawn – a movement called 'Sovereignty'. 'There's an operation of ethnic substitution co-ordinated by Europe,' said Salvini. A CasaPound activist, Mauro Antonini, became the spokesman for one of the Lega's most outspoken extremists, Mario Borghezio (the man who said 'Hitler did many great things'). Salvini, it was clear, had gone all-in on the Identitarian gamble. At another rally, under the 'Stop Invasion' slogan, he proclaimed: 'There's an attempted genocide [of native Italians] going on...'

That sudden inversion of roles, with white Europeans cast as a threatened species, was beautifully beguiling because everyone wanted to be told they were victims. It shifted the blame else-where. If there were a conspiracy organized by powerful forces, we were absolved of responsibility, which is always a relief. It meant that nothing was our fault because we're oppressed. The simplicity of the narrative erased all the epic complexities of modern life, replacing them with a binary black-and-white solution. But the seductive argument had a grim and hidden catch: the need to finger those who are responsible, to find the familiar scapegoats – invariably Americans, Semites, Muslims and immigrants. Because if we're suppressed, it requires defence and then liberation, it calls for *squadristi* and soldiers.

For the resurgent extremists, there was one clear precedent

of what they called 'ethnic cleansing' at the expense of loyal, Italian nationalists. The Foibe are the karst sinkholes in modern-day Slovenia and Croatia into which hundreds (no one knows the precise number) of Italians were thrown to their deaths between 1943 and 1947. An acutely controversial topic, the Foibe massacres were in part an operation by Yugoslav (and Italian) partisans against fascist forces but were also an attempt by Tito's forces to rid Istria and Dalmatia of Italians and so pave the way for annexation. Hundreds of thousands of Italians fled their homes. The subject had been almost taboo in Italy during the First Republic but ever since a new law was passed by Berlusconi's government in 2004, 10 February has become a day of remembrance for the 'exiles and the Foibe'. For Italian fascists, it naturally became one of the most sacred dates in their calendar, a chance to commemorate not only the dead but also to persuade sceptics that the eradication of Italian patriots wasn't a fantasy but a historical reality.

In many ways the ultras were the yeast in this rapidly rising, far-right dough, frequently sliding from the terraces into political parties. Yari Chiavenato, the man who had hanged a black mannequin in Verona's stadium in 1996, had become a leader of Forza Nuova. He had parked cars in the shape of a swastika as a joke, and then become an electoral candidate for the Lega. He was also the chairman of Fortress Europe, another white-supremacist organization whose name echoed Hitler's *Festung Europa*. Andrea Arbizzoni, former *capo-ultra* of Monza, was part of a neo-Nazi organization called Lealtà Azione and was elected to the city council. Checco Latuada, an ultra from Pro Patria (a club in the Lombard town of Busto Arsizio) had, in 2007, celebrated Hitler's birthday in his pub. He became a town councillor in Berlusconi's Freedom Party. (When Pro Patria ultras booed Kevin Prince Boateng, the Ghanaian then playing for Milan, Latuada defended them by saying: 'Almost all the terraces, almost all the organized groups have the style and symbology of the extreme right.') It's true that they were very minor political figures, but others made it to parliament: Domenico Furgiuele, a former ultra for the Calabrian side Sambiase, and Daniele Belotti, an ultra from Atalanta (Bergamo), were both elected to the Camera as MPs for the Lega party (which by now had dropped its 'Northern' prefix). Belotti once claimed 'I've always whistled [jeered] Balotelli,' the black Italian striker.

At the genesis of the movement the ultras had borrowed the phrases and slogans of political extremism but now the exact opposite was happening: Italy's far right was copying the rhetorical rhyming couplets of ultra banners. At many political rallies and protests, banners are now unfurled using the ubiquitous Ultras Liberi font as if the terraces' slick sloganeering has been recognized as the surest way to get a photograph into the papers or the evening news. Nuance of thought was threatening, a sign of dandification, whereas the punchier the message, the more likely it was to get noticed. One-liners – like Salvini's incessant tweets – spoke straight to the belly of the electorate. (Even opposition to Salvini – expressed through thousands of bedsheets hung on balconies – owed much to the tradition of punchy *striscioni*.)

As well as the means of delivery being comparable, the message itself was often identical. That old fascist dictum (actually borrowed from Roman legionnaires and gladiators) '*Usque Ad Finem*' – 'To the End' – was a battle cry for both the ultras and far right. Many ultra groups had been called 'Indians' back in the 1970s and 1980s, partly out of an instinctive anti-Yankeeism but also because it enforced the notion of indigeneity. Now, in an era of so-called Identitarianism, that boast of belonging, so central to ultra mentality, was easily converted into an anti-immigration political message. All the language and imagery of the ultras, forever pitting an 'us' against outsiders, was suddenly useful for politicians who wanted to play the race card. The object pronoun had a long, if troubled, political pedigree. '*A noi!*' – 'to us' – was an old D'Annunzian motto during the occupation of Fiume, and later a rallying cry for any territorial expansionism, be it in Abyssinia or on the terraces. Salvini's use of '*noi*' – '*Noi con Salvini*' – was a shrewd piece of political positioning, identifying him with us and, the subtext went, against 'them'. The Northern League had always had a 'them' against which to define itself (the South of the country) but now a combination of political ambition and a new scapegoat meant that the League dropped its Northern prefix. It mutated into its opposite, no longer a secessionist movement (it had started out wanting the North to split from the South) but a patriotic and nationalist one. A new slogan – '*Prima Gli Italiani*' ('Italians First') – was coined.

June 2015: Padre Fedele absolved

Padre Fedele was almost eighty by the time he was cleared of the accusation of being a rapist. He still wore the brown habit, even though he had been expelled from his order. It was slightly stained now and covered with loose, white hairs. His eyes were the same light brown, surrounded by a head and beard of white hair, but he was weary, weighed down not just by age but by an accusation that had hung around his neck for almost a decade. He kept saying to everyone that he had lost his mother when still a young boy, and how women had always been for him, first and foremost, mother figures. 'It's strange,' he told me, 'the older I get, the more I feel my mother's absence.'

For the last few years he had been in and out of courtrooms. The guilty verdict of the initial trial was upheld on appeal, but the Cassazione, the Italian Supreme Court, annulled that verdict and sent the case back to the appeals court. There, in June 2015, over nine years after he had first been arrested, he was cleared of all the charges. It had emerged that the victim had repeatedly fabricated other attacks – two in Rome and one in Reggio Calabria. There, too, the stories had been cinematically graphic – kidnappings and druggings – even though the photographic and medical evidence gave no credence to her story. The whole case was a tragedy. The nun in question was perhaps trying to communicate or explain some sexual activity but, unable to do so within the normal parameters because of her ecclesiastical position, she had invented extraordinary fantasies around what had happened. Padre Fedele had spent the autumn of his life fighting to clear his name and even now he had his reputation back, it wasn't the same. He wasn't allowed to say mass any more, and so much mud had been slung that he kept talking about the case for years afterwards.

He would park his Ford Fiesta around the city, with its peeling plastic letters on both sides: 'The Paradise of the Poor'. It was his new initiative. He wanted to build a new Oasis and was trying to raise the funds for it. There was a mobile number on the side of the car and an offer: 'I listen to all.' As he sat there, waiting for people to ask him for help, Cosentini would just come up and shake his hand. But he looked broken. He could still work up a decent head of steam when he was angry but he was quieter now. It was now his former teenagers – Luca, Claudio, Paride, Ciccio, Drainpipe and all the rest – who were keeping an eye out for him. As in loving families, everyone had learnt to forgive each others' faults.

That profound bond between a Franciscan friar and his ultras is one of the most fascinating stories of this whole sub-culture. Because although they originally seemed poles apart ideologically, in the end they seem very similar. Like so many men within the movement, Padre Fedele was mourning his absent parents from a young age. Lacking a family after most of his relatives moved to America and Canada, he found his on the terraces. In many ways, he was as hard-up, short-tempered and blue-collar as any of the lads with whom he rubbed shoulders.

But perhaps more surprising were the ways in which the ultras came to seem not dissimilar to Padre Fedele. Apart from Pastachina, few ever found his faith (Drainpipe was so disgusted by the Church that he paid €14 to be *un*baptized). But all were inspired by Padre Fedele's charitable example. Within days of his best friend Piero's death, Drainpipe set up a charity called La Terra di Piero, which opened playgrounds for disabled children and dug wells in, and took provisions to, Africa. One of his volunteers, Plato, calls it 'going on a mission'. Gianfranco started his People's Boxing Gym inside the San Vito stadium with a sign on the door: 'This gym repudiates all forms of racism and fascism.' 'We're always aiming,' he says above the thumps and kicks, 'to improve the lot of the most disadvantaged in society. If someone has money, they contribute. If they don't, they train just the same.'

Thanks in part to Padre Fedele, the ferment and froth of the terraces had been harnessed by visionary leaders to create countless social projects for the benefit of the dispossessed. Those leaders were still, as you would expect, uncompromising: 'Never a backwards step' is the slogan of Gianfranco's gym. They hadn't gone, in any sense, soft. When CasaPound militants attempted to set up an office in Cosenza they were run out of town. But the Cosentini's uncompromising stance wasn't about attacking enemies, but rather about inclusivity. The astonishing openness of the *curva*, so evident at the movement's genesis, had been taken into the city. Padre Fedele somehow taught atheist guerrillas the essence of his Gospels. 'How can anyone say they're not believers,' he ticks me off, 'when you see what they do?'

But if they had, in one sense, an atheistic faith, those men had lost all trust in the Italian state. After Claudio and Gianfranco were imprisoned on charges of political terrorism and Padre Fedele tried for sexual violence, the Cosenza ultras felt that they were being punished for being revolutionaries. The fact that the policeman who investigated Padre Fedele was married to a local judge, herself the daughter of a powerful local politician, convinced them that the Establishment had a hand in his downfall. The Italian state has never enjoyed much consensus in Calabria but amongst the ultras it was, by now, non-existent. 'The real Mafia,' Claudio wrote in a novel thinly disguising the Cosenza story, 'nestles in the police station.' 'If you want to be someone here,' he wrote in another passage, 'you have to be a mason, a criminal, a card-carrying politician or else linked to the underground sectors of the Church.'

On 26 September 2011 a sailing boat seemed to be drifting near Alghero, on Sardinia's northwest coast. The boat was flying under a French flag, with the name *Kololo II*. There was something suspicious about the boat's position and when the Guardia di Finanza went aboard, they found a man called Roberto Grilli. In the hull were 477 clingfilmed bricks that turned out to contain 503 kilogrammes of pure cocaine.

Arrested and imprisoned, Grilli began cooperating with investigators and revealing everything he knew about the criminal underworld of Rome. What emerged from his testimony was a city in which various criminal gangs and Mafias coexisted on their own turfs, called *batterie*. There was no domineering organization but instead a complex web of connections between the highest, and lowest, of Roman society. The spider at the centre of that web was a former terrorist from NAR, the Armed Revolutionary Nuclei, the most lethal fascist group of the Years of Lead. Massimo Carminati was nicknamed 'the Blinded' because he had once lost an eye in a shootout with police. Many within his inner circle were ultras, both from Roma and Lazio. One of his closest collaborators was 'Rommel', leader of Roma's Opposta Fazione group and present at the armed robbery, back in 1994, that cost Kapplerino, his accomplice, his life. Another of his regular contacts was Mario Corsi, 'Marione', the former NAR militant and now host of a Roma fans' radio station.

Investigators placed many phones under surveillance and overheard one man talking about a gang operating in the north of Rome, in the Ponte Milvio area. 'The Neapolitans and Albanians are one thing... [but] these are shit people, these are evil people.' He was referring to the *batteria* belonging to Diabolik. He had links, it seemed, to a Neapolitan mafioso called 'the Madman' (so called as he was so adept at faking psychiatric illnesses to avoid prison time). The Neapolitans were supplying Diabolik with narcotics that, with his commercial nous and distribution network, he would sell in his stronghold just north of the Tiber. In one bust the police seized 185 kilogrammes of hashish. It looked like clingfilmed blocks of chocolate.

In the midst of the investigation Lazio enjoyed one of their greatest games. It was the first time the team had ever met their hated rivals, Roma, in a cup final. It was the Coppa Italia, May 2013. The Laziali's main banner displayed the defiant saying of a Roman centurion during the sack of Rome, quoted by Livy and borrowed by D'Annunzio: '*Hic Manebimus Optime*' ('We'll be fine here'). After Lazio's 1–0 victory – thanks to a tap-in by the Bosnian Senad Lulić – the ultras paraded with the cup, wearing T-shirts saying 'We are legends'. Mr Enrich was in the middle of the 'O' of '*Noi*' ('we'). Not for the first time, the ultras were mythologizing not the team, but themselves.

The investigation into the drug-dealing was slow-moving. In June 2013 one of the Irriducibili, Toffolo, was kneecapped near Caffarella park. (He had already been kneecapped in August 2007 when men dressed as police officers shot him on his doorstep.) Most people assumed it was a warning to keep his mouth shut. Diabolik was arrested in October 2014, having been on the run for a month using a fake ID. Police tracked him down thanks to the delivery of a pizza to a remote address during a televised Lazio game in the Europa League. When they arrested him, they found in his hideout baseball bats, truncheons, axes, swords, a pistol, blank and live ammunition and telephone jammers. The Guardia di Finanza subsequently estimated Diabolik's accumulated, and now confiscated, wealth at €2.3 million. He had various bank accounts and owned two villas, three cars and company shares. Judges later described his criminal gang as 'particularly fierce and dangerous'.

Over the following months and years, it became obvious that the Irriducibili were major drug-dealers in the Italian capital. On 27 September 2014 Toffolo was again arrested in possession of marijuana and cocaine. Then, on 11 August 2015, a fisherman was walking along the no man's land between the railway, the ring-road and the river in northeast Rome. He glimpsed something unusual on the banks of the Aniene, a tributary of the Tiber. When he looked closer, he saw that it was a left foot. On it was a tattoo: 'Today is a beautiful day to die, Irriducibili Lazio.'

Forensic tests suggested the foot had been severed using a chainsaw and then stored in a fridge. The tattoo made it easy to identify the victim. He was Gabriele Di Ponto, who had been missing since July. His had been a short, sad life. He had lost both parents aged five and had committed his first robbery aged eighteen because he had never eaten roast chicken. That's the story he told his wife, an Italo-Tunisian to whom he had been married for six weeks until she left him because of his violence. Di Ponto had the word 'Psycho' tattooed around his belly button and a pistol inked on his left hip. He had a long criminal record for robbery and drug-dealing, and had only recently come out of prison. It was thought that he tried to start dealing again on his old turf, between Tor Sapienza and San Basilio, and used force with the wrong people. The rest of his body was never found and the investigation came to nothing.

Di Ponto was on the fringes of the Irriducibili but his murder, though unsolved, was further evidence that certain members of the ultra group doubled as wholesale drug-dealers. The irony was that Lazio's Curva Nord was implacably opposed to any narcotics. Like many other terraces with far-right leanings, drug-use is scorned as the irresponsible stupidity of left-wing hippies and those without martial rigour.

The vast majority of Italian ultras, however, don't recognize the Irriducibili as an ultra group at all. It says a lot about the purist conception of what an ultra is that the criticism of the Irriducibili from other ultras centres neither on drug-dealing (outside the far-right terraces, many are anti-prohibitionists), nor on the political extremism (which is so widespread on the terraces) but on the one aspect that society considers normal and legitimate: the profiteering. It's the monetization of fandom, the exploitation of the terraces to make millions, which most ultras find heretical. They see the Irriducibili as no more representative of the ultra mentality than Rockefeller is of communism.

The theoretician of group dynamics, Bruce Tuckman, once came up with a quartet of rhyming phases through which all groups usually pass: forming, storming, norming and performing. Years later, a fifth was added: mourning (also called adjourning or transforming). In many ways it seems that the ultra movement is in this last stage, not just grieving the departed ultras but also, in some ways, the end of the movement itself. Many old hands say that what passes for an ultra now is so far removed from the original version as to be unrecognizable. Being an ultra is not, like football, a game any more. Too much is at stake. Teenage tearaways have been replaced by middle-aged men, the carefree by the calculating, chaos by order, insurgency by tradition. A movement that once empowered the penniless is now bossed by rich, autocratic *capi*.

One of the most poignant interviews I did for this book was with a semi-retired ultra, now in his late fifties, in his attic. There he had a miniature football stadium, the size of a pool table, for Subbuteo tournaments with friends. Every detail – the advertising hoardings, the scoreboard, the shirts – devoutly recreated the 1970s. 'This is the football from when I was little,' he said wistfully. 'Now it's all finished.' Perhaps that, too, is a reason for the melancholia of ageing ultras. Not just that the movement has changed, but that the times have too. Football is a reminder, as one ultra memoir put it, of 'days which won't return, days in which we were happy'.

Some ultras decided they wanted to recapture the simplicity of the old days. They just wanted to play again, or at least – if they were a bit long in the tooth – set up football clubs where kids could have a kick-around. Disillusioned with industrialized football, they founded new clubs. Various Cosenza ultras created Brutium Cosenza in January 2011 as a protest against 'racism, corruption, business and gratuitous violence'. Ovidiana Sulmona was founded in 2014 by ultras from Sulmona, the town in Abruzzo where Ovid was born. There were also Atletico San Lorenzo Roma, Stella Rossa Napoli and Ideale Bari Calcio. These clubs seemed to recapture the simple fun of sport (one team was called 'Lebowski' after the cult stoner film). 'Despite the sparkling football of Serie A,' the founders of Lebowski said, 'we were tired of seasons without surprises.' Many of these new clubs were self-financing. It cost twenty euros to join Palermo's 'Calcio Popolare'. Their ideals sounded almost identical to what the ultras were hoping to do way back in the late 1960s: 'We will bring belonging to our city and attachment to the shirt on the pitch. We will bring pranks, warmth, passion and rivers of beer, because popular football belongs to the people.'

For many, these new associations were a way to return football to its origins. RFC Lions Ska in Caserta was actively trying to bring locals, refugees and asylum-seekers together. The San Precario ('Saint Uncertain') club was founded in Padua in 2007 with similar aims (their slogan captured that sense of idling in the face of nastiness: 'Playing against racism').

Alessio Abram was among those who decided to take the game back to the grassroots. Throughout the 1990s he had been one of the leaders of Ancona's terraces. Short, with thick black hair, he was the opposite of the caricature of many ultras: not only was his ideological home the autonomous left, he also had

Jewish ancestry. (The notoriously far-right Ascoli fans once held up a banner, in response to Ancona's Cuban flag, saying 'Your Head-Ultra is a Jew'.)

He was one of the many far-left agitators who saw the ultra world as a place of countercultural rage and energy. He felt that sport was a rare means to bring people together to fight, rather than reinforce, prejudice. The Ancona ultras were active within the Ultra Resistance movement and in 2001 Abram began bringing people together informally to work out in a gym and play football. So many people got involved that a year later, he and friends organized a 'Mundialito', a multicultural 'World Cup' for all the immigrants living in and around Ancona. It was awarded a prize by FARE ('Football Against Racism in Europe') and in 2003 Abram decided to take it a step further and found a sports club.

It was originally called Assata Shakur (after the American civil rights activist – or criminal, depending on your point of view – who has lived in exile in Cuba for the last thirty years). A local branch of the Italian FA objected to the name and it was changed to Konlassata (because so many activists complained that they were happy with the name as it was, *con l'Assata*). Its symbol was a white hand shaking a black hand in front of a football. The slogan was simple: 'Who loves sport, hates racism'. None of it felt like a departure from the ultra movement but simply its continuation. A T-shirt you often see in the Ancona stands says bluntly 'Racism divides'.

Abram never pretended to be a saint. He saw the ultras as 'the armed part of social resistance'. He received various stadium bans and because one ban was outstanding, Abram's presence in the Konlassata club was considered an infringement of his restriction order. He was arrested and spent eighteen months in prison, and over a year under house arrest. There were major protests in the city and banners in the terraces. It felt, as with Claudio's arrest in Cosenza, completely stupid. It often seemed to the minority – but nonetheless sizeable – contingent of left-leaning ultras as if they were being punished far more heavily than those on the far-right who committed more serious crimes.

In prison, Abram felt like a political prisoner. 'You wonder why you're there,' he says, now released. 'You don't understand why you're inside and what you're paying for. But that gives you strength: obviously I've done something right.' Unlike many prisoners who are adamant that they don't belong there, Abram is actually accepting. 'Sure, there were grounds for me being there. I just said that maybe' – he smiles – 'I was paying too much.'

Both political wings of the movement are united in the conviction that ultras are treated differently to every other citizen. Someone who escapes from prison is given an additional six months of detention when caught; an ultra who fails to sign in at the police station on match day can be sentenced to three years. Lorenzo Contucci, both a lawyer and a Roma ultra, says 'the stadium has become an extraterritorial space, less for the behaviour than for the laws which are applied there. In the street, throwing a dangerous object is punished with a minimal fine; if the same gesture happens even outside the stadium but in a sporting context, the punishment is from one to four years.'

All civil rights movements are initially dismissed by the mainstream, meeting with responses that vary from negation ('things aren't that bad') to celebration ('you had it coming'). It's particularly difficult for ultras to argue that they're the victims of institutional discrimination when, for decades, they've seemed to revel in the scorn that they've provoked. But there is something dangerously dictatorial, they say, about legal measures that the Italian state has adopted. On the terraces there are many university lecturers and lawyers and they have begun to pick apart how police now act as judges. Even though Article 27 of the Italian constitution says that 'the accused isn't considered guilty until a definitive conviction', a Daspo can be imposed by a chief of police – the *Questore* – without trial. Even preventative measures against suspected mafiosi, says Contucci, have to come before a judge, not a police officer. A Daspo can stop you going to games and force you to sign in at the police station twice during matches, for up to eight years. As one Milan banner once wrote: 'A punch on the pitch – banned for 8 games; a punch on the terraces – 8 years. Disgrace.'

It would take immense naivety to imagine that the system isn't open to abuse, especially since the police are the enemy of the ultras and might be looking to settle scores. A Daspo can be issued for not sitting in an allocated seat (nobody does) or for lighting a sparkler. One can receive a Daspo simply for wearing a T-shirt, or singing a song, considered to be seditious. There are 'group daspos', in which the entire passengers on, say, a coach can be banned from games because of the behaviour, or luggage, of a single fellow traveller. It's obvious that if police want to dismantle a group that is politically or ideologically inconvenient, the means are at their disposal. The measure can even be preventative, issued if there's the perception that someone could cause trouble.

The numbers involved are pretty astonishing. In one section of one comparatively small city (Cosenza's Curva Sud) there were, at the last count, 145 Daspo-ed fans. Nationally, the number varies but it is between four and six thousand fans. It's a form of martial law, the ultras say, that is being tried out on society's scapegoats and could easily be rolled out for other black sheep, be they drug-addicts, agitators, protestors or immigrants. As one banner from the Viareggio ultras said: 'Special laws: today for the ultras, tomorrow for the whole city.'

Hence the repeated lament of modern ultras that they're facing repression. It's not just the miserable crowd-control where everyone is filmed, barcoded and kettled. There are pointless truncheonings, arrogant rough-handlings and the deliberate detention of fans so that they miss long periods of the actual match. The main gripe is that, according to another human-rights lawyer, Giovanni Adami, 60 per cent of fans are cleared of their offence once they've already served the sentence.

So, in some ways ultras have reinvented themselves as spokes-people for fans' rights: for cheaper tickets, more amenable match times and for the demilitarization of policing. No longer immoral iconoclasts, the ultras now present themselves as the guardians of an older, more innocent football, or else the least unethical element of it. 'If you look,' says Abram, 'at everything Italian football has produced – match-fixing, doping and so on – are we really convinced that the ultras are the baddies?' It's a line you hear repeatedly and see held up in banners at every other game: 'All straight things lie,' said a banner of the Pescaresi, 'every truth is a... curve.'

On 25 November 2014 investigators made a breakthrough in their search for links between the Juventus ultras and organized crime. Andrea Puntorno, the thirty-nine-year-old Sicilian boss of the Bravi Ragazzi, was arrested for importing heroin and cocaine from Sicily and Albania. Despite his many houses and cars, between 2004 and 2011 Puntorno had only declared an income of €2,600 per annum. Soon after his arrest, his wife was threatened by men who had, it seems, been investors in the ticket-touting scheme. Now that Puntorno was inside, they wanted their money back. The woman's car was burnt and, after constant harassment, she decided to turn state's witness, revealing everything she knew about the touting operation. She confirmed what investigators had long suspected: that professional criminals were using ultra groups to add interest to their cash through ticket-touting.

Whether those investigators tipped off the Juventus hierarchy is unknown but by late 2014, it seems that Juventus was aware that they had allowed wolves into the building and that more were trying to get in. The club had been pressured to give building work at the new stadium to particular builders in order to avoid vandalism and the intimidation of workers. Andrea Angelli nobly resisted the intimidation but could surely read all the signs. In discussion with his childhood friend, his security manager Alessandro D'Angelo, Agnelli was heard by investigators talking about his concerns regarding one *capo-ultra*, the head of the Vikings, Loris Grancini. 'The problem is,' says Agnelli, 'he has killed people.' His friend corrects him: 'He commissioned a killing.' (Grancini is currently in prison, having been convicted of attempted murder.)

From San Severo, Ciccio Bucci was trying to plot his comeback and, in November 2014, called Alessandro D'Angelo. He alluded, albeit in typically veiled terms, to Rocco Dominello's Mafia links. Bucci called Dominello 'that type of person'.

'Ah, OK,' said D'Angelo.

'Only at that point,' commented the Public Prosecutor in the subsequent arrest warrant for Rocco and Saverio Dominello, 'does D'Angelo seem to understand.'

So, throughout that 2014–15 season Juventus was trying to disinfest its dealings with the ultras. Perhaps nudged by the police and the secret services, for whom Bucci was an occasional informant, the club decided that Bucci was one of the few straight ultras with whom they could still do business. The commercial director of the club, Francesco Calvo, said that Bucci was a man who 'inspired empathy'. The club's elderly lawyer, Andrea Galassi, told me he was 'a simple, sunny, enthusiastic, clean guy'.

A plan was hatched to give Bucci an official role, to use him as a barrier between dark forces and the decorated football club. He would work alongside the club's SLO (supporter liaison officer), negotiating with the ultras who had, effectively, expelled him. It would turn him from a poacher to a gamekeeper. From down South, Bucci phoned D'Angelo to pitch how he would work with the ultras. 'The goose can continue to lay the golden egg,' he said cryptically, 'but a bit of water needs to get in.' He was offering to wash off the dirt, or maybe even water down, the 'compromise' whereby Juventus had a safe stadium and the ultras made their millions.

By the start of the 2015–16 season, Ciccio Bucci was back in Turin. His exile down South was over and it seemed that his childhood dream had come true. He was working for the club he had always loved. The last time the club's lawyer saw Bucci, on the occasion of the Torino–Juventus derby in March 2016, he received an enthusiastic hug. 'I'm an official figure,' Bucci had said, beaming happily. All the years of hustling, of sourcing and slinging tickets, were over. He had a proper job.

The trouble was that he had, in his words, 'a foot in both rivers'. He was aiming to satisfy the demands of Juventus, the ordinary fans, various ultra groups and even the police ('They call me every day,' he complained). Like in his school days, he was trying to be friends with everyone. His old mates, the Drughi, didn't want any watering down of the compromise, and he was ostracized and branded a traitor to the cause. Whilst his dream of working for Juventus had come true, after a year it was no longer quite so charming. He would always peer into a bar to see who was there before going in. He would look over his shoulder when walking the streets late at night. He knew that he was a target. In the spring of 2016 his mother died and he felt more alone than ever.

On 1 July 2016 Rocco and Saverio Dominello, and thirteen others, were arrested for a variety of Mafia-related crimes. On 6 July Bucci was questioned as 'a witness to the facts'. That night, he phoned his ex-wife and she felt that he was jabbering and barely making sense. He apologized to her and their son for any 'lack of respect'. She didn't understand and Bucci could only say that he was 'totally paranoid'. It's possible that he felt responsible for the arrest of the mafiosi, and was sure there would be reprisals. At the very least, he thought, the club he loved, Juventus, would sack him. He kept saying to his wife that he would have to sell his house. He would have no income any more.

Nobody knows what exactly happened in the next few hours. It seems highly likely that Bucci – given the bruises to the side of his head and the organic material found on his sunglasses – had been roughed up. The Italian press later speculated that his son had been threatened and that the crime of 'instigation to suicide' had been committed.

On 7 July, after watering his ex-wife's plants, Bucci parked his car on that long viaduct on the way back to Turin. Two workmen witnessed him get out of the car and stand on the edge of the road. He acted alone. But as he stood there, Bucci must surely have blamed others for what he was about to do. He had been shunned and beaten. Maybe he knew that all corrupt societies seek a scapegoat to cleanse themselves of their sins, and it was his shit luck to be that goat.

After his death, there were no loose ends. The server on which phone-taps were recorded was wiped between 10.38 a.m. and 1.30 p.m. on the day of his death, meaning that there was no record of who had been in contact with Bucci in those crucial hours. The small bag from which he was inseparable was missing, and was only later returned to Bucci's ex-wife by Juventus staff. It was almost as if all traces needed to be erased. When I spoke to someone within the club hierarchy to ask how Juventus was dealing with the death, he smiled ruefully: 'In silence.'

Many within the club, however, and the vast majority of Juventus supporters, were convinced that the Faustian pact between the Juventus ticket office and its ultras was operating elsewhere. Probably every big club had a similar quid pro quo in which tickets were illicitly slid under the counter to ultras in return for the ultras agreeing to suspend their instinct for insurgency. One Napoli director said that it had been standard procedure at the club to supply hundreds of tickets to fans for 'over twenty years'. That's just the way it was. A famous lawyer in Turin, who has represented both Juventus and ultra leaders, told me that 'the compromise between Juventus and the ultras was simply the compromise between the rules and the realities'. It sounds uncannily like a metaphor for Italian life.

Present Day: Livorno v. Cosenza

It's the first game since fifty-five ultras from the Curva Sud were given a stadium ban, so all the banners are hung upside down. A large, spray-painted portrait of Francesco, who has just died, is taped up on the plexiglass. Many of the chants are defiant:

'The mistrusted are always present' and 'You'll never have us as you want us'. A few minutes into the first half, a paper banner is unrolled. Twenty metres long, it says: 'You've done nothing to us.'

The stadium is only a fifth full. Livorno was in Serie A only a few years ago but is now bouncing along, with Cosenza, at the bottom of B. The cherry-and-yellow seats aren't shiny but aged, with grass and moss growing out of the holes in their middles.

Behind our terrace, through the railings and the maritime pines, you can see the distant oil-tankers static on the sea. On the far side of the Livorno terrace are the butterscotch high-rises. The Livornesi have a banner celebrating their lowly rank. '*Ultimi sì*', it says ('yes, last'), which could be taken as both the team being bottom or the ultras being dispossessed, 'but with honour and dignity'.

Livorno ultras are known for being the most ideologically left-wing of all their peers. Unlike the anarchic, egalitarian autono-mists of Cosenza, the Livornesi have often been proudly Leninist or Stalinist, creating a yellow hammer-and-sickle choreography or even replacing the Italian tricolour (on a ferry to Palermo, much to the captain's annoyance) with the Soviet flag. The group that cemented this reputation was BAL, the 'Autonomous Livorno Brigades', active from 1999 until the 2003–04 season. For years the portraits of Che, Castro, Stalin and Lenin fluttered in the Tuscan wind.

A neat game is going on. Boozy Suzy and I are queuing for another beer in the middle of the first half, albeit still singing along. Claudio is here. Despite his stadium ban, Chill is sud-denly among us, being complimented on his camouflage. The singing is repetitive and hypnotic, with One-Track banging out the rhythm on the drum: 'For the love of the shirt, Come on Cosenza, score a goal'.

But they don't. Livorno nudge one in from a corner. Tutino, the Cosenza striker, is sent off. Livorno score a penalty. 2–0. There are groans but you sing through it. If anything, it's more raucous now, as the only way to rescue the afternoon is to make it into a memorable party. We stay for an hour after the end singing, 'We're not leaving here' to the tune of the chorus from Bobby McFerrin's 'Don't worry be happy', until the police are almost begging us to move on. Another Sunday afternoon has slipped by and Cosenza are being sucked back into the relegation zone.

2017–18, Fermo

They're selling scarves saying 'Amedeo is with us' under the steps of the terraces. One old man mutters something to the lad behind the rickety counter. The lad doesn't like whatever he's said and tells him to fuck off, bouncing his fingertips up and down at waist height. A 'Free Amedeo' sticker has been pasted up, crooked, next to the fire hydrant. They think he's a victim of a repressive state. There's a concrete bog in the corner of the stadium. Inside is the usual graffiti: 'Live aflame but never getting burnt.' There are slap-dash Celtic crosses, a symbol not of piety but of anabolic right-wingery.

The game is one of those harum-scarum matches between top (Fermana) and fourth (Vis Pesaro). It's an end of season derby with all to play for. The midfielders spend plenty of time clutching shins or backs as they crash to the ground with a shout. The ball is moved side to side pretty neatly until the Fermana left-back slices it into the stands again.

Fermo is a small city of thirty-five thousand souls clinging to the summit of the Girfalco hill (the place of 'circling falcons'). The city's name has an implication of stubbornness. It comes as recognition of the place's reliability as an ally of the Roman Empire during the Second Punic War: '*Firmum Firmae fidei romanorum colonia*' – 'Fermo, Roman Colony of Firm Faith'. In the middle ages they used to say around here that '*Quando Fermo vuol fermare, tutta la Marca fa tremare*' ('When Fermo wants to be intransigent, all of the Marche region trembles'). The town's name simply means 'stop'.

That solidity mixes with an exquisite civility. At sunset the Piazza del Popolo has groups of old men talking football and politics. Couples sit in bars with tall glasses of neon-orange or blood-red *aperitivi*. Toddlers race around in front of the Palazzo dei Priori, giggling as they chase each other. The mayor is a fanatic follower of Fermana football club. He's worked as the defence lawyer to the ultras and now walks around the bars chatting amiably with anyone who calls him over. In one bar, he quietly pays for peoples' drinks. '*Ha pagato il sindaco*' is the shout from the barman half an hour later. 'The mayor has paid.'

To the northwest of the Girfalco, on the next-door hillock called the Colle Vissiano, is a seminary. It mixes Soviet-like architecture with twentieth-century Italianate materials of light ochre bricks and reinforced concrete, rising above the grey-green olive groves and cypresses like a hospital or prison. Its size is a reminder of decades past, when a common career choice for thousands of Italian boys was to become a priest. But by 2014 this place was almost empty. A few priests were hanging on, waiting for a religious revival that never came.

But it all changed in April that year. There was one priest who was always filling beds. Don Vinicio had spent much of his life creating his Comunità di Capodarco and its satellite communities. The first one was on little hillock a couple of kilometres east of the seminary towards the sea. All the other subsequent communities had borrowed the name of that first group: Capodarco. Decades of working with the lesser-abled, with the addicted and those recently released from hospital or prison had made Don Vinicio both weary and commanding. He was always approachable and informal but no word was wasted. 'Has this been done?' 'What's happening about that?' He took the calls and called the shots.

In April 2014 Don Vinicio was sitting in his grand, high-ceilinged office in that original community. Surrounded by religious figures, cartoons, footballs, files, fossils and rocks, he was chain-smoking straw-thin cigarettes under a rectangle of light. His secretary came to the door and told him that the Bishop was on the phone.

The Bishop explained to the priest that the Prefect had a problem. The Ministry of the Interior had decided that Le Marche had to offer shelter to fifty asylum-seekers. It was a tricky wicket for any astute politician. If you were too hospitable in this time of crisis, you would lose your electoral base. But if you appeared uncooperative with the Ministry of the Interior, your superiors might go sour on you and your career. So, the Prefect knew he had to go with the flow but he needed an ally on the ground who could accommodate the asylum seekers. The Prefect had turned to the Bishop who had turned to his old ally, Don Vinicio.

According to legend, Don Vinicio said the seminary was the place. He got to work and two days later, he had beds ready for fifty souls. The seminary became an asylum, suddenly filled with those who had braved the deserts of North Africa and the waters of the Mediterranean to reach Europe. Over the following months the rooms of the building were painted in bright colours: pastel greens, pinks, oranges and yellows. Don Vinicio appointed a nun who was tough but gentle. Suor Rita was in her thirties, a tall woman who was part of a new order of nuns called the 'Little Sisters of the Visitation', founded in 2008 and inspired by the radicalism of a French priest murdered in Algeria, Charles de Foucauld.

Over the next two years, Suor Rita and Don Vinicio learnt about human trafficking and its consequences. When migrants arrived on Italian soil, they had nothing – no documents, no money, no self-esteem. All they had was their story, full of suffering and, sometimes, bullshit. Suor Rita and Don Vinicio became expert at spotting the bull. But many didn't need to embellish anything. They had thought home was hell until they tried to leave it and things only got worse. There were few who hadn't witnessed first-hand rapes, robberies and even murders. If they were tetchy and needy when they rolled up on the elegant streets of Le Marche, it wasn't surprising.

The walls of Suor Rita's office became covered with mugshots of asylum seekers: large, A4 prints of dark faces. She only had a few staff working with her and was overwhelmed by the documents she had to deal with. Just feeding fifty people was hard but over the years, the numbers grew to over one hundred. The rules began to take shape: no alcohol, no drugs, a midnight curfew and so on. The operation was constantly getting bigger, with more people being referred each month. Quite often, the young men would get voluntary work, endearing themselves to locals and making friends. If all went well, some would be offered an apprenticeship. Other times, they would cause problems – rioting, throwing food, getting aggressive – and were quickly removed. Suor Rita, on appearances such a simple woman, had steel in her spine.

Until late 2015 the asylum seekers had only been men. But then, in September that year, a couple arrived. Nobody knew quite how long Emmanuel and Chinyeri had been together. The story went that their house in Nigeria had been burnt by Boko Haram, killing Chinyeri's parents and the couple's daughter. She said she had suffered a miscarriage on the journey through Libya. The two of them lived as common-law man and wife in the seminary. Emmanuel was tall with a boy-next-door face, serious but smiley at the same time. Chinyeri was tougher than him, more astute, even though, at twenty-four, she was twelve years younger. She was the only woman allowed to live amongst what were now 126 male asylum seekers at the seminary. Don Vinicio married them on 6 January 2016 in San Marco alle Paludi. It was an elegant ceremony, a charming mixture of Italian style and African exuberance: flowers, high-heels, drums and dancing.

But not everyone in Fermo was so accommodating. There was a man called Amedeo who was notorious for throwing peanuts on the cobbles outside the bar where he drank when the asylum seekers walked past. 'You hungry, monkey?' he would taunt as they walked on. Amedeo Mancini had a long criminal record for firearms offences, public affray and violence within the stadium, usually involving stone throwing. Over the years, he had received three Daspos.

Worse than the peanuts chucked on the floor were the bombs placed outside various churches throughout the spring of 2016. They were rudimentary but still dangerous. There were explosions outside the Duomo, the city's Cathedral, and outside the San Tommaso church in the Lido Tre Archi suburb. The entrance to San Marco alle Paludi had been badly damaged when a bomb exploded there on the night of 12–13 April. It was thought that the target was Don Vinicio, by now notorious for his work with

371

migrants. In May an unexploded bomb was found outside San Gabriele dell'Addolorata.

On Tuesday, 5 July 2016 there was a queue of immigrants waiting for the bus to the coast and the nearest railway station. The bus stop was at a semi-circle promenade by the side of the hairpin bend in Via Veneto. It's a stunning spot. The whole range of the Sibylline mountains are in front of you, their peaks covered with snow that looks impossible in the heat. There's an angled map to help you identify which summit is which: Monte Vettore, Cima del Redentore and, of course, Monte Sibilla. Chinyeri had stopped to drink at a water fountain and her husband, Emmanuel, was looking at his reflection in the black window of a parked car.

As Chinyeri straightened up, two men were walking towards her. She recognized one of them – that good-looking tough who hung out in the bar halfway between here and the seminary. He used to chuck peanuts at her. He was wearing a T-shirt of the far-right rock band ZZA, fronted by the CasaPound leader Gianluca Iannone. 'Until the end' it said.

'Monkey,' said Amedeo.

'Who's a monkey?' Chinyeri asked, incensed.

Then he walked over towards Emmanuel. 'Why are you looking in the car? What the fuck are you doing, you black shit? You trying to steal our cars as well?'

By now Chinyeri was shouting 'Racist, racist.'

Amedeo Mancini's friend tried to diffuse the situation. '*Amadé*,' he said. 'Leave it, she's a woman. Don't react.'

The eye-witness accounts of what happened next are conflicting. Some said that Emmanuel, angry at the abuse his wife was receiving, picked up a metal traffic sign – one of those temporary notices held in place by sand bags – and hit Amedeo

Mancini with it, knocking him to the ground. Others say he wasn't aggressive in any way.

It seemed like the confrontation was over. Two traffic wardens, and others who had seen the scuffle, began to walk away. But Mancini was a trained boxer and didn't like to retreat. He had been insulted by someone he considered his inferior and he was steaming. He walked over to Emmanuel and punched him hard. The Nigerian fell to the ground, hitting his head on the pavement. Mancini then waded in with kicks and punches.

'Look how well I caught him,' Mancini said in the local dialect. '*Lo sò allungato.*' – 'I've laid him out.'

Emmanuel never regained consciousness. He had the appearance of someone who had been in a high-speed car crash. He had cranial fractures, his lips were so swollen that they looked like a bike's inner tube, his jaw, ribs, legs and arms were purple.

Suor Rita's main concern was reprisals from her boys. The atmosphere in the seminary was tense. Everyone was talking about what had happened and quite a few thought it was time to take matters into their own hands. There were so many journalists around that Suor Rita eventually had to evict them all.

Don Vinicio was incensed. Emmanuel was being demonized as if he were at fault. There was an attempt to create an equivalence between the two men, and Don Vinicio didn't buy it. Emmanuel had been battered like a rug in a spring clean and Mancini didn't have a scratch. For a priest in the provinces, Don Vinicio was well connected in Rome. He knew many of the famous names in the Italian media – Enrico Mentana at La 7 TV station, Carlo Rosella at Channel 5 – and he called them all, telling them he was going to hold a press conference.

The day after the attack, whilst Emmanuel was still in a coma, Don Vinicio sat at a small desk, flanked by Suor Rita and a lawyer representing the Nigerian couple, and shot from the hip. 'I don't want this to be passed off as a black peoples' brawl. There's been a gratuitous provocation from some ultras, and I believe the thing can be linked with the bombs.' They were part of the same 'climate' he said: 'A container of magma formed of violence, aggression, frustration and exhibitionism.' The people responsible weren't organized, he said, but formed of 'mad splinters able to coagulate if needed'.

He went even further, accusing the city itself of indulging the activities of its local thugs: 'There's a cover-up which isn't explicit but treacherous. I call it cowardly.' He finished the press conference by expressing the hope that none of the nineteen Nigerians in the seminary would take revenge. 'Hatred brings only hatred,' he said. Shortly after the press conference, at half-past-three the day following the attack, Emmanuel was declared dead.

A week after the killing, on 13 July 2016, the Curva Duomo ultras wrote on their Facebook page: 'We want to applaud all the lads from the *curva*, especially the youngest ones, for the way in which they have managed the media pillory of recent days. From this story we will emerge with heads held high: Stronger! More mature! More united!... This is what being an ultra is about: not abandoning a friend in difficulty.' In another post on 7 August 2016, addressed to Amedeo Mancini and entitled '*Un mese senza di te*' ('A month without you'), they wrote: 'We feel your absence. In the paths of the centre, and especially Sunday in the *curva*, there on those steps where we have grown up together... you have always been and always will be the soul of Curva Duomo.' As often happens, the rhetoric of the ultras eerily echoed religious phraseology. Instead of 'God be with us,' the new chant at the stadium quickly became '*Amedeo Con Noi!*'

– 'Amedeo is with us!' Later, the ultras set up a bank account to pay for Mancini's legal expenses.

Mancini was released under house arrest in October. Although he always denied any racial motivation to the attack, he subsequently plea-bargained, admitting 'involuntary murder aggravated by racial hatred'. To many, the sentence handed down on 18 January 2017 was ludicrous: four years of house arrest with permission to go out for work during the day. He was freed from even that light sentence in May 2017 when his house arrest was lifted for good behaviour. Less than a year after the murder, the only obligation on Mancini was to sign in once a day at the local *Carabinieri* station. Meanwhile, Don Vinicio was still trying to raise the 5,000 euros necessary to repatriate the body of Emmanuel back to Nigeria. A tip-off from a young woman led police to identify two other Fermana fans as the authors of the rudimentary bombs outside churches. Emmanuel's widow, Chinyeri, was in hiding.

But at the stadium, if you're on the look-out for racism, you don't see it. There's a black girl with her man at the centre of the *curva*, watching the game. Plenty of mixed-race kids in their teens are clapping along to the constant 'Amedeo is with us' chant. In this imitative world, you often follow a lead without understanding its meaning. You're absorbed into something greater than yourself, which is part of both the enchantment and the risk. The bliss of being bound together means that, sometimes, you're also blinded.

Ten minutes from the end, Edoardo Ferrante – a ginger-bearded central defender – bangs in a goal with his forehead right in front of the ultras. They sprint to the glass wall separating them from what is now a player pile-on on the other side. 'You're shit,' they sing to the Pesaresi, 'and you'll always be shit.'

The next quarter of an hour is bliss. The sun has come out and you can see the Adriatic, reminding you it's almost summer again. Fermana seem certain to go up into Serie C and the whole repertoire of songs are yodelled. It's as if the hope of promotion is lifting the whole city. On the way out, Paolo the mayor, just rolling up from a funeral, says hello. 'As you see,' he says, 'it's a tranquil place.'

Nobody knows why but, out of the blue, in 2016 the leadership of Lazio's Irriducibili suddenly decided they liked the club's owner, Claudio Lotito. The cynics suggested that some sort of deal must have been struck between the two sides. Some of the Irriducibili were so outraged by this *volte-face* that they left the group. Despite his house-arrest, Diabolik issued a communiqué in January 2016 inviting all Lazio fans to an open-air reunion. He lamented the 'sad moment' on the terraces and urged: 'Come on, my friends and fans. Today is the moment to reunite, to see each other again, to go to away games together like the old days… all fans, let's close ranks. It's time to march!'

Most ultra communiqués are issued solely in the name of the group. There are no names. But this was highly personalized. The word 'Irriducibile' was singularized. It was signed by that playfully devilish moniker, Diabolik. And there was a subtle edge to it, hinting at what might happen when his house arrest was over: 'I swear I feel like a lion in a cage… and more than that, hungry. Sooner or later this will end, and my place will return to being the same as it always has been – amongst you, amongst my people, my group, my terrace.' It sounded strangely like the threatening growls of an ageing dictator who suspected a coup.

Within a year, his group had retaken control, hanging their

banner in the centre of the Curva Nord once more. Almost immediately, the grim, familiar stunts returned. Three mannequins, dressed in Roma shirts, were hanged in the city centre, with a message: 'No offence, just advice: sleep with the light on.' At one training session prior to a derby, the ultras screamed at the mute, almost scared players: 'This is more than a battle for us, this is ethnic warfare.'

In 2017 the Irriducibili distributed style guides for Lazio fans. With two fans side-by-side – one from Lazio, the other a generic alternative – orders were given about how to dress: the baseball cap had to face forwards, the only sunglasses allowed were Ray-Ban and Persol, shoes had to be New Balance or Clarks. There was even advice about the height of the crotch on trousers. It expressed disdain for the long-haired types from 'Brescia and Bergamo' and the 'gypsies' from Pescara. There was nothing ironic or tongue-in-cheek about the orders. This was an attempt at sartorial despotism expressed in mangled prose.

The flier eloquently expressed the essence of the Irriducibili: the arrogance of imposing on thousands of people how they should dress, the fogeyish dismay at some imagined cultural decline, the idea that there was a rigid hierarchy in which the front row was for the bosses, and the back rows for the slobs. Instead of the exuberant rebellion of the ultras from decades before – a rebellion implying the rejection of Italian sartorial homogeneity – the Irriducibili were now demanding conformity. It twisted the famous ultra mentality into mannerism, and there was, as always with the Irriducibili, a crude capitalistic agenda. If tens of thousands of Lazio fans assumed a uniform, those who controlled the merchandising could make a lot more money.

In July 2017, shortly after taking repossession of the terraces, the group released another communiqué: 'We want to clarify the following: for some months the little group, Lazio Hit Firm, has not existed. It won't exhibit either flags or banners any more. To the lads of the terraces, and to the youngsters who will come, we remind and clarify that in our Curva Nord the line to follow is, and remains, that of the sole group...' Not for the first time, the totalitarian tendencies of the gang were evident: no opposition or rival would be tolerated.

A few months later, in October, Lazio fans put up stickers of Anne Frank wearing a Roma shirt in the Curva Sud of the Stadio Olimpico. It was a reiteration of the old, tasteless joke that your rival was Jewish and destined to die young. The same had been going on for years. Back in April 2001 a Lazio banner had taunted Roma fans with the line: 'Team of niggers, terraces of Jews.'

To redress the antisemitism, the Italian footballing authorities decided that passages of Anne Frank's diary should be read at all grounds, followed by a minute's silence, the next weekend. Maybe it was laudable in its intentions but in reality, it was surreal, with stadiums becoming like schoolrooms for those in detention and needing re-education. No ultra likes to be lectured, especially by the footballing powers, and Juventus ultras turned their backs and sang the Italian national anthem. Whilst the Lazio players wore white T-shirts with the familiar face of Frank and 'No to antisemitism' written below, its ultras – in the Bologna stadium, the Dall'Ara – chanted that old Mussolini slogan '*Me ne frego*' ('I don't give a shit'). Ascoli's ultras deliberately only entered the ground after the minute's silence, issuing a statement that said: 'We don't want to be complicit in a media and institutional theatre which forgets earthquake victims and our elderly but which is always ready to exploit ten stickers.'

The minute's silence, often used at the beginning of matches, was always an open goal for ultras. In October 2013, after an estimated 368 refugees had drowned near Lampedusa, stadiums were again asked to observe a silent sixty seconds. During the silence, the Juventus ultras sung the national anthem, while Lazio's chanted *'Forza Lazio olé'*. The Lazio ultras' opinions on immigration were very clear. Another of their banners read 'To the ultras stadium bans and prison, to immigrants safe spaces to deal drugs and rape. This is your Europe.'

Any kind of commemoration was becoming an excuse for ultras to parade their politics. When, in November 2017, the ninety-eight-year-old Dante Unti, a Tuscan survivor of the Holocaust, was presented with a pennant of the local team, Lucchese, on the pitch prior to a local derby, the notoriously far-right ultras avoided the occasion. At the end-of-season party for the Curva Sud of Hellas Verona in the summer of 2017, Luca Castellini (a Forza Nuova bigwig) was on the microphone: 'Who allowed this party, who paid for everything, who was the guarantor? He has a name: Adolf Hitler.' It would be easier to dismiss his words as the rantings of a lunatic if the crowd hadn't started laughing and cheering, breaking into that old rhyming song that Hellas Verona was a *'squadra fantastica'* made with the 'swastika'.

Now that the Irriducibili had retaken the terraces, they imposed their ideology. Another flier, left on seats all over the Curva Nord in August 2018, banned women from the front ten rows. 'The "North" represents, for us,' the flier said, 'a sacred place, an environment with a non-written code to be respected. We have always lived in the front rows as if they were trenches. Within them, women, wives and girlfriends are not admitted, so we invite them to position themselves from the tenth row back.'

As yet another media storm engulfed the terrace Talibans, the Irriducibili replied by issuing a prolix communiqué that seemed almost deranged. It railed against 'drunk, unsteady' women who lost sight of their children for the sake of a selfie, against 'freaked out feminism', against 'paedophilia' and 'short-sighted ideology'. But amidst the meandering nonsense, there was a very sober threat. The group warned Lazio's PR spokesman (who had attempted to distance the club from the group's men-only imposition) not to 'separate himself from lads who might also be friends with his own daughter'.

Other ultra groups backed up the Irriducibili. The Siracusa terraces boasted, without irony, that 'there's no sexism or discrimination towards women who occupy the back rows', because those women had been brought up 'with order and discipline'. The group's female section, Le Aretusee, promptly disbanded in protest. 'We distance ourselves from this way of thinking,' they announced.

The expulsion of women from the front rows was symbolic of the Irriducibili's territorial occupation. For a group that had staked out their drug-dealing turf in the Italian capital, taking control of the *curva* was simple. But many fans, even plenty of ultras, were dismayed by that occupation. Groups like We Love Lazio bravely denounced the idiocy of the Irriducibili. 'There's no possible justification for the repeated debasement,' they wrote after the Anne Frank stickers had appeared. 'It's not a prank, it's human misery.' There's a 'Lazio and Anti-fascist' organization, which battles against the stereotypes of the 'Lazi-fascist' label.

A few months later, I met one of Diabolik's lieutenants at a Lazio game at the Stadio Olimpico. An enormous, muscular man in his mid-forties, Franchino isn't the sort of person you can just walk up to. You have to work your way through his entourage of heavies, filters, fixers and friends. When you eventually get to him, you're granted a few minutes as if it's an audience with a feudal lord. I asked him if there wasn't a huge amount of arrogance in this group. He smiled coldly and shook his head. 'It's very unlikely that a Lazio fan would dare to raise their voice… who is arrogant will be automatically marginalized because we are very hierarchical and very militarized.' He was unwittingly confirming arrogance by saying it was unthinkable: it didn't exist because everyone knew their place.

What was once inconceivable outside the terraces was now becoming normal. Twenty bronze cobbles commemorating victims of the Holocaust in Rome were ripped up and stolen. The sign for the Anne Frank school in Pesaro was spray-painted with a swastika and the 'dogs forbidden' sign was changed to 'Jews'. Skinheads from a neo-Nazi organization called Veneto Fronte Skinhead, all wearing black bomber jackets, interrupted a meeting of the Como Without Borders association, accusing the volunteers of plotting the substitution of the European peoples by helping immigrants. One of those skinheads was a Piacenza ultra who had previously served six years for knifing two people in 2009. A beach resort in Chioggia was revealed to be a fascist theme park, a self-styled 'anti-democratic zone' with Mussolini memorabilia on sale and 'no entrance' signs replaced by 'gas chamber' ones.

Each instance was, in some respects, only a minor news story but the constancy with which these things happened persuaded *Il Tempo* newspaper to call Benito Mussolini its 'person of the year' for 2017. It wasn't being facetious but factual, because the *Duce* barged into the news agenda every week. What was noticeable was that it wasn't just a few rogues who were nostalgic about the *ventennio*, but often those with institutional positions. A neo-

Nazi flag was hung up in a *Carabinieri* barracks in Florence. A teacher in Rivarossa boasted about being fascist. Another teacher, from a secondary school in Massa Carrara, published a photograph of himself waving an RSI flag (from Mussolini's Repubblica di Salò) on top of the Monte Sagra in the Apennines.

Every political party on the right always defended the nostalgics. The alarmist left, they said, was deliberately creating a *spauracchio*, a 'bogeyman' because – other than anti-fascism – the left had no ideology left. It was honourable, they said, that neofascists from CasaPound and Lealtà Azione were marching to the Campo X, in Milan's cemetery, to remember the fallen from the RSI. The organization of a pilgrimage to Predappio by Lazio ultras (€50 a head) was no longer even news.

The shooting of black bystanders in Macerata by Luca Traini was an almost inevitable result of this atmosphere of hatred. Traini was a troubled man: his father had abandoned the family when he was young and he had been brought up by his grandmother. He had been excluded from a local gym because he used to give a Roman salute on entering. He was nicknamed Wolf because he had the 'Wolfsangel' rune (a symbol used by both the SS and Italy's 'Third Position') on his forehead. Despite that evident signalling of extremism, he was on the fringes of Lega politics, having met Matteo Salvini once at Corridonia. On 3 February 2018 he took his Glock pistol to his Alfa Romeo 147 and drove around town shooting at migrants. He hit six blacks before going to a war memorial and, draped in an Italian flag, gave a Roman salute.

The aftermath of that shooting showed that mainstream politicians on the right blamed immigration, not Traini: Berlusconi spoke of a 'social bomb' created by foreigners. Italy, he said, needed to repatriate 600,000 illegal immigrants. In an atmosphere that felt akin to the American Deep South in the early 1960s, Establishment politicians blamed the victims: Matteo Salvini said that 'it's clear and evident that an immigration which is out of control… leads to social conflict'.

Traini's legal fees were paid by Forza Nuova and the Lazio ultras hung a banner at Ponte Milvio saying 'Honour to Luca Traini'. Those two worlds were, by now, one and the same. A parliamentary report, published before the shootings in December 2017, had said that 'the presence of ultras in all the recent cases of political demonstrations by the far right creates concern'. On 24th April 2019 the Irriducibili paraded in Milan, doing Roman salutes, behind a banner which read: 'Honour to Benito Mussolini'. When a handmade bomb exploded days later outside the Irriducibili's HQ in Rome, Diabolik said: 'If they want the terrorism of the 1970s to come back we're ready. In fact, I can't wait. Of course we're fascists, we don't renounce anything.'

Perhaps the key question regarding the ultras is how far there is an overlap not just with political extremism, but with organized crime. Daniele Segre, the documentary-maker who made the *Stadium Kids* documentary in the 1970s, said in an interview in 2007: 'I've followed them over the years, and many of them have become criminal labourers… There was [in the 1970s] a large entanglement between organized crime and the extreme fringe of fandom.'

In many ways, that entanglement happened because both sides were doing something very similar. The ultras had always been about the territory, and that devotion to the streets obviously brought them into contact with mafiosi whose power is based on territorial control. A 2017 report from the parliamentary anti-Mafia commission studied this 'infiltration, or better contamination, of organized fans by organized, Mafia criminals' and, not surprisingly, found many examples. Particular fan groups had become the public representatives, the boots on the ground, of specific clans. They were used to exert influence on both players and presidents: to throw games, to provide more tickets, to disrupt matches and so on. But perhaps those ultra groups' most important service to the mafiosi was simply persuasion. The fear ultra groups could instil in the public was a crowd-controller for Mafia families, a ground-level intimidation that could escalate if someone was messing with your business. One police chief interviewed by the commission spoke of the Mafia seeing the terraces as 'an opportunity to increase not only the field of illicit dealing and the recycling of dirty capital, but also to insinuate itself in a creeping and pervasive way into the social fabric'. It was as if certain ultra groups were being turned into a public relations operation for criminal clans.

But perhaps the true overlap between ultras and organized crime is a way of being. Ultras protest continually and since there's plenty to protest about, many groups bravely bear witness to injustices. But ultra protests throughout the peninsula are often intimidating. They can be manipulated. The show of muscle sometimes replicates criminal threats. Even Osvaldo Pieroni, who wrote – without condescension – about the Cosenza ultras' 'simplicity of spirit', also noticed that some would 'point their fingers with an air of the mafioso.' There's no generous mellowness to being an ultra. Even someone who loves the football and the insider-status it offers, who relishes the partying and singing, who can even understand that men like fighting, struggles with the sheer arrogance of this world. When you've seen enraged men screaming at everyone around them (demanding a player's shirt which has been caught by a kid, punching a fan who is singing their own song, pushing a woman down the stairs because she has the wrong tattoo), you tire of it all. There's just too much *straffottenza* ('attitude' or 'arrogance').

Present Day: Another Game

It's mid-winter, mid-week, and a 2,000-kilometre round trip to watch a cup game that is nothing more than tidy and perfunctory.

We haven't come for the football though. Antò died yesterday and this is our way of showing this Northern town that we remember our own. '*Antò è qua, e canta con gli ultra*' – 'Antò is here and is singing with the ultras.'

In Italian the 'here' ('*qua*') rhymes with '*ultrà*' but the rhyme isn't the only reason we're chanting the word again and again. The hypnotic repetition of '*qua*' and '*ultrà*' reminds you of where, and who, you are. You are here, and you are ultra, so you're present but you're also beyond. All the old paradoxes flood back through that simple chant: an individual's name is only chanted when they're not with us. And, Left-Behind says, Antò is far more important that those 'shits' – he chins towards the players in the gleaming away kit – who are borrowing our shirt for a season or two.

We unfurl a banner 2 metres high and 6 wide. It just says 'Antò'. Someone lights a red flare beneath it, which smokes hard in our faces as we're chanting: 'Antò is here and is singing with the ultras.'

The banner catches light and two firemen rush towards us. We close ranks around it and stamp out the flames. The firemen back off. Any pyrotechnics are banned from stadiums but you have to smuggle in something when there's a death, because the colours have to smoke up into the dark December skies like a funereal pyre.

That insistence on the presence of the departed chimes well with everyone. Because the absences aren't just due to death, but because of all the Daspos too. 'The mistrusted are always present', we chant occasionally, clapping our frozen hands. It reinforces the idea that there's honour in being distrusted, that you'll be remembered the more mistrusted, or dead, you are. You get the feeling that any scorn that comes our way is uplifting. Because we're here and we reckon we're sticking it to the authorities by being here.

In many ways, the terraces are now spaces to eulogize and memorialize the dead. Banners showing the names of late fans or players are held up at games. The list of those who have gone is obviously long. Exactly ten years to the day since Roma lost that iconic cup final against Liverpool, the Roma captain, Agostino Di Bartolomei – depressed at his exclusion from the game since his retirement and, given the date, clearly still mourning that loss against Liverpool – shot himself in the heart. Both Giorgio Chinaglia and the Taxi-Driver died in 2012. The great Cosenza striker Gigi Marulla passed away in 2015. Their faces are spray-painted onto concrete walls outside the stadiums. Sometimes, those remembered are former club owners or favourite players but normally it's the ultras who are inscribed onto the stadium. Parma's Boys renamed the Curva Nord the Matteo Bagnaresi terrace after a twenty-six-year-old who was crushed by a bus. Many websites have long dedications to brothers and sisters who have fallen. The 'AsRomaUltras' website even has a page of threnodies under the refined Latin heading of *Sit Vobis Terra Levis* ('May the earth be light on you').

Ultra banners have often played with the gladiators' pledge to the dignitaries in the arenas of ancient Rome: 'Those who are about to die salute you.' One of the earliest mottos of Roma's Boys was 'beyond death'. It's as if the ultras are reminding everyone, absurd as it sounds, that they are prepared to die for this creed. Sacrifice is constantly invoked. Those who are scornful of the ultra world have often perceived a fascistic death cult on the terraces, but maybe being an ultra is simply another way to commemorate our ancestors, to tell their stories and sacralize the spaces where they, and we, used to come together.

It's a truism to say that the stadium is a temple, but it consciously functions as such. More people pray on the terraces, or at least plead with fate, than in the pews. The funeral processions, of both ultras and iconic players, always pass around the athletics track. When you see those funerals, you remember that it's called a ground, that a terrace is to do with the earth. The rotundity of the *curve* isn't only fertility, but a barrow. With the coffin there in the stadium, with the coloured incense and the rowdy hymns of the terraces, it begins to make sense.

When tragedy befalls a city, it's now the stadium, more than the cathedral, that marks the moment. In August 2018 Genova's Polcevera Viaduct (better known as the Morandi Bridge) collapsed, killing forty-three people and making 566 homeless. Long before the footballing authorities decided that the two matches involving Genoa and Sampdoria should be postponed, their ultras announced their absence. 'Our city is in mourning,' the Genoa ultras wrote in a press release, 'and for dignity, respect and sorrow, the Genoa fans will not be present at Sunday's match at the San Siro Stadium. Our sector will be completely deserted.' It was another example of how ultras saw football, in certain circumstances, as a desecration. And their language was, intentionally or otherwise, religious: 'La Superba [that nickname of the city] is wounded but will rise again.'

From Cosenza, Drainpipe wrote an open letter to the city, calling it 'a magnet of tragedies'. He wrote about his admiration for the Genovese, particularly their bluntness, speaking 'without frills, without finery and lexical twirls'. His letter, using the word 'love' sixteen times, showed how much leaders on the terraces had taken on the role formerly assigned to priests of publicly marking a tragic moment, of accompanying and consoling. At Genoa's next game, the ultras decided to remain silent for forty-three minutes to mark the forty-three dead. There, too, the religiosity was recurrent: 'We are proud and always will be of our beloved Genova, which will know how to resurrect herself.'

Although police insist that the ultra world is an 'adhesive' for criminality, it's also a much deeper form of social glue. Ultras are always frustrated with those who don't see the good they do. Cosenza is maybe an extreme example of the goodness but many terraces do something similar. After the Aquila earthquake in 2009, dozens of ultra groups moved in, clearing ground, bringing tents, cooking meals. The Mayor of Amatrice later said that 'the ultras have done more than thirty years of politicians'. One Christmas, Spampinato's group in Catania raised €3,000 and filled four vans with Christmas presents for kids who wouldn't get any otherwise. One Torino group sent money to a Napoli group in order to replant Vesuvius with saplings after a forest fire. When Livorno or Genova were hit by severe flooding, the ultras – including from rival cities – helped out. Phonelines and lifeboats and ambulances and braille-printers have been financed by them. Many scoff that this is mere 'metapolitics' (that cultural persuasion that the far right borrowed from Gramsci) but actually this charity often comes with no agenda. It is just an extension of being attached to place and to people.

I recently went to see a friend who had been in a motorcycle accident. He had always lived his life as an ultra, not just in the sense of the terraces but in terms of excess and passion. He had played bass in a hardcore punk band and every time I played football against him (he was a chunky central defender) he gave it, and you, everything he had. He was a Torino obsessive but is now in a coma, only his huge eyes moving.

There, in the room, were cherry-coloured scarves and a man was talking to him about recent results. By his bedside was a book about Torino and, maybe because I couldn't understand how this bull of a man could now be immobile and emaciated, I read the closing pages: 'Toro is severely religious, even mystical. If Juventus didn't exist, Toro fans would have had to invent her, to suffer more and to feel more tense and sharp and inferior, an inferiority of an evangelic type: sacred, saintly, poor...' Maybe that is what fandom does. It habituates you to loss and creates the occasions to share it with other people.

It's the last day of the Serie B season. Because there are only nineteen teams in the league, Cosenza isn't playing. But the team is safe from relegation following recent victories against Spezia and Salernitana.

Left-Behind, Boozy Suzy, Chill and I are walking up to the Svevian castle to toast the end of the season. The castle is perched on top of the Pancrazio hill, a beehive of lanes, narrow staircases and petite piazzas which make up 'old Cosenza'. There are artisan workshops – cobblers, coffin-makers, luthiers – but nothing has been gentrified. This is a place of rugged survival; where people live at such close quarters there are few secrets. You can hear every argument. Skinny kittens scamper up steep paths which disappear into front rooms. Weeds grow out of the cracks. Many buildings are empty or have got a belly, and cement has been slapped here and there to patch up the ancient stone.

There are great murals everywhere. Yellow cartoon faces, monkeys giving birth, wiggly nudes, buccaneering horses, seascapes, tributes to the Faraca cyclists from this city. '*CZ merda*' it says everywhere ('Catanzaro is shit'). When you wander around it's like half the *curva* is here. By chance, Egg comes out of a dented metal door, asks what we're doing, and joins the walk up the hill.

The view from the castle is stunning: olive groves, wooded mountains and narrow bridges crossing the city's rivers. But Suzy is scornful. 'There's not a patch of land they haven't built on,' she says. Blocks of flats spill across the valley as far as the eye can see.

'Never-ending *palazzi*,' shrugs Left-Behind, 'and not one for us.'

The Curva Sud has recently been evicted from its squat, the *Casa degli Ultrà*, and is homeless. Those who most express belonging now have nowhere they belong. But that sense of exclusion makes them feel even more integral to, or rooted in, the city: they're not in the corridors of power, but in the streets, the ditches and the gutters. They know the lie of the land better than anyone. And although their way of life is a constant expression of love for their city, they're also eloquent critics of its corruptions and crimes.

Chill is unscrewing the lid of a tall bottle. He slops the Silan liqueur into small plastic glasses, lining them up on the fat wall of the castle. We each take one, and raise them to the red-and-blue shirt… then to the city… then to Denis Bergamini, and to Piero, and to each other, until by then we've drunk too much and Egg is talking shit again. 'Next season,' he grins, 'Serie A'.

Afterword

In the spring of 2019 Ciccio Bucci's body was exhumed for further examinations. In 2017 the body of Donato Bergamini was exhumed and a new autopsy conducted. Results seem to suggest he had been suffocated and strangled. The investigation is ongoing.

Pino Coldheart remains the undisputed leader of Juventus' Drughi. In September 2019, he and eleven other capo-ultrà were arrested, accused of blackmailing Juventus in order to acquire free tickets. They are currently awaiting trial.

On 7th August 2019, Diabolik was sitting on a park bench in Parco degli Acquedotti in the south-east of Rome. Shortly before 7 p.m., a man dressed as a jogger – wearing a cap and neck-scarf – ran past the bench and fired a 7.65 calibre pistol into Piscitelli's left ear. He died almost instantly, sliding off the bench as the murderer ran off. It had all the hallmarks of a professional hit. His murder remains unsolved.

Antonio Bongi and Grit still live and work in Rome.

Puffer and Scotto continue to lead, respectively, Genoa's Gradinata Nord and the Genova Insieme cooperative.

Michele Spampinato is still chairing meetings between the petrol pumps in Catania's Piazza dei Miracoli.

The Inter ultras responsible for the ambush of their Napoli

counterparts in which 'Dede' – Daniele Belardinelli – lost his life were convicted of 'aggravated assault'. Although given stadium bans of up to eight years, none of the ultras received a custodial sentence.

In February 2019 the Roma ultra who reduced the Liverpool fan Sean Cox to a coma received a three-and-a-half-year prison sentence.

Ciccio Conforti has become a Buddhist and runs a Bed & Breakfast in his 16th century family home, Palazzo Conforti, in the hills outside Cosenza.

Claudio teaches in a middle school and has written, and edited, many books about the ultra lifestyle.

Gianfranco manages his 'peoples' gym' inside Cosenza's San Vito stadium.

Paride is the director of the Lucana Film Commission.

Drainpipe still lives in Cosenza and frequently takes his charity, La Terra di Piero, to Africa.

The Curva Sud and Anni Ottanta are trying to get along.

Padre Fedele is still sitting in a car in the city, offering to listen to anyone who needs.

Acknowledgements

I am, above all, grateful to the ultras of many different terraces for their hospitality, patience and generosity. The list of people to thank in Cosenza is too long to mention everyone but I owe a particular debt to Marco, Simona, Francesca, Olga, Gianluca, Alberto, Emmanuele, Arturo, Gabriele, Marcellino, Ciccio, Danilo, Silverio, Robertino, Achille, Marco, William, Piero, Claudio, Gianfranco, Vincenzo, Pietro, Francesco, Barbara, Luca, Sergio, Katia, Mena, Paride and Padre Fedele. It's been a blessing to have met Monica Levantino and Vincenzo Reda.

Every time I write an essay or a book about Italy, I'm amazed by the generosity of Italian journalists. I'm greatly indebted to Massimiliano Peggio, Jacopo Ricca, Marco Grasso, Massimo Calandri, Jacopo Forcella, Giuseppe Scarpa, Mario Salvini, Pierluigi Spagnolo, Gianluca Marcon, Marco Di Mauro, Raffaele Vitali, Andrea Luchetta, Simone Meloni and Timothy Ormezzano. I've benefitted from the expertise and contacts of Richard Hall, Luca Hodges-Ramon, John Foot, Max Mauro, Guido Polini and Sergio Sinigaglia. Mattia Fossati, Antonio Broso, Pasquale Ancona and Sacha Malgeri helped with legal documents and dialects. Matteo Galloni and Filippo Ziveri have constantly lent me their books and their ideas. I've been very lucky to have alongside me Daniela Calebich, Laura Lenzi and Matteo Diena, and am grateful to Francesco Pedrona and il Vascio for introducing me to all the fine '*calciatori distrutti*'.

The Society of Authors gave me a generous grant to finance moving back to Italy, and without the heroic Mark Loveys we might never have made it. Mary Massey, Bob Jones, David and Vandana Jones, Paul and Marija Jones, Andy and Marion Street, Richard and Sheena Brooke, Andrea and Russell Hartley and Steve and Susannah Baker all put their trust in us and kept Windsor Hill Wood alive. I'm very grateful to Christopher Somerville and Pete Dennis for their visionary generosity. Huge admiration to Chris, Katharine, Josh and Natty Thompson, who understand the agonies of playing, and watching, football. Thanks, too, to Shaun Wolff, Franco Tomasi, Costanza Gambarini and Guido Bizzarri for being such good neighbours; and to Gildo Claps, Andrew Wigley, Paolo Mortarotti, Glen Alessi and James McConnachie for being so giving.

Jonathan Shainin, Clare Longrigg and David Wolf of the *Guardian*'s 'Long Read' kindly published my essay that became the genesis of this book. I'm grateful, too, to Rob Yates and Paul Webster at the *Observer* for continuing to commission my work. Ben Donald has been constantly supportive.

I'm in awe of the editorial skills of Neil Belton, who mysteriously helped me finish a book that seemed never-ending.

Thanks also to Anthony Cheetham and everyone at Head of Zeus. Walter Donohue and Enrico Basaglia have, as always, offered invaluable advice. Georgina Capel, Irene Baldoni, Rachel Conway and Simon Shaps at GCA have offered continual, and concrete, encouragement. Thank you.

Francesca, Benedetta, Emma and Leonardo have put up with months of absences and have indulged my notion that drinking beer at football matches is actually work. Everything I've learnt about belonging, love and rootedness is thanks to them.

Select Bibliography

Memoirs

Anonymous, *Brigate Neroazzurre Atalanta* (private printing)

Barillaro, A., *Ultras Grigi* (Canepa, Spinetta Marengo, 2007)

Bisceglia, F., *Io, frate detenuto* (Pubblisfera, San Giovanni in Fiore, 2006)

Califano, A., & Cuccurullo, G., *Una vita da molosso* (Coessenza, Cosenza, 2016)

Cametti, S., *I Guerrieri di Verona* (private printing)

Casolari, A. and Landini, F., *Gruppo D'Azione*, (Hellnation / Red Star Press, Rome, 2015)

Dionesalvi, C., *Mammagialla* (Rubbettino, Soveria Mannelli, 2003)

Franzo, B., *Via Filadelfia 88* (Novantico, Pinerolo, 2013)

Franzo, B., *80 Voglia di Curva Filadelfia* (NovAntico, Pinerolo, 2014)

Greco, S., *Faccetta Biancoceleste* (Ultra Sport, Rome, 2015)

Grinta, A., *Anni Buttati* (Settimo Sigillo, Rome, 2015)

Luraschi, I., *La Violenza negli stadi* (SEB, Cusano Milanino, 2003)

Ruello, N., *Il Vento della nord* (private printing)

Spampinato, M. & Pulvirenti, L., *Quando saremo tutti nella nord* (Euno Edizioni, Leonforte, 2014)

Various, *Noi Siamo Dorici* (Punto, Ancona, 2015)

Secondary Sources

Augé, M., *Il Calcio come fenomeno religioso* (EDB, Bologna, 2016)

Beha, O., *Il Calcio alla sbarra* (Rizzoli, Milan, 2011)

Berizzi, P., *Bande Nere* (Bompiani, Milano, 2009)

Berizzi, P., *Nazitalia* (Baldini & Castoldi, Milan, 2018)

Carchidi, G., *Profondo Rossoblù* (Editoriale Progetto, Cosenza, 2003)

Casanova, M., *Tifose* (Odoya, Bologna, 2018)

Coccia, P, *Un'impresa degli ultrà* (Rai Eri, Rome, 2004)

Dal Lago, A., *Descrizione di una battaglia* (Il Mulino, Bologna, 1990)

Dal Lago, A. & Moscato, R., *Regalateci un sogno* (Bompiani, Milan, 1992)

De Rose, M., *Controcultura Ultrà* (Coessenza, Cosenza, 2011)

Dionesalvi, C., *Scritti Ultrà* (Coessenza, Cosenza, 2016)

Ferreri, A., *Ultras* (Bepress, Lecce, 2008)

Foschini, G. & Mensurati, M., *Lo Zingaro e lo scarafaggio* (Mondadori, Milano, 2012)

Garsia, V., *A Guardia di una fede* (Castelvecchi, Rome, 2004)

Lanna, L. & Rossi, F., *Fascisti Immaginari* (Vallecchi, Florence, 2003)

Marchi, V., *Ultrà* (Hellnation / Red Star Press, Rome, 2015)

Marchi, V., *Il Derby del bambino morto* (Alegre, Rome, 2014)

Marchi, V., *Stile maschio violento* (Costa & Nolan, Genova, 1994)

Mariottini, D., *Ultraviolenza* (Bradipo Libri, Torino, 2004)

Mariottini, D., *Tutti Morti tranne uno* (Bradipo Libri, Torino, 2009)

Martucci, M., *11 Novembre 2007* (Sovera, Rome, 2008)

Massucci, R., & Ferrigni, N, *C'era una volta l'ultrà* (Eurilink, Roma, 2013)

Morello, N., *La Religione Granata* (Yume, Turin, 2017)

Mungo, D., Abbatantuono, V., Viganò G., *Noi Odiamo Tutti* (La Città del Sole, Naples, 2010)

Mungo, D. & Ranieri, G., *@Ultras* (Galeone, Rome, 2017)

Mungo, D., *Cani Sciolti* (Boogaloo, Rovereto, 2008)

Nastasi, S., *Il Caso Speziale* (Bonfirraro, Enna, 2013)

Ormezzano, G. & Ormezzano T., *La Bibbia della Fede Granata* (Sperling & Kupfer, Milan, 2018)

Pasqua, G. (ed), *Il Mio Cosenza* (Pellegrini, Cosenza, 2014)

Petrini, C., *Il Calciatore Suicidato* (Kaos Edizioni, Milan, 2001)

Pieroni, O., *I Pedatori dell'arca perduta* (private printing)

Pozzoni, S., *Dove sono gli ultrà?* (Zelig, Milan, 2005)

Romani, P., *Calcio Criminale* (Rubbettino, Soveria Mannelli, 2012)

Roversi, A., *Calcio, tifo e violenza* (Il Mulino, Bologna, 1992)

Roversi, A., *L'odio in rete* (Il Mulino, Bologna, 2006)

Russo, P., *Gol di Rapina* (Edizioni Clichy, Florence, 2015)

Salvini, A., *Il Rito Aggressivo* (Giunti, Florence, 1988)

Salvini, A., *Ultrà* (Giunti, Florence, 2004)

Scandurra, G., *Tifo Estremo* (Manifestolibri, Castel San Pietro Romano, 2016)

Spagnolo, P., *I Ribelli degli stadi* (Odoya, Bologna, 2017)

Tassinari, U., *Fascisteria* (Castelvecchi, Rome, 2001)

Triani, G., *Tifo and Supertifo* (Edizioni Scientifiche Italiane, Naples, 1994)

Triani, G., *Mal di Stadio* (Associate, Rome, 1986)

Triani, G., *Bar Sport Italia* (Elèuthera, Milan, 1994)

Turani, G., *Fuori gioco* (Chiarelettere, Milan, 2012)

Valeri, M., *Che Razza di tifo* (Donzelli, Rome, 2010)

Fiction

Arena, A., *Io, Ultras* (Eretica, Rome, 2001)
Balestrini, N., *I Furiosi* (DeriveApprodi, Rome, 2004)
Dionesalvi, C., *BDD* (Coessenza, Cosenza, 2013)
Milazzo, G., *Fuoco ai mediocri* (Hellnation/Red Star Press, Rome, 2016)
Specchia, G., *Il Teppista* (Stefano Olivari, Milan, 2011)

In English

Arendt, H., *On Violence* (Allen Lane, London, 1970)
Armstrong, G. and Testa A., *Football, Fascism and Fandom* (A&C Black, London, 2010)
Bosworth, R.J.B., *Mussolini's Italy* (Allen Lane, London, 2005)
Canetti, E., *Crowds and Power* (Gollancz, London, 1962)
Carroll, S., *Cultures of Violence* (Palgrave, London, 2007)
Cohen, S., *Folk Devils and Moral Panics* (Routledge, London, 2011)
Doidge, M., *Football Italia* (Bloomsbury, London, 2015)
Duggan, C., *Fascist Voices* (The Bodley Head, London, 2012)
Eco, U., *Travels in Hyperreality* (Harcourt, New York, 1986)
Elias, N., *The Civilising Process* (Wiley-Blackwell, Hoboken, 2000)
Elias, N. and Dunning, E. (Eds), *Quest for Excitement* (Blackwell, Oxford, 1986)
Fagan, G., *The Lure of the Arena* (Cambridge University Press, Cambridge, 2011)
Foot, J., *Calcio* (4th Estate, London, 2006)
Hebdige, D., *Subculture* (Methuen, London, 1979)
Maffesoli, M., *The Time of the Tribes* (Sage, Thousand Oaks, 1995)

Martin, S., *Football and Fascism* (Berg, Oxford, 2004)

Hebdige, D., *Subculture* (Routledge, London, 1979)

Murphy, Williams and Dunning, *Football on Trial* (Routledge, London, 1990)

Thompson, H.S., *Hells Angels* (Penguin Classics, London, 2003)

Žižek, S., *Violence* (Profile, London, 2009)

Articles

Armeni, G., 'Sorpasso in Curva Nord', *Limes*, 3, 2005

Balestri, C. & Podaliri, C., 'The ultras, racism and football culture in Italy' in *Fanatics* ed. Brown, A. (Routledge, London, 1998)

Bindi, R. & Di Lello, M., 'Relazione su Mafia e Calcio' (Parliamentary Anti-mafia Commission, Rome, 2017)

Bromberger, C., 'Football as World-View and as Ritual', *French Cultural Studies*, 6, 1995

Dal Lago, A. & Di Biasi, R., 'Football and identity in Italy' in *Football, Violence, and Social Identity*, eds. Giulianotti, R., Bonney, N., & Hepworth, M. (Routledge, London, 1994)

De Biasi, R. & Lanfranchi, P., 'The importance of difference. Football identities in Italy' in *Entering the field: New perspectives on world football*, eds. G. Armstrong, G. & Giulianotti, R. (Berg, Oxford, 1997)

Eco, U., 'Ur-Fascism', *The New York Review of Books*, June 1995

Luchetta, A., 'Curve rette', *Limes*, 3, 2014

Marchi, V., 'Sono ultrà e sono contro', *Limes*, 3, 2005

Roversi, A. & Balestri, C., 'Italian Ultras Today', *European Journal on Criminal Policy and Research*, 2, 2000

Scalia, V., 'Just a few rogues?', *International Review for the Sociology of Sport*, 1, 2009

Testa, A. and Armstrong, G., 'Words and actions: Italian ultras and neo-fascism', *Social Identities*, 4, 2008

Testa, A., 'UltraS: An Emerging Social Movement', *Review of European Studies*, 2, 2009

Tuckman, B., 'Developmental sequence in small groups', *Psychological Bulletin*, 6, 1965

Zani, B. and Kirchler, E., 'When violence overshadows the spirit of sporting competition', *Journal of Community and Applied Social Psychology*, 1, 1991

Filmography

Quel Ragazzo della Curva B (Dir. Romano Scandariato)
Ultrà (Dir. Ricky Tognazzi)
E Noi Ve Lo Diciamo (dir. Giuseppe Marcon)
Farebbero Tutti Silenzio (Dir. Andrea Zambelli)
ACAB (Dir. Stefano Sollima)
Secondo Tempo (Dir. Fabio Bastianello)
Il Potere dev'essere bianconero (Dir. Daniele Segre)
Ragazzi di Stadio (Dir. Daniele Segre)
Eccezzziunale... veramente (Dir. Carlo Vanzina)
Estranei alla Massa (Dir. Vincenzo Marra)
Ovunque Tu Sarai (Dir. Roberto Capucci)
L'Ultimo Ultras (Dir. Stefano Calvagna)
Diaz (Dir. Daniele Vicari)
Sulla Mia Pelle (Dir. Alessio Cremonini)

Websites

https://www.sportpeople.net/
http://www.asromaultras.org/
https://www.tifonet.it/
https://www.iogiocopulito.it/
https://www.pianetaempoli.it/
http://www.boysparma1977.it/
https://www.rivistacontrasti.it/
http://www.rivistaundici.com/
http://www.osservatoriorepressione.info/
https://www.thetotallyfootballshow.com/
https://www.secondcaptains.com/
http://www.ecn.org/antifa/
https://www.fanseurope.org/en/
https://farenet.org/
https://gentlemanultra.com/
http://www.mondialiantirazzisti.org
https://www.football-italia.net/
http://www.tuttocurve.com/

About the Author

Tobias Jones is the author of seven previous books, including *The Dark Heart of Italy*, *Blood on the Altar* and *A Place of Refuge*. He has written and presented documentaries for the BBC and for RAI, the Italian state broadcaster, and has been a columnist for the *Observer* and *Internazionale*. He is the co-founder of Windsor Hill Wood and an occasional midfielder for the England Writers' football team. He lives in Parma, Italy.

@Tobias_Italia
www.tobias-jones.com